OBJECT RELATIONS THEORIES AND PSYCHOPATHOLOGY

FRANK SUMMERS

Object Relations Theories and Psychopathology

—

A Comprehensive Text

THE ANALYTIC PRESS

1994   Hillsdale, NJ   London

Published by The Analytic Press, Inc.
365 Broadway, Hillsdale, NJ 07642

Set in Palatino by Magazine Graphics, Westwood, NJ

Library of Congress Cataloging in Publication Data

Summers, Frank
    Object relations theories and psychopathology : a comprehensive text
    Frank Summers.
        p. cm.
    Includes bibliographical references and index.
    ISBN 0-88163-155-8
    1. Object relations (Psychoanalysis) I. Title.
    [DNLM: 1. Object Attachment. 2. Psychopathology. WM 460.5.02
S955o 1994]
    RC455.4.023S85   1994
    616.89' 001 – – dc20   93-39264
                                                                                CIP

Printed in the United States of America
10 9 8 7 6 5 4 3 2 1

To Renée

Contents

Acknowledgments

I wish to express my gratitude to Dr. Paul Stepansky for the exceptional effort he put into editing this manuscript. His helpful suggestions improved the manuscript with respect to both content and style. I also wish to thank Toby Troffkin for a quality job of copy editing and Eleanor Starke Kobrin for her assistance. I want to give special thanks to my students over the years in the Division of Psychology, Northwestern University Medical School, for their stimulating, thought-provoking discussion, and persistent encouragement, without which this book would never have come to pass.

Preface

THIS BOOK IS INTENDED FOR BOTH BEGINNING AND EXPERIENCED CLINICIANS who may be interested in either learning about object relations theories for the first time or integrating these theoretical approaches more fully into their work. While the contributions of many different theoreticians are worthy of inclusion in a text of this type, this book concentrates on object relations theorists who are most clinically relevant. For this reason, such highly regarded and influential theorists as Margaret Mahler and Edith Jacobson, although discussed, are not subjects of intensive investigation. It is hoped that the reader will gain an appreciation for the way each theoretician (and his or her followers) deliberates upon and uses clinical material to further the therapeutic process. Only in the last chapter is an effort made to move toward an integration of these diverse clinical approaches, and even then there is no attempt to blur critical clinical distinctions. Each chapter is an invitation to the reader to step into the theoretical worldview of the theorist and approach clinical material without uncritical acceptance of it.

A word about the chapter sequence is in order. Although the chapters are roughly chronological, a strictly temporal sequence was not adopted. Although Klein's writings antedate those of Fairbairn, the chapter discussing her work follows that devoted to Fairbairn and Guntrip. Although many of the significant writings of Klein and Fairbairn were contemporaneous and each theorist influenced the other, Fairbairn's work is more easily grasped and represents a cleaner break with classical analytic theory. For these reasons, his work serves better as an introduction to object relations theorizing than does Klein's writing. In addition, although Kohut's major theorizing began before Kernberg's primary contributions, the continuity of the text is best maintained by placing Kernberg's work, as well as Winnicott's, directly after the discussion of Klein because both theorists were influenced by her whereas Kohut was not. The chapter on the interpersonal theorists follows the chapters on the object relations theorists to enrich the reader's appreciation of the contributions of this related school of thought and to provide deeper understanding by contrasting the two theoretical approaches.

This book aims to give the reader a comprehensive understanding of the major object relations theories. Each theory is presented from the viewpoint of those primary assumptions and principles out of which its ideas of pathology and treatment grow. Further, and perhaps most important, the emphasis here is on the clinical process. Each theory has critical implications for the conduct of psychoanalytic treatment, implications that grow organically from its view of development and pathology. In the discussion of each theory, the emphasis is on what its principles mean for the practicing clinician.

CHAPTER 1

The Origins of
Object Relations Theories

OBJECT RELATIONS THEORIES HAVE BEEN WIDELY READ AND DISCUSSED IN recent years as psychoanalytic theorists, and clinicians who have begun to question traditional psychoanalytic theory have turned increasingly to object relations theories to broaden or even supplant their theoretical and clinical understanding. Nonetheless, there is a great deal of confusion regarding the nature of many object relational theories and their clinical application. Object relations theories differ widely with respect to key concepts, assumptions, and principles and are often confusing and difficult to digest.

In addition, the general trend of object relations theories has been subject to widely different interpretations. Greenberg and Mitchell (1983) view object relations theories as part of a wider movement to supplant drive theory with a relational model of psychoanalysis; Kernberg (1984) and Winnicott (1960a) tend to see object relations concepts as an addition to drive theory applicable to more primitive emotional disorders; and Bacal and Newman (1990) view object relations theories as a bridge to self psychology. An object relations theory as defined here and used throughout the text signifies any systematic effort to account for personality development and pathology on the basis of the internalization of relationships with others. This model is contrasted with the drive–ego model, according to which the drives and their vicissitudes (however disguised, sublimated, or neutralized), along with ego mechanisms, account for personality development.

In an attempt to consolidate knowledge of object relations theories, Greenberg and Mitchell (1983) presented the first comprehensive review of each of the major theories. Serving the critical purpose of familiarizing clinicians with the major concepts of these theories, their text has probably made the single most significant contribution to the dissemination of information about object relations. Despite the invaluable contributions of their discussion of object relations theories, however, there are two key drawbacks to their work. First,

Greenberg and Mitchell do not present each theory as an integrated whole; they discuss the various ideas of each theory in isolation without full appreciation of the unifying principles on which the individual ideas are based. Thus, the reader fails to obtain a sense of the overall thrust of each theory. Second, Greenberg and Mitchell pursue the discussion of each theory primarily in terms of its proximity to either the drive/structure or the relational/structure model. While this issue is pivotal theoretically, their focus on thus categorizing each theory gives short shrift to its clinical implications. Nor is it clear from their theoretical discussions how drive/structure and relational/structure models differ clinically.

Since the publication of their book, both Mitchell (1988) and Greenberg (1991) have offered clinical theories that involve relational concepts. These theories, which will be discussed in chapter 7, do not, however, address the clinical implications of the major object relations theories.

The contributions of the various object relations theories to the psychoanalytic process remain unclear. This obfuscation may be due partly to the cumbersome and difficult language often used by theorists. A large share of the difficulty, however, is due to the fact that object relations theories were developed by clinicians dissatisfied with the clinical and theoretical limitations of the classical psychoanalytic models. We will see in our discussion of the various theorists that they differ on whether their ideas are an addition to the classical viewpoint or a replacement of it, and at times, the theorist is unclear about the relationship between his or her ideas and the classical model. Each object relations theory breaks away from the major tenets of the model of endogenous drives to some degree, but, because of this confusion, the clinical implications of this theoretical shift are not readily apparent. It is a major task of this book to show the connection between theory and clinical intervention in each major object relations theory.

Because each object relations theory is a reaction to the classical theory, one cannot grasp the meaning and importance of its concepts without an appreciation of the history of the psychoanalytic ideas which preceded them. Object relations theories developed because each theorist found some limitation in the drive-ego model that pushed his or her thinking to new concepts and, ultimately, ways of practicing psychoanalytic therapy. Consequently, to understand the contributions of the object relational theorists, one must first grasp the major trends in psychoanalytic theory. Therefore, we shall review in detail the major developments in ego psychology so as to clarify the ego-psychological view of psychic structure, development, pathology, and treatment. From this conceptual clarification, we can see the growth of object relations theories from their roots in ego psychology to the critical step of separation from it in the development of new theorizing. As we will see, some object relations theorists take this step more dramatically than others—hence the differences among them in their degree of adherence to the classical model.

This chapter describes the shift from drive to ego psychology and presents the major theoretical and clinical developments within the ego psychology tradition. It highlights the major theoretical bridges from ego psychology to object relations theories. This discussion sets the context for the presentation of object relations theories in subsequent chapters.

THE ORIGINS OF EGO PSYCHOLOGY

When Freud abandoned the theory of sexual trauma as the etiology of neurosis in favor of endogenous drives, psychoanalytic theory shifted to consideration of the internal workings of the mind. Freud (1915a) began to focus on inborn drives as the motivating force of psychopathology and eventually extended this focus to personality development in general. As drives and their vicissitudes came to be considered the critical factor in development, psychoanalytic theory made a decisive move away from external events, including trauma, toward the functioning of the mind, now conceived as a product of the drives, or biological tension states, that aim for gratification through tension reduction. According to this drive model, human motivation originates in the press of biological drives that gain psychological expression in the form of wishes that power psychological functioning. Psychopathology, in this model, is caused by the repression of wishes, not of memories of external trauma (Freud, 1915b). The pathogenic conflict is between preconscious censorship of conscious thoughts and unconscious wishes for instinctual gratification (Freud, 1915c). When the repression barrier is broken through by disguised expressions of unconscious wishes, symptoms result. The clinical implication of this shift from the trauma theory to the drive model is that the goal of the analytic process becomes the uncovering of unconscious wishes, the repression of which is considered the cause of neurosis.

The study of unconscious wishes and their manifestation in psychopathology dominated psychoanalytic theory and practice from 1897 to 1923. This situation began to change when Freud (1923) pointed out in *The Ego and the Id* that the unconscious cannot be equated with wishes, nor the conscious with the forces of repression because the mechanism of repression is unconscious. These facts led Freud to superimpose his structural model of ego-id-superego upon the topographic model of unconscious-preconscious-conscious: the ego, consisting of repressive mechanisms, is largely unconscious; and the superego, which is the moral system motivating the repression of unacceptable wishes, has a conscious component, the conscience, as well as an unconscious component in the form of unconscious guilt. From the viewpoint of this structural model, psychological conflict takes place not between the unconscious and the conscious, but between the unconscious components of the ego or superego and the id. Psychopathology is a compromise formation between an id content, such as a sexual wish, that is otherwise blocked from consciousness, owing to its unacceptability to the moral system, or superego, and an ego defense mechanism, such as repression. Psychopathology is, therefore, a result of conflict between competing psychological structures. This shift in Freud's theoretical thinking marked a change in psychoanalytic theory and practice away from the exclusive focus on drives to an equal emphasis on the forces opposing it (Freud, 1937).

With this theoretical shift, the ego now assumed the central role in the functioning of the psyche. The degree of health or pathology of the personality, from this viewpoint, is a function of the ability of the ego to manage the press of drive-based wishes for discharge as well as the constraints of reality on such gratification. The ego must also change the moral constraints from within (in the form of the superego), which constitutes an additional counterpressure to drive discharge. Ego strength, or the capacity of the ego to handle the conflicting demands of id, reality, and superego, now assumes the pivotal role in the well-being of the personality. To the degree that the ego is not able to accomplish a functional balance, the personality will fall ill. For example, if the ego is forced to use excess repression, wishes will seek substitute expressions of discharge and hysterical symptoms will result. To the extent that the ego displaces unacceptable wishes onto the environment, phobic fears ensue. Thus does ego psychology include the functioning of the ego in all psychopathology, with every symptom implying a failure of the ego to balance effectively the need for drive discharge with the constraints of superego strictures and reality (Fenichel, 1945).

Freud (1926) changed his concept of anxiety in accordance with the structural model. Whereas he had originally viewed anxiety as the result of dammed up libido due to repression, he now reconceptualized anxiety as a warning signal to the ego. When the ego senses danger from unacceptable wishes, it experiences anxiety; it then employs a defense mechanism to ward off the threatening affect and restore balance, sometimes at the price of a symptom outbreak. From the viewpoint of the structural model, anxiety is not a product of repression, rather, it motivates repression and other defenses. This reconceptualization of anxiety reflects the central role of the ego in balancing the various pressures to which the psyche is subject.

The structural model resulted in the concept of psychological organization: the ego is not simply a group of mechanisms but a coherent organization whose task is to master the competing pressures of the id, superego, and relations with reality. This concept led Freud to question how such mastery is possible given the biological origins of the psyche. He had to account for the establishment of a psychological organization, the structured ego, that opposes the gratification of the drives, from which all human motivation originates.

Freud's answer was that the ego develops from drive frustration. Simple drive gratification is never all the child wants, even in the best of circumstances; eventually, the preoedipal tie to the mother is given up, and later the oedipal object must be relinquished (Freud, 1923). The loss of these early objects, according to Freud, forces the child to set up a substitute: an internal psychological representation of the parents to replace the abandoned objects of childhood longings. As the early attachment to the mother is given up in reality, she is taken in psychologically. The object cathexis of the mother is replaced by identification with her. In the oedipal phase, which Freud considered decisive for identifications, the longing for the parent of the opposite sex is given up and the child either intensifies identification with the same sex parent or identifies with the opposite sex parent in response to the loss. These identifications will determine the gender identification of the personality and concomitantly form the superego-ego ideal complex. Each relinquishment of a childhood object results in an identification that helps form the ego structure:

> When it happens that a person has to give up a sexual object, there quite often ensues an alteration of his ego which can only be described as a setting up of the object inside the ego. . . .the process, especially in the early phases of development, is a very frequent one, and it makes it possible to suppose that the character of the ego is a precipitate of abandoned object-cathexes and that it contains the history of those object-choices [Freud, 1923, p. 29].

In Freud's formulation, the id drives the organism to seek object contact to achieve instinctual gratification. When reality forces the relinquishment of these objects, they are taken in through identification and form the basis of the ego. Thus, the ego develops out of the frustration of id wishes and is formed by becoming like the objects reality forces the id to relinquish. Likewise, the superego is a "precipitate of abandoned object-cathexes of the id," but it is also a reaction formation against those choices in the form of moral objection. Thus, both the ego and the superego are formed from the internalization of previously cathected objects.

THE CLASSICAL EGO PSYCHOLOGISTS

Freud's pioneering suggestions regarding the importance of the ego and the mechanisms of its development became the basis for ego psychology, which extended the concept of the ego even further than Freud did. Anna Freud (1936) enumerated a variety of defensive mechanisms used by the ego to keep wishes unconscious. She pointed out that the various defenses used by the ego become resistances in the analytic process; thus, psychoanalytic treatment is focused equally on ego mechanisms and id wishes. She drew further implications from the structural model by pointing out that psychoanalytic assessment of development and psychopathology must include the functioning of the ego.

Subsequent ego psychologists have extended further the concept of the ego's autonomy from the id. Hartmann (1939) pointed out that some of the mechanisms used by the ego, such as perception, motility, and memory, do not develop from frustration but are autonomously developed functions, which he termed "apparatuses of primary ego autonomy," which later become integrated and are necessary for the functioning of the ego. Hartmann pointed out that since these ego functions exist from birth and originate outside of conflict, one cannot properly speak of the ego as developing "out of" the id; rather, both ego and id gradually develop from an undifferentiated matrix and become separate systems. This concept removes the original dependence of the ego on the id that characterized Freud's formulation. Hartmann referred to that part of ego functioning which is not in conflict at any given time as the "conflict-free ego sphere." For example, while fantasy is at times a product of frustrated wishes and conflict, it is also a useful means for the consideration of alternatives in solving problems.

The concept of autonomous ego apparatuses does not mean that Hartmann disputed Freud's view that drive frustration leads to the structuralization of the ego. Indeed, in Hartmann's view there are

two sources of ego development: the motivation of inborn apparatuses of primary autonomy and the frustration of drives, which results
in secondary autonomy. With regard to the second source, Hartmann
agreed with Freud that energy from libidinal frustration is used for
the organized ego; however, in his view aggression, rather than
libido, is a more significant factor in ego structuralization. (Hartmann,
Kris, and Lowenstein, 1949). Hartmann pointed out that since the
intent of the aggressive drive is to destroy the object, its discharge is
more dangerous than that of the libidinal drive and, consequently, its
neutralization is more critical. For the same reason, in the view of
Hartmann and his colleagues, permanent object relations are more
dependent on the sublimation of the aggressive than of the libidinal
drive. Neutralized aggression leads to structuralization of the ego,
which allows for good object relationships and object constancy and
which, in turn, make possible the further neutralization of aggression.
Unneutralized aggression, on the other hand, is accorded a primary
role in much of psychopathology (for example, when unneutralized
aggression attacks an organ, psychosomatic illness results). According
to Hartmann (1953) when aggression is not neutralized, no counter-
cathexis is possible, aggression erupts over the organism, object
relations are not possible, and a schizophrenic process results.

In Hartmann's view, the ego is a group of functions, including
defenses and adaptive mechanisms. These functions are organized
into a system Hartmann called the "synthetic function" of the ego.
This system is not simply an outgrowth of the id but an organized,
adaptive capacity that controls healthy functioning and has its own
sources of growth in addition to frustration of wishes. Nonetheless,
complete ego autonomy is not possible, in Hartmann's view, because
the ego uses energy from the drives, especially the aggressive drive.
Thus, the organized ego is always linked to the id and achieves only
relative autonomy from it.

Rapaport (1951, 1957) viewed the id as a constitutionally given and
the ego as the created personality. Although he agreed with
Hartmann that the ego develops from an undifferentiated ego-id
matrix, Rapaport pointed out that in healthy development the emer-
gent ego organization obeys its own laws, distinct from and independent of the elements from which it emerged. To the extent that the ego
is independent of the id, it is better adapted to reality and more capable of functioning; the extent to which the ego is unable to achieve
autonomy from the id is the degree to which it will be a slave to it,
with a resultant inability to adapt to the demands of reality. The
health of the personality, in Rapaport's view, is a function of ego

autonomy, that is, the ability of the ego to manage id pressures. The actual content of id wishes and the conflicts to which they give rise are of little moment to Rapaport, as the same wishes and conflicts may exist in healthy and pathological personalities; the difference lies in the ability of the healthy ego to achieve autonomy from the id so that it can manage its conflicts without symptomatic outcome.

Arlow and Brenner (1964) extended Hartmann's concept of ego autonomy by pointing out that the topographic model was not modified by the structural model but replaced by it. In contrast to the common ego-psychological view, as represented by Hartmann and Anna Freud, that the topographic model can be used along with the structural model, the view held by Arlow and Brenner is that the two models are, in fact, contradictory because anti-instinctual forces are unconscious. With the introduction of the structural model, conflicts were no longer considered to be between the preconscious and unconscious; both instinctual wish and the force that opposes it are seen as unconscious. The concept of the preconscious had been obviated by the central role of the ego in psychic conflict; because the preconscious could not determine the nature of the psychic content with which the instinctual wish is in conflict, it was replaced by the ego.

In agreement with Rapaport, Brenner (1981) endorses Hartmann's view that the ego and id develop from an undifferentiated matrix. He points out, however, that since all mental phenomena include some degree of compromise between ego and id, the two are not separable except under conditions of conflict. The ego as executant of the id must find a way to help it achieve instinctual gratification. To accomplish this goal, the ego must negotiate the dangers to which all id wishes give rise. Therefore, according to Brenner (1976), mental phenomena are products of a compromise formation including wish, guilt, anxiety, and defense. The id wish conflicts with feelings of guilt, creating anxiety that is warded off by defense. The task for the ego is to find a way to allow instinctual gratification within the limits set by guilt feelings and anxiety.

To perform this task, the ego uses a variety of mental mechanisms, such as fantasy, perception, cognition, and the functions typically labeled "defense mechanisms" (Brenner, 1981). In this view of mental functioning, defenses are not a specialized group of mechanisms, as conceptualized by Anna Freud (1936) and Hartmann (1939); that is, one cannot label any particular ego function as a "defense" since all ego functions have both defensive and adaptive value (Brenner, 1981). Healthy, socially acceptable behavior is no less a compromise formation than is a symptom. When instinctual gratification is excessively compromised to satisfy the demands of guilt and anxiety, symptoms or pathological character traits result. The decisive factor in health or illness for Brenner (1976) and Arlow (1963) is the ability of the ego to execute a compromise formation that allows instinctual gratification without symptoms.

White (1963) took the final step in the theoretical movement toward the concept of the autonomous ego with his view that the ego has its own independent energies. Unlike other ego psychologists, White based his position on animal and child development research. He pointed out that there is abundant evidence from animal research to support the concept of nonbiological motivation: a variety of animals will learn mazes and solve problems when all their drive needs are satisfied. Further, rats and other animals that have been studied will learn complex material solely for the experience of novelty and the opportunity to explore, and among rewards of novelty they prefer objects they can manipulate and have an effect on. White noted that Harlow's monkeys would learn solely for the reward of looking outside and that the learning curve for this experience was similar to that achieved for biological rewards. White concluded that there is a drive for mastery over the environment, which he termed "effectance motivation."

White believed that experimental and naturalistic observation of infants and young children supported the notion of the existence of a need for "effectance" independent of biological motivation. He noted that observations of infants as early as the first few days after birth show that they spend some time in exploration and that time for this activity gradually increases until one-year-olds spend about six hours a day in playful exploration. Infants perform activities during this "playtime" for no reward other than the successful completion of the behavior. White noted Piaget's observation that infants as young as three months learn to repeat behavior for the sole purpose of having an effect on the environment—and show clear signs of delight when they are successful. White also pointed out that children sometimes choose to perform activities that, in fact, delay gratification but lead to the mastery of a skill. For example, children prefer to use a spoon rather than their hands to eat, thus delaying instinctual gratification but promoting the joy of mastery.

White concluded that the need for effectance is not only separate from, but may also be in conflict with, biological drives. In White's view, effectance motivation is fueled by energies inherent in the ego apparatus that are totally independent of instinctual needs. Hendrick (1942, 1943), from a more purely psychoanalytic viewpoint, also came to the conclusion that a drive for mastery of the environment fuels the organization of the ego. Hendrick (1942) resolved the issue, however, by postulating a drive "to do and learn to do" (p. 40). White pointed out that the motivation to have an effect on the environment shares none of the characteristics of a drive per se, that it has neither somatic source nor consummatory pattern nor specificity of aim. White's argument is that only independent ego energies can account for the animal and child research data and that, therefore, the ego does not develop from a common matrix with the id but is separate and autonomous from birth. White's position is the final step in the evolution of ego psychology toward the liberation of the ego from its dependence on the id.

In White's formulation there is no role for abandoned object cathexes in the development of the ego. Independent ego energies require no object relations to achieve structuralization; the parents' role in ego development is to provide identificatory objects for modeling effectance. The child wants to be like the father in order to achieve competence in affecting the environment. This concept of identification is very different from Freud's (1923) view of "taking the object in" in order to withstand the pain of loss. White viewed identification as a form of imitation, not as an incorporation of the object, as it was for Freud.

Whether ego psychology views the ego as completely independent of the id, as in White's formulation, or more functionally autonomous, as in the theories of Hartmann and Rappaport, the ego is seen as a separate organization from the id. This model of the mind, consisting of drives and an ego organization that has some autonomous ability to regulate their discharge is referred to here as the "drive-ego model." From this viewpoint the crucial issues in development are the vicissitudes of the drives and the concomitant organization of the ego, the adaptive capacity of the organism. As can be seen from this review, within ego psychology there are two views of ego autonomy: the view of Hartmann and Rapaport that the ego originates from both inborn apparatuses and the neutralization of drives and the view of White and Hendrick that the ego is formed solely from its own energies. For Hartmann and Rapaport, who adhered to Freud's notion that the ego is formed partly on the basis of drive frustration, ego autonomy is relative. By contrast, White's more complete break with Freud led to an abandonment of the frustration model of ego development and the notion of structuralization through frustration. White was able to marshall considerable experimental and observational evidence to support his view of total ego autonomy; consequently, he gave only a minimal role to object relationships in the development of the ego. White viewed the ego as originating in psychic energy, similar to the energy fueling the id. By contrast, Hartmann and Rapaport saw in their view of the relative autonomy of the ego, a direct connection between the vicissitudes of object relations and ego development, with frustration in drive-fueled object relationships leading to the structuralization of the ego. Their derivation of the ego from id energy was speculative, however, lacking the evidential support of White's theory.

EGO PSYCHOLOGY AND THE PSYCHOANALYTIC PROCESS

The classical ego psychologists tended to emphasize theory, but they did draw some clinical implications from their view of the importance of the ego in development and pathology. Rapaport (1954) pointed out that the clinician cannot make an assessment solely on the basis of knowledge of the patient's drives and their vicissitudes. Such an assessment would leave out of account the functioning of the personality and its strengths and weaknesses and would not be sufficient to determine the patient's prognosis and suitability for analysis. Owing to the influence of ego psychology, psychoanalytically informed assessment now typically includes judgments regarding the patient's ego strengths and weaknesses as well as its structure. Psychopathology is understood not simply in terms of the conflicts that produced it but also from the way the individual handles the conflict, that is, by the ego mechanisms used for this purpose. From the ego-psychological viewpoint, the structure of the ego is as necessary to understanding pathology as is the conflict with which the ego is grappling.

With regard to the psychoanalytic process, it has been mentioned that Anna Freud (1936) adopted the view, endorsed by her father (Freud, 1940), that analysis is only half about unconscious wishes, the other half being concerned with the ego and superego, their structure and functioning. Interpretation is geared toward the ego mechanisms as much as toward what they conceal. Although this may seem like a self-evident technical principle from the contemporary viewpoint, it is a clear departure from the position Freud (1895) adopted in *Studies on Hysteria* in which he advocated using any means to circumvent the patient's defenses to bring forth repressed material. Ego psychology shifted the theory of technique to defense interpretation, according this aspect of the process a role equal to that of interpreting unconscious wishes.

Arlow (1987) and Brenner (1976) extended the concept of defense analysis by drawing out the clinical implications of the view that symptoms are compromise formations effected by the ego. They point out that defense analysis is not a clinical process distinguishable from the analysis of wishes; that is, one does not analyze defenses first. Since every symptom is a compromise formation, its analysis includes interpretation of the wish, guilt, anxiety, and defense that compose it. As the psychology of mental conflict, psychoanalysis is always concerned with the unconscious conflict between a wish pressing for instinctual discharge and the danger situation that its gratification would produce. The analysis of the danger situation that motivates defense may be termed ego analysis, but it is inseparable from other aspects of interpretation. Indeed, in Arlow's (1963, 1969) view, both the id wish and the danger to which it gives rise are unconscious fantasies; thus, pathology is considered to be ultimately a product of unconscious fantasies, one from the side of the id and the other motivating the ego's defense.

In the view of both Arlow (1987) and Brenner (1976), the role of the analyst is solely to interpret unconscious conflict. The analytic task, therefore, is to understand psychic conflict and make conscious the compromise formations to which it gives rise. The patient tries to enlist the analyst to gratify the unconscious wish; by not complying, the analyst facilitates its expression (Arlow and Brenner, 1990). For Brenner (1979), there is no role for the development of an analytic alliance, nor any noninterpretive behavior by the analyst to form a relationship with the patient. If the patient pressures the analyst for an alliance, the analyst's role is to interpret the conflict that underlies that wish, not to comply with it. Brenner's (1979) contention is that analysts in the presence of severe emotional symptoms, such as excessive dependence, suicidal ideation, and depression, too quickly forget the importance of analyzing conflict, that the success of the analysis is a function of the analyst's ability to maintain the analytic stance irrespective of the severity of the conflict.

Because conflict is ubiquitous, defenses will still operate and a new compromise formation will be effected after all the elements of the conflict are made conscious (Brenner, 1976). However, the defenses, now less intense, will result in a new compromise formation that allows greater control and integration by the ego and increased instinctual gratification. According to Arlow (1987) and Brenner (1976), the result of a beneficial analysis is not a change in the defenses but a new compromise formation that allows instinctual gratification without symptom formation.

Despite these clinical implications of ego psychology, another group of ego psychologists believes that there has been a "developmental lag" between the advances in ego psychological metapsychology and the clinical theory derived from this theoretical shift (Gray, 1982). Their contention is that, despite widespread acceptance of ego psychology as the metapsychological foundation of psychoanalysis, practice has continued to employ an id model. Gray points out that Freud's original technique of circumventing the defenses in whatever way necessary still has undue influence on technique, although in more subtle fashion than overt suggestion and manipulation. For example, if the patient is angry at the analyst, interpreting this quickly as an aggressive drive derivative from childhood bypasses the negative transference and the defenses against it, thus increasing and perhaps preserving resistance. To the extent that the analyst relies on quick interpretation of impulses, she is using id, rather than ego, psychology, in conducting the clinical process. If the analyst insists on confronting impulses that the patient is trying to keep unconscious, he will necessarily meet resistance, and it may appear that suggestion or manipulation is in order. According to Gray, however, such interventions are not called for. The reason for the increased resistance and apparent need for noninterpretive intervention is to be found in the analyst's technique of bypassing the defenses.

Gray (1990) proposes, instead, a technical model based on the recognition that the patient's symptoms are a product of the defensive processes of the ego. According to this model, the analyst listens for drive derivatives but does not intervene until the patient's ego unconsciously interferes with the flow of material. This resistance reflects the defensive functioning of the ego, and attention is directed to it. In opposition to Arlow and Brenner, Gray believes that interpretation is best approached from the side of the defense. He assumes that the patient's resistance is caused by a fantasy of danger if certain words are spoken to the analyst. By directing attention to the immediate resistance, this fantasy will be addressed and may itself be revealed as a defense. The goal of this type of intervention is to increase the patient's awareness of his unconscious ego rather than to bring impulses into consciousness.

Gray's fundamental point is that a strict adherence to the principles of ego psychology dictates a focus on ego functioning within the analytic session as the best means for understanding the way the ego defends and adapts. Because the purpose of interpretation is to help the patient give up his defenses, he must be shown how they work in the analytic relationship. In Gray's (1973) view, a major advantage of this approach is that it leads the patient to become self-observing.

Gray points out that the patient is most likely to become self-analytic if he sees his defenses operating on a moment-to-moment basis.

Gray (1987) has applied the same reasoning to the treatment of the superego. He feels that analysts tend to overlook the analysis of the superego because Freud was pessimistic regarding the subjection of this psychic agency to analytic scrutiny. Freud (1920, 1926) saw the superego as a form of resistance linked to the death instinct and, therefore, unanalyzable. In Gray's view, the superego is an alienated part of ego functioning and should be analyzed like any symptom, with the goal of making it conscious. As the nature and origins of the superego become conscious, it is brought under the control of the ego. Whereas Freud believed the superego could be influenced mostly by suggestion, Gray sees it as an analyzable portion of the ego that will enhance ego functioning when made conscious.

Weiss (1971) also emphasizes the importance of here-and-now defense analysis, but his views depart more radically from the classical theory of analytic technique. Weiss argues that unconscious urges do not become conscious owing to frustration caused by the neutrality and abstinence of the analytic setting. If this were so, he argues, their eruption into consciousness would be disruptive rather than helpful. Weiss points out that defenses are given up when the ego feels it is safe to do so, indicating that the lifting of the defenses is under the unconscious control of the ego. When the ego judges reality to be safe, it lifts the defenses, and the ego defenses change from being a segregated portion of the ego to an ego-syntonic control mechanism in harmony with the rest of the ego. In the analytic setting, this means that the patient will test the analyst to judge whether the analyst can safely endure the revelation of anxiety-provoking impulses. When the analyst is so judged, unconscious impulses can become conscious and will then be subject to ego regulation. According to Weiss, this process explains why making the unconscious conscious is helpful rather than disruptive. Weiss contends that classical theory has remained within the outmoded frustration theory and has therefore failed to appreciate the role of the ego in the clinical process, a state of affairs metaphorically referred to as a "developmental lag" between the metapsychology of the ego and clinical theory. The value of defense analysis, according to Weiss, is that it changes the relationship of the defenses to the rest of the ego, a psychic shift that makes possible the appearance of unconscious wishes.

Weiss (1988) has reported empirical evidence to substantiate his claim regarding the operation of the analytic process. On the basis of blind ratings of clinical protocols in a limited number of cases, his data show that when repressed contents became conscious, the patients' anxiety was lower and their experience more vivid. The classical theory would predict the opposite, but the data support Weiss's hypothesis that the unconscious becomes conscious when the patient feels safe rather than disrupted. In addition, Weiss found that after the patients' unconscious demands were frustrated by the analyst, the patients tended to feel less anxious, bolder, and more relaxed. If the patient tested the analyst to have the demands gratified, as predicted by the classical model, the patient would be more anxious. This finding confirms Weiss's hypotheses that patients test to see if the analyst is safe and that if the analyst shows he or she is safe by maintaining neutrality, patients feel relief and be able to bring forth more material.

In a similar study Weiss reported that patients' intensity of experience and insight was aided by interpretations that tended to disconfirm unconscious beliefs and that patients who did better in analysis tended to receive such interpretations. In Weiss's view, these results explain why some interpretations work and others do not. If an interpretation tends to confirm a patient's anxiety-provoking unconscious belief, say, that he is inadequate, the interpretation will not help, but if the interpretation tends to disconfirm the belief, as, for example, by indicating the belief is a fantasy, it will bring relief. Weiss uses these findings to support his contention that the analytic process works by defense interpretation and maintenance of a neutral analytic stance, both of which help the patient feel safe, and that this sense of safety opens the patient to previously warded-off impulses, resulting in analytic success.

This group of ego psychologists has applied the insights of ego psychology to a reconceptualization of analytic technique. The importance of drive interpretation recedes in their model in favor of detailed attention to the operation of the defensive functioning of the ego in the analytic setting. According to this model, impulses need not be directly addressed, but will emerge when the defenses are properly interpreted and when the patient feels safe after having successfully tested the analyst's neutrality. To the degree that the analyst is able to make the setting safe by adherence to analytic neutrality and defense interpretation, progress toward the analytic goals will be made. The approach of this group is a clear and consistent application of the structural model to the analytic process.

EGO PSYCHOLOGY AND OBJECT RELATIONSHIPS

All the ego psychologists discussed thus far have either ignored or minimized the role of object relationships in the formation of the ego.

In contrast, the third branch of ego psychology views ego formation as a function of object relationships. This viewpoint, which provides the foundation of object relations theories, is based on Freud's (1923) concept of the ego as the "precipitate of abandoned object cathexes" (p. 29). W. R. D. Fairbairn in Scotland and Melanie Klein in London, working independently, both inferred from this statement that the ego consists of internalized object relations. Fairbairn (see chapter 2) endorsed the concept of the ego's autonomy from the drives but pointed out that the growth of the ego is dependent on satisfactory object relationships. His protégé, Harry Guntrip, whose theoretical and clinical contributions are also examined in the second chapter, further developed the relationship between early object relationships and the growth or arrest of the ego. Klein (see chapter 3) also believed that ego development is a product of internalized object relationships. Klein, unlike Fairbairn and Guntrip, contended that endogenous libidinal and aggressive drives give rise to object relationships and that from the earliest phase of infancy these form the basis of the ego. The significance she accorded the drives sets her theoretical views apart from those of other object relations theorists, but her theoretical and clinical system was based on the concept of ego growth through the internalization of objects. Klein's modifications of psychoanalytic theory spawned a group of followers who adopted the fundamentals of her conceptual scheme but revised certain aspects of it (see chapter 3).

Klein's views were sharply criticized by Anna Freud (1927), who, as we have seen, adopted the more traditional ego psychological position that the ego was formed from the frustration of drives. The result was a split in British psychoanalysis between the "Kleinians" and the followers of Anna Freud (Segal, 1980). Analysts who neither fully accepted the Kleinian system nor rejected all of its postulates became known as the British "middle school," or "independents" (Rayner, 1991). Fairbairn and Guntrip are often included in this group along with Michael Balint and Donald Winnicott (Sutherland, 1980). Balint (1968), like Fairbairn, emphasized the importance of the primary love relationship as the foundation of ego development. Winnicott was influenced by Klein's object relations theory, but his views regarding the relationship between early object relations and ego development emphasized the mother-child bond rather than drives. Winnicott's theoretical and clinical views, the subject of chapter 4, are the most comprehensive system of thought to come from the British middle school.

Edith Jacobson and Margaret Mahler

In America Edith Jacobson (1964) was the first theoretician to link object relationships and the building of ego structure. In her view, drive development, ego maturation, and the growth of object relationships are all aspects of a unified developmental process. She agreed with Freud that pleasure and unpleasure are the primary infantile experiences, but she pointed out that in the earliest phase of infancy the child cannot distinguish pleasure from its source. In this phase, the child's fantasies of merger with the mother form the foundation of all future object relationships. Jacobson's contention was that the concept of the oral stage had to be expanded beyond feeding and oral erotism to a whole range of experiences that cluster around oral gratification and frustration.

In Jacobson's view, at about three months the maturation of the ego leads the child to differentiate the love object from the self. At this point the beginnings of self- and object-images are formed, and they cluster along the lines of the drive organization. Gratifying experiences become libidinally organized self-object units distinct and independent from the aggressively organized self-object units born of frustrating experiences. In this phase every experience of closeness or gratification leads to the temporary experience of return to the early merger state. These fantasies are incorporative, or introjective, in the sense that the child wishes to *become* the mother. Jacobson viewed introjection, in contrast to customary usage, as a primitive mechanism of incorporating the object in fantasy mechanism whereby the object becomes the self. Analogously, she viewed projection as the primitive experience of ejection, whereby the self becomes the object. In this view, the earliest identifications consist of the re-fusion of self- and object-images and are not true ego identifications.

According to Jacobson, if the mother is able to "tune in" to the discharge pattern of the infant, sometime in the first year the infant begins a more active form of primitive identification by imitating the parent. This new behavior is a developmental step forward because the infant is active and utilizes an ego mechanism, motor behavior. Nonetheless, Jacobson pointed out that imitation is not a true ego identification because it is founded on the magical fantasy of *becoming* the mother rather than on the wish to be *like* the mother. Imitation, in Jacobson's view, is merger through activity rather than through physical contact.

In the second year the child learns to distinguish the features of the love object, and the temporal sense develops. These two capacities allow the child to be *like* the object without the fantasy of *being* the object. At this point selective identification begins to replace fusion as a true ego identification, and the child is thus able to differentiate wishful and real self-images. The child's wishful self-image and the identification with the idealized parent form the ego ideal; this benign structure compensates for the lost fusion. Concurrently, the negative self-image built from frustrating experiences, realistic parental prohibitions, and the ideal self- and object-images combine to form the superego.

Jacobson pointed out that unless the child admires qualities of the parents, he cannot form a meaningful identification in which the ego is modified to assume characteristics of the object. Although she believed that all identification has a component of separation, and therefore of aggression, her contention was that the formation of the ego is dependent primarily on the mother's attunement to the infant's discharge needs. This attunement is the basis for the libidinal object relationship, which fosters the development of positive self- and object-images. These internalized positive images are the basic units out of which the healthy ego is formed. Aggressive object relationships are inevitable, but if the positive self-images and object-images are strong, they keep frustration within manageable limits, preventing excessive aggressiveness. In turn, the strong ego is better able to withstand gratifying experiences without merging and to experience frustration without returning to primitive identifications. The interrelationships among drive discharge, ego maturation, and object relations are complex and reciprocal from Jacobson's point of view. The healthy formation of ego and superego is inseparable from maternal attunement to the child's discharge needs and the satisfaction of the resulting object relationship.

Jacobson, unlike traditional ego psychologists, gave a primary role to the nature of the early object relationship in the formation of psychological structure. Her view of the importance of this relationship emphasized both gratification and frustration of drive needs, and both are included in her concept of ego identification. For Jacobson, the crucial process in early development is the shift from the fantasy world of *being* the mother to *being like* the mother. This gradual movement from fantasy to reality is made possible by the reciprocal influences of object relationships and identification. Jacobson's view that the ego develops in accordance with early object relationships and resulting identifications extended the connection between ego development and object relationships well beyond Freud's concept of abandoned object cathexes. In Jacobson's view, the nature of the real relationship between mother and child is crucial, and the bond that grows out of this relationship is central in ways that go beyond its frustrating component.

Like Jacobson, Mahler believed the real relationship between mother and child is the crucial factor in the development of psychological structure. Mahler, Pine, and Bergman (1975) saw the birth of the psychological self as the outcome of the separation-individuation process. They define separation as awareness of separateness from the primary object and individuation as the assumption of individual characteristics. Although Mahler and her coworkers conceptualized this process as intrapsychic and therefore not directly observable, they believed it could be inferred from systematic observations of the behavior of infants and young children with their mothers.

Mahler agreed with Jacobson that in early infancy self and object cannot be differentiated. According to Mahler's developmental scheme, after a brief "autistic" phase devoid of object contact, the infant of one to six months is in a "symbiotic phase" in which all experience is fantasized as part of the self. The separation-individuation process begins with the child's emergence from symbiosis and lasts until the onset of the oedipal phase at about 36 months. The first subphase, from six to ten months, is termed "differentiation" and is characterized by the child's first awareness of its difference from the environment. From about 10 to 16 months, the child engages in "practicing," moving away from the mother both physically and emotionally to explore the world. According to Mahler, in the "rapprochement" phase at about 16 to 25 months, the child suddenly seems to realize that there is danger in moving away and seems to want to return to the earlier bond. Nonetheless, the child still needs to separate, and this resistance to losing its gains results in an "ambitendency." Eventually, the child moves away again toward independence, and one can infer the existence of internalized emotional object constancy in the child at this phase.

In Mahler's view, the intrapsychic process of separation-individuation, if successful, results in the internalization of whole objects with both good and bad qualities. If the process is disturbed at any point, however, the ego's development will be impaired and either a preoedipal form of pathology will result or, at minimum, oedipal development will be distorted. Thus, Mahler, like Jacobson, viewed object relationships as an inherent part of ego development. Mahler saw the bond formed between mother and child, and the child's ability to use it, as the crucial component in the child's internalization process and consequent ego development. Like Jacobson's theory, Mahler's view of ego development extended the role of object relationships well beyond the concept of frustration.

The clinical implications of Jacobson's and Mahler's revisions of psychoanalytic theory extend psychoanalytic treatment to severe psychopathology. Jacobson's view of ego development led her to treat depressives, borderline patients, and even psychotic persons by analytic means. She did, however, acknowledge that the treatment of preoedipal psychopathology requires modification of the strict interpretive stance. Pregenital fantasies may often be used for the treatment process rather than interpreted. For example, Jacobson (1954) allowed the idealizing transferences of depressed patients to go on for extended periods without interpretation because she believed such patients were attempting to recover their lost ability to love through "magic love" of the analyst. To interpret such a transference quickly is to interfere with the patient's need to use the analyst in a way that can ultimately lead to restored functioning. Jacobson's primary contribution to technique was to show that analytic treatment could be successful with severely disturbed patients as long as the analyst is willing to be more flexible regarding interpretation than classical technique allows. Jacobson appeared to draw no clinical conclusions from her theoretical views for the analytic treatment of neurotic patients and, consequently, made no effort to modify the classical model for the treatment of such patients.

Mahler (1971, 1972), too, derived from her own theory a reconceptualization of the treatment of severe pathology. She viewed severe forms of childhood psychosis in terms of her developmental theory: infantile autism is fixation at the autistic level of development, and childhood schizophrenia (Mahler, 1952, 1968) is a pathological fixation at the symbiotic phase. Mahler's contribution in these areas is a new conceptualization of these severe illnesses based on an empirically derived developmental model.

Although these conceptualizations in themselves are highly original, Mahler (1971, 1972) made perhaps her most unique contribution to the understanding of pathology in the application of her developmental model to the borderline syndrome. In Mahler's view, the borderline patient is caught in the rapprochement conflicts of the 16-to-25-month-old child. The borderline patient, like the child of this age, wishes to cling but fears the loss of his fragile sense of self, wishes to separate, but fears the dangers of moving away from the parental figure. In Mahler's view, treatment of the borderline patient, who is fixated at the rapproachement crisis, should focus on the patient's inability to resolve the separation-individuation process. However, Mahler provided no specific recommendations for treatment technique.

Although Mahler's clinical theory tends to focus on preoedipal pathology, she, unlike Jacobson, did believe that her developmental model had implications for neurosis. In Mahler's (1975) view, "the infantile neurosis becomes manifestly visible during the oedipal phase, but may be shaped by the rapprochement crisis *that precedes it*" (p. 332). Conflicts in negotiating the rapprochement subphase render more difficult the successful resolution of the oedipal phase and thereby contribute to a neurotic outcome. In particular, Mahler thought that neurotic patients who oscillate between desires for merger and defense against it suffer from unresolved conflicts in the rapprochement subphase. While she believed that her delineation of preoedipal developmental phases had significant implications for at least some neurotic patients, she did not construct a detailed therapeutic model for use with such patients.

The work of Klein, Jacobson, and, to a lesser degree, Mahler exerted a strong influence on Otto Kernberg (see chapter 5). Kernberg adopted Jacobson's blend of drives, object relations, and ego structuralization to create a developmental theory based on the internalization of drive-based object relations. Kernberg, like Jacobson, views development as a series of object relationships with increasing degrees of structuralization and differentiation. Like Klein and Jacobson, he believes drives fuel psychological structure, but in his view drives are inherently object relations and the ego is formed from object relations units.

Heinz Kohut's work does not clearly bear the stamp of Jacobson's theory, but her theoretical influence can be seen in his abandonment of the concept of the ego in favor of that of the self. While other object relations theorists use the concept of the self, Kohut was the most explicit in substituting self-structuralization for ego formation as the foundation of the developmental process. Kohut, like all other object relations theorists, viewed early object relationships as the key to the formation of psychological structure, but he conceived of the psyche as a self structure rather than as an organization of ego mechanisms. Kohut's clinical theory was influenced by Jacobson's principle that transference idealization in disturbed patients must be allowed to continue for an extended period uninterrupted by interpretation. Kohut applied this concept to the analysis of narcissistic disorders, for whom he believed that a protracted period of idealization of the analyst is a necessary step for the eventual recovery of narcissistic balance. His systematic views on the development, pathology, and treatment of the self (see chapter 6) have spawned self psychology as a separate "school" within psychoanalysis.

CONCLUSION

In Freud's view, abandoned objects form ego structure through the process of identification. The concept of ego autonomy, first introduced by Hartmann, challenged the contention that frustrating object relations alone motivate ego development. If the ego has its own sources of motivation, its development is not fueled by frustration. It is true that if the ego has *some* degree of autonomy but is *partly* motivated by drive neutralization, then Freud's concept of ego development from abandoned objects can still play a role in the structuralization of the psyche. It is unclear, however, how such a speculative transformation of psychic energy comes about, and in any case White showed that ego functioning occurs in the absence of drive frustration. Furthermore, Jacobson and Mahler showed that the mother-child relationship includes much more than frustration and that aspects of the whole relationship are internalized to form the ego and superego structures. Their work demonstrated that the concept of ego autonomy is not in conflict with the view that ego formation is a product of object relationships. All the major object relations theorists have departed from Freud in adopting the view that psychological structure is a product of object relationships and not simply their frustrating aspects.

From the viewpoint of classical ego psychology, then, there is a conflict between object relations and ego autonomy because ego formation derives from the frustration of drives. Because White viewed object relations as rooted in drive frustration, he could not admit them into his theory of autonomous ego development. Although he provided impressive evidence of learning that was not drive motivated, subsequent evidence indicates even more decisively that the infant and growing child seek object contact independent of the drives almost from birth (Bowlby, 1969; Lichtenberg, 1983; Stern, 1985). For example, neonates seek the gaze of the parent and even search for it if it is not there; in addition, they differentiate the mother from other figures very early. Animal research shows that a variety of animals attach to maternal figures for no reward other than contact itself. More evidence of this type will be presented in chapter 8; here it suffices to observe that there is abundant evidence that contact with objects is not reducible to more primary drives. White, who had no concept of autonomously motivated object relations, could understand ego development only in terms of psychic energy.

Once the assumption is abandoned that psychological structure necessarily grows out of frustration, it is possible to view personality formation as a matter of the internalization of autonomously motivated object relationships. From this viewpoint, object relations theories become an extension of the concept of complete ego autonomy and also of the notion held by Freud, Hartmann and Rapaport that the ego develops from object relations, though shorn of its assumption of drive frustration. All object relations theories view the personality as a complex product of early object relationships. Different object relations theorists accord the drives different roles in this process, but none of these theorists links the frustration of drives to the structuralization of the personality.

This notion of the roots of personality organization is easily confused with interpersonal theory. Indeed, the concept of relational origins of the psyche has been carried even further than the object relations view by the interpersonal theorists. Beginning with Sullivan's (1953) interpersonal theory of the personality, the Sullivanians have developed a theory of personality formation, psychopathology, and psychoanalysis based on the principle that all psychological phenomena are interpersonal. Until recent years the Sullivanians have remained outside mainstream psychoanalysis; however, with the publication of Greenberg and Mitchell's (1983) book showing the relationship between Sullivan and both the interpersonalists and the object relations theorists, the interpersonal viewpoint has been given greater consideration within established psychoanalytic theory (see chapter 7). Despite the shared emphasis on the relationship between self and other in object relations and interpersonal theory, the relative neglect of the internalization process in favor of the interpersonal situation in the latter distinguishes the two types of theory.

Psychoanalytic work within the object relations paradigm is based on a group of theories that, although differing considerably, have as their underlying commonality the view of development and pathology as products of the internalization of early interpersonal relationships. Consequently, the conceptualization of the psychoanalytic process in the paradigm is of a treatment focused on the manifestations of these internalizations in the form of object relationships. Each object relations theory has a different view of the critical factors in development and pathology and a distinct concept of the significant ingredients of successful analytic treatment. As we shall see, some theories tend to accord the drives a major role, whereas other theories abandon drive theory entirely. The theories also differ on the role of the environment versus constitution in pathology and on the critical environmental variables implicated in questions of health and pathology. In their conceptualizations of the treatment process, they differ on both the role and content of interpretation and on the extent to which other interventions are desirable. Consequently, we cannot speak of a single object relations theory.

Object relations is an umbrella concept for any theory that derives its principles of human motivation from the need for early relationships and consequently views the primary goal of psychoanalytic treatment as modification of the object relationships that have grown out of these early relationships. Precisely how the personality develops from early relationships and what the implications of this are for treatment is answered differently by each theory, and we now turn to the individual object relations theories to see how each variant of this model addresses these issues.

The Work of W. R. D. Fairbairn And Harry Guntrip

W. R. D. FAIRBAIRN

Basic Concepts of Fairbairn's Theory

W. R. D. FAIRBAIRN (1949, 1951) SOUGHT TO RECONCEPTUALIZE PSYCHOAN-alytic theory by recasting it as an object relations model of personality development and psychopathology. His interests remained the theoretical reconceptualization of the psychoanalytic theory of development, mental structure, and pathology until near the end of his life, when he began to draw out the clinical implications of his views. Unfortunately, owing to his ill health and premature death, Fairbairn was never able to complete his clinical theory, and it was left to his analysand and protégé Harry Guntrip to provide the clinical drama for Fairbairn's object relations theory. Indeed, Fairbairn published no case studies demonstrating his theoretical views. The theoretical focus of Fairbairn's detailed reconceptualization of psychoanalytic theory, the clinical application of which is often difficult to discern, gives his writing a dry, abstruse quality. Nonetheless, there is a great deal of theoretical innovation in Fairbairn's work, and Guntrip's writings provide much of its concrete clinical application.

Fairbairn viewed as ground-breaking discoveries Freud's concept of the unconscious and his interpretation of psychopathological phenomena and dreams as products of unconscious mental processes. However, Fairbairn felt the limitation of Freud's thought lay in his "impulse psychology," or drive theory, a limitation that led him to formulate his alternative object relations psychology. For Fairbairn, impulses, whether conscious or unconscious, exist only within an ego structure, however primitive or undifferentiated it may be, and derive their relevance from this. They do not somehow exist prior to the development of the ego, either temporally or logically. For Fairbairn, human experience can have meaning only in terms of an ego. Consequently, he disputed Freud's (1923) concept of an original id out of which the ego is born as well as Hartmann's (1939) concept of an undifferentiated matrix from which both ego and id develop. For Fairbairn, the ego exists from birth. The baby's needs exist within an experiencing organism, however undifferentiated it may be, a viewpoint that led Fairbairn to a primary theoretical postulate, namely, that structure exists before energy. Fairbairn (1946) disagreed with Freud's concept of a directionless psychic energy existing from birth that must be harnessed as psychic structure develops; for him, the concept of psychic energy is meaningful only insofar as it is associated with an ego structure. Fairbairn ultimately disputed Freud's tripartite structural model of id, ego, and superego, viewing all divisions in the psyche as parts of the ego.

According to Fairbairn (1951), not only do all impulses emanate from an experiencing ego but they always have objects. In this regard he was influenced by the work of Melanie Klein. As will be discussed in detail in chapter 3, Klein (1952b) believed that ego growth is a process of internalizing objects. Fairbairn used Klein's concept of the internal object as the building block of the personality to develop his own object relations theory of development and psychopathology, believing that Klein's object relations theory was too dependent on the drive concept. In Fairbairn's (1949, 1951) view, libido is "object seeking." The infant cannot exist without an object, and, indeed, objects are needed throughout life, although the type of need and the nature of the relationship with the object changes. Infantile libido, like all stages of libido, is conceptualized as object seeking. Thus, Fairbairn reverses the primacy of libidinal zone and object. Freud (1905a) and Abraham (1924) held to the erotogenic zone theory of development, dividing the epigenetic stages of child development into the oral, anal, and genital libidinal zones. In opposition to this view, Fairbairn pointed out that the infant is oral not because of the primacy of the mouth, but because the mouth is the appropriate organ for the breast. The child becomes genital when it is able to have a more mature form of object relationship. In other words, the erotogenic zone the child uses is defined by the kind of object relationship it seeks and is capable of.

Throughout his work Fairbairn (1946) used the word libido to refer to positive affective charge. However, he criticized as a hypostatization Freud's notion of libido as existing originally in a directionless, "pure" state. Fairbairn's (1944) view that libido exists within an ego seeking an object from the beginning caused him to dispute the importance of the pleasure principle in normal development and to postulate that libido is reality oriented, not pleasure seeking, from the start, although the relationship with reality is initially immature.

Pleasure, according to Fairbairn, is a "signpost" to the object. When pleasure is sought for its own sake, the psyche has broken down; a personality dominated by pleasure seeking is pathological, even in the earliest stages of development.

Fairbairn's defense of this view is that there is no other way to understand the devotion of children and adults to their objects. Freud (1920) recognized the problem of reconciling object attachment with the pleasure principle when he raised the question of why neurotics are so attached to painful objects; he resolved this dilemma with his concept of the death instinct. Fairbairn's view, which does not require the postulation of an abstract, unverifiable concept like the death instinct, is that neurotics are attached to their bad objects because they need them for survival, that any object contact is better than none at all. If the organism were pleasure seeking, Fairbairn reasoned, the internalization of bad objects would not be explainable, nor would the attachment to objects no longer valued as sources of pleasure.

Fairbairn's rejection of the concept of the id in favor of the concept of an ego present from birth did not mean he disputed Freud's notion of psychic structures in conflict with each other. Instead, Fairbairn (1944) reconceptualized Freud's structural model into three types of ego, each of which has a corresponding object. In developing this conceptualization, Fairbairn was again influenced by Klein (1952b), who, as we shall see in the next chapter, conceived of the early division of the psyche as splits in the ego. In Fairbairn's theory, the dynamic of psychic division is repression, as it is in Freud's. However, the nature and developmental origins of psychic differentiation are quite different for the two theorists. To understand Fairbairn's conceptualization of psychic structure, one must understand his developmental model, and it is to this aspect of his reconceptualization of psychoanalytic theory that we now turn.

Development

Fairbairn was influenced by Klein's (1957) concept of ego development as a series of phases of object relationships. Like Klein, Fairbairn (1940) redefined developmental stages in terms of the characteristic manner of relating to objects. However, he opposed Klein's retention of the concept that object relations are a function of the drive organization.

In Fairbairn's (1944) view, the earliest stage, in which orality is so prominent, is properly called the stage of infantile dependence because its outstanding feature is the dependence of the infant on its caretakers. The only mode of object relationship possible in this phase is complete identification with the object of dependence. Fairbairn termed the relationship between the infant and the mothering figure "primary identification" in order to describe the process of incorporating the object so completely that the distinction between ego and object is blurred. This equation of incorporation with a type of identification differs from customary psychoanalytic usage, in which identification means becoming like an object rather than incorporating it, as for example in Jacobson's theory (see chapter 1). Fairbairn called this more common meaning "secondary identification" because it is based on differentiation between ego and object, and he believed that this type of identification becomes the prominent mode of object relating in the "phase of mature dependence." In this stage objects are sought that can be incorporated. Since the breast is the most easily and usefully incorporated object, it is the preferred object in this phase. Orality becomes salient because the mouth is the path of least resistance to the object. This fact makes orality a prominent feature of this phase but, according to Fairbairn, does not justify postulating the primacy of orality over the nature of object relations. The child is oral because it seeks the breast; it does not seek the breast because it is oral.

The infant's desire for the breast is inevitably frustrated when the desired object does not meet the infant's needs. When the sought object does not appear, the infant feels that its love, its sucking, has destroyed the object. Once the infant makes such an interpretation, a problem arises, for satisfaction appears to make the object disappear. This interpretation leads to the fundamental conflict of this phase: the infant seeks to incorporate the object but doing so "destroys" the object. From the infant's viewpoint, its own desire for the object threatens its existence. The result is a conflict between longing for the object and fear of it and a tendency by the infant to withdraw from the object in order to save it. Because of this conflict Fairbairn termed this phase of his scheme the "schizoid position." He believed the schizoid position to be the fundamental psychological position and considered schizoid phenomena universal because frustration of some degree is inevitable.

Fairbairn agreed with Abraham's division of the first developmental phase into two subphases. Abraham (1924), who defined the stage by its orality, subdivided it into an earlier, oral sucking, phase and a later, oral biting, or sadistic, subphase. Fairbairn believed that the key distinction in the two subphases is the emergence of ambivalence toward the object in the second subphase as differentiated aggression appears. Fairbairn called the first subphase "preambivalent" because aggression does not yet appear as an affect distinct from libidinal longing. His conceptualization of the second subphase is another instance in which his thinking was heavily influenced by Klein. As will be seen in chapter 3, Klein (1937) believed that the second phase of infancy is marked by the infant's awareness of its love and hate for the same object, which she called the "depressive position." In Fairbairn's view, it is when frustration eventually leads to differentiated aggression that the ambivalent subphase of infantile dependence begins, as the infant is now aware of loving and hating the same object. The danger to the object now comes from the infant's aggression rather than its love, as in the preambivalent subphase. Like Klein, Fairbairn conceptualized the depressive position as the intent to injure the loved object. The problem of the schizoid position is to love without destroying; the problem of the depressive position is to hate the loved object without destroying it.

In both the schizoid and depressive positions the object becomes "bad," but the infant forms different interpretations of the "badness." In the schizoid position, the object is loved, but when it frustrates, it becomes a "deserter" and is experienced as "bad" by virtue of its unattainability. In the depressive position, the object is also loved, but when it becomes frustrating, it is hated. The infant desires to injure the ambivalent object in the depressive position but has no such intent in the schizoid position.

In both the schizoid and depressive positions, the infant is forced to master the anxiety of object loss. In the schizoid position, the infant fears that its love threatens the object. The only means the infant has to manage the anxiety of potential object loss in this incorporative ("preambivalent") subphase of infantile dependence is to internalize the object. For Fairbairn, the motive for all internalization is the effort to control the bad object. In the depressive position, the internalized object is ambivalently experienced, a condition that creates an intolerable internal situation and leads to the need to "dichotomize" the object. To protect the object, it is split into an "accepted" and a "rejected" object. "Rejecting" now becomes a crucial technique for mastering the anxiety of object contact, and its use marks the beginning of the transitional phase of development.

While Fairbairn believed that the orality observed in infants justified its salient position in a conceptualization of the infantile dependence phase, he saw no such justification for the concept of anality. He agreed that the "oral phase" has a libidinal object, the breast, but saw no libidinal object of anality. The infant does not seek the feces. The developmental period others refer to as the "anal phase" is characterized by rejecting behaviors, but for Fairbairn anality was only a symbol. Fairbairn saw the child in this period as still dependent on the object while using rejecting techniques to differentiate itself from it. Because of this combination of dependence and rejection, Fairbairn labeled this phase, which embraces the periods transitionally termed "anal" and "phallic-genital," as "transitional."

The transitional phase, according to Fairbairn, begins with the use of rejecting techniques to differentiate self from object. Continuing the ambivalence of the second subphase of infantile dependence, the infant needs both to accept and reject objects. If the object relationships of infantile dependence are satisfactory, the infant is able to dichotomize the object, utilize rejection, and achieve differentiation. This process has both internal and external aspects. Interpersonally, the child now becomes capable of forming a relationship that is not based on primary identification. However, the growing child is still dependent on the mother, and it now confronts a new type of ambivalence. If the child is too close to the external object, it will be in danger of regressively becoming identified with it, thus risking its newly emerging differentiated sense of self; but if it moves too far away, it faces the danger of abandonment. The conflict between engulfment and isolation are the characteristic anxieties of the relationship with the external object in the transitional phase. Fairbairn's view of the relationship between the growing child and the caretaker in the transitional phase is close to Mahler et al.'s (1975) view of the separation–individuation process (as discussed in chapter 1). Both saw the developmental task of this phase to be the separation from the caretaker while maintaining a meaningful bond that is not threatened by merger, or the obliteration of self–object boundaries. The dilemma for the toddler in this phase, in addition to the isolation–engulfment conflict, centers on the expulsion and retention of internal objects: expulsion achieves autonomy but risks the emptiness of life without objects whereas retention achieves fullness but risks loss of differentiation from the object. According to Fairbairn, the child in this phase must manage rejection and acceptance of both internal and external objects. From a developmental perspective, the critical task of the transitional phase is to reject objects without losing them; the child must learn to form dependent object relationships while maintaining differentiation between self and object. Successful completion of this task prepares the child for the mutual dependency that Fairbairn believed was characteristic of all mature object relationships.

Fairbairn gave little attention to the phase of mature dependence, most likely because he postulated that all psychopathology originates in the earlier phases. The importance of this phase, according to

Fairbairn, lies in its representation of the goal toward which all development is aimed. Successful resolution of the transitional phase allows the child to maintain a dependent tie to a differentiated object. The ability to form a nonincorporative object relationship requires complete differentiation so that the object can be accepted for who he/she is. Both the accepted and rejected objects must be "exteriorized" for this to occur. When infantile dependence is completely relinquished, the object can be given to and dependence can be mutual. This mode of object relationship allows for genital sexuality.

Psychological Structure

According to Fairbairn, psychic division originates in the infant's experience of the unsatisfactory object. Here again Fairbairn was influenced by Klein (1952b), who emphasized ego splitting as a normal process in early development to manage the anxiety of frustration. According to Fairbairn, if the object provides a satisfactory experience, ego integration and development are fostered, yet if an infant were to experience complete satisfaction, no psychic division would occur. All unsatisfactory experience leads to the internalization of a bad object, which is both exciting and frustrating. Since the infant seeks an object that is not responsive, it feels that its own love is unacceptable and an internalized rejecting object is set up within the psyche. In an effort to diminish the intense pain and anxiety of feeling its own love rejected, the infant splits the unsatisfying object into "exciting" and "rejecting" objects, both of which are repressed.

Since for Fairbairn all objects give rise to a corresponding ego structure, this internalization of objects results in a psychic division into libidinal and anti-libidinal egos. The satisfying object, which he calls the "accepted object," remains within the ego and becomes the "central ego." The "exciting object" becomes the libidinal ego, which, like the central ego, is dynamic; however, the libidinal ego is relatively more infantile and less reality oriented than the central ego. The "rejecting object" becomes structured as the "internal saboteur" and uses aggression produced from the frustration by the unsatisfactory object to repress the libidinal, ego-exciting object structure. The central ego rejects both the libidinal ego and internal saboteur, and in this reaction it too uses aggression. The central ego deploys aggression to reject the exciting and frustrating objects, or the libidinal ego and internal saboteur, and the latter structure uses aggression to repress the exciting object and its subsidiary, the libidinal ego. The configuration of the central ego, or accepted object, repressing the internal saboteur-rejecting object and the libidinal ego-exciting object while the internal saboteur represses the libidinal ego is what Fairbairn calls the "basic endopsychic situation."

It should be noted that in Fairbairn's scheme the aggression deployed for repression is wholly a result of frustration. Fairbairn saw no evidence for an aggressive drive, or even aggression analogous to libido, embedded in an ego structure seeking objects. His view was that aggression appears only when libido is frustrated by an unsatisfying object, resulting in ambivalence. To remove the danger to the good object, aggression is deployed for the object splitting that is necessary to manage the pain of frustration.

Fairbairn's (1954) case of Olivia illustrates his theory of the dynamics of psychic division. The patient was anorexic and agoraphobic. Her developmental history revealed early feeding difficulties and constant crying. Her father, unable to tolerate her crying, adopted the strategy of holding her down until she stopped crying. This method worked so well that Olivia learned to "hold herself down." Her father generally interfered with her life by adopting an overprotective, stifling attitude toward her. This interference excited her, but her father was also a rejecting figure who inhibited her oral needs and general spontaneity. Olivia "held herself down" by relentlessly attacking her own needs from within. This internal rejecting object constituted a primary identification with her father and was tantamount to her antilibidinal ego attacking the libidinal ego that longed to have its needs met. The success of the antilibidinal ego resulted in the almost total inhibition of Olivia's craving for the oral incorporative object, and anorexia was the outcome of this massive repression. The exciting object, which was also represented by the father, had to be split off from the rejecting object and repressed owing to the intense frustration of needs.

This case illustrates Fairbairn's understanding of the formation of psychic structure: it describes the internalization of the frustrating object and its splitting into the rejecting and exciting objects, which results in the division of the ego into the libidinal and antilibidinal egos that split off from the central ego. Although Olivia was highly symptomatic, Fairbairn believed that her dynamics differed from the normal situation only in degree and that while people who are not symptomatic do not repress the libidinal ego with such severity, the repression, its motivation, and the resulting psychological division of the ego are characteristic of the human personality.

Is Fairbairn's "basic endopsychic situation" simply a relabeling of Freud's structural model of ego, superego, and id? Fairbairn believed that his concept of mental structure was not a mere change of nomenclature and that his model possessed distinct advantages over Freud's concept of the tripartite division of the psyche. First, from a metapsychological viewpoint, Fairbairn believed his theory to be more elegant. He did not have to stipulate impersonal impulses and then explain how ego structure could be derived from them. Fairbairn believed that by divorcing energy from structure Freud required cumbersome postulates of transformations of energy into structure that are difficult to justify; in chapter 1, we saw how this problem informed the efforts of the ego psychologists to account for the autonomy of the ego. Second, Fairbairn regarded his theory as closer to the experience of patients and criticized the "id" as an impersonal theoretical artifact, not something actually experienced. Even more important for Fairbairn (1943) was the fact that his theory, unlike Freud's, could account for the attachment of libido to its object. To resolve the perplexing problem of the stubborn attachment of libido to painful objects Freud was compelled to adopt his highly speculative, questionable concept of the death instinct, which ultimately explained little. With his object relations model Fairbairn pointed out that when an object is repressed, an ego structure is formed and that giving up the object is, consequently, losing a part of the ego, resulting in annihilation anxiety. By equating the internalization of objects with the formation of ego structure, Fairbairn believed he accounted for the adhesiveness of object attachments, including the clinically frequent tenacity of ties to painful objects. This explanation has implications for the concept of resistance, as will be discussed presently.

Fairbairn also believed that his theory employed a more satisfactory concept of aggression. According to Freud's dual drive theory, repression uses aggression, but aggression is also a drive, concepts which lead into the quagmire of trying to explain how one aggressive drive can repress another aggressive drive. According to Fairbairn's (1944) theory, aggression is a response to frustration and repression becomes "one structure using aggression to repress another ego structure with an aggressive charge" (p. 119).

Further, Fairbairn contended that his concept of the internal saboteur had a great advantage over Freud's concept of the superego. The internal saboteur performs many of the functions of the superego but in an amoral fashion. Because tempting, overstimulating objects excite without satisfaction, they must be repressed. While Freud's superego represses impulses that conflict with a moral sense, Fairbairn's internal saboteur rejects threat and pain, and morality has no meaning to it. According to Fairbairn, the superego is a higher level structure that has little to do with the basic endopsychic situation—and even less relevance for psychopathogenesis. As will be shown later, Fairbairn believed that psychoanalytic theory made a fundamental error in its emphasis on guilt in the theory of neurosis.

In accordance with his metapsychological reformulation and recasting of the stages of development, Fairbairn (1944) reconceptualized the meaning of the Oedipus complex, a situation that he believed arises as the child is able to relate to two objects rather than only one. When the child's needs become genital, it experiences new frustrations because the genital needs are never satisfied. This ambivalence results in the internalization of a bad maternal and a bad paternal genital object, each of which is split into an exciting and rejecting object. To simplify this complex emotional situation the child perceives one parent as the exciting object and the other as the rejecting object, perceptions that result in the Oedipus complex.

In Fairbairn's view, neither the desire for the oedipal object nor the triangular situation produces guilt. "Pseudoguilt" issues from the Oedipus complex to the degree that demand for parental love is not fulfilled. From this rejection of its needs, the child concludes that its own love is bad. Unfulfilled longing for love in the phase of infantile dependence results in feelings of *shame*. If shame is the outgrowth of that period, the unmet oedipal longings will also be experienced as shameful, and this feeling will be masked by pseudoguilt. On the other hand, if the object relationships from the infantile period were satisfactory, there is little reason for guilt in response to unfulfilled oedipal longings. This deemphasis on the Oedipus complex and guilt in favor of shame and weakness in the dynamics of pathology is another instance in which Fairbairn's views presaged Kohut's (1977) later formulations of self psychology.

As might be guessed from this view of the Oedipus complex, Fairbairn saw no major role for guilt in development. He believed that one of the primary mistakes of the classical psychoanalytic theory of development was an overemphasis on guilt. Hence, guilt is not a significant variable in pathogenesis. What, then, are the crucial variables in the onset of psychopathology for Fairbairn? To answer this question, we now turn to his reconceptualization of the psychoanalytic view of psychopathology.

Psychopathology

Fairbairn's (1941) theory of psychopathology was as developmentally based as the traditional psychoanalytic view, but his reformulation of crucial developmental issues resulted in a markedly different understanding of every form of neurosis, character pathology, and psychosis. In accordance with his view of the schizoid position as the earliest developmental stage, Fairbairn (1940) believed that the schizoid character is the most severe form of psychopathology. Since the infant's earliest need is to have its love accepted, the most severe trauma is the feeling that one's love is rejected, a feeling that arises from excessively frustrating object relationships in the first subphase of infantile dependence and that leads to feelings of shame, weakness, and helplessness.

The lack of responsiveness from the object in the earliest developmental phase intensifies the normal schizoid position by producing intensified desire to possess the object. If the deprivation is strong enough, the desire becomes so strong and desperate that the infant wishes to devour the object to secure it. To the infant, its the craving to possess the object that now threatens to destroy it, a perception that intensifies anxiety over losing the object. According to Fairbairn's conceptualization, this is the most painful anxiety a child or an adult can face because it renders all object contact potentially destructive. Every move toward the object elicits the fear of destroying it; the object can be protected only by withdrawing from contact. The need to withdraw exacerbates the normal splitting of the ego as the libidinal ego withdraws from contact with reality. In this emphasis on ego splitting Fairbairn is again indebted to Klein. Although his concept of the schizoid split has an emphasis different from Klein's concept of ego splitting, he adopted Klein's (1957) view that ego splitting is characteristic of severe pathology.

The withdrawal from all object contact is dangerous. As the emotional investment in object contact is withdrawn, the ego loses contact with reality and begins to lose the sense of its own existence. Clinically, this state appears when the patient talks of feeling nothing or of feeling dead, as though he or she has ceased to exist. Need for the object is intensified as a result of the deprivation, and the schizoid can find satisfaction nowhere. Objects can be neither reached nor avoided: Object contact imperils the existence of the object needed for its survival; and withdrawal endangers the ego directly. Ultimately, the schizoid fears the loss of the ego whether he or she moves toward or away from objects. The dilemma of this dual anxiety results in the feeling of futility so characteristic of the schizoid.

It was Fairbairn's contention that this schizoid dilemma—intense need for the object and fear of destroying it through contact—results in adult schizoid pathology. According to Fairbairn, the schizoid patient possesses four basic attitudes. First, the schizoid is oriented toward partial objects, not whole objects. Owing to the fixation at the oral level, others are treated like preambivalent breasts, as objects to be incorporated for the patient's gratification. For example, when Fairbairn (1940) asked a schizoid patient if he was happy in his marriage, "a look of surprise at my question spread over his face, followed by a rather scornful smile. 'That's what I married for,' he replied in a superior tone, as if that provided a sufficient answer" (p. 13). Fairbairn believed that by adopting such an attitude, the patient was treating others as he had been treated. Mothers of schizoid patients are either indifferent or possessive toward their children, whom they do not see as having value in their own right, and the patients take the easy route of maintaining the relationship they know.

Second, such patients are oriented more toward taking than toward giving, again as a result of fixation at the oral incorporative mode, but also because they are so fearful of emotional contact that all emotion is repressed and its contents overvalued. Eventually, all emotional expression becomes associated with depletion, and giving is equated with loss. Fairbairn mentions one patient for whom this dynamic became so extreme that he was unable to pass an oral examination because he was not able to give answers, even those he knew to be correct. The schizoid can only take and must ultimately withdraw into a remoteness detached from all emotional contact with others.

These two characteristics suggest how Fairbairn would view patients who today would be characterized as having narcissistic personality disorders. Clearly, Fairbairn viewed patients who treat others as objects for their own gratification, who can only take but not give, as schizoid. The self-absorbed and exploitive attitudes of the narcissistic orientation, according to Fairbairn's formulation, emanate from the schizoid fixation at the preambivalent level of infantile dependence. The patient can relate to objects only with an attitude of "primary identification," an oral-incorporative attitude. To protect the object, the patient withdraws from all object contact, but when he or she does come into contact with objects, the ego attempts to incorporate them in accordance with the only way it knows to form object relationships.

This dynamic is closely linked to the third schizoid characteristic, which Fairbairn calls the "incorporative factor." Since schizoids equate relations with others, or any form of giving, with depletion, relationships with objects are transferred to the realm of inner reality, where they have value. This preoccupation with depletion also characterizes the schizoid character's orientation to creative endeavor. When such a person does create, he or she tends to regard the product as worthless because to value the creation means to lose something valuable and therefore to be impoverished. With this formulation, Fairbairn offered an alternative viewpoint to a customary interpretation. The devaluation of one's own products is typically viewed as a narcissistic issue, reflecting self-devaluation or the protection of grandiosity. For Fairbairn, it is most commonly the schizoid fear of losing something valuable.

Among some schizoid patients, this issue is manifested by a "substitution of intellectual for emotional value" (Fairbairn, 1941, p. 20). Such patients resort to an intellectual thought process in order to maintain the overvalued emotions within, a process that results in an intellectualized character style. Intellectualization, for Fairbairn, is not simply a defense against affect; it is an effort to maintain a stranglehold on overvalued emotions that the patient cannot bear to give up.

The fourth characteristic is the "emptying of the object." As a consequence of deprivation in the preambivalent object phase, the infant feels it has emptied the breast by its incorporative strivings for it. To contact the object is to empty it, thereby destroying it. Again, the result is avoidance of object contact to preserve the object.

It is clear that in Fairbairn's discussion of schizoid characteristics he reinterpreted many typical symptoms and character styles as manifestations of schizoid dynamics. One can see in his attitude toward narcissism and intellectualization, for example, a clear clinical alternative to the traditional view of these symptoms. It was not simply a case of his recasting impulses as object relationships; his view of psychopathology was founded on a basis different from all other psychoanalytic conceptualizations of pathogenesis. Specifically, Fairbairn conceived of many pathological features, such as narcissism and intellectualization, as desperate efforts to avoid object contact. The schizoid's presenting pathological picture hides the intense fear of object contact that reflects the primitive incorporative mode of longing for objects, a longing found so shameful by the patient. The clear clinical implication is that unless the clinician sees this schizoid root of the presenting symptom picture, the depth and severity of the pathology is likely to be missed.

Whereas schizoid pathology in Fairbairn's model is rooted in the preambivalent phase of infantile dependence, depression is seen as originating in the ambivalent subphase. If in the preambivalent phase the infant's need to love is accepted and it feels its love is acceptable, it will be able to feel aggression toward the loved object and in the ambivalent phase will dichotomize the object into the hated and loved objects. If however, the infant does not feel that its love has been accepted by the object, in the ambivalent phase of infantile dependency it becomes anxious that its aggression will destroy the loved object. Attempting to master the anxiety, it incorporates the ambivalent object in a desperate effort to save it. Such an infant has not mastered the ability to hate the loved object without feeling that it is destroying it and is beset with unresolved ambivalent feelings toward the incorporated object, which is now repressed.

The repressed ambivalent object determines further object relations and is activated in the future by aggressive feelings toward the loved object. Constantly fearful that its aggression will destroy the loved object, the child suffers from chronic anxiety regarding object loss. When later object relations evoke ambivalence, anxiety over loss of the object may result in depression. Thus, in Fairbairn's view, the repressed ambivalently valued object is the root of adult depression. Nor is the depressive state considered a defense. The schizoid and the depressed states are both primary psychopathological constellations resulting from unsatisfactory object relations in the phase of infantile dependence leading to the repression of bad objects. The schizoid represses the exciting and rejecting object and so must avoid all object contact. The depressive represses the ambivalent object and, unlike the schizoid, can love and derive some degree of satisfaction from object relations; however, relations with others will always be fragile because aggressiveness can easily disrupt them.

All other forms of psychopathology, according to Fairbairn, are efforts to manage the conflicts of the transitional phase rooted in the schizoid or depressive positions. If there is unresolved conflict in either the schizoid or depressive positions the transitional phase becomes pathogenic. Both conditions involve fixation to objects in the infantile dependence phase, which renders impossible the resolution of the transitional phase in the direction of differentiation and the capacity to give to the object. Consequently, defensive techniques must be used in the latter phase, and these defenses constitute the various forms of neurosis. Fairbairn described four such defensive techniques, each corresponding to a psychopathological syndrome.

Since the developmental task of the transitional phase is to differentiate the object and surrender infantile dependence, rejective techniques are prominent. The incorporated object must be "expelled" to achieve differentiation, but this expulsion results in separation anxiety and a sense of isolation. Retaining the object, however, means primary identification—and thus failure to differentiate from the object and loss of any movement toward autonomy—and is experienced as feeling "shut in" or engulfed. According to Fairbairn, all phobic states are defenses against one side of this conflict. Although he did not discuss specific phobias in detail, it is clear that agoraphobia, acrophobia, and phobias of darkness would be considered defenses against the anxiety of differentiating from the object in the transitional phase. Claustrophobia and relationship phobias would be defenses against the anxiety of engulfment.

If there is intense anxiety over expelling the incorporated object, the conflict can present itself as between emptying and retaining contents. In this case, expelling is experienced as the anxiety of draining the insides and retention as bursting from overflowing within. Mental states, especially affects, are retained and overvalued to keep the patient "filled up" and to thereby avoid the anxiety of loss. However, this state of "fullness" produces the intense anxiety of bursting from internal tension, which can become manifest in such symptoms as somatic complaints. The patient oscillates between the push to expel and the urge to retain, is paralyzed by the inability to make decisions, and attributes exaggerated powers to thoughts. Whereas the phobic externalizes the incorporated object and enacts the conflict with external objects, the obsessional keeps the object within and vacillates between letting go of the object and retaining it.

Instead of treating both the accepted and rejected objects as either internal or external, the patient may incorporate one object while externalizing the other. If the accepted object is kept within and the rejecting object is externalized, the latter becomes a persecutor and the patient feels that the goodness within is under threat from without. The anxiety of the inside being under attack from the outside is Fairbairn's formulation of the paranoid state.

The reversal of the paranoid state would be internalization of the rejected object and externalization of the accepted object. Such a state results in an overvaluation of the external object and a clinging demand for it to compensate for the rejected internal object. The result is a feeling of badness within and goodness without. This configuration represents the hysterical state, according to Fairbairn. Because of the historical importance of hysteria in the development of psychoanalysis and the considerable attention Fairbairn gave to the disorder in his reconceptualization of psychoanalytic thought, his views on hysteria are worth considering in detail.

The hysterical response to the dilemma of the transitional phase is differentiated from the other neurotic techniques by the excessive intensity of the exciting and rejecting objects, an intensity that results in the repression of both (Fairbairn, 1954). The overexcitement and overrejection of objects originates in the failure of the environment to meet the infant's needs to love and have its love accepted. In the future hysteric, the trauma of this unfulfilled need results in the enhanced desirability of the exciting object, which remains elusive, and a commensurate need to reject the object out of the frustration of craving an unresponsive exciting object. Aggression turns from the object to libido and represses the libidinal ego with excessive severity, creating a deep ego split, the symptomatic expression of which is the dissociative state of the hysteric.

It is the mother—or, more accurately, her breast—that both excites and rejects. The future hysteric reacts to this exciting and frustrating object relation with a premature libidinalization of the genitals in infantile masturbation. Fairbairn's view is that genitality enters the picture as the overexcited child identifies the genitals with the breast. To the hysteric, sexuality is oral, as can be seen in the clinging, incorporative needs of the hysteric. Repression is not directed to genital sexuality but to the objects of infantile dependence with which the genitals are associated. When the child reaches the transitional phase, it is still very much attached to these objects, a condition that compromises its ability to differentiate from them. In lieu of differentiation, the child overvalues the external object, seeking the infantile object under the guise of sexuality while repressing the bad object. Although Fairbairn did not dispute the traditional psychoanalytic view that hysteria involves repression of genital sexuality, he viewed the sexuality of the hysteric as a fundamentally infantile dependent object relation.

In Fairbairn's view, oedipal conflicts assumed importance in the clinical picture of the hysteric only because, in order to simplify a complex emotional state, the child identifies one parent with the accepting object and the other parent with the rejecting object. Fairbairn considered oedipal conflicts to involve representations of the traumatizing exciting and rejecting objects, repressed long before the oedipal phase. Owing to the traumatizing early object relations, the organ systems of the future hysteric become libidinally charged as substitutes for the frustrating objects. When an external situation breaks through the repression barrier, it revives the early trauma of rejecting object relations and somatic symptoms appear as substitutes for them. The hysterical focus on the body and bodily complaints constitutes, according to Fairbairn, a hopeless effort to achieve through the body what had been frustrated in the early mother-child interaction. That is, the hysteric seeks an oral incorporative object relation through the body.

Because of the premature erotization of the sexual organs, the hysteric also seeks oral object contact through the genitals. Like somatization, oral eroticism, masturbation, and other autoerotic activities result from object frustration. This premature genitalization of orally sought objects creates the conditions for overvaluation of the external object in the transitional phase. The hysteric uses the body and the overvaluation of the external object as the means for attempting to achieve the object contact which was frustrated in the phase of infantile dependence.

Fairbairn's (1954) formulation of hysteria is illustrated in his discussion of his patient Olivia. As stated earlier, Olivia suffered from anorexia and agoraphobia and eventually became withdrawn to the point of almost total passivity. Her first years were characterized by severe feeding difficulties and the father's holding her down in response to her hunger cries. The mother tried breastfeeding to no avail and had difficulty first in getting Olivia to feed from a bottle and then finding suitable food for her to take. Because the mother was unable to feed Olivia properly, she became the first object to be both exciting and rejecting to her, and when her father held Olivia down, he also filled both roles. In addition, her father teased her in a sexually provocative way, inhibited her freedom in order to protect her sexually, and yet did not prevent her from being sexually traumatized. Each parent assumed the role of an exciting and rejecting object, but Fairbairn believed that the mother's assumption of both roles in infancy represented the "nucleus round which the hysterical personality is characteristically built" (p. 113). The simultaneous excitement and rejection of the infantile object accounts for both the orality of the hysteric and the severe repression of the libidinal ego when the exciting object is attacked mercilessly by the antilibidinal ego.

In her childhood Olivia's greatest delight was to be given the top of her father's egg at breakfast. After her brother grew old enough to compete for the egg, she abruptly stopped eating breakfast with her father and assumed a distant attitude toward him. In analysis, Olivia dreamed about eggs to represent her father's penis. The egg symbol illustrates that "whereas the sexuality of the hysteric is at bottom extremely oral, his (or her) basic orality is, so to speak, extremely genital" (Fairbairn, 1954, p. 114). Fairbairn believed that the case of Olivia illustrated not only the extreme repression of the libidinal ego in hysterical states but also the premature excitement of genital sexuality, thus leading to a fusion of orality and sexuality. This connection is supported by another case of Fairbairn's involving a patient who verbalized an experience of being "a baby at the breast" but also "wanted something between my legs" (p. 114).

In all four types of transitional-phase psychopathology, the pathogenic conflict involves overwhelming anxiety about object contact,
whether because love destroys or because aggression destroys in loving. Except for hysteria, Fairbairn offered no explanation for why one
of these four defensive techniques is preferred in a given case. He did
make clear that the distinction between patients in the two primary
psychopathological conditions and patients who utilize one or more
of the four defensive techniques lies in the greater degree of trauma
suffered by the former group in the phase of infantile dependence.

Regardless of why a particular technique is preferred in the transitional phase, Fairbairn's contention was that the Freud-Abraham
equation of psychopathology with libidinal position missed the
crucial issue in each syndrome. Fairbairn concluded that, by miscon-
struing defensive techniques as libidinal positions, the traditional psychoanalytic view ignored the fundamental depression or schizoid
state beneath the defensive constellation. For Fairbairn, at the root of
all psychopathology is an unfulfilled childhood longing expressed by
an infantile ego, ashamed and anxious of its longings for dependence.
There is no higher level pathology produced by conflict between
impulse and guilt, as there was for Freud, who felt that only such conditions were analytically accessible. Such a fundamental reconceptualization of the psychoanalytic view of psychopathology has direct and
potentially far-reaching implications for treatment, and it is to this
issue that we now turn.

Treatment

Despite Fairbairn's extensive critique of psychoanalytic theory and his
radical transformation of it, he said little about the concrete therapeutic implications of his views until very late in his career. This is particularly surprising in the light of his often-repeated statements that
impulse psychology limited and even distorted practice by encourag-
ing an impersonal style of interpretation (Fairbairn, 1944). That there
was so little focus on clinical theory until later presents some difficulty
in interpreting Fairbairn's clinical views, but they can be discerned
from various comments throughout his writings and from his last
papers, in which he began to formalize a clinical theory (Fairbairn,
1958).

I have already indicated that Fairbairn's reconceptualization of all
psychopathological conditions seems to imply a technical approach
different from that suggested by drive theory. For example, the classical analyst who views hysteria as primarily repression of genital sexu-

ality due to oedipal conflicts will tend to interpret anxiety over sexuality as the basis for somatic complaints and hysterical emotional states. Clearly, Fairbairn viewed such interventions as failing to reach the depths of the patient's pathology. As we have seen, he viewed the repression of sexuality in hysteria as a withdrawal of the libidinal ego due to intense anxiety generated by object contact. Fairbairn felt that the treatment of the patient must, at some point, reach this deep fear of emotional contact in order to achieve a genuine therapeutic process. Interpretation of the patient's repression of excitement as oedipal guilt avoids this anxiety and thereby colludes with the patient's defenses.

Analysis informed by the impulse–conflict model tends to target relief of guilt. Fairbairn's (1943) view was that hysterics, as well as other patients, prefer to view underlying guilt as the source of their problems because guilt defends against their fear of object contact. To feel guilt over sexual longing is far more acceptable than to acknowledge the fear that one's love is not good enough, along with the resulting shame, withdrawal, and regressive longing for the object of infantile dependence. The use of guilt to mask these painful feelings is what Fairbairn called the "guilt defense," a defense that tends to be fostered by the impulse–conflict model. One of the major clinical implications of Fairbairn's theoretical views is the position that guilt should be interpreted primarily as a defense against schizoid withdrawal and regressive longing.

Since all intrapsychic conflict is between ego structures, according to Fairbairn, the distinction between intrapsychic conflict and structural defect is blurred. All people suffer some degree of ego splitting, and the more severe psychopathological states differ only by their relatively deeper ego cleavage. Symptoms result from ego splits in all patients, whatever the degree of pathology. Consequently, the fact that structural defect is a component of psychopathology does not imply a reduced accessibility to analysis. In the traditional viewpoint, structural defects are not analyzable because only the id is dynamic, the ego being conceived of as static. Fairbairn eliminated this problem with his concept of dynamic structure, that portions of the ego are in dynamic conflict with each other, each with a dynamic charge. Analysis of conflict between the libidinal and antilibidinal egos aims at resolution of conflict and concurrently heals an ego "defect." For Fairbairn, structure itself is dynamic; therefore, problems within it are accessible to analysis. Criteria for analyzability cannot rest on the assumption of an "intact ego," since no such ego exists.

As the splitting of the ego is always a component of the symptom picture, the ego must always be addressed in clinical interventions

(Fairbairn, 1944). It was Fairbairn's contention that interpretations geared to impulses allow the ego to become a detached observer of the clinical material. The patient can, and often does, assume the spectator vantage point from which he or she may well elaborate the material endlessly in order to defend against engagement. In this way, Fairbairn believed, impulse psychology lends itself to collusion with schizoid defenses. Fairbairn contrasted this type of intervention with the more personal object relations interpretations that are addressed to the experiencing ego. According to Fairbairn, this personalization of interpretations allows less possibility for defense.

When Fairbairn (1958) finally did begin to formalize his theory of technique shortly before the end of his life, it was this "personalization" of the psychoanalytic process that he most emphasized. He ultimately decided to apply to the treatment process his theory that ego development is based on satisfactory object relationships by emphasizing the therapeutic importance of the personal relationship between analyst and patient. Indeed, Fairbairn went so far as to state that impulse psychology cannot account for the analytic emphasis on the transference. According to Fairbairn, if impulses are of primary importance, their interpretation outside the transference should be sufficient. However, if symptoms are best resolved within the patient–analyst relationship, a conclusion that is well accepted by analysts, then problems with impulses are problems within a personal relationship, and impulse psychology has no tools for explaining this. However, from an object relations perspective, emphasis on the transference is to be expected, as impulse problems are symptoms of anxiety in object contact and can be resolved only within an object relationship; it follows that in the clinical setting impulse problems can only be meaningfully addressed within the transference context.

This emphasis on the "personalization" of the analytic process led Fairbairn (1958) to a reconceptualization of resistance. He pointed out that analysis has changed emphasis from uncovering childhood traumata to analyzing the current relationship with the analyst. To Fairbairn, this change implied that the patient's resistance is not directed against the unconscious past but against the inner reality of the present. The patient defends against the repressed ego and resists the analyst's efforts to bring this portion of the personality into the treatment; the patient's resistance is directed against bringing his or her inner reality into contact with the analyst. That is, what is ultimately resisted, according to this view, is not the process but the analyst.

Similarly, Fairbairn conceptualized the transference as the patient's effort to bring the analyst into his or her inner world of object relations. The analyst attempts to alter the structure of this world, and the patient not only resists the analyst as a threatening intrusion but also perceives and experiences the analyst in accordance with this inner world in order to maintain it. This view of transference and resistance dictates a treatment focus on the transference as the here-and-now representation of the patient's object relations inner world. In this respect, Fairbairn anticipated crucial elements of Gill's (1981) view of the analytic process (see chapter 8).

Although Fairbairn insisted on the crucial role of the transference in treatment, he believed that the therapeutic action of psychoanalysis lies in the whole of the patient–analyst relationship, not just in its transference component (Fairbairn, 1958). In adopting this view, he believed he was beginning to carry out the clinical implications of his view that patients are crippled by the distorted object relations of their inner reality which originates in the object relations of early childhood. He reasoned that one cannot expect these inner relations to change by interpretation alone, even if they are focused on the transference. Interpretations can only be of benefit in the context of a relationship with a "reliable and beneficent parental figure" (Fairbairn, 1958, p. 379). Such a figure allows for a satisfactory object relationship that can begin to replace the early traumatic relationship. This emphasis on the importance of the way the analyst relates to the patient is similar to Winnicott's view of the analytic process (as will be seen in chapter 4) and presaged Kohut's work on empathic attunement (discussed in chapter 6).

This reasoning eventually led Fairbairn (1958) to yield some of the traditional psychoanalytic strictures. He stopped using the couch because he felt the couch technique interfered in the establishment of a personal relationship between patient and analyst. He dismissed arguments in favor of the couch as rationalizations designed to maintain a distance perhaps desired by the analyst, but contraindicated for the patient. Since the therapeutic efficacy of psychoanalysis, in his view, is dependent on the maintenance of a positive object relationship between patient and analyst, it is the analyst's responsibility to provide the setting most conducive to such a relationship. Fairbairn opposed the restrictiveness of the traditional setting. He believed that to maintain it was to put the purity of a prescribed method before the well-being of the patient; that since the patient is the priority, restrictions should be minimized and treatment method flexible enough to adapt to the patient; and that to the extent restrictions are needed it should be acknowledged that they are for the analyst, not the patient. Fairbairn believed that if a patient did not improve in a traditional setting, the analyst should ascribe the poor outcome to the failure of the analysis to adapt to the patient rather than concluding that the patient was unsuitable for analysis.

While the concept of a more flexible relationship may seem vague, there are hints in Fairbairn's writings indicating what he meant. In discussing a case of hysteria to explain his concept of conversion, Fairbairn (1954) mentioned an incident in which the patient referred to seeing a play the night before and he responded by commenting that he had attended the program and had noticed that she was there. Mention of this incident was dropped casually into Fairbairn's discussion of the case, but it indicates concretely by the very ease with which he bent the classical framework, the flexibility in his technical approach. According to the classical viewpoint, such a remark was a violation of the analytic stance; from Fairbairn's vantage point, it was a move toward the establishment of a personal relationship, without which an analysis cannot succeed.

The good parental figure provides the environment for the release and derepression of internalized bad objects without threat of destruction. Since all internalized bad objects are ego structures, as they are made conscious the ego begins to reintegrate. Thus, the personal relationship between patient and analyst becomes a critical therapeutic ingredient in ego integration.

As can be seen from this discussion, Fairbairn's (1958) approach leads to a recasting of the aims of psychoanalytic treatment from making the unconscious conscious to repairing ego splits and reintegrating the personality. Topographic shifts are meaningful, according to Fairbairn, if they repair the ego but if unconscious impulses are rendered conscious without such a reintegration, they do not aid personality growth. Fairbairn recognized that some classical theorists, such as Gitelson (1962), considered the goal of psychoanalytic treatment to be the general maturation of the personality. While he welcomed such discussion, Fairbairn's contention was that the drive–ego model was unable to explain how psychoanalytic treatment causes general psychological maturation to occur. For Fairbairn, psychological maturation is tantamount to the healing of rifts in the ego, and therefore can be explained only on the basis of an ego-object relations model of personality change.

As discussed earlier, resistance, for Fairbairn, is the patient's continued adherence to his or her inner reality despite the analyst's efforts to bring it into the outer reality of the analytic relationship.

According to Fairbairn, the personal relationship is the only means the analyst has to break through resistances. The transference is the patient's "counter effort" to bring the analyst into his or her inner world. As long as this inner world remains self-contained, it cannot be changed, and the result is the "static internal situation" (Fairbairn, 1958). The patient maintains the internal configuration because the patient is attached to the internal bad objects resulting from the frustration of early experiences that led to overwhelming anxiety and hopelessness regarding contact with external objects and subsequently to withdrawal to the inner world; this is the only object contact the patient has and feels capable of having. The analyst attempts to breach this closed system, but the patient attempts to hold to the transference perception, that is, to the perception that is in accordance with his or her inner object world. The analyst's leverage is derived from his or her ability to form a personal relationship with the patient that does not fit the transference perceptions.

The patient who is able to accept the analyst's "outer reality" has moved from a closed to an open system. For Fairbairn, the transference, as well as the resistance with which it is identified, is resolved more by the new relationship that develops during the analysis than by insight. Nonetheless, analysis of the here-and-now transference is at the center of Fairbairn's technical recommendations: transference analysis is considered therapeutic when it leads to a new relationship that breaches the patient's previously closed system of object relationships.

It is clear that Fairbairn had begun to develop a new model of psychoanalytic therapy based on his object relations theory. This model was in process when he ceased writing owing to his failing health. Despite its incomplete nature, Fairbairn's clinical theory had already provided new ways of understanding many types of psychopathology, had eliminated the distinction between intrapsychic conflict and structural defect and the use of this distinction to assess analyzability, and had begun to revise the concepts of transference and resistance as well as to reconceptualize the process and aim of psychoanalytic treatment.

Because Fairbairn's published work gives little indication of how he put his theory into clinical practice, the most extensive case discussion of his work is Harry Guntrip's (1975) description of his own analysis with Fairbairn. His protégé experienced Fairbairn as a detached "technical interpreter" who was surprisingly orthodox and formal, showing little capacity for personal relatedness within sessions. Equally surprisingly, Guntrip described Fairbairn as relying heavily on classical theory, remarking to Guntrip at one point that the "oedipal

complex is central for therapy, but not theory" (p. 451). Guntrip's discussion of his analysis with Fairbairn seems to contradict the theoretical
model Fairbairn worked so hard to develop. Guntrip was well aware
of this, and he attributed it to both Fairbairn's personality and illness
(Fairbairn was sick during the major part of the analysis). Whatever
the cause of Fairbairn's behavior, his analysis of Guntrip raises the
question of whether he adopted his own model of treatment.
Especially troubling is Fairbairn's remark that the oedipal complex is
"central for therapy" inasmuch as he had based his theoretical and
clinical apostasy on his opposition to the centrality of this very concept. At minimum, we have far too few clues from Fairbairn as to the
clinical implementation of his model. For this, we must turn to his
most famous analysand, Harry Guntrip himself.

THE WORK OF HARRY GUNTRIP

Basic Concepts of Guntrip's Theory

Harry Guntrip, Fairbairn's protégé and analysand, did more than any
other theoretician to popularize and extend Fairbairn's theory of object
relations. Viewing his own theory as an extension of Fairbairn's
thought, Guntrip (1961a) agreed with his mentor's contention that the
infant seeks objects, not pleasure, and that personality growth depends
primarily on the quality of object relationships. He also adopted
Fairbairn's view that the earliest developmental phase is infantile
dependence and that unsatisfactory object relationships in that phase
are the root of schizoid pathology, the most primitive psychological
state. Further, Guntrip concurred with Fairbairn's view that the ego is
born whole, if primitive, and that the result of unsatisfying object
relationships is ego splitting and the formation of psychological structure.

He agreed with Fairbairn's critique of an impersonal id, believing
that meaningful experience exists within the ego. Guntrip extended
Fairbairn's critique with his view that once Freud developed his concepts of narcissism, the distinction between ego and libidinal drives
was eliminated, rendering any distinction between ego and id meaningless. Further, the recognition of an unconscious ego in conflict with
the repressed unconscious indicated that split-off experience is part of
the ego. In Guntrip's (1971) view, the elimination of the id makes
ego psychology a personal, or human, psychology in which the ego,
interacting with others, is a personal center of experience. He contrasted this concept of the ego with Hartmann's (1939) "system" ego,
an apparatus for controlling the drives.

Guntrip (1961a) was even more thorough and piercing in his attack on the biological grounding of psychoanalysis than was Fairbairn. He also pointed out that one does not see the operation of the pleasure principle except in cases of severe pathology, when the personality has broken down. Similarly, sexuality and aggression only become problems within a fractionated ego owing to frustrated object relations; when the ego is coherent and strong, sexuality and aggression are experienced joyfully and help the ego grow. In adopting these views, Guntrip anticipated many of the points Kohut (1977) would later make in the development of his self psychology (as will be seen in chapter 6, Kohut held similar views but used the concept of the self, rather than the ego in his reformulation of psychoanalytic theory).

According to Guntrip, since the growth of the ego is dependent on object relations, it is the relationship between ego and object that is crucial to the health of the personality, not the vicissitudes of the drives. The natural progression of ego psychology, according to Guntrip, is from a psychology of ego and id to one of ego and object.

Guntrip (1961a, 1971) was well aware that "object relations thinking" could be construed as shifting psychoanalysis toward an interpersonal theory. He discussed the interpersonal theorists at length to demonstrate that such a view was misguided. Focusing on Fromm, Horney, Adler, and Sullivan, he pointed out that since these theorists viewed personality as a reflection of the social environment, their theories are more sociological than psychoanalytic. Guntrip attacked the "cultural pattern" theorists for abandoning the depth psychology begun by Freud rather than building on it, and for ignoring the complexity of unconscious human motivation, especially in psychopathology. This point is critical to Guntrip's clarification of object relations theory and to the current resurgence of interest in interpersonal theory. Since the publication of Greenberg and Mitchell's (1983) *Object Relations in Psychoanalytic Theory*, the distinction between object relations theories and interpersonal theory has become blurred. Guntrip's critique of the "cultural pattern" theorists makes clear that he would have been in clear disagreement with such a merger of what he considered to be two different views of human motivation. In chapter 7 the interpersonal theorists are discussed in some detail, and the contrast between their views and the ideas of the object relations theorists will be explained more clearly. Suffice it to say that Guntrip believed interpersonal theory was an abdication of psychoanalysis whereas what was needed was a reconstruction of its theoretical edifice.

Psychopathology

Guntrip took as his starting point for understanding psychopathology Fairbairn's view that the infant's first need is to love and be loved and that the first object relationship is organized around this need. If the infant's need to love is rejected, it experiences the most painful emotional state: the feeling that its love is unacceptable. Like Fairbairn, Guntrip (1969) believed that all psychological division originates with the ego splitting that begins when the infant feels its love is rejected. This unsatisfactory object experience leads to the internalization of the bad object in an effort to master the experience. Guntrip, too, believed the bad object was split into the exciting and rejecting objects. However, he emphasized a different aspect of the bad exciting object: he pointed out that the object that is longed for but not found is desirable, but deserting, and he called it the "desirable deserter." This is more than a change in nomenclature. Guntrip believed that the experience of rejected love, whether in the adult or the infant, results in the feeling that the object is deserting, rather than simply exciting, as Fairbairn described it. This shift has significant implications for the understanding of schizoid dynamics, as will be shown presently. For now, the important point is that in Guntrip's schema the bad object is split into the desirable deserting object and the rejecting object. The former is tantalizing and, according to Guntrip, more painful than the latter, because it continually frustrates and threatens abandonment whereas the rejecting object is simply bad. The deserting object generates the anxiety of object loss; the rejecting object, loss of the object's love. Of the two, the ego much prefers the latter, as it is less threatening to its existence.

Guntrip's writings provide illustrations of desirable deserters in which the patient appears to be apathetic or depressed, whereas the therapeutic material indicates intense, frustrated longing for objects, often symbolized by dreams and fantasies of food. For example, a school teacher who complained of depression and lack of interest in school had a dream of going to a camp school where "the Head walked away when I arrived and left me to fend for myself and there was no meal ready for me" (Guntrip, 1969, p. 27). The patient went on to describe his preoccupation with eating despite minimal food intake, and then remarked that he typically eats alone and feels "totally cut off" (p. 28). Guntrip interpreted the dream as reflecting both the patient's longing for deserting objects, symbolized by the Headmaster, and the resulting frustration, which leads to withdrawal that appears to be depression. This example also indicates both the way signs of apparent depression can be used to mask schizoid dynamics and the frequently seen association between food and desirable deserters.

When the need to love is frustrated in the phase of infantile dependence, the infant fears loss of the object and seeks the object with greater intensity. The more the need to love is frustrated, the greater becomes the need to cling to the object. This is Guntrip's understanding of why patients cling to bad objects, a view that has, in fact, been amply confirmed by the findings of ethological research (Bowlby, 1969). (More will be said about the connection between this line of research and object relations theories in chapter 8.) According to Guntrip's presentation of the dynamics of schizoid pathology, if love is frustrated so that the anxiety of object loss becomes unbearable, the infant longs to devour the object in order to keep it. However, this desire leads to a more intense fear of object loss: the infant's desire to devour the object triggers its worst fear—destruction of the object—and now the infant itself is the potential source of the destruction. Because the infant fears that its love will destroy the object it so desperately needs for survival, it withdraws from object contact. This is why, according to Guntrip, the schoolteacher's associations to his dream, cited earlier, led to his feeling of being "totally cut off." The patient so longed for the object represented by the Headmaster that he wished to devour it, as symbolized by the preoccupation with gobbling food; consequently, to preserve the objects of his desire he withdrew from all object contact. Guntrip's formulation of the schizoid position is that "love gone hungry" leads to "love as destructive" and the anxiety of destroying the object results in schizoid withdrawal to preserve the needed object.

This pattern is shown clearly in the connection the schizoid patient makes between need for the object and craving for food. Guntrip (1969) discussed one patient who became ravenously hungry whenever she saw her husband. She wanted to gobble food and drink in a single gulp, yet in the presence of food she immediately lost her appetite. More will be said later of the relationship between object hunger and eating; the critical point for now is that hunger for the object leads to the desire to devour it, to gobble it like food. "This anxiety about destroying and losing the love-object through being so devouringly hungry is terribly real. . . . The schizoid person is afraid of wearing out, of draining, or exhausting and ultimately losing love-objects" (Guntrip, 1969 p. 30). The woman who was hungry for her husband commented that she had "an urge to hold him so tight that he [couldn't] breathe, shut him off from everything but me" (Guntrip, 1969, pp. 29–30). She also expressed desire to kill the analyst.

Because of the fear that desire for the object will destroy it, any affective bond threatens the existence of the object. Because the ego needs objects to survive, the anxiety of object loss is ultimately the anxiety of ego loss. There is no psychological structure in this first phase of development, so all anxiety is experienced as traumatic, threatening the very existence of the ego. The result is a careful avoidance of all emotional contact with objects. However, this schizoid withdrawal generates anxiety of loss of all contact with reality and threatens, once again, the very existence of the ego. Objects are needed as much as they are avoided. Consequently, object contact, though terrifying is sought. According to Guntrip, this situation leads to intense "all or nothing" object relationships, which he called the "in and out program." Schizoids can tolerate neither the presence nor the absence of object contact. They desire to fuse with the object to secure it, but this very desire threatens both the object and the ego and leads ultimately to the futility so characteristic of schizoid psychopathology.

Guntrip (1969) formulated the schizoid conflict as the inability to *"be in a relationship with another person nor out of it, without in various ways risking the loss of both his object and himself"* (p. 36). Each side of the dilemma risks ego loss, and this anxiety propels the patient to the other side of the conflict. Guntrip illustrated the "in and out" program with the following statement uttered by a nurse residing in a hostel:

> The other night I decided I wanted to stay in the hostel and not go home, then I felt the hostel was a prison and I went home. As soon as I got there I realized I wanted to go out again. Yesterday I rang mother to say I was coming home, and then immediately I feel exhausted and rang her again to say I was too tired to come . . . . as soon as I'm with the person I want, I feel they restrict me [p. 37].

It is common for clinicians to interpret such ambivalence as fear of intimacy, and Guntrip would not disagree with such a description. However, his contention was that such an extreme fear of intimacy is a product of hunger for the object so powerful as to result in fear of all object contact. Oedipal conflicts, however severe, cannot account for the severity of this withdrawal.

Object contact is so threatening that a defensive character structure is erected to protect the ego and allow an apparent affective bond with a minimum of threat. According to Guntrip, there are two broad categories of defenses that may be utilized in the service of defending against schizoid withdrawal. The most common type of defense is involvement in object fantasies that appear to be primary issues.

Guntrip regarded oedipal conflicts and longings for the breast as the most typical of these issues. By including oral desires, Guntrip is clearly extending Fairbairn's views another step. Both theorists saw oedipal conflicts as primarily defenses against schizoid withdrawal, but Guntrip believed longing for the breast typically served the same function. For Fairbairn, longing for the breast is the underlying issue for most schizoid pathology, but Guntrip believed such a longing enables patients to defend against the underlying withdrawal from all object ties by allowing them to believe that their wish is to possess the breast. According to Guntrip, schizoid patients typically seek not the breast but the cancellation of all object ties. The predominant under-lying fantasy is to return to the womb, to prenatal existence, when nothing was longed for and nothing was needed (Guntrip, 1961b).

Guntrip did not make clear whether womb fantasies are a desire to return to a "remembered" phase or are adult fantasies of what intrauterine existence is like. In either case, it is fair to say that the adult desire to achieve an objectless state does not imply memory of prenatal life. Guntrip's point is that the adult schizoid longs to with-draw from all object ties and that his predominant fantasy therefore becomes the return to the womb, the symbol of an objectless state.

To illustrate the way oedipal conflict defends against the regressive longing to return to the womb, Guntrip (1969) described a patient who suffered from "apparent depression," experiencing great diffi-culty finding interest in anything. Analysis uncovered a clear castra-tion fear that greatly exacerbated the apathy and resulted in crippling difficulty performing daily tasks.

> He lay in bed all day, curled up and covered over with bed clothes, refusing food and conversation and requiring only to be left alone in absolute peace. That night he dreamed that he went to a confinement case and found the baby sitting on the edge of the vagina wondering whether to come out or go back in, and he could not decide whether to bring it out or put it back. He was experiencing the most deeply regressed part of his personality where he felt and fantasied a return to the womb, an escape from sheer fear of castration [p. 69].

Guntrip went on to state that the patient had, indeed, suffered repeated castration threats from both his mother and an aunt that were often accompanied with gestures with knives or scissors. The "well-founded castration complex" was the result of his mother's hos-tility, according to Guntrip, leading to the patient's regressive with-drawal into himself. Although Guntrip acknowledged the castration complex, he believed that in itself it would not lead to such a crippling illness. The desire to remain in a womblike state indicated that the primary anxiety was not so much about losing the penis as about any type of object contact. In Guntrip's view, maternal deprivation led the patient to attempt to withdraw from all object contact, and the anxiety about losing the penis was primarily a symptom of the patient's terror.

The other major category of defensive constellation against schizoid anxiety reveals more clearly the underlying schizoid withdrawal. Some patients present with an aloof, superior, affectless, apparently self-sufficient interpersonal style. The need to deny the need for objects is so great that the defense involves a presentation of complete indifference to others. The schizoid personality reveals in this defensive constellation, neurotic defenses of oedipal and breast longings, a lack of connection to objects. This defense is intended to mask from patients themselves and from others their intense need for dependence and the overwhelming anxiety associated with it. Object contact is so threatening to the ego that it must believe in its total self-sufficiency, resulting in a withdrawal into private grandiosity. This defensive constellation is the essence of Guntrip's conceptualization of what has over the past two decades come to be known as the narcissistic personality. (Guntrip's formulation of self-sufficiency as a defense fits with Kernberg's concept of the narcissistic personality, to be discussed in chapter 5, but Kernberg, 1975, believed the defense was directed primarily against oral aggression rather than object hunger. As will be shown in chapter 6, Kohut's, 1971, views differed from both theorists inasmuch as he attributed stable grandiosity to developmental arrest rather than to defensive need.) From Guntrip's viewpoint, narcissistically aloof patients who believe themselves able to do anything and who believe their need for others is nonexistent, are defending against a terrifying longing to love and have their love accepted. This desire in them has become so intense as to threaten their very sense of self if any object contact is made. Consequently, aloof withdrawal is the only way to maintain a sense of "autonomy." The only alternative is merger which means loss of the sense of personal existence.

Such patients typically display this defensive constellation in their attitudes of self-sufficiency, superiority, and coldness. For example, Guntrip (1969) discussed one patient who disdained children's games and all other normal activities of youth. "As a child I would cry with boredom at the silly games the children played. It got worse in my teens, terrible boredom, futility, lack of interest. I would look at people and see them interested in things I thought silly. I felt I was different and had more brains" (p. 43). Such an attitude of superiority, according to Guntrip, reflects the deep fear of object contact character- istic of the schizoid. Guntrip (1969) quoted another patient who described his relationships this way: "I don't feel drawn to anyone. I can feel cold about all the people who are near and dear to me. When my wife and I were having sexual relations she would say 'Do you love me?' I would answer: 'Of course I do, but sex isn't love, it's only an experience.' I could never see why that upset her" (p. 44). These attitudes of superiority and affectlessness are, Guntrip believed, defenses against intense object hunger.

A personality structure of this type successfully defends against the longed for merger between self and object. The defense allows the patient to function and experience a minimal sense of connection with reality without affective contact with objects, but requires constant vigilance inasmuch as interactions with others continually threaten to break through the defensive constellation by evoking affect. Since interpersonal affect represents the most terrifying threat to such people, their lives tend to be lonely, empty, and withdrawn.

Patients who are not able to defend so successfully become psy- chotic. In Guntrip's formulation of psychogenic psychosis the illness represents the breakthrough of the desire to merge and involves a blurring of self–object boundaries. The result is withdrawal from real- ity and concurrent self–world fusion. The psychotic is neither in the world nor separate from it. By contrast, the schizoid personality, who does successfully defend against the blurring of self–object bound- aries, maintains the boundary at the cost of withdrawal from the world. Guntrip (1969) saw the schizoid character structure as a des- perate effort to "preserve the ego." From this point of view, all nonpsychotic psychopathology, whatever the cost of the symptoms, has the value of preserving the ego and, perforce, the connection with reality.

It can easily be seen from this formulation that Guntrip viewed the defensive structure of the schizoid personality as ultimately a defense against psychosis. This is an important concept in Guntrip's theory; it underscores the gravity of schizoid illness, as we shall see in the next section, defines the goal of psychotherapy with such a patient as reaching the core schizoid withdrawal underlying the defenses. If treatment achieves its goal, it must run the danger of potential psychosis.

Guntrip (1962) followed Fairbairn in the belief that when the infant begins to feel ambivalence to the maternal object, the second phase of infancy begins. For Guntrip, this is the phase in which the infant needs to know not so much that its love is acceptable but that it can love without "destroying by hate." This sounds like Fairbairn's view of two pathological positions, the schizoid and the depressed. In many of his writings Guntrip appeared to adopt such a position, even at times adding paranoia as a third psychopathological position. However, Guntrip seemed ultimately to endorse no more than one psychopathological position.

Guntrip (1962) agreed with Freud (1917) that depressives suffered from repressed hatred of the loved object, but he questioned the traditional psychoanalytic formulation that hate is rooted in the aggressive drive (Freud, 1920). In Guntrip's view, because one can only hate the object one loves and is attached to, hate implies an attachment, albeit a frustrating one. Therefore, the opposite of love is not hate but indifference; the object one hates is the object one seeks satisfaction from but finds frustration in. From this Guntrip concluded that hate is frustrated love, leading to the desire to attack and devour the object. To preserve the object the hatred is repressed and turned against the self, and depression results. The root of depression, then, according to this view, is frustrated love, which leads to anxiety of object loss. But this is essentially the same dynamic that Fairbairn and Guntrip proposed as the root of schizoid pathology. This reasoning led Guntrip to the conclusion that depression is a defense against schizoid pathology. All his clinical vignettes and illustrations of depression were ultimately formulated as examples of the schizoid position as in the clinical illustration described earlier.

Guntrip believed depression was the most significant defense against schizoid pathology because of the strong preference patients have for believing themselves to be depressed when they are, in fact, emotionally withdrawn into a schizoid state. Indeed, Guntrip (1969) broadened his discussion to a general human preference—to be found in the history of ideas, including those of Freud himself—to view man as bad, rather than weak. Guntrip's contention was that classical psychoanalytic theory was dominated by the self-delusion that human problems are due to guilt over "badness," a delusion that he believed to be a denial of man's weakness. One of Fairbairn's most critical contributions to psychoanalytic theory, according to Guntrip, was the movement away from this view and toward the understanding that all psychopathology, whatever its presenting clinical picture, is a product of fears with which the patient is unable to cope. Guntrip pointed out that guilt implies strength but "badness"; that people prefer to feel they have the capacity to act, since this means they can control their own fate. To admit that we would like to behave otherwise but do not have the capacity is shameful because it exposes an inadequacy: Freud's theoretical edifice, built on the guilty repression of unacceptable affects, fits the human need to believe that one *can* and colludes with the defensive needs of all patients who are fearful, feel ashamed of inadequacy, and are unable to acknowledge their incapacity.

Guntrip's view was that the rejection of love evokes feelings of weakness because the infant longs for a response to the deepest need it has but is unable to make the response occur. The infant's most precious offering is inadequate, with the result that it feels weak, helpless, and ashamed of its own needs. This "weakened ego" is fearful and attempts to avoid exposure continually. To avoid recognizing this painful weakness, the ego attacks itself for this very weakness, creating the illusion that its badness is the source of its problems. Guilt is superimposed upon the sense of badness and unworthiness, adding to the feeling that the ego is undeserving and fostering the illusion that the reason for unhappiness and symptoms lies in the feeling of unacceptability. Guntrip stressed that patients will quite readily admit to feeling guilty because they are unconsciously relieved to avoid confronting their fears and weakness. In this sense, he believed that Freud had not grasped the magnitude of his own discovery. While Freud succeeded in demonstrating that mental life is filled with a vast array of desires that it hides from itself, he saw the source of the unconscious as the unacceptability of these wishes. From Guntrip's point of view, this conception does not go to the deepest root of man's lack of self-awareness. Guilt masks the parts of the self the ego is most afraid to know; namely, the feelings of weakness and helplessness and the resultant sense of shame. All of this has profound ramifications for treatment in general, as shall be seen shortly, but it has special implications for the understanding of depression.

Recall that for Guntrip ego weakness always means the desire to withdraw from all object contact and consequently evokes the threat of ego loss. The patient turns his hatred against his own weakness in a desperate effort to feel real. Guilt, self-hatred, and depression are the price paid for this tenuous hold on reality. According to Guntrip, depression is the prototype for all neuroses. All supposedly neurotic conditions traditionally conceptualized as products of intrapsychic conflict between affect and a moral standard are defenses against the regressive longing to withdraw from all object contact and against the resulting incipient loss of reality. Regarding the longing to return to womblike security, Guntrip (1969) stated, "I regard this as the basis of all schizoid characteristics, the deep secret flight from life, in seeking a defense against which the rest of the personality lands itself in a variety of psychotic and psychoneurotic states, among which one of the most important is depression" (p. 144). For Guntrip, the regressive longing for the pre-object state is at the core of all depression.

The two patients cited earlier illustrate the regressive core of depression. The schoolteacher who dreamed of the Headmaster walking away and leaving him without food represents the schizoid withdrawal of an apparently depressed patient. The patient who had such great difficulty getting out of bed demonstrates the regressive longing even more clearly. Both patients suffered from depressive symptoms, but in analysis the longing to return to prenatal security emerged. Guntrip (1969) discussed in some detail a third case, a manic-depressive man who suffered prolonged periods of depression, characterized by guilt and inactivity, alternating with phases of hyperactivity and overwork. During the course of the analysis, the focus shifted from his guilt over sex and aggression to his fears of facing the world. The patient could not relax, had difficulty quieting his mind, and had great difficulty sleeping as a result. He feared that if he "let go" in sleep, he would never "get started" again. Guntrip used this as a clue to the underlying "frightened self" seeking a retreat from life, and for the first time the patient's schizoid characteristics were revealed. The patient's "frightened child self" and a spate of fantasies and desires to be warm and secure with the analyst emerged. He expressed a longing to "let go," and during one session, he slept for about 40 minutes. Guntrip's contention is that this type of material is typical of depressed patients if the analysis is allowed to proceed without premature interpretations or interruptions.

Guntrip was able to fit addiction into his formulation that all psychopathology is rooted in the schizoid position. His view was that when schizoid dynamics are operative, substitute objects are sought. In some cases new human objects are used, but the despair in schizoid withdrawal tends to draw the ego to nonhuman replacements such as food, drugs, and alcohol. Substances are more easily controllable and are therefore unlikely to repeat the frustration already experienced in human relationships. Further, it is in the nature of schizoid withdrawal to prefer nonhuman modes of gratification. Recall that for Guntrip the goal of schizoid withdrawal is the cancellation of all object relationships. The schizoid seeks nonhuman forms of gratification in an effort to achieve the satisfaction missing in early object relationships and in a manner that will not evoke the anxiety and frustration of human contact. Food, drugs, and alcohol all serve this purpose. Since the longing is for human contact, however, the substance cannot succeed in providing the needed gratification, and it must be continually sought in a desperate effort to avoid the anxiety of schizoid withdrawal without the danger of human contact. The result is substance addiction, which defends against regressive schizoid longing by providing a sense of reality contact. As soon as the substance wears off, the sense of reality threatens to disappear. Addiction, being a desperate effort to maintain a sense of existence, becomes inevitable.

Eating disorders fit especially well into Guntrip's formulations. Recall the connections alluded to earlier between the longing for the tantalizing love object and food. As we have seen, the dreams of the schizoid are frequently about food, and especially food that is not eaten or eatable. The dream of the schoolteacher in which the Headmaster left him without food is illustrative of this relationship. Guntrip (1969) cites another patient who dreamed that she was enjoying her favorite meal, only to have her mother snatch it away when she came to the best part. The schizoid need to devour the object links the "desirable deserter" with food and renders the latter a natural substitute for the former, particularly given its relative availability. According to Guntrip, in all eating disorders, food symbolizes the tantalizing early object. It is a simple matter to extract from this conceptualization a formulation for each major form of food pathology. Binge eating is an uncontrolled desire to secure the object by ingesting it. Bulimia has the same root but includes the fear of having destroyed the object by devouring it, a fear that leads to the need to expel the object to save it. If the craving to devour the object is overwhelmingly intense, it may threaten ego loss, resulting in an overwhelming fear of the longed-for object and a stubborn defense against it. Anorexia is a schizoid defense against the desire to devour the object. Typical of the latter is the patient, cited earlier, who became hungry whenever her husband came home. She craved food, desiring to devour it in a single gulp, but her appetite disappeared at the sight of it. For such patients, the "in and out program" is enacted in the domain of food and eating.

A similar assessment can be applied to the borderline personality disorder. Guntrip did not use this label, but he described many patients with the intense hostility, chaos, disorganization, overwhelming anxiety, and intensely devaluing and idealizing object relationships so characteristic of borderline psychopathology. Without detailed examination of the various symptoms of borderline psychopathology, Guntrip made clear that all these features were desperate efforts by the ego both to form such minimal object contact as the patient was capable of making, and to protect itself from being over-whelmed by any object contact. All the characterological features of borderline pathology were seen by Guntrip as symptoms of either the longing for merger or the fear of loss of the ego via withdrawal.

Patients in all these categories of psychopathology are beset by internalized bad objects, the experience of which is usually extremely painful. Nonetheless, psychoanalytic inquiry is not to be ended at the uncovering of represented bad objects. Guntrip's crucial point is that the bad objects are themselves defenses against ego loss. This may not seem like a credible view, given the extreme pain bad object experi-ence can bring, especially in self-hating depressive and borderline patients. However, Guntrip insisted that it is only the conception of bad objects as defenses that can account for the stubbornness with which patients cling to them. As painful as bad object experience is, the pain provides a feeling of reality; the anxiety of loss of existence is more threatening. The only alternative to bad object experience is regression to a withdrawal so deep as to threaten the existence of the ego.

In this view of psychological rock bottom, Guntrip parted company with Fairbairn, who despite his emphasis on the schizoid position had no concept of schizoid regression. It was his insistence on the impor-tance of longing for regression to the pre-object state that led Guntrip to alter Fairbairn's theory of endopsychic structure.

Psychological Structure

Guntrip accepted Fairbairn's division of the psyche into the central, libidinal, and antilibidinal egos; however, he questioned the concept of the libidinal ego as the deepest, most repressed, ego structure, being unable to accept the view that libidinal excitement by itself could lead to severe repression and psychopathology. In a very real sense, Guntrip came to believe that Fairbairn's view of the libidinal ego as the seat of repressed material suffered from the same failing as Freud's view of the id, namely that it could not account for severity of symptoms; internalized bad objects; and, above all, psychological weakness, shame, and feelings of inadequacy and helplessness, which Guntrip believed were endemic to psychopathology.

As a result of the findings of his investigation into the depths of psychopathology, Guntrip postulated a further division of the libidi-nal ego into an active, oral, sadomasochistic ego and a regressed ego. The former corresponds, although perhaps imprecisely, to Fair-bairn's libidinal ego, and the latter is Guntrip's effort to explain the schizoid core he saw in all psychopathology. The difference between these two divisions of the libidinal ego is the distinction between an ego invested in bad object relations and an ego seeking to return to the prenatal safety of no object relations. The aspect of the libidinal ego that is excited by objects is to some extent involved in a connection with reality. Such an ego is possessed of breast and incest longings and fantasies. It has not lost its desire for objects; it seeks primitive objects. This active ego has sexual and aggressive investments in early objects, with all the conflicts and guilt resulting from oedipal and preoedipal conflicts. However, the futility of unsatisfactory object relations, as discussed earlier, leads not to bad object relations but to the longing to withdraw from all object contact. As Guntrip (1969) states, this is a "passive regressed ego which seeks to return to the antenatal state of absolute passive dependent security" (p. 74).

The attack of the antilibidinal ego is directed against this passive dependence, not against excitement. Guntrip viewed the self-hatred of the depressive as a good illustration of such an attack: depressives appear to be turning aggression from the object to the self, but they are simultaneously attacking their longing for passive, absolute dependence and defending against the awareness of it. According to Guntrip, all people have this division of the libidinal ego and the potential for withdrawal from object contact; those with psychopathology are characterized by a greater degree of dominance of this regressive longing.

In Guntrip's view, the concept of the regressive ego is the final outcome of the shift in psychoanalytic theory from drive psychology to object relations theory. Fairbairn had taken a major step in this direction with his reconceptualization of psychic structure into ego divisions based on internalized objects. However, his concept of the libidinal ego bases his theory of mental structure on a fear of excitement, rather that anxiety about object contact and, therefore, according to Guntrip, fails to address the depths of patients' anxieties. Intense feelings of shame, weakness, and dependence imply a fear that is far more powerful than excitement. In Guntrip's view, the concept of the libidinal ego as the deepest part of the psyche represents Fairbairn's failure to move his theory far enough from Freud's drive psychology. With his concept of the regressed ego, Guntrip believed he had taken the final step in the development of the psychoanalytic theory of psychopathology from a drive to an ego–object relations psychology. It was this concept of the regressed ego that he felt made sense of the fear and shame in the deepest levels of patients' psyches.

Consequently, he believed this concept had far-reaching implications for psychoanalytic therapy, and it is to the therapeutic process as conceptualized by Guntrip that we now turn.

Treatment

Guntrip's clinical recommendations follow directly from his concept of the regressed ego at the core of all psychopathology. On the basis of his formulation that psychopathology is rooted in the desire to regress to an egoless state, Guntrip believed that psychoanalytic therapy must reach this regressive longing in the patient. In traditional analytic therapy the aim of the process is to make conscious affects, impulses, and wishes, and the mode of verbal interpretation is apposite to this end. However, Guntrip, following Fairbairn's formulation of schizoid dynamics, proposed a shift in the goal of the therapeutic process; rather than bring discrete affects to consciousness, the psychoanalyst should bring forth a split-off ego. This is not simply a matter of interpreting correctly, but a process of allowing the patient to experience a previously buried part of the self for the first time.

Once this component of the personality is apparent, the patient must feel safe enough for its emergence in the analysis. The realization of the existence of regressive longings is itself insufficient for therapeutic efficacy; the buried personality must be experienced within the context of the therapeutic relationship. (In this sense, Guntrip's thought is in agreement with Weiss's, 1971, ego-psychological view that unconscious material emerges when the patient feels safe. The primary differences are that for Weiss unconscious material consists of impulses and safety is equated with analytic neutrality, whereas for Guntrip the unconscious is split-off portions of the ego, and safety can be provided in other ways, such as by reassurance against abandonment.) With his prescription for the emergence of regressive longings, Guntrip believed he was carrying out the direct therapeutic implications of his and Fairbairn's object relations theory of psychopathology. A consistent object relations approach to analytic therapy, according to Guntrip, requires the relationship between patient and analyst to be a critical component of the therapeutic process, as it was for Fairbairn (1958). Guntrip went beyond Fairbairn by describing more specifically the needed therapeutic relationship. Since the patient's problems are a product of unfulfilled early object longings, the resolution must come from a new object relationship that to some degree, satisfies the unfulfilled childhood longings. In Guntrip's view, a part of the ego is "left behind" and continues to cripple the growth of the personality. To unblock the ego, its split-off portion must be reintegrated with the rest of the personality; this requires a personal relationship that allows the emergence and integration of the regressed part of the ego.

As we will see in chapter 4, Guntrip's concept of regression in the analytic relationship is similar to Winnicott's notion that the analytic process consists of belated ego maturation by the provision of a new relationship. Winnicott, who was Guntrip's second analyst, had a profound influence on Guntrip. Although we will discuss Winnicott's theory of technique in chapter 4, it should be noted here that when Guntrip extended his theory of technique to the fostering of regression to ego arrest, he blended Fairbairn's object relations theory with Winnicott's technical emphasis on belated ego maturation.

According to Guntrip, the regressed ego is a product of trauma in the child's longing for love and its offering of love. It is the original unsatisfactory relationship that leads to the splitting off of the infantile longings into the buried part of the self. If this traumatized component of the personality is to reemerge, a new relationship must be experienced in which the child does not fear a reinjury to the infantile ego. In this way the relationship the analyst offers to the patient becomes crucial to the success of the treatment. The attitude of the analyst, according to Guntrip, is critical for the provision of the safe conditions necessary for the emergence of the regressed ego. The analyst must be a demonstrably "better parent" than the original parenting figure.

In Guntrip's view, it is the analyst's ability to identify with the patient that determines whether he or she can provide the atmosphere necessary for the patient to take the risk of allowing the withdrawn component of the self to meet reality for the first time. Since the patient must take a risk never before attempted, the analyst must offer a relationship never before experienced. In emphasizing the analyst's role in providing the necessary therapeutic relationship, Guntrip was again influenced by Winnicott, who (as we will see in chapter 4), believed the analyst's role is to adapt to the patient's needs. According to Guntrip (1969), what concerns the patient is "whether the therapist as a real human being has a genuine capacity to value, care about, understand, see, and treat the patient as a person in his own right" (p. 350). Only such a relationship has a chance of allowing the patient's long-buried individuality to emerge.

Nonetheless, no sooner does the patient begun to experience this emerging individuality than he or she experiences renewed threat. The relationship offered by the analyst is itself a source of anxiety, since the regressed ego now experiences the object contact it withdrew from the world to avoid. The threat of ego loss becomes very real, and the previously withdrawn ego craves regression. As Guntrip (1969) states, "*The weak schizoid ego is in urgent need of a relationship, a therapeutic relationship capable of filling the gap left by inadequate mothering. Only that can rescue the patient from succumbing to the terrors of ultimate isolation. Yet when it comes to it, the weak ego is afraid of the very relationship that it needs*"(p. 231). Guntrip points out that the ego cannot integrate and grow without a relationship but that "*the weakened ego always fears it will be swamped by the other person in a relationship*" (p. 231) Consequently, the patient is continually moving toward and away from the analyst as he or she enacts the in-and-out program in the therapeutic relationship. Each time contact is made with the regressed ego, it will seek to rebury itself in the withdrawn state from which it is trying so hard to emerge. This situation frequently leads to a therapeutic stalemate. The therapeutic process then becomes a continual effort by both patient and therapist to overcome this dilemma.

Two of Guntrip's clinical vignettes illustrate this enactment of the in-and-out program in the therapeutic relationship. Guntrip (1969) discusses one case in which the patient showed marked improvement after working through the trauma of having been rejected by her grandfather, a trauma that had resulted in a fear of trusting others (p. 231). When Guntrip linked this fear to her relationship with him, the patient initially showed further improvement. However, one day, she arrived late, had not wished to come, and was hoping to be able to leave before Guntrip could see her. When the interpretation was made that she was fleeing the therapist because she had been more trusting of him recently, she responded this way:

> She sat silent, pale, cold, uncommunicative, and then said that she had told her mother that she felt her heart was a frozen lump inside her, and she was frightened that she would never all her life be able to feel warm and responsive and loving to any one. She added that she was afraid to get too close to people, they were too much for her, and she revived a fear . . . of becoming pregnant and having a baby, a fear which would make marriage impossible [p. 232].

The patient went on to say, in response to Guntrip's interpretation of her fear of closeness, that she was overwhelmed at the thought of being close to anyone and could only feel safe at a distance. This schizoid patient's flight reaction was part of her enactment of the in-and-out program she had in response to a closer connection to her therapist.

The second case illustration involves a woman who suffered from a severe regression and occasional nightmares in which she would scream for her mother and feel as though she were dying. As she began to feel that Guntrip could fill the gap of utter isolation that led her to seek her mother in her dreams, the nightmares diminished and her condition improved. At this point two close friends of hers were killed, and the patient began to feel that she was on the verge of collapse. She found it impossible to turn to Guntrip; she began to argue stubbornly with him, and her nightmares resumed. However, she then had a dream in which a headwaiter, who symbolized Guntrip, was going away but then decided to stay on her account; in the same dream she had a baby she had forgotten to feed. Guntrip pointed out to her that she had been doing without him and had therefore been repressing, not feeding, the baby in herself and that this withdrawal had led to a fear of abandonment. Guntrip interpreted to her that her increasing dependence on him led to anxiety over losing her autonomy, thus motivating the push away from him.

This vignette demonstrates the typical schizoid response to therapeutic improvement: the patient feels closer to the therapist, becomes anxious, and then withdraws from the process. Both cases presented here illustrate well the continual oscillation between connection with the therapist and symptom improvement, on the one hand, and withdrawal and exacerbation of the clinical condition, on the other. Looking at the analytic process from this point of view, the concept of resistance assumes a new meaning. Resistance in the process Guntrip describes refers to the patient's continual effort to withdraw from contact with the analyst and return to the regressed objectless state. This is Guntrip's application of Fairbairn's principle that the patient resists the analyst not the analysis. Because the objectless state threatens such sense of ego as the patient has been able to sustain, the resistance tends to manifest itself most frequently in a "compromise relationship," in which the patient can neither fully accept nor fully reject the analyst, as to do either risks ego loss. The resistance may manifest itself in a variety of defenses, such as intellectualization and isolation of affect, but the value of the defense is always to maintain whatever sense of connection the patient is capable of. As was shown earlier, schizoid states always serve a critical function for the patient: they maintain the reality sense. In the treatment process the patient's defenses must be seen as providing the only type of contact he or she can achieve, even as they simultaneously block the progress of the treatment. In sum, the resistance must be analyzed, but it must also be appreciated as the form of object contact the patient is currently capable of.

Guntrip did exactly this in both of the aforementioned cases. To the woman who pushed him away out of fear of betrayal, Guntrip interpreted that she had come late and had sought to withdraw from him in order to see if he could accept her independence rather than abandon her in the face of her need for withdrawal. This is a good example of what Guntrip meant by appreciating the patient's need for the defense rather than simply interpreting it as a resistance to involvement with the therapist. Similarly, in the case of the woman whose friends had died, Guntrip interpreted her need to argue with rather than rely on him as her need for independence; he stated clearly that he accepted this need and would not abandon her nor even change his attitude toward her in response to it.

Despite the effectiveness of interpretations in these two cases, in Guntrip's view interpretations themselves are insufficient for analytic movement because making unconscious contents conscious does not lead to the reintegration and growth of the ego. "Analysis must be seen as 'exposing' a developmentally arrested psyche to the support and new stimulus of an understanding relationship in which the therapist, like the parent, must wait while the child grows" (Guntrip, 1969, pp. 178–179). This concept of resistance as a form of object contact and of its treatment as the "exposure" to a new relationship presaged Kohut's concept of allowing the patient's defenses to form the transference relationship until they are gradually relinquished in the context of the new relationship (see chapter 6). Thus, Guntrip's concepts of resistance and defense resolution anticipated some of Kohut's fundamental concepts of the analytic process.

Both case illustrations also demonstrate Guntrip's view of the transference. In the first case, the patient feared Guntrip would be like her rejecting grandfather; in the second, the patient feared Guntrip would not allow her independence without abandoning her, as her mother had done. In both clinical situations the transference became apparent as the patient began to feel the therapist was useful and dependable. The anxiety of this potential view of the therapist was stimulated in both cases by the image of the most painful, rejecting figure of the patient's past. The figure most closely identified with the patient's anxiety in object contact becomes the transference figure and, as such, interferes with the advance of the treatment process. The transference is the most stubborn obstacle to the progress of the relationship between patient and therapist and, consequently, to the appearance of the regressed ego. Its interpretation is crucial for the new relationship between patient and therapist, which is necessary for the development of the therapeutic regression. For example, Guntrip's interpretation to the first patient that she feared that he would be like her grandfather allowed her to begin once again to depend on him.

These case examples also show the ease with which Guntrip intervened noninterpretively. In the first case, after interpreting to the patient that she feared he could not allow her autonomy without losing touch with her, he told her that he would be there when she needed him. In the second case, he was even more direct and reassuring: after interpreting that the patient feared she would lose her independence, Guntrip (1969) told her that her dependence on him "did not aim at robbing her of independence based on inner strength, and [that he] could accept her independence as well as her dependence" (p. 235). Guntrip believed such reassuring remarks helped foster the patient's feeling of safety and security in the patient–therapist relationship that is required for the eventual emergence of the therapeutic regression. These examples demonstrate that Guntrip's concept of the therapist's role is a plain departure from the traditional near-exclusive reliance on interpretation. Guntrip clearly believed that the priority for the therapist is to make contact with the regressed ego rather than offer the most apt interpretation and that any intervention that furthers that goal is preferable to interpretation.

Guntrip refers to three stages in the analytic process. Initially, the oedipal object-related conflicts, involving sexual and aggressive feelings and guilt are addressed. However, according to Guntrip, such dynamics are always to some degree defenses against the exposure of the weak, immature component of the personality with its infantile dependency. Consequently, when the oedipal conflicts are interpreted, the infantile dependency longings and the shame associated with the regressed ego threaten to appear and the schizoid compromise becomes manifest. The treatment task at that point is to overcome this stalemate. This critical breakthrough can be achieved only by a combination of the safe therapeutic atmosphere, and the therapist's persistent interpretation and appreciation of the patient's resistance to the emergence of the regressed ego. The third phase of treatment involves regression to the infantile ego and the rebirth of the ego as a reunited whole. The therapeutic action, for Guntrip, lies in regression and rebirth rather than in the content of interpretations. In this sense, Guntrip reconceptualized the therapeutic process of psychoanalytic treatment, and in so doing he believed he had arrived at the logical clinical application of Fairbairn's and his own object relations theory of mental structure and psychopathology.

Guntrip was realistic in his assessment of the possibility of such a radical treatment in every case of psychoanalytic therapy. He acknowledged that such a deep treatment was often not possible, but he believed that his concept of the therapeutic process provides the therapist with a model that fits the patient's needs and issues far better than does the traditional interpretive model. Even though every analysis will not be carried through to the deepest point, the model Guntrip proposed sensitizes the therapist to the defensive nature of such seemingly bedrock issues as oedipal conflicts and internalized bad objects. The realization that even such painful issues can be used as defenses against a still deeper regression, with longings to devour and return to a womblike existence, helps the analyst guide the therapy to a deeper level, even though a complete regression and rebirth may not occur.

Perhaps the clearest view of analytic therapy conducted according to this model was presented by Guntrip in his lengthy discussion of the manic–depressive case described earlier. The patient led a miserable life, oscillating between the sluggish inactivity of depression, at times accompanied by guilt, and hectic overwork, punctuated by sexual and aggressive outbursts. In the treatment process it became apparent that the guilt was a feeling of contempt directed at his weakness and inability to function. He used somatic symptoms to defend against the depression, often falling ill for long periods during which he could do almost nothing. Guntrip used the somatization to focus the treatment effort away from his guilt over his "bad" sexual and aggressive impulses and toward his feeling of weakness and his wish to withdraw. The patient acknowledged that he had to force himself to function against deep feelings of inadequacy and fear. It will be recalled that he was unable to relax for fear that if he "let go" he would lapse into a completely nonfunctional state. During therapy the patient came to understand that his manic drive was a desperate attempt to avoid such an outcome; ultimately, he feared the recognition of his infantile, regressed ego and used the mania to maintain contact with reality. The crucial intervention at this point was Guntrip's (1969) interpretation of the patient's apparent depressive guilt as a component of his "self-forcing" and therefore, as a defense against the recognition of his *"'frightened child' self who was in a state of constant retreat from life"* (p. 158). After three and one-half years of analysis, the patient entered a period during which his schizoid character came to the fore; then after a retreat to the most regressed part of himself, he embarked upon a course of steady and irreversible improvement. The regression began when the patient evinced no discernible reaction to his father's death, remarking that his father cared little for children and adding that he himself was quite sensitive to their sufferings. Guntrip remarked that the patient inflicted great suffering on "the child within." The patient replied that he had the wish that Guntrip would put him to sleep so that he could awake and find all his troubles solved. This comment, which marked the start of the patient's recognition of his desire for regression and dependence on his analyst, led to their intensification. At this point, the patient began talking frenetically and dreamed of a man buried alive in a coffin. Guntrip pointed out that the withdrawal he feared was so deep that he felt as though he would be buried alive and his rapid speech defended against this recognition.

The transference became the focus of the patient's schizoid conflict between yielding to the longing for infantile dependence and forcing himself into pseudoadulthood. He had fantasies both of smashing Guntrip's car and of being in the car with Guntrip, of leaning against him and putting his arm around him or of curling up in the back seat as Guntrip drove. Guntrip (1969) interpreted these fantasies as follows: "His hostile resistances to me and fantasied aggressions against me earlier on were clearly a defense against his fear of helpless dependence on me, and masked a fantasy of a return to the womb" (p. 159). In a crucial session the patient began with an attitude of impersonal, unfeeling detachment, and Guntrip pointed out that this was a withdrawal in fear from his deepening attachment, dependence, and trust of him. The next session began the patient's steady improvement; he reported a dream of going through a tunnel, which Guntrip interpreted as a fantasied return to the womb. In the same session, the patient expressed a desire to fight, because "a love relationship is smothering " (p. 160). Guntrip interpreted this wish to do battle with him as the patient's defense against his developing feelings of closeness and dependence.

Subsequent material continued the theme of the patient's wish to surrender to Guntrip's care (for example, he reported feeling greater comfort on the couch) and his desire to flee in fear. However this tolerance for his dependence and regressive longings irreversibly increased, as did his clinical improvement. In one session he slept most of the time; in the next analytic hour he reported that the previous session had changed him by giving him a feeling of greater calm and strength. Guntrip reports that the manic–depressive condition never returned and that eighteen months after the case report was written the patient's gains were still evident.

This case, which he reported in great detail, provides a good illustration of how Guntrip applied his treatment principles. One can see that Guntrip interpreted the patient's guilt as a defense against regression. By remarking on the patient's abuse of his "child within," Guntrip elicited his first acknowledgment of his dependent and regressive longings. After that point the treatment took on the character of the in-and-out program, with the patient seeking both complete dependence and total detachment. Womb fantasies appeared as a manifestation of the regressed ego, and eventually the regression achieved its deepest enactment when the patient slept for most of a session. The transference manifested itself most importantly as the patient's deep need for and fear of trusting and surrendering himself to the analyst, and its interpretation served to help the patient overcome this fear. When the patient trusted the analyst enough to allow the regressed portion of the ego to appear in the analytic relationship, therapeutic movement occurred.

In this case and others like it, Guntrip brought to fruition his and Fairbairn's far-reaching theoretical revision of Freud's concept of human motivation, development, and psychopathology. Guntrip's description of the therapeutic process indicates that he, unlike Fairbairn, viewed object relations theory as providing the rationale for a clearly different, but nonetheless psychoanalytic, model of psychodynamic treatment, a model he implemented in his work with patients. Guntrip went beyond Fairbairn in developing this model in some detail. Guntrip believed that in his application of his and Fairbairn's reconceptualization of psychoanalytic theory, he was able to demonstrate how psychoanalytic therapy is conducted on a human object relations, rather than a drive, model.

CRITIQUE

Fairbairn developed the most systematic object relations theory of personality and pathology. He was the first theorist to build a theory on the concept of autonomy of object attachment, and his view that object seeking is a primary function has been supported by the research on attachment in animals and children, as we have seen in chapter 1 (Bowlby, 1969). This object relations theory is closer to patients' experience by avoiding the reductionism of classical theory. This type of theorizing was later lauded as "experience-near" (discussed in chapter 6) by Kohut (1977). Fairbairn must be given due credit for the development of a comprehensive theory of personality development and pathology containing a minimum of unfulfilled nonexperiential concepts. His "personalization" of psychoanalytic concepts is a forerunner of recent efforts to make psychoanalytic theory more of a psychology of persons rather than of impersonal forces (for example, Mitchell, 1988; Stolorow, 1985).

Another of Fairbairn's major contributions is his emphasis on the dependency–autonomy conflict in the dynamics of psychopathology. Fairbairn was a pioneer in the recognition that the failure to resolve the need to both attach and maintain independence accounts for many human problems. The influence of Mahler and her colleagues has led to wide acceptance of separation-individuation as a key developmental process and force in pathology, but Fairbairn understood the significance of this developmental trajectory before Mahler's work appeared. Fairbairn also used it to understand neurotic pathology, whereas Mahler and her coworkers have confined their clinical application of the concept primarily to severe pathology.

Perhaps the most significant of Fairbairn's and Guntrip's contributions to the theory of psychopathology is their appreciation of schizoid dynamics in a range of pathological conditions, including apparent neurosis. Both Fairbairn and Guntrip pointed out that the overuse of guilt and structural conflict in psychoanalytic formulations often masks a deeper level of pathology characterized by shame, fear, and feelings of inadequacy, and both theorists were instrumental in applying these concepts to a variety of symptomatologies. They pointed out that treatment must often touch a deep level of schizoid withdrawal, fear of object contact, and shame in order to reach the patient. This view has been adopted to some degree by several more recent psychoanalytic movements, such as self psychology (Kohut, 1977; Bacal and Newman, 1990), Winnicott and his followers (Khan, 1974), and interpersonal theory (Mitchell, 1988). Fairbairn and Guntrip must be considered leaders in this general thrust of psychoanalytic theory toward the appreciation of psychological deficit. In addition, they developed a unique approach to deficit with their theory of schizoid dynamics.

As is frequently true of theories, the strength of schizoid dynamics is also its most glaring drawback. In their zeal to underscore its importance, Fairbairn and Guntrip made the error of reducing all pathology to the schizoid position. While Fairbairn theoretically recognized two pathological positions, the schizoid and the depressive, his discussion of pathology (and especially his limited case material), focused exclusively on the schizoid fear of destroying the object with love. Guntrip yielded all pretense of belief in any other dynamic by formulating depression as a schizoid condition. Ultimately, Fairbairn and Guntrip reduced all human problems to a single issue. The drug addict, the demanding borderline patient, the anxiety neurotic, and the depressive all suffer from the same "disease"—fear of object love. The theories of Fairbairn and Guntrip cannot provide an explanation for why these syndromes are different, and they are limited in their ability to explain the particular issues in each clinical condition and the individual dynamics of each patient. Their homogenization of pathology is undoubtedly a primary reason for the limited influence of their theories. Although recent interest in object relations thinking has led to a greater degree of recognition for their work, their impact has not been extensive even among relational theorists with few exceptions (e.g., Mitchell, 1988, and Celani, 1993).

Fairbairn's work is so theoretically dominated that there is insufficient clinical material to see how his theory works in practice. While the clinical work Guntrip reported is often impressive, it suffers from the same limitation as Fairbairn's object relations theory: its application of one basic principle. For Guntrip, the analytic task is to meet the needs of the patient's regressed ego, and while he reported some cases in which this technical approach seemed to be quite successful, it is the only type of intervention he advocated. One is left with the impression that Guntrip believed in meeting a need for regression in all patients, an error of homogenization of pathology in the clinical arena. If Guntrip believed that some patients could be treated in another way, this possibility is not indicated in his writing.

Fairbairn and Guntrip are primary advocates of what Mitchell (1988) has called "developmental arrest theory," the belief that pathology is a block in the developmental process that must be undone in treatment (see chapter 7). Unfortunately, their approach to the concept of developmental arrest is so narrow in its single-issue focus on schizoid withdrawal that the range of applicability of their theories is limited. It remained for Winnicott to create a developmental arrest theory which took into account a variety of developmental issues that could be the source of a pathological outcome. Winnicott's views have a strong connection to the theories of Fairbairn and Guntrip, but they will be postponed until chapter 4, after the presentation of the theoretical system of Melanie Klein, by whom he was also greatly influenced.

The Work of Melanie Klein

MELANIE KLEIN DEVELOPED THE FIRST SYSTEMATIC BRANCH OF PSYCHOANA-
lytic thought that retained Freud's concept of the dynamic unconscious and remained within the psychoanalytic movement. Her ideas
are difficult to categorize because she based her thinking on innate
drives but always emphasized the significance of object relationships
in development and psychopathology. She stressed the importance of
the ego in development but advocated an aggressive clinical style of
interpreting impulses rather than systematically interpreting defenses.
Despite the confusion surrounding her work, she is considered here—
as she often is (for example, Greenberg and Mitchell, 1983, and
Guntrip, 1971)—as an object relations theorist because she viewed
development, despite her emphasis on drives, as organized around
the vicissitudes of object relationships and conceptualized the dynamics of all forms of psychopathology as object relationship conflicts. She
differed from most other object relations theorists, such as Fairbairn
and Guntrip, in the importance she gave to drives in the development
of object relations and in her aggressive interpretive technique.

Unlike many other psychoanalytic theorists, Klein developed a systematic conceptual framework that she used to account for all clinical
syndromes and symptoms. The basis for her theory is Freud's (1920)
dual-drive formulation, as set forth in *Beyond the Pleasure Principle.*
Klein (1946, 1958) adopted Freud's view that the infant is born with
both libidinal and destructive impulses and that the ultimate fate of
the personality rests with the development of these drives and the
relationship between them. Indeed, Klein believed that analytic theory
had erred by focusing too much on libidinal drives and failing to
grasp the critical importance of the aggressive drive. She believed that
the aggressive drive is more potentially pathogenic than libido and
that psychoanalytic intervention at the deepest layers of mental functioning cannot be conducted without focusing on aggressiveness. To
gain a clear view of Klein's understanding of psychopathology, one
must approach her theory from a developmental perspective.

74   Chapter 3

DEVELOPMENT AND PSYCHOPATHOLOGY

The Paranoid Position

According to Klein (1935, 1948b), the problem in the earliest phase of development stems from the fact that the infant is born with the aggressive drive, giving rise immediately to annihilation anxiety. Aggressiveness, for Klein, is the death instinct, or the drive to destruction; thus, the ego is born with the anxiety of its own destructiveness. Although the infant is also born with the life instinct, or libido, this positive force is not inherently strong enough to dissipate the death instinct completely; therefore, the primitive ego must use the mechanisms at its disposal to assuage annihilation anxiety. The first and most dependable mechanism is projection. The infant attributes its own destructiveness and the attendant anxiety to the breast, which frees the primitive ego from the anxiety of being destroyed from within (Klein, 1948a, 1957, 1958).

Klein (1957, 1958) drew two key implications from this view of the origins of psychological life. First, she pointed out that innate aggressiveness leads immediately to an object relationship. Because of the immediacy of the projection of destructive impulses, mental process from its origin has an object. Consequently, Klein disputed Freud's notion of the stages of autoerotism and primary narcissism. While she did not disagree with the notion of objectless states, she viewed them as coexisting with the early relationship with the breast, and thus rejected the idea of objectless stages of development. Second, she believed that the cost to the primitive ego of the projection of aggressiveness onto the breast is the preconception of a new state of danger from without, as the breast holds the threat of destruction that once resided within the ego. All the vicissitudes, mechanisms, anxieties, and feelings associated with this earliest object relationship of a primitive ego fantasizing attack from a bad breast constitutes the "paranoid position," the earliest developmental phase (Klein, 1948a, 1957).

Because of the immediacy and importance of the ego's early relationship to the object, Klein (1935) concluded that the infant's mental development from the earliest phase is a function not only of libidinal position but also of the nature of the object relationship: "For where we deal with etiology it seems essential to regard the libido-disposition not merely as such, but also to consider it in connection with the subject's earliest relations to his internalized and external objects. . . ." (p. 267). For Klein, a good object relationship is a bond in which the infant has an overall feeling of contentment and satisfaction. Only one component of this object relationship consists of feeding. The defenses are also crucial to the internalized object relationships that form the ego and superego even in this early phase. Furthermore, Klein (1952a) noted that infants as early as the second month will interrupt feeding to look lovingly at the mother. From such infant behavior she concluded that the infant derives as much gratification from the "object that gives the food as the food itself" (p. 96). Indeed, Klein (1952a) believed that direct observation of infants supported the view that a good object relationship makes feeding more gratifying. She pointed to the fact that "sleepy satisfied" babies suck better if the early object relationship is positive and that the "good suckers" become less aggressive and greedy if the initial object relationship is good.

In this context Klein (1958) developed her position on the relative importance of constitution and environment. She felt that the emotional well-being of the infant is dependent on its ability to form positive early object attachments and that this, in turn, depends on the relative balance of destructive and libidinal impulses. While frustration is a major contributor to the amount of aggression in the early object attachment, the infant's ability to tolerate frustration is the other key variable. Both Zetzel (1951) and Guntrip (1961a) criticized Klein for neglecting the role of the environment. Mitchell and Greenberg (1983) adopt the view that Klein saw aggressiveness as originating within and libido as originating without. However, Klein (1937, 1952a, 1957) made clear that she believed that both libido and aggression are constitutional drives greatly influenced by environmental factors and cannot be separated from the vicissitudes of object relations. Development within the paranoid position is a function of the amount of innate aggressiveness and libido with which the ego is born, as well as of the consistency of good feeding and good overall handling, which determines the degree of frustration to which the infant is subjected. She pointed out both in her theoretical and case discussions that the extent of parental gratification and good handling has a profound effect on the infant's development. All libidinal gratification reduces persecutory anxiety, allowing the infant to bear frustration more easily. Similarly, frustration exacerbates fear of the object, intensifying the bad-object relationship and leading to greater difficulties in bearing negative experience. Ultimately, it is the relative strength of the early object relationships, Klein believed, that determines the outcome of the paranoid position.

All good feeds and good handling are initially projected onto the good breast, just as negative experience and handling are projected onto the bad breast. The battle for the fate of the infant's psyche is waged between, on the one hand, innate aggressiveness, frustrating experience, and negative handling, all of which lead to the buildup of the bad object, and, on the other hand, innate libido, gratifying experience, and positive handling, all of which lead to the buildup of the good object.

The Projective and Introjective Cycles

The initial projection of positive and negative experience onto the good and bad breasts, respectively, is the first step in the projective and introjective cycles that Klein (1952b) considered the essence of the paranoid position. According to Klein's view, the infant reacts to all frustrating experience by sadistically attacking the breast in fantasy, thus endangering it. These fantasied attacks quickly become attacks on the mother's insides as the breast is believed to have the object that gratifies but is refusing to provide it. This early oral aggressiveness is projected onto the breast to protect both the ego from its own destructiveness and the breast from the ego's sadistic attacks. Klein believed the fantasied attacks on the breast and the mother's insides dissipate annihilation anxiety but produce a different threat: the infant is now under potential attack from without, from the breast itself. The bad object is now outside and possesses the destructiveness that once threatened from within. Thus, the projective process transforms annihilation anxiety into persecutory anxiety.

To reduce the danger of attack from outside, the ego introjects the bad breast in an effort to control the danger (Klein, 1952b). Klein's thinking is similar in this regard to Fairbairn's concept of introjection as an effort to master the anxiety of the bad object. Introjection is the next step in the projective-introjective cycle; like all other maneuvers in this process, it assuages one type of anxiety but generates another. The danger to the ego now resides within once again. It may appear that the infant has gained nothing by shifting aggressiveness from inside to outside and back again, but this is not the case, according to Klein. Each step in the projective-introjective cycle does reduce anxiety, but its success depends on the relative balance of good- and bad-object experience. Persecutory anxiety inevitably creates the need for introjection, but the anxiety produced by the internalization of the bad object is assuaged by the buildup of the internal good object from satisfying experiences. If there has been a strong buildup of the good internal object, the internalized aggressiveness will not result in an overwhelming annihilation anxiety, and persecutory anxiety will be reduced.

The introjection of the bad breast is the core of the malignant, harsh aspect of the superego (Klein, 1948a, 1958). This introjected persecutory anxiety is experienced by the verbal child or adult as internal verbal self-abuse. This view of early superego formation allowed Klein to explain the persecutory nature of the superego in children as well as various types of pathology characterized by psychological self-flagellation. She believed that all children suffer from severe superego strictures because the bad breast is introjected so early. Similarly, the introjection of the good breast forms the core of the benign superego. The balance of the good and bad introjected objects determines the relative severity of the superego.

Klein (1948a, 1958, 1959) viewed the persistent, vicious verbal self-attacks so common in both adult and child character pathology as fixation in the paranoid position due to excessive introjected persecutory objects; such self-attacks are to be distinguished from guilt over injury to the object, which is a depressive position dynamic (to be discussed shortly). Internalized persecutory anxiety is rooted in anxiety of attack defended against by the introjection of the bad object. According to Klein, if the ego is fixated at this level, the mature superego will not develop. It should be underscored that although the introjection of persecutory objects reduces the threat from without, it generates anxiety from within and thus poses a threat to the ego, the extent of which depends on the buildup of the good internal object.

Anxiety from within can become overwhelming if the internal good object buildup is insufficient to counteract it; now the need is not only to expel the bad object but also to control it. The primitive ego makes a desperate effort to control its aggressiveness by projecting the bad object "into" the breast and identifying itself with the object; that is, the infant attempts to control its own aggressiveness by endeavoring to control the aggressiveness in the object. Klein (1948b) viewed this mechanism of projective identification as the prototypical aggressive object relationship. It should be noted that in recent years projective identification has come to be regarded as an interpersonal process in which the object of the projection must actually feel the affects projected into him or her (Ogden, 1982). This view, discussed further later, is an extension of Klein's concept of projective identification as a fantasied process in which to reduce the anxiety of internal persecution, the infant fantasies putting its self-hatred into the mother.

Projective identification, like every step of the projective-introjective cycle, generates anxiety of its own. The object now becomes even more dangerous since it contains the aggressiveness and must be controlled. The fate of this mechanism, too, depends on the relative balance of good and bad object experience. If the internal good object has some degree of strength, projective identification may dissipate the anxiety of attack. However, if good object experience is insufficient and the buildup of the internal good object is weak, the infant does not feel it can control the destructiveness of the object. To defend against this new danger from the outside, the primitive ego uses the only mechanism it has at its disposal: introjection of the object. This re-introjection is now a "forceful entry" into the psyche, resulting in the feeling of being controlled from the outside, a dangerous level of introjection that Klein (1948b) believed was the source of paranoid delusions of mind and body control.

According to Klein (1952b), in normal development all these steps in the projective-introjective cycle are experienced to some degree as the internal good object is never strong enough to eliminate completely the need to reproject aggressiveness. The extent to which the ego is forced to rely on projective identification is a major factor in the movement of the ego toward growth or pathology. The more the balance of object relations is weighted in favor of bad object experience, the more the ego, in increasingly desperate efforts to control its own aggressiveness, is forced to utilize the primitive mechanisms of the paranoid position, such as projective identification and its re-introjection. Conversely, the more dominant the good object experience, the less the ego needs to use defenses against aggressiveness and the greater the movement toward ego integration and growth.

Although Klein (1952a) has been quite justifiably criticized for unfounded speculation on the infant's mental processes, she felt that the data of infant observation confirmed her views of good and bad object experience. The terrifying screams of the small baby who has been left were evidence for Klein that such an infant feels subjected to attacks from a bad object. Similarly, the fact that the infant eventually calms down when the mother returns or when it is comforted by another meant to Klein that the infant could re-establish the good object.

The mechanisms of good object experience are critical for ego development. In an effort to combat the threat of the internalized bad object, that is, to combat the dangers within caused by the introjection of the bad breast, the good breast is also introjected. This internalization of the good object forms the core of the ego. We have already seen that the superego is formed by the internalization of good and bad objects. The ultimate strength of the ego and superego structures is primarily a function of the balance of good and bad object buildup at this early developmental phase (Klein, 1952c, 1958). Because object relationships, ego, and superego structures are all intimately related, one cannot separate object relations from mental structure. Klein believed her views in this regard were an expansion of those of Freud, for whom the ego was a "precipitate of abandoned object cathexes" and for whom the superego was also an internalized object (Freud, 1923).

Splitting

The fantasied destructive attacks threaten not only the primitive, helpless ego but also the good breast. To protect the good breast, or gratifying object, unspoiled by aggressiveness, the infant splits the breast into good and bad (Klein, 1937, 1957). Because of the need to protect the good breast from the fantasied destructive attacks, the splitting of the object occurs simultaneously with the projection of destructive impulses onto the breast. Splitting thus becomes a primary defense mechanism of the paranoid position. Klein made clear that splitting is never total. She believed that even in the earliest phase of infancy there is some mingling of the good and bad breast in the infant's mind; however, if this contact between the two objects is transitory, the good breast remains intact. The use of splitting prevents the infantile ego from having to experience the anxiety of injuring the good object.

The internalized good object assuages anxiety to some degree because of the inevitable contact between the good and bad internalized objects, but such contact is threatening to the good object at this phase because of its fragility. Consequently, the ego must be split into good and bad selves. This ego splitting protects the bad self, but mitigates the effects of the internalized good object on the internalized bad object. Just as object splitting protects the good object, or breast, so too does ego splitting protect the good self. Nonetheless, according to Klein, every internalization of good object experience fosters ego integration by providing a counterbalance to the internalized bad object. The structure of the ego is a product of the internalization of good and bad objects. As good feeds and overall good handling lead to the strengthening of the internalized good object, the core solidity of both the ego and superego is strengthened. To the extent that bad object experience interferes with this development, the ego is weakened and the persecutory internalized object influences the development of the superego.

The result of splitting is an ego so weakened as to lack cohesiveness. If splitting is unsuccessful in defending against bad object experience because of insufficient buildup of the good object, a more severe form of splitting will take place. To defend against persecutory anxiety, the good object will be exaggerated into the idealized object, now fantasied to provide unlimited gratification (Klein, 1946, 1952d, 1957). The idealized object is identified with the ever-bountiful breast and thereby serves as a defense against persecutory anxiety. The fantasied availability of this everflowing breast obliterates all frustration and negative experience. If the idealized object disappoints in some fashion that breaks through into awareness, the disappointment results in the emergence of the persecutory object. Thus, Klein's theory makes a crucial distinction, not always made so clearly in psychoanalytic theory, between the good object and the idealized object. The former is an inherent part of good experience; the latter is a defense utilized only when the ego feels threatened by persecutory anxiety and resorts to a more severe form of splitting, the cleavage between the persecutory object and the idealized object. This degree of splitting always reflects an excessive degree of persecutory anxiety that is not well defended by the projective-introjective cycles alone (Klein, 1957).

The idealized object can also be introjected, and the ego will take advantage of this opportunity to defend against dangers from within. The idealized object is then identified with the self, and a feeling of omnipotence results. This omnipotence diminishes annihilation anxiety in a fashion analogous to the way the idealized object protects against persecutory anxiety. The fantasy of omnipotence provides the infant with the feeling of having unlimited control over its own fate and simultaneously obliterates awareness of all negative experience, helplessness, and frustration. Both idealization and omnipotence, which tend to go together, defend against the helplessness and persecutory anxiety of the paranoid position, resulting in the denial of all frustration and negative experience. Thus, the ability to deny reality becomes another primary defense in this stage of development.

The Dynamics of Envy

The helplessness and dependence of the infant in the paranoid position makes the need for gratification aggressive. No sooner is the infant aware of its need for the breast than it feels envious of the good breast for having the supplies necessary for its survival (Klein, 1957). Believing that the infant is aware very early that the source of its gratification is outside itself, Klein did not recognize an initial state of merger. The very fact of the good object existing outside leads to envy of the good breast. Further, since the bad breast is withholding, it too is envied. To the infant, frustration always means being withheld from, so envy is elicited in both gratification and frustration.

Envy goes beyond hatred to the desire to injure. The hatred of the breast for having or withholding needed supplies produces the desire to injure the breast. Klein believed that the desire to spoil and remove the good object and replace it with the bad is inherent in envy. Since envy is dangerous to the good object, it must be defended against with the means available. The most useful initial defense against envy is devaluation because denigration involves denial of the need for the object. Alternatively, the object can be idealized to protect against the recognition of the hateful desires to spoil the object that are inherent in envy. However, since it exaggerates the good qualities of the object, idealization can also incite envy even while attempting to defend against it. In this case the object is devalued to defend against the idealization, thus providing a layered defensive structure. The child with excessive envy may also split off the envy and become compliant, making exaggerated efforts to please the mother.

Psychopathology

The primary defenses of the paranoid position are projection, introjection, projective identification, splitting, idealization, omnipotence, and denial (Klein, 1946). All these defenses serve the purpose of defending against aggressiveness and its associated anxieties, whether in the original form of annihilation anxiety; its projected form, persecutory anxiety; or introjected persecutory anxiety. These defenses will be utilized by all infants, but the degree to which they are employed to protect the ego determines the propensity for the ego to become fixated in the paranoid position.

Various types of pathology may originate from fixation in this phase of development. If the good object buildup is virtually nonexistent, the projective-introjective cycle ends in the desperate "forceful entry" of the projectively identified object, which results in delusions of being controlled (Klein, 1946). According to Klein, psychosis results from a failure of projective identification. However, this mechanism will be more successful if there is sufficient good object buildup to allow it to allay anxiety. This same principle applies to projection, introjection, denial, idealization, and omnipotence. If the internalized good object is fragile but provides a significant portion of the ego and superego structures, these defenses will become a major fixation point of the personality. One can identify borderline conditions, narcissistic character disorders, and other severe character disorders as types of psychopathology characterized by reliance on these defenses. It should be emphasized that, according to Klein, the entire personality need not be fixated at this level for paranoid position dynamics to be operative. Neurotic patients frequently make use of paranoid position defenses even though their personality is not organized around them.

The organization of defenses at this level implies a weak, unintegrated ego. A stable defensive structure relying on splitting and the projective-introjective defenses arrests the development of the ego by preventing the integration of split ego and object states. For Klein, the ego with adequate balance between the good and bad objects and good and bad selves moves naturally toward the integration of ego and object (the details of which will be discussed in the context of the depressive position). However, an imbalance arrests the ego in the early split state, preventing this movement and inhibiting further ego growth. The result is a permanently weak, incohesive ego that lacks the integration of internalized objects.

Such an imbalance also arrests superego development. The internalized bad objects are ruling the personality by their continual threat, preventing the movement toward a realistic, reasonable superego composed of the integration of good and bad objects. In lieu of an integrated superego structure, the personality is ruled by the internalized persecutory object. The constant self-flagellation of the borderline and those with other severe personality disorders is testimony to this inhibition of superego development. The internalized good object, which in normal development would form the core of the benign superego, is weak and split off and has minimal influence on the internalized bad object, which tyrannically rules the ego. The use of paranoid position defenses; the arrest of ego development in a weak, incohesive state; and the failure of superego development all reflect fixation in the paranoid position and constitute severe character pathology.

Furthermore, according to Klein, when frustration interferes with good object buildup, not only is the internalized good object fragile but its instability results in greed and the desire to incorporate and devour. When a good object is introjected, it is greedily devoured in fantasy in an effort to protect it against potential enemies. The desire to devour threatens the internalized good object, further contributing to its fragility. The result is a cycle of greed and anxiety as the ego desperately searches for good objects by indiscriminately identifying with external objects. This cycle represents Klein's understanding of the chameleon-like identity changes characteristic of some types of severe pathology the most extreme form of which is the "as if" personality.

As we have seen, in projective identification the external object must be controlled in order to manage the aggressiveness projected into it. The ego with insufficient buildup of the internal good object feels under extreme threat and will cling to the external object in a desperate effort to control it. If the defense works well enough to stabilize the ego at this level, there is no forceful reintrojection of the external object as seen in psychosis, and the personality is characterized by the clinging dependence so typical of borderline patients. Thus, in Klein's view, the demands, excessive expectations, and inability to separate, so characteristic of the severe character pathology of borderline patients, are all rooted in the desperate attempt to control the aggressiveness projected into the other (Klein, 1946).

It should be noted that this "compulsive tie to the object" has a different dynamic from Fairbairn's and Guntrip's understanding of hunger for the object, as discussed in chapter 2. Klein did not see excessive clinging to the object as evidence of a primary need unmet in childhood, as did Fairbairn and Guntrip. It is true that she clearly viewed early frustrations as a major source of psychopathology; however, she believed that the reason the external factor is so important is that early frustrations lead to an increase in aggressiveness, build up of the bad object, and persecutory anxiety, thus intensifying the projective and introjective cycles. Thus the "compulsive tie to the object" is not a direct manifestation of early need but the effect of the projective mechanisms initiated by the anxiety of aggressiveness, a dynamic that sets Klein's views in direct opposition to the theories of Fairbairn and Guntrip.

Klein was in agreement with Fairbairn and Guntrip that the projective identificatory process is a schizoid mechanism and can often result in schizoid withdrawal (Klein, 1946), but she arrived at this conclusion in a sharply different way. When the mechanism of projective identification dominates the personality, the external object becomes a representation of the self. The ego is so governed by the anxiety of controlling aggressiveness that it views the object solely as an aggressive threat, the aggressiveness being originally the ego's own. Since the object is now identified with the self, such object relationships, in Klein's view, are narcissistic. Clinging to the object potentially intrudes upon it and blurs object boundaries, threatening such integrity as the ego possesses. To protect the fragile ego boundaries a schizoid withdrawal from object contact is effected; that is, in order to ensure sufficient distance from objects, the emotional part of the personality must be split off. In effect, schizoids destroy a major component of their personalities to protect a minimal sense of boundaries.

Because this withdrawal is characteristic of fixation in the paranoid position, Klein, acknowledging the influence of Fairbairn's views, modified her name for this phase and called it the "paranoid-schizoid position."

Klein acknowledged the importance of schizoid mechanisms in the paranoid position but arrived at the concept of schizoid withdrawal by a markedly different route from Fairbairn and Guntrip. The withdrawal from object contact, for Klein, is always rooted in aggressiveness even though the function of the withdrawal is ultimately to protect the fragile integrity of the ego. The pathogenic feature of frustration, in her view, is always the increase in aggressiveness and bad object buildup to which it gives rise. Klein also agreed with Fairbairn that schizoid defenses attempt to split off, even destroy, a part of the personality, but her understanding of this effort is that only effective withdrawal can protect the object from the patient's projected aggressiveness. Schizoid pathology, then, in Klein's schema, is one form of fixation at the paranoid position.

Any of the defenses against the paranoid position can become character constellations if envy is so excessive that it threatens the good object. In such cases the personality is arrested at the paranoid position, and many of the character defenses are directed against the awareness of envy. That is to say, the dynamics of envy, according to Klein, are a major source of severe character pathology.

The defensive layering motivated by envy of the primal object is illustrated by Klein's (1957) discussion of a female patient who suffered from strong schizoid and depressive symptoms but whose severe pathology was not recognized until she experienced some professional success. At that point in the analysis the patient had a dream in which she was flying on a magic carpet and looking down through a window where a cow was munching an endless strip of blanket. It had already been established from previous dreams that the analyst tended to be symbolized by a cow. The patient's associations indicated that the endless blanket represented the analyst's words, which she now had to swallow since the patient felt she was becoming superior to her. The strip of blanket reflected the worthlessness of the analytic interpretations. The patient was shocked at this devaluing attitude toward her analyst, whom she consciously admired. According to Klein, this dream and other material convinced the patient that she possessed feelings of hatred and poisonous envy toward her analyst and wished to injure and humiliate her, forcing upon her the awareness of a split-off, aggressive part of her personality. The result of this recognition was a severe depression, as the patient could not bear her destructive desires nor reconcile them with her idealized picture of herself. "She felt bad and despicable. . . . Her guilt and depression focused on her feeling of ingratitude towards the analyst . . . towards whom she felt contempt and hate: ultimately on the ingratitude towards her mother, whom she unconsciously saw as spoilt and damaged by her envy and destructive impulses" (Klein, 1957, p. 209).

This vignette illustrates the importance of envy in the aggressiveness toward the primal object, as well as the layering of defenses against it. The patient had an idealized view of herself and the analyst in large part to defend herself against the awareness of envy. Her professional success broke through the defense by revealing a contemptuous attitude toward the analyst. This devaluation masked the envy and desire to injure, feelings from which the analyst had been protected. Once this protection was removed, the patient fell into a severe depression, convinced she had injured the analyst whom she relied upon—and, ultimately, her mother, the primal object whom she felt she had irreparably injured with her envy.

The foregoing describes Klein's view of character pathology organized around defenses against envy. If the envious threat to the good object is extreme, however, envy interferes with its introjection, and the ego, now lacking the internalized good object, is further weakened. A weak ego tends to envy any potentially good object all the more. A downward cycle takes place in which envy blocks introjection and ego growth and the arrested ego becomes increasingly envious. Further, the intent to destroy the good object leads to premature guilt, which the ego is too undeveloped to manage and which must be projected. This early form of guilt is a sadistic attack on the ego. Its projection shifts the source of attack to the outside, leading to persecutory anxiety. In this way, the object becomes a persecutor. Thus, according to Klein's formulation, envy is a primary source of paranoia; this fact explains why guilt is so often confused with persecutory anxiety in the paranoid patient. When guilt is prematurely generated in the paranoid position, it is so burdensome to the ego that it can only be projected, resulting in persecutory anxiety.

These dynamics of the paranoid position are illustrated in Klein's discussion of an obsessional neurosis in a six-year-old girl, Erna (Klein, 1946). The little girl suffered from sleeplessness precipitated by her fear of robbers; obsessional activities, including head banging, rocking, thumb sucking, and masturbating; depression; and a severe learning inhibition. She also dominated her mother, whom she watched over compulsively, and she felt responsible for all her mother's illnesses and expected punishment for them. Erna had shared her parents' bedroom and witnessed the primal scene. In her therapeutic play Erna provided abundant evidence of her hatred and envy of both parents. For example, she played the mother and had the analyst suck on two "red, burning" lamps, which she then put in her own mouth. (Klein interpreted the lamps as mother's breast and father's penis). The play was always followed by "attacks of rage, envy, and aggression against her mother, to be succeeded by remorse and by attempts to make amends and placate her" (Klein, 1946, p. 68). Erna also played intensely rivalrous games with the analyst in which she came out ahead. She cut paper and said that "blood was coming out." Erna played at being a washerwoman, a role in which she punished and humiliated a child. Once she changed from a washerwoman into a fishwife; she turned on the water tap, wrapped paper around it, drank greedily from it, and chewed an imaginary fish. Klein (1946) believed this play material showed "the oral envy which she had felt during the primal scene and in her primal phantasies" (p. 70).

Erna also played at cheating the analyst, but since she had a policeman on her side, the analyst was helpless against her. She also showed her hostility to and envy of her mother by pretending to be a queen or a performer admired by spectators while the analyst, in the role of a child, was mistreated and tormented. While the patient and her husband ate delicious food, the child had gruel and was made sick. The child was made to witness sexual intercourse between the parents and was beaten if she interrupted them. In one game a priest gave a performance and turned on the water tap; his partner, a woman dancer, drank from it while the child, named Cinderella, could only watch and remain motionless. At this point Erna let loose a rage attack that "showed with what feelings of hatred her phantasies were accompanied and how badly she had succeeded in dealing with those feelings" (Klein, 1946, p. 72). Every educational measure, every limit set upon her, was interpreted by Erna as her mother's sadism. The little girl, feeling persecuted and spied upon by her mother, was terrified of her.

Klein interpreted the child's anxiety, sleeplessness, and fears of robbers as rooted in her hostility and envy toward the mother and her desire to damage her insides. Erna's destructive impulses were projected onto the mother, resulting in persecutory anxiety that was displaced onto fears of robbers, thus leading to sleeplessness. Her sadism and envy were also projected into the mother via projective identification, leading to the need to maintain constant vigilance over her. Thus, the control the little girl attempted to exert over her mother was, in Klein's view, a product of the projective identification of her aggressiveness and of her sadism and envy.

Klein viewed Erna's pathology as so rooted in overwhelming aggressiveness that she did not consider the child's witnessing of the primal scene as pathogenic in itself. She believed that the child wished to do what her mother did with her father and that because she could not, the observation of the primal scene led to an increase of aggressiveness, envy, and sadism. The primal scene became pathogenic because the child's ego could not cope with her destructive impulses toward her mother which led to the projection of her aggressiveness and sadism both onto and into her. Further, Klein interpreted the obsessive thumb sucking as rooted in fantasies of biting and devouring the mother's breast. The learning inhibition, in Klein's view, resulted from the association of writing and arithmetic with sadistic attacks on the mother's body. In brief, Klein believed that the child's overwhelming envy and aggressiveness toward her mother constituted the crucial dynamic underlying all her symptoms.

The case of Erna illustrates Klein's understanding of pathology originating in the paranoid position as well as her view of neurotic cases: she believed neurosis is rooted in the psychotic anxieties of the paranoid and depressive positions. Erna's primary defenses were projection and projective identification, and her anxiety was clearly persecutory in nature. Klein believed this case illustrated the pathogenesis of excessive aggressiveness and envy, which can dominate the ego and lead to its reliance on the paranoid defenses of projection and projective identification.

The good object acts as a counterbalance to envy and hate, just as it counterbalances the internalized bad object. Good experience produces good internalized object relationships and enjoyment; a natural product of the enjoyment is gratitude. The degree of enjoyment experienced in the paranoid position expands the capacity for gratitude later on, whereas, excessive aggressiveness and arrest in the paranoid position inhibits the development of the capacity for gratitude. The interference of intense envy and destructive impulses with enjoyment and gratitude explains the lack of a capacity for gratitude in severe character pathology.

A variety of severe character pathological constellations may originate in the paranoid position. While a complete deterioration of the defensive system results in delusional paranoia, more frequently, unresolved anxieties from the paranoid position are arrested at a more advanced defensive level. If the projective-introjective cycles allay anxiety at the level before the deterioration to delusion, the personality is fixated at the level of projective identification, and the result is severe character pathology. Fixation at the nonpsychotic paranoid position involves the following characteristic defenses: idealization, omnipotence, denial, devaluation of the object, and splitting. An ego structure reliant on these defense constitutes severe character pathology tantamount to what is now commonly referred to as the borderline personality. Conditions now typically labeled narcissistic personality disorders are conceptualized in a similar fashion, with emphasis on the idealization and omnipotent defenses and the use of schizoid mechanisms to regulate ambivalence in object relationships. As we shall soon see, some of Klein's followers have formalized these views into more precise conceptualizations of narcissistic and borderline pathology (Rosenfeld, 1971, 1978; Segal, 1983). As is discussed in chapter 5, Kernberg's (1975) formulation of and treatment approach to borderline and narcissistic personality organizations are based largely on Klein's concepts. If the schizoid mechanisms become the dominant force in the personality, the emotional component of the personality is buried and a schizoid personality is the result.

The commonality of all these forms of psychopathology is that the ego feels endangered by the projection of its own aggressiveness. The ego in its primitive, incohesive, and fragile form is always a victim, experiencing itself as ill equipped to mount a defense against the powerful, hostile forces it feels subjected to. When the ego begins to move toward the experience of itself as an agent, that is, to develop a sense of responsibility, a new developmental phase is initiated.

The Depressive Position

If early positive experiences and innate libido have been strong enough to result in a solid internalized good object, the growing ego will be able to begin to recognize that the good and bad objects are the same. Although some contact between good and bad objects occurs in the paranoid position, Klein (1937) believed that a new developmental phase is initiated when the infant ceases to use splitting as a major mechanism for the organization of its object relationships and begins object integration. Klein believed that this shift begins at about three to four months and is completed at about six months, when, she believed, the oedipal phase is initiated. The integration process appears to be conceptualized primarily as a developmental unfolding given satisfactory early experiences and innate libido. In Klein's view, however, this movement is also motivated by the anxieties of the paranoid position. The most positive response to persecutory anxiety is to begin object integration.

When the infant becomes aware of the fact that the object it hates and desires to injure and destroy is the same object it loves and depends on for gratification, it has begun to move from the "part object" level of object relations to the experience of whole objects (Klein, 1935, 1940). Simultaneously, the infant begins to remove itself from the painful role of victim, a role characteristic of the paranoid position; it now feels its desire to injure the object of its love. This recognition enables the growing ego to experience a feeling of agency, the power to injure. Rather than experiencing itself as the passive victim of persecution, the infant believes itself to be the agent of injury; the persecution is now of the object rather than the ego, and the source of danger is within rather than without. Klein called the realization that one can injure the object of its love the"depressive position" and the anxiety that this feeling engenders "depressive anxiety."

According to Klein (1948a), guilt originates from the anxiety of injuring the loved object. Because integrated object perception stimulates the recognition of the desire to injure, whole object perception is inevitably accompanied by guilt and anxiety. This view represents a major disagreement between Klein and followers of classical psychoanalytic theory. Klein believed that guilt stems from destructive wishes toward the loved object, rather than from sexual longing, and that it appears long before the consolidation of the oedipal phase at about three years of age. Moreover, Klein believed that because guilt arises in this way it is closely linked to the anxiety of loss, as the ego fears for the loved object, and inevitably results in the reparative desire. Guilt, then, is the bridge between the destructive desire and reparation.

The movement toward object integration is halting and oscillatory, since whole object perception inevitably gives rise to depressive anxiety, resulting in the urge to regress to the paranoid position. Some movement backward is an inevitable component of the lengthy process of object integration, but if good object internalization is well established, the infant will be able to sustain whole object integration. Despite the chronological priority of the paranoid position, Klein (1937) often seemed to regard the depressive position as the fundamentally more important developmental phase. She tended to emphasize it in her discussions of psychopathology and, in fact, formulated it before she conceptualized the paranoid position. Indeed, the distinction between these two critical developmental phases is not always clear: envy presumably originates in the paranoid position, and yet it involves the desire to injure the gratifying object. Klein did not seem to regard envy in the paranoid position as dependent on the object integration of the depressive position.

If the infant is able to feel in its fantasies that it has repaired and restored the injured object, guilt will not become crippling. Reparative experiences are crucial to overcoming the burdensome guilt anxiety of this phase. The capacity for repair is dependent both on the introjection of the good object in the paranoid position and on continued good handling, which allows for the perception of good external objects. If these conditions occur, the positive experiences provide the child with the opportunity to feel that its aggression has not irreparably damaged its loved object, a feeling that mitigates its guilt. However, if the introjected good object is weak and unstable or the experiences in this phase are predominantly negative, the infant's personality will tend to become dominated by excessive unresolved guilt and feelings of unworthiness. (As will be seen in chapter 4, the concepts of ambivalence toward whole objects and repair to mitigate the ensuing guilt greatly influenced Winnicott's developmental theory and treatment approach to character pathology.)

Klein believed that the ability to love and sustain love relationships in later life is dependent on the experience of reparation in the depressive position. Without this experience the personality remains chronically fearful that its aggressiveness will injure or destroy the loved object. The result is constant uncertainty regarding love relationships, especially when aggressive feelings appear. For this reason, Klein believed that good object relationships in adult life depend to a large extent on the outcome of the depressive position. She also believed, however, that successful love relationships in later life can help to complete unfinished reparation from the depressive position (Klein, 1937). The problem with this later life resolution is that if reparation is blocked completely, successful love relationships are not possible. The reparative experience in the infantile depressive position must be sufficiently complete in order for later love relationships to develop to the point where they can resolve arrested infantile efforts at repair.

Parental love and the provision of good care eases the child's anxiety of its destructive fantasies and aggressiveness by proving that they have not destroyed the good mother (Klein, 1937). All good experience in this phase, according to Klein, proves to the child that its internal fantasies of destruction have not been carried out in reality, rendering the child's feelings of danger to the object less severe. All negative experience increases the child's aggressiveness and belief in its power to injure. If experience in this phase is excessively frustrating, the child will feel that its aggressiveness has in fact destroyed the loved object, resulting in intolerable guilt. However, parental care is not the only variable. If the child possesses extreme innate aggressiveness and minimal ability to tolerate frustration, its perception of the parents will be dominated by aggressiveness even if they love the child, and the child will feel that much more burdened by excessive guilt. Similarly, some children receive bad treatment and continue to perceive the parents positively because they do not have a great deal of innate aggressiveness to project onto parental figures. In this case, guilt is minimal despite mistreatment.

Awareness of the fantasied ability to injure the loved object increases envy and greed (Klein, 1957, 1958). As the child begins to feel the anxiety of losing the loved object, it feels less certain of it and feels more greedy for and envious of the good object it cannot secure. As envy and greed increase, fear of destroying the good object is exacerbated, leading to more greed and envy, and a pathological cycle ensues. The counterbalance to this negative cycle is the internalization of good objects and reparation, both of which allay the anxiety of losing the good object. If positive experiences are not sufficient to counteract the pathological cycle of envy and depressive anxiety, emotional organization becomes fixated at the depressive position and a pathological result ensues.

Defenses in the Depressive Position

Because the anxiety of losing the loved object is so painful and the consequences so potentially disastrous, defenses are erected against depressive anxiety. The infantile ego is so weak that to manage the overwhelming anxiety of intending to injure the loved object, it resorts to the omnipotent defense of fantasizing restoration of the parental figure. Because the reparative experience includes the omnipotent belief in the magical ability to control bad objects and restore good objects, mania is a normal accompaniment of the depressive position (Klein, 1940). In Klein's view, omnipotence is the fantastic belief in absolute control and therefore involves denial of psychic reality. Aggressiveness, bad objects, and dependence on real objects are denied, and good objects, believed to be under omnipotent control, are idealized. The denial of psychic reality is therefore an inevitable component of the infant's need to master the depressive position.

Excessive depressive anxiety is, therefore, defended against by massive denial of the dangers to the good object (Klein, 1935). In the manic state all dangers to the good object disappear and the object is magically restored. Thus, the importance of good objects in reality is denied, as is all object danger. In this way, all guilt and dread disappear. Thus, the manic defense, for Klein, is the ego's denial of both external and psychic reality and the flight to the exaggerated internal-ized good object. The manic state so massively defends against the anxiety of losing the loved object that all dependence on objects is denied and the only object relation is to the internalized, idealized object with which the ego now identifies itself.

In the normal developmental process frustration and negative experience inevitably occur, forcing reality upon the child to some extent. Consequently, fluctuations between the manic and depressive positions are continuous throughout this period as the infant alter-nately denies and perceives psychic reality (Klein, 1935, 1940). When the manic defense fails, the child is forced into reliance on obsessive mechanisms in a desperate effort to repair the object over and over again to prevent psychic disintegration. In Klein's (1935) view, this mechanism constitutes the origin of childhood obsessional symptoms. Because the early aggressive intent was not successfully repaired, the child is attempting to control magically the object it fears it has destroyed. Since the manic defense never works perfectly, some degree of obsessional behavior is an inevitable part of childhood. The adult obsessive is fixated in this endless effort to repair magically the fantasied injury to the loved object.

Psychopathology

Unresolved depressive anxiety leads to a defensive arrest that may assume a variety of pathological forms. If reparative efforts are not felt to be successful, the continued need for reparation may appear in a desire for perfection. Work inhibitions, in this view, are rooted in the fear of imperfection that results from the need to reassure oneself that one has not irreparably damaged the loved object. The obsessive worker who cannot commit to a project for fear of committing an error is, in Klein's view, experiencing the work project as an opportunity to repair the damage to the loved object, but an opportunity doomed to failure since only a perfect product can relieve the guilt. If guilt is so overwhelming that no reparation is considered possible, it will be massively repressed. In this case, the superego is crushed and the source of damage is externalized, resulting in sociopathy (Klein, 1933). Criminality, in Klein's view, is a product not of a gap in the superego but of an excessively burdensome superego that is repressed.

If the child does not feel it can repair the damage to the good object, the ego may become fixated in the manic defense. The mania of the adult manic-depressive is, according to Klein (1935) the equivalent of the normal child's temporary defense against depressive anxiety. If the child feels its aggressiveness toward the good object is so dangerous that its very existence is threatened, the ego will continue to deny all psychic reality. The result is an ego reliant on the manic defense, and when depressive anxieties are aroused in adulthood, the result will be manic–depressive illness.

These views have clear implications for the mourning process. Klein (1940) agreed with Freud's (1917) view that the task of mourning is to introject the lost object. However, Klein departs from Freud in her view that the loss evokes depressive anxiety. According to Klein, the infantile fantasy of having injured or destroyed the parents is inevitably activated by adult loss. Thus, the outcome of mourning will depend on the degree of successful resolution of the infantile depressive position. If the infantile object was felt to be repaired, when the infantile depressive position is activated by adult loss, the mourner will be able to repair and restore the newly lost object internally by restoring the injured parents from infantile fantasy life. The reparation of the early objects and their reinstatement allows for overcoming grief and making peace within. If, on the other hand, there is unresolved guilt for having damaged or destroyed the parents in fantasy and the early objects are not repaired, the mourner feels that he or she has once again destroyed the loved object. Just as he or she did in the infantile depressive position, the mourner fears retaliation for the injury, and fears of punishment and persecution become part of the grief reaction. In this situation, the mourner becomes paralyzed by the guilt of destroying the lost object in fantasy and by the ensuing anxiety of retaliation. The guilt is too much to bear and the outcome is an inability to overcome the grief of mourning. Since the reinstatement of good objects does not occur, when adult loss is responded to in this way, mourning becomes melancholia and results in the same efforts to escape depressive anxiety as are found in melancholia: mania, obsessional defenses, paranoia, and "flights to the object."

The most typical pathological outcome of unresolved depressive anxiety is a chronic fear of injuring the loved object that results in clinical depression (Klein, 1935, 1937, 1940). The melancholic, according to Klein's model, has been unable to overcome the anxiety of damaging its loved objects and, consequently, has repressed all aggressiveness. The relentless internal self-persecution of the depressive, according to Klein, is a product of its self-hatred for having injured the loved object. Not having the opportunity for reparation, the melancholic attempts to save the object the only way it can; namely, by turning its aggressiveness toward itself. The self-abuse of the depressive is not only a product of guilt but also a desperate effort to protect the good object. All enduring relationships are subject to rupture and even ruin because the individual feels, however unconsciously, that he or she is dangerous to the early object of its love. As soon as gratification from an object becomes possible, the depressive unconsciously fears injuring or destroying the object of its love. If such gratification does occur, the individual feels guilty, however unconsciously, and a depressive episode will ensue.

According to Klein (1937), unresolved guilt from the depressive position also explains why some depressed patients become so hopelessly attached to their objects that they have great difficulty separating from them. Unconscious anxiety from potential destructiveness to the loved object requires constant contact as reassurance that the destruction has not taken place. By attaching tenaciously to the object, such patients have found a way to maintain object contact despite unresolved intent to destroy. The price of this quasi resolution is the endless reassurance needed to maintain the certainty of the object's preservation and the continuation of the relationship. This type of excessive object attachment is to be distinguished in Klein's work from the "compulsive tie to the object" based on persecutory anxiety as illustrated in the treatment of Erna. According to Klein, all difficulties in separation from an external object originate in aggression toward the object and are therefore motivated by either persecutory or depressive anxiety. This view is in clear disagreement with the Fairbairn–Guntrip position (discussed in chapter 2) that excessive object attachment is a deprivation-induced arrest of the normal developmental needs to depend on a reliable object. On the other hand, Klein's view that extreme dependence is a defense against hostility to the object at either the depressive or paranoid levels had a profound influence on Kernberg, who (as we shall see in chapter 5) based his conceptualization of severe character pathology on the pathogenicity of excessive aggressiveness.

How far Klein (1960) extended this concept of separation anxiety can be seen in her treatment of Richard. Because she treated this ten-year-old boy during a planned four-month-stay in a small Scottish town during the war, the analysis had a prearranged ending. As the time for Klein's return to London and termination of the analysis drew near, Richard began to react to the impending separation. Richard was staying with a man, Mr. Wilson, whom he felt was strict. In the 76th session, Klein had some oranges in a parcel, and Richard "looked white with anger and envy, but said he did not like oranges" (p. 388). When later in the session Richard begged Klein to take him with her and let him sleep in her bed, she interpreted "Richard felt that because Mrs. K. did not let him stay with her, give him the oranges, and love him, she had become the ally of Mr. Wilson, who was now felt to be the bad Daddy. This made his need for reassurance and love from her all the greater" (p. 389). Richard was restless and depressed throughout the session and at one point talked of a tornado razing two houses to the ground. Later in the session Klein interpreted that his depression was due to her going away and to his jealousy of her grandchildren and the other patients she would see in London. She told him he wanted to raze her house because he was angry with her for leaving and "therefore his fear of losing her forever was very great" (p. 390). This vignette demonstrates the emphasis Klein placed on aggressiveness and the fear of destroying the loved object in the dynamics of separation anxiety, an emphasis she maintained even when the loss was real and imposed from the outside. In this case, as opposed to that of Erna, the interpretation was focused on the anxiety of loss due to aggression toward the loved object.

The easiest path of escape from the depressive position is regression to the splitting of the paranoid position, (Klein, 1937). When the good object is not established well enough within, depressive anxiety is excessive and the defense of least resistance is to resplit the object to immediately allay the anxiety of loss. This regression evokes the persecutory anxiety of the paranoid position, rendering the infant helpless once again; its need to gain control of its persecutors will now motivate a renewed advance to the depressive position. This oscillation is Klein's explanation for why so many patients cycle between paranoia and depression. The target of their aggressiveness continually shifts between the object and the self as they oscillate between forward movement to the depressive position and regression to the paranoid position.

Escape from depressive anxiety may also be effected by denial of dependence on the object. At the neurotic level the individual turns away from all loved objects, fearing dependence on them (Klein, 1937). Consequently, the neurotic pattern of inability to commit to a partner and remain in a relationship is always at root the unconscious fear of injuring the loved object. This theoretical outlook provides a slant on this neurotic syndrome, seen so much in today's clinical practice, that is different from the common conception of narcissistic vulnerability (discussed in the context of Kohut's theories in chapter 6). Indeed, Klein (1937) viewed the fundamental dynamic of the Don Juan syndrome, or any type of chronic infidelity or promiscuity, as the need to reassure oneself that one is not dependent on one object and therefore not in danger of doing it harm. Klein believed the source of dependence anxiety lay in the identification of the current loved object with the original loved object, which in fantasy has been irreparably injured by the aggressiveness directed toward it. In some cases the outcome is an avoidance of affective life as a whole; the individual with such a constricted personality has renounced all affective bonds in order to avoid reexperiencing the original injury to the object.

The "flight to the external object" as a means of escaping the depressive position can also occur in milder forms. The guilt of the depressive condition, according to Klein (1937), is the primary reason for inferiority feelings. Unconscious hatred of the loved object in the infantile position makes the adult feel unworthy of being loved. This neurotic level of feelings of unworthiness and low self-esteem is to be distinguished from the internal persecution of the paranoid position and is characterized by a continual need for praise and admiration from external objects to assuage the guilt and low self-esteem that result from the unconscious intent to injure the original loved object. The need for esteem from the environment may assume the form of excessive concern over competence, beauty, work, or many other specific areas of life. For Klein, the root of all such self-esteem anxiety is unconscious guilt, and the effort to assuage this guilt constitutes the neurotic outcome of unrepaired desires to injure in the depressive position. This excessive dependence on the object's opinion is neurotic, rather than more severely pathological, because the need for admiration tends to be specific, rather than all-consuming and the dependence is on the other's admiration, rather than a clinging object tie. According to Klein (1937), the determining factor of whether dependence on others is neurotic or more severely pathological is the timing of the trauma and guilt fixation. If the fantasy of damage to the loved object occurs in the early part of the depressive position, when only a minimal degree of integration has occurred, anxiety of injuring the loved object will be pervasive and dependence will tend to be extreme. However, if the ego has achieved substantial whole object and ego integration, the fear of damage will be less extreme and the need for reassurance from the object will apply only to a specific area of functioning. In either case, the dependence on the object rooted in the depressive position is to be contrasted with overdependence originating in the paranoid position, which, as discussed earlier, is motivated by the infant's fear of the bad object and need to cling to the good object for protection.

Other forms of psychopathology can be rooted in either depressive or paranoid anxieties (Klein, 1935). For example, eating disorders can be due to the identification of food with persecuting objects, in which case food is experienced as a poisonous attack on the body, or with the good object, which is endangered by being taken in. The fear of destroying or injuring the good object by biting or chewing is depressive anxiety displaced onto food whereas the anxiety of being damaged by the ingestion of external substances is the paranoid type. Similarly, hypochondriasis can be symptomatic of either type of anxiety. If the body is felt to be under attack, bad objects taken from the outside are felt to be persecuting the body. If, however the hypochondriacal symptoms result from internal warfare in which good objects are under attack from internalized bad objects, the anxiety is depressive. In both cases the result is preoccupation with danger to the body, but in the first case the danger is felt to come from outside persecutors and in the second type the danger is to the object experienced as within. The comparison between the roots of these two clinical syndromes, eating disorders and hypochondria, illustrates the essential distinction between persecutory anxiety and depressive anxiety: the former is danger to the ego and the latter is danger to the object. In almost all of Klein's clinical cases there is some degree of mixture of the two, (although one type of anxiety will tend to predominate in a given case), and within a particular session or theme either depressive or persecutory anxiety will come to the fore.

Klein's (1935) views on fixation in the depressive position and its relationship to hypochondria are illustrated in her discussion of patient X. The analysis of this case is discussed more fully later; the part of the analysis relevant to this discussion occurred in the patient's movement from paranoid to depressive anxiety. When this change took place, X became deeply depressed and his hypochondriacal pains shifted: in the first phase of treatment the analyst had been identified with a fantasied tapeworm and other substances attacking his insides; after the shift to the depressive position X had a fear that cancer would eat away through his stomach. But X wanted to protect the analyst—identified with the internalized mother—from attack by his own sadism and greed, which he equated with the cancer and in consequence of which he felt despairing, unworthy, and deeply depressed. When paranoid anxiety was predominant, X was hypochondriacal, but he felt attacked rather than concerned for the object. According to Klein, when X shifted to the depressive position, he no longer felt attacked but now feared that his illness, a cancer, would injure the analyst; in consequence of this fear, the patient became depressed.

The dynamics of fixation in the depressive position are also well illustrated in Klein's (1935) discussion of two dreams of patient C, who also suffered from severe depression, paranoia, and hypochondria. In the first dream C's parents were elderly, and he was "managing" (taking care of) them on a trip in open air. The parents were lying in bed, their beds end to end, and the patient found it difficult to keep them warm. With the parents watching, the patient urinated. He noticed that his penis was very large; he felt uncomfortable because he believed that he would be humiliated if his father saw the size of his penis. However, he also felt he was urinating to save his father the trouble, and he commented that he felt as if his parents were a part of himself. The next night C dreamed that he heard a frying sound. He felt that a live creature was being fried. He tried to explain to his mother that to fry something alive was the worst thing to do, but she did not seem to understand. He associated to beheading and acknowledged that he used to think about torture.

According to Klein's (1935) interpretation, the urinating represented the early aggressive fantasies toward the parents, especially toward their sexual relationship: "He had fantasied biting them and eating them up, and among other attacks, urinating on and into his father's penis, in order to skin and burn it and to make his father set his mother's inside on fire in their intercourse. . . . Castration of the father was expressed by the associations about beheading" (p. 281). Klein added that the patient's wish to humiliate the father was shown by his feeling that he ought not to do so. His sadistic fantasies were represented by his mother's inability to understand that she was in danger from the biting penis inside her. Klein interpreted the position of the beds to indicate both C's aggressive and jealous desire to separate his parents during intercourse and anxiety that sexual contact would injure or kill them, as was his wish. C now felt overwhelming anxiety that his parents would die.

There is much more material in C's dreams, but this brief account shows that his dominant anxiety was distress and concern for the loved object, the danger C imagined them to be in coming from his own aggressive desires toward them. Klein (1935) comments:

> The patient deals with the depressive position in different ways. He uses the sadistic manic control over his parents by keeping them separated from each other and thus stopping them in pleasurable as well as in dangerous intercourse. At the same time, the way he takes care of them is indicative of obsessional mechanisms. But his main way of overcoming the depressive position is reparation. In the dream he devotes himself entirely to his parents in order to keep them alive and comfortable [p. 283].

These dreams are illustrative of the way Klein believed the mechanisms of the depressive position work. In order to love his parents, C had to repress his sadistic desires toward them and repair the loved objects in fantasy, as represented in the first dream by his over-solicitousness and caretaking of elderly parents. Because the patient felt overwhelming guilt for these desires, he had a need to repair and control his parents, which resulted in the overattached "management" of them in reality.

In summary, Klein was able to explain a great deal of psychopathology as fixation at issues embedded in the depressive position. Not only did she view depression itself as originating in this developmental phase, but she conceptualized many other manifestations of psychopathology as attempts to escape from depressive anxiety. In some cases the link with depressive position dynamics is evident, as in mania and unresolved mourning, but the depressive position dynamics of other types of pathology are not so obvious. Klein also conceptualized obsessive neurosis, some forms of paranoia, neurotic character pathology, and many of the symptoms in cases that today would be labeled borderline or narcissistic as rooted primarily in the drive to escape the anxiety and guilt of the depressive position. Because depressive position dynamics imbued so many types and levels of pathology, Klein gave the depressive position the central role in her theory of pathogenesis and seemed frequently to speak of it as the fundamental conflict of childhood even to the point of equating it with the infantile neurosis. According to Klein, the extent of success in overcoming the anxieties of this fundamental conflict is the most critical feature in emotional development and in preparing the child for oedipal conflict.

The Oedipus Complex

As we have seen, Klein believed that the superego originates in the early introjective process and that guilt originates in the depressive position. This distinction would seem to set her views in opposition to Freud's belief that the Oedipus complex is the source of guilt and the superego. However, instead of opposing Freud in this way, Klein adopted the position that the Oedipus complex begins long before the origin ascribed to it by traditional psychoanalytic theory (Klein, 1928, 1933, 1945). Klein (1926) believed that observations of children and the findings of child psychoanalysis, of which she was a pioneer provided "evidence" for the existence of guilt, the superego, and the Oedipus complex in children much younger than three years of age. Klein pointed to the fact that children show preference for the parent of the opposite sex as early as the beginning of the second year as evidence that the Oedipus complex originates at least that early. In children as young as two-and three-quarters to four years old, Klein (1933) saw evidence of early, harsh superego strictures in their fantasies of creatures that bite, devour, and attack. It was Klein's contention that only the existence of oedipal ambivalence and rivalry could account for the severity of the superego and the accompanying fear of parental retribution in children this young and that the "full-blown" Oedipus complex in the fourth or fifth year is therefore a result of a process begun in infancy.

By placing the origins of the Oedipus complex in the period of the projective–introjective cycles, she was able to equate early persecutory anxiety with the maternal retribution of the oedipal phase. In Klein's view, by the beginning of the second year sadistic impulses and persecutory anxiety are related to oedipal rivalries. This contention links persecutory anxiety, the early sadistic superego, and the origins of the Oedipus complex.

According to Klein, the oedipal phase begins with the height of the depressive position in weaning when the infant searches for a new object; the second object, in Klein's (1945) view, is the father's penis. If the breast was gratifying, the good object is sufficiently internalized that new objects will be sought at this point. If the breast was unduly frustrating, the infant will turn to new objects to escape the frustration. According to Klein, the breast and penis in this phase are both oral objects and both are split into good and bad. To the degree that the good breast has been solidly introjected, the penis will be viewed as good; likewise the strength of the bad breast will determine the influence of the bad penis. One can see that Klein did not view libidinal positions as discrete, sequential phases of development. She believed that the introjection of objects begins to become genital as early as six months of age, although the organs are oral. Similarly, she believed that the aggressiveness of this phase quickly becomes anal sadism as the infant desires to expel introjected objects. Oral, anal, and genital aggressiveness intermingle as the oedipal phase dawns. Envy plays an important role in the beginning of the oedipal phase as both good breast and bad breast envy motivate the infant to turn away from the breast to search for the penis.

This view raises the question of how an infant could have knowledge of the sexual organs and attribute meaning to them. Klein treated many children who had witnessed the primal scene, and she attributed their knowledge of sexuality to this observation. Although she realized that not all disturbed children have this experience, she felt that the content of their play indicated unconscious awareness of sexual intercourse. Klein (1946) was forced to adopt the hypothesis that children are born with innate knowledge of sexual intercourse.

All that has been said thus far regarding the Oedipus complex is true for both sexes. However, the boy and girl experience the shift from breast to penis differently (Klein, 1946c). The little girl wants her father's penis but fantasizes that her mother has it, a fantasy that initiates rivalry with her mother and fantasies of attacking her mother's body and stealing its contents. In fear of retaliation, the little girl turns to the father. In Klein's view, the little girl wishes to have a penis to escape maternal retaliation; thus penis envy is a *product* of oedipal conflicts, not a cause. If the aggressive feelings toward the mother are not excessive and the good object has been sufficiently internalized, the little girl will eventually identify with her mother as she realizes that her wish for her father's penis is futile. However, if she has excessive oral sadistic wishes toward her mother from earlier phases, she may not be able to overcome her fear of maternal retribution and will not be able to enter the oedipal phase or, at best, will be unable to resolve her oedipal rivalry. Her wish for the father's penis may endure, or if given up, it will result in regression, rather than identification with the mother. Thus Klein's contribution to oedipal theory is that, unless the paranoid and depressive position resolution has modulated the little girl's aggressive wishes toward her mother, she will have great difficulty even entering the oedipal phase, much less mastering it. For example, if the girl feels she has injured the mother, she may have to disavow her aggressiveness toward her mother and regress to splitting, a sequence that leaves her unable to enter the oedipal rivalry and arrests the personality in the preoedipal phase.

Klein's (1945) patient Rita is a prime example of a little girl so traumatized by her unresolved aggressiveness toward her mother that she was unable to master the oedipal phase. Rita was two-and-three-quarters years old at the onset of her analysis and already suffered from a variety of symptoms—anxiety, appetite disorder, depression, obsessional symptoms, and inability to tolerate frustration. She had great initial difficulty accepting the bottle and later resisted yielding the bottle for food. She had witnessed the primal scene and felt that her father was sadistically damaging her mother. At the beginning of her second year, she switched her preference from mother to father and tried to exclude mother. At 18 months, her mother became her favorite, and at that time Rita developed phobias and nighttime terrors and began clinging to her mother so intensely that she could not separate from her. Klein pointed out that Rita's relationship with her mother was dominated by persecutory fear and depressive anxiety.

She feared her mother, who was her loved and needed object but whom she "endangered" with her aggressive wishes. Rita was clinging to her mother to protect the needed object from her own aggressive wishes. Consequently, when Rita began the oedipal phase at the beginning of her second year, she could not tolerate the anxiety of the rivalry and regressed to the helpless, clinging dependency of earlier infancy. Nor could she really desire her father, for she felt he had sadistically damaged her mother and was therefore a threat to her, a fear that also fostered her regression.

This case could be discussed from many perspectives, the point in the current context is that Rita's unresolved destructive wishes toward both parents, but especially her mother, rendered the Oedipus complex insurmountable. Klein believed that the clear shift in Rita's preference for the father at the beginning of her second year and for the mother at 18 months proves irrefutably that the Oedipus complex begins much earlier than at three or four years of age, as postulated by traditional analytic theory. Rita's oedipal phase was begun but then retreated from because of the overwhelming anxiety and guilt that the oedipal rivalry heaped upon the preexisting anxiety and guilt of both the paranoid and depressive positions. The witnessing of the primal scene also stimulated excessive aggressiveness, as the little girl believed her father was damaging her mother. Klein believed that this case illustrates the pathogenicity of excessive aggressiveness both in the earlier phases and in the oedipus phase. For the oedipal phase to consolidate identifications and superego formation, the aggressiveness of the paranoid and depressive positions must first be allayed so that the anxiety and guilt of the Oedipus complex can be tolerated.

For the boy the original oedipal constellation is not the positive but the negative position. Both boys and girls shift the object of desire from the breast to the penis, but for the boy this means the adoption of the first homosexual position (Klein, 1945). This feminine position remains to some degree throughout life, resulting in some degree of feminine character traits in all men. According to Klein (1945), "If the boy can turn some of his love and libidinal desires from his mother's breast towards his father's penis, while retaining the breast as a good object, then his father's penis will figure in his mind as a good and creative organ which will give him libidinal gratification" (p. 411). Conversely, if the boy is unable to make this shift from the negative to the positive oedipal position, the penis will become a hostile, retaliatory, attacking organ. The crucial factors are the solidity of the good internalized breast and the relative balance between the good and bad internalized objects. The oral sadistic attacks on the mother's breast become transferred to the penis with the result that the boy wishes to bite off the father's penis. According to Klein, this wish constitutes the first expression of the boy's rivalry with his father and leads to castration anxiety. If the aggressiveness toward the breast is excessive, the penis becomes a persecutory object, castration anxiety cannot be resolved, and the Oedipus complex cannot be mastered. Further, the boy identifies with his father's penis, so that the bad, persecutory penis becomes his own negative masculine identification. Conversely, if the internalization of the good breast is strong enough, the penis will be viewed with sufficient positive affect to combat castration anxiety. Klein believed that the boy's view of his penis, the strength of his masculine identification, and the outcome of his Oedipus complex all hinged ultimately on the ability of the internalized good breast to combat the internalized bad breast. If the good object has been irreparably damaged by the bad object in the depressive position or split off in the paranoid position, the penis remains a persecutory object and castration anxiety is too severe to allow for the resolution of oedipal anxieties.

Klein's (1945, 1960) view of the boy's oedipal development is best illustrated in her discussion of Richard, the 10-year-old patient discussed earlier. Richard was a severely inhibited boy who was afraid of other children (his refusal to go out by himself made it difficult for him to attend school), preoccupied with his health, and given to frequent bouts of depression. He was precocious and gifted, and, preferring adult company, he often disdained other children. The history indicated that Richard had had a brief, unsatisfactory breast-feeding period and was frequently ill as a child, undergoing two operations between his third and sixth year.

The case of Richard is the only analysis Klein (1945) described fully; the discussion of the clinical material is detailed and lengthy, but only a fragment need be presented here to illustrate her view of the boy's Oedipus complex. After the first interruption of the analysis, Richard played at bumping a vampire, representing himself, into a ship named Rodney, which represented his mother. He immediately became defensive and rearranged the ships, including one representing his father, in a row. This defensive arrangement, which Klein interpreted as Richard's belief that peace and harmony could only exist in the family if he repressed his oedipal longings, was associated with the boy's chronic anxiety of injuring his mother. After remarks about his mother or the analyst, he often asked, "Have I hurt your feelings?"

Richard made drawings in which red (indicating his rage, according to Klein) represented himself and blue his mother. In one drawing the blue parts are separated by an elongated red section that the patient himself interpreted as a genital. Klein suggested that the object could be a tooth and interpreted this material as "symbolizing the danger to the loved object from the oral-sadistic impulses, the latter the danger pertaining, as he felt, to the genital function as such because of its penetrating nature" (p. 380). The penis represented to Richard a dangerous object that could damage his beloved mother's insides. Consequently, he split his mother into the idealized breast mother and the hostile, retaliatory mother with whom he associated genitality. Out of fear, Richard withdrew to the pregenital longing for the breast and the idealization of the mother–infant relationship, and consequently, was attached to his mother in an infantile way.

Klein believed that the early feeding difficulties led to overwhelming oral aggressiveness and to its projected form, excessive fear of the bad breast. Richard's paranoia was shown clearly in one session when he frequently looked out the window and stated that two men he saw talking were spying on him. Klein linked this persecutory anxiety to his hypochondriacal fears, as he unconsciously feared poisoning from his parents. This interpretation appeared to have lessened Richard's anxieties, for the next day it appeared that his mood shifted from depression to elation. He described how much he loved his breakfast and how the world looked beautiful to him. Klein believed this shift to a hypomanic defense reflected his renewed belief in his internalized good mother.

In this session Richard proceeded to discuss two drawings from the previous day in which his mother was represented by a "very horrid" bird with an open beak in the colors representing himself and his brother. His mother "now appeared as greedy and destructive. The fact that her beak was formed by red and purple sections expressed Richard's projection on to his mother of his own (as well as his brother's) oral-sadistic impulses" (p. 388). It was significant to Klein that Richard had equated this drawing with another drawing representing himself, indicating his introjection of the devouring, retaliatory mother.

Richard assuaged his fear of the bad breast by his idealization of the good breast, but that meant regression to the oral level. The fears of the bad breast were transferred to his father's penis, leading to fear of that organ and to overwhelming anxiety in the early positive oedipal position. His fear of his father's penis led to severe castration anxiety and fears of persecution, and he feared that his own penis would injure the mother he loved. These fundamental anxieties and their associated guilt led to repression of genitality, depression, severe inhibitions, and fear of other children.

In Klein's view, Richard's transfer of the bad, retaliatory, devouring breast onto the father's penis resulted in severe castration anxiety and regression not only from the oedipal phase but also from the depressive position, since the mother was split into the genital bad mother and the idealized good breast mother. Further, the hostile genital breast was both a projection of Richard's sadistic wishes toward it as a result of early frustration and constitutional deficiency, and the introjection of the retaliatory breast, leading to severe anxiety that provoked regression. Ultimately, Richard's unresolved castration anxiety and failure to master the oedipal phase, in Klein's view, could be traced to excessive aggressiveness in the paranoid position. She considered this and similar cases to be evidence of the close connection between persecutory, depressive, and castration anxiety and of the impossibility of considering oedipal issues in isolation from these early phases of development.

It is clear from this view of the Oedipus complex that Klein viewed the pathogenicity of this developmental phase to reside in the degree of aggressiveness toward the same sex parent which is itself ultimately rooted in unresolved aggressiveness toward the breast. Even viewing the primal scene, as in the case of Rita, was considered pathogenic by Klein only because of the excessive aggressiveness it stimulated. In Klein's view, libidinal desires are not pathogenic of themselves even when directed to the opposite-sex parent. Klein (1945) viewed the sexual excitement of childhood masturbation as inevitably rivalrous with the opposite-sex parent, leading to aggressive wishes toward that parent. This desire to injure provides the potential pathogenicity of childhood masturbation. The child becomes anxious, according to Klein, not because of the sexual excitement per se but because the rivalrous aggressiveness threatens the parent of the opposite sex.

In the discussion of the cases of Rita and Richard, one can find some indications of the way Klein used her theory of development and psychopathology in treatment. Her interpretations follow her theory of the significance of the paranoid and depressive positions, excessive aggressiveness, and their influence on oedipal conflicts. However, it is not possible on the basis of the foregoing discussion to appreciate fully the uniqueness of Kleinian technique, and it is to her treatment approach that we shall now turn.

TREATMENT

Klein believed herself to be an adherent of traditional psychoanalytic principles of reliance on transference and resistance and in an absolute adherence to the interpretive method for resolving emotional difficulties (Klein, 1926, 1946c, 1952d). Indeed, her strict devotion to interpretation was one cause of her disagreement with Anna Freud, who believed that for children and adolescents the analyst must use noninterpretive means to build a treatment alliance before interpretive work can begin (A. Freud, 1927). Klein considered her primary contributions to psychoanalytic technique to be her emphasis on aggressiveness in interpretations, her expansion of the psychoanalytic method to severely disturbed adults and children, her belief in early interpretation with children, and her advocacy of play technique for children.

In all the case material she published, Klein emphasized in her interpretations paranoid and depressive anxieties and their influence on the Oedipus complex, the primal scene, and excessive aggressiveness, as well as envy, greed, and jealousy. Oral sadism, included in both persecutory and depressive anxiety and often expressed as fantasies of attacks on the mother's insides, plays a central role in her interpretations. Klein believed these issues were present in all psychopathology because they are central aspects of development. Consequently, interpretation must be focused on aggressive wishes and their attendant anxieties whether the central pathology is organized around the paranoid or depressive anxieties or their manifestation in oedipal conflicts.

One direct result of this spectrum conceptualization of psychopathology is a broadened view of analyzability. Since all forms of disturbance are separated only by degree, the same type of treatment approach is applicable whether the presenting symptom picture is schizophrenic, neurotic, or in the range in between. A direct consequence of Klein's theoretical system is the belief that psychotic cases can be analyzed by the same methods used for neurotic cases, the issues differing only in severity. The advocacy of strict interpretive psychoanalysis in psychotic and borderline cases was one of her more controversial positions, but it also made her a pioneer in a trend that has been called "the widening scope" of psychoanalysis (Bibring, 1954).

Klein's (1952d) claim for the analyzability of severe pathology is linked to her broadened view of the transference. Klein (1952b) believed that transference originates in the same developmental processes that provide the initial full object relationship. Klein (1952d) deduced from her view of the origins of mental life that this early object relationship becomes a part of all analyses and that it forms a major component of the transference of severely disturbed individuals. In Klein's view, the issues of psychotic patients always manifest themselves in primitive negative transferences based on these early object relationships, which, like neurotic conflicts, can be altered by the "good feed" of interpretations. While Klein recognized that patients often do not make direct references to the transference for a long time, her argument was that transference must be viewed as a much broader phenomenon than this behavior indicates. Klein disputed Freud's (1912) concept of transference as a libidinal object cathexis across the repression barrier; in contrast, she believed that the patient transfers the "total situation" from infancy to the consulting room. Since the transference is rooted in the earliest object relationship and deepest layer of the unconscious, its manifestations exist from the very beginning of an analysis, even in the patient's reporting of his or her history. It is not just that one can see the functioning of the ego early in the treatment; according to Klein, the patient's every presentation reveals defenses against the anxiety of the transference, an anxiety that is eventually revealed in the analysis.

For similar reasons, Klein (1946c) believed in the applicability of psychoanalysis to children. Since childhood emotional disturbance is rooted in the same anxieties as adult psychopathology, Klein (1926) adopted a strict interpretive method in her work with all age groups, even very young children. As children are often not able to verbalize their experience, she used play to stimulate clinical material; she then applied interpretive principles in the same way as she did with adults. Her advocacy of this approach with children made Klein a pioneer in child analysis.

In the treatment of children, Klein (1948c) believed strongly in early interpretation. While she acknowledged that the material must be adequate to warrant transference interpretation, she also pointed out that children provide sufficient material early in the course of treatment:

> As soon as the small patient has given me some sort of insight into his complexes—whether through his games or his drawings or phantasies, or merely by his general behavior—I consider that interpretation can and should begin. This does not run counter to the well-tried rule that the analyst should wait till the transference is there before he begins interpreting, because with children the transference takes place immediately, and the analyst will often be given evidence straight away of its positive nature. But should the child show shyness, anxiety or even only a certain distrust, such behavior is to be read as a sign of a negative transference, and this makes it still more imperative that interpretation should begin as soon as possible. For interpretation reduces the patient's negative transference by taking the negative affects involved back to their original objects and situation [pp. 46-47].

Although Klein's writing is replete with evidence of early interpretation, her examples are typically of interpretations of the Oedipus
complex, the primal scene, and the destructive impulses associated
with them and only rarely refer to the transference. For example,
Trude, age three-and-one-quarter years, in her first analytic hour
requested that flowers be removed, threw a toy man out of a cart,
wanted a man taken out of a picture book, and said that cushions had
been thrown into disorder by a dog; Klein interpreted to Trude that
she wanted to do away with her father's penis because it was playing
havoc with her mother. Her patient Peter, of the same age, in the first
hour bumped together a horse and carriage and later did the same
with two toy horses, saying, "That's not nice"; in the second session
he played again at knocking, bumping, and dangling, and Klein interpreted that these were all symbols of his mother and father bumping
their genitals together to produce his brother. These comments are
representative of the type of interpretation Klein made to children
early in treatment, although both interpretations are genetic, not
transference, interpretations. Indeed, one of the cardinal principles of
her technique in child analysis was to reduce the intensity of affects by
continually interpreting them back to the "original situation."

In her treatment of Richard, discussed earlier, Klein (1960) did in
fact make reference to the transference in the first session. Richard
spoke of Hitler's bombs, and Klein asked if he was worried about his
mother. He replied that he worried that a tramp might break into his
mother's room and hurt her. Klein interpreted that Richard knew
Klein herself was Austrian and was also concerned about injury to
her. However, she focused her attention during the session on the
boy's mention of a tramp, which she interpreted as symbolic of the
father who Richard feared would hurt his mother with his genital.
Despite the reference to the transference, Klein's interpretive focus
was on Richard's anxiety regarding his parents' sexual intercourse as
damaging to his mother. It appears that despite her theoretical adherence to early transference interpretation, Klein preferred early genetic
interpretations and there is little evidence that she interpreted early
material as transference.

Klein's (1926) justification for deep, early interpretations in child
analysis was that in children the demarcation between the unconscious and conscious is weak, so that early interpretations can be
effective immediately. Her contention was that because children tend
to blend the unconscious with the conscious, such interpretations
strengthen the child's weak ego (although she was not clear about
how this happened). When Trude asked that flowers and other objects

be removed from the consulting room, she was, according to Klein, already close to awareness of the wish to have her father's penis removed from her mother; Klein believed that her interpretation reduced the child's anxiety by making her wish completely conscious. Conversely, she argued that if such material remains uninterpreted, anxiety increases. Klein concluded that early, deep interpretations in child analysis are not only possible but desirable. They may even be necessary in many cases for the continuance of the treatment: if the transference is initially negative, early interpretations are necessary to form an immediate positive bond with the child, thereby reducing anxiety by tracing the aggressiveness "back to the original objects and situation" (Klein, 1946, p. 48). If the immediate transference is positive, conditions are already present for the therapeutic efficacy of interpretation.

These illustrations also indicate Klein's criterion of sufficient evidence to warrant interpretation. Although she stated that the clinical material must justify interpretive content, these clinical vignettes show that the child's play need not in any way be connected by the child to the content of the interpretation. When Trude's play centered around the notion of removing, Klein interpreted that the little girl wanted her father's penis removed from her mother. Children's play in itself seemed to Klein to justify its interpretation as symbolic of early hostile fantasies and anxieties. Klein's (1952d) rationale for this criterion is based on her broadened view of transference, as discussed earlier, although the interpretations focused on the past rather than the transference.

This advocacy of early in-depth interpretations without substantial evidential basis in the associative material would seem to contradict the time-honored analytic principle of gradually interpreting ego defenses so as to not overwhelm the ego with anxiety and to allow a gradual working through of defenses. Klein (1926, 1946) was very clear in her belief that to conduct child analysis on this adult model fails both to "establish the analytic situation" and to reduce the child's anxiety. Resistance, she believed, increases if the child is not helped to see the unconscious meaning of his or her play and behavior. Further, she believed the interpretation offered must be deep because unless it is directed to the most intense anxiety and guilt of the child's mind, it will be ineffective and may even increase resistance. Consistent with her stress on the pathogenicity of aggressiveness, she believed that excessive aggressiveness and negative transference were the "deepest strata of the mind" and that interpretation at this level loosens the most stubborn resistances and thereby "establishes the analytic situation" by reducing anxiety. Klein felt that children's anxiety required this type of interpretation, unnecessary in the adult.

Early interpretation does not resolve this deep level of anxiety, but it "opens the door" to the unconscious and to the analysis. She recognized that much effort was still ahead, in helping the young patient work through and resolve the anxiety and integrate the interpretations into the ego. For example, she interpreted to Peter in the second hour that his play with "broken men" was his wish to "kick his father out" and his fear of his father's retaliation; seven months later these fantasies were still being worked on in the analysis.

Klein's concept of early interpretation of material that is continually worked on throughout the analysis can be clearly seen in her treatment of Richard, which is the most detailed case study she published (Klein, 1960). As has been mentioned, Klein interpreted Richard's fear of his father hurting his mother in sexual intercourse in the first session. In the next session Richard talked about colliding planets, and Klein once again interpreted this as a manifestation of anxiety regarding sexual intercourse between the parents. Richard commented in his response that he hated Hitler and would like to hurt him, as well as Ribbentrop, who dared to accuse England of being the aggressor in the war. In this session Klein added that not only was he concerned about his father hurting his mother but that he also might be afraid his parents were enjoying themselves, in which case he "would be jealous and angry with them for leaving him 'lonely and deserted'" (p. 25). She then referred to his comment about Ribbentrop, interpreting that if he was angry and jealous of his parents, he would be the aggressor owing to his desire to make trouble for them.

This theme—Richard's desire to injure his parents out of oedipal rivalry rooted initially in oral sadistic desires to injure his mother—was repeated throughout the analysis. In our discussion of the Oedipus complex, it was pointed out that Richard's drawings, produced about four weeks into the analysis, were interpreted as representations of his destructive wishes toward his mother's insides and his fear of her retaliation, wishes that led to Richard's splitting his maternal introject into good and bad. In the 55th session Klein interpreted the boy's desire to injure and destroy his mother and his analyst while pretending to be an innocent lamb. In the next session Richard drew an eagle inside a coat and pulled his coat over himself to demonstrate the eagle. Klein interpreted that he saw himself as an eagle inside his mother's and his analyst's stomach harboring a wish to damage their insides. Finally, as mentioned earlier, at the end of the prematurely terminated analysis Klein interpreted Richard's anxiety about her leaving as his fear that his envy and rage were so great that he could destroy her.

Klein believed that this type of interpretation, of which only a small illustrative sample can be given here, helped Richard to begin to introject her as a good object, a process that aided in the diminution of his persecutory and depressive anxieties. Whatever the validity of this claim, the same analytic issues were interpreted from the beginning to the end of the analysis. It seems clear that in child analysis Klein believed in interpreting the same fundamental issues throughout the analysis rather than allowing a gradual unfolding of material.

As can be seen from these clinical examples, the content emphasis in Kleinian child analysis is no different from the interpretive focus in adult analysis. Klein believed that the child's unconscious aggressive feelings toward the parents, including all doubts and criticisms of them were central in all childhood conflicts. She also felt that the making conscious of sexual fantasies is crucial to the reduction of anxiety; however, she believed that the pathogenic component of these sexual fantasies lies in their aggressive nature, which the child's mind perceives as a threat to the parents.

Klein (1945) believed that oedipal conflicts were central to pathology but could not be separated from persecutory anxieties. In the case of Rita, Klein's oedipal interpretations focused on the child's hostility toward her parents in sexual intercourse. For example, Rita played that she was traveling with her teddybear to a "good woman" who was to give her a treat, but on the way she got rid of the engine driver who kept returning to threaten her and they battled over her teddybear. Klein interpreted that the bear represented her father's penis, which she had stolen in order to take his place with her mother. To this oedipal interpretation, Klein added that the fantasied penis robbery was an effort to repair the fantasied damage done to the mother's body by her oral sadistic attacks. Recall that Rita had witnessed the primal scene. Klein interpreted to her that when she observed coitus she wanted to do with her father what her mother was doing, that she sadistically wished to injure her mother out of jealousy. Klein interpreted the teddy bear play as evidence of Rita's failure to overcome her sadistic wishes toward her mother.

Similarly, Rita had a bedtime ritual of being tightly tucked in with her doll to prevent a mouse or "butzen" (her word) from coming in through the window to bite off her "butzen." Again, Klein interpreted the oedipal level: Rita feared that her father's penis would bite off her imaginary penis just as she desired to castrate him. However, Klein added that the fear of entry through the window also represented the fear of her mother's retaliatory attack upon her for her sadistic wishes to attack her mother's body. The phobias and nighttime terrors were all interpreted as Rita's fear of maternal retaliation, and her wish for a penis as a wish to repair her mother's damaged body. Klein also interpreted Rita's inability to separate from her mother as evidence of her continual need for reassurance that she had not damaged her mother with her sadistic wishes. Klein considered her difficulty accepting the bottle and then her resistance to yielding it for food as symptomatic of this same anxiety.

One can see from these examples that Klein's interpretive focus for the solution of Rita's multiple symptom picture was on the little girl's unconscious hostility toward the parents and the resulting depressive and persecutory anxieties. Klein's view of Rita's oedipal conflicts, as we have seen, was that they were pathogenic because of her unresolved oral sadistic wishes toward her mother's body, which resulted in the persecutory anxiety of retaliation and the depressive anxiety of having done fantasied injury to her mother's body. It was this interpretive focus on the anxiety of doing damage to the mother and the resulting fears of retaliation and loss that Klein felt was mutative in her treatment of Rita.

This emphasis on aggressive wishes was also seen in the case of Ruth, a four-and-one-half year-old who refused to be alone with Klein (1946), and thus treatment had to be conducted with Ruth's older sister in the consulting room. The child had an overly strong attachment to her mother and some, but not all, other women. She was timid, had great difficulty making friends, and suffered from severe anxiety. Once when the sister was ill, Ruth had to enter the consulting room by herself, which led to a severe anxiety attack; meanwhile Klein played at feeding dolls, as Ruth had done in the previous session. When the analyst put a wet sponge near one doll, Ruth screamed that the big sponge was only for grown-ups and must not be given to the doll. As in the previous session, the material related to envy of the mother; Klein now interpreted that Ruth "envied and hated her mother because the latter had incorporated her father's penis during coitus, and . . . wanted to steal his penis and the children out of her mother's inside and kill her mother" (p. 56). Klein went on to explain to Ruth that her fears were due to her anxiety of having killed her mother with her rage. Klein reports that after this interpretation Ruth's anxiety dissipated considerably in the session and that after a few more sessions she had very little anxiety entering the consulting room. Klein analyzed Ruth's anxiety attacks as a repetition of *pavor nocturnus*, which she suffered at age two when her mother became pregnant and she wished to steal the new baby and kill it. The guilt from this wish resulted in her over-attachment to her mother, with Ruth needing to be constantly in her mother's presence to reassure herself that she had not killed her mother. When she went to sleep, Ruth feared she would never see her mother again. In this case, as in the case of Rita, the source of the pathology, according to Klein, is to be found in the sadistic wishes to attack the mother's body, resulting in both the persecutory anxiety of retaliation and the depressive anxiety of guilt and fear of loss. The case of Ruth also demonstrates the increasingly central role envy came to play in Klein's understanding of the pathogenicity of aggressiveness. Ruth did not simply hate her mother but envied her, and Klein believed that envy was the root of Ruth's wish to damage her mother and her mother's body. For Ruth, unlike Rita, the full force of the anxiety was felt toward the analyst and was the basis for an intense negative transference.

In accordance with her view of the pathogenicity of aggressive and envious object relationships, Klein considered the negative transference to be a critical component of all analytic treatment, since the patient projects the early pathogenic hostile object relationship onto the analyst. Since envy is inevitably an aspect of the transference, the analyst's interpretations, especially if they are good and potentially helpful, are envied. In Klein's (1957) view, a good interpretation symbolizes a good feed. Therefore, to accept a helpful interpretation is to acknowledge that the analyst has good supplies that the patient lacks; envy follows, along with its desire to devour. To defend against envy of the analytic "good breast," the patient may reject the interpretation. Klein was well aware of the possible dangers of this view: if misused, it allows the analyst a way to blame the patient's rejection of interpretations on the patient's envy. However, she did not view all patient rejections of analytic interpretations as envy; she was referring only to interpretations that have been helpful. Recall that the infant is envious of the good breast for having and of the bad breast for withholding. The same phenomena become an inevitable component of the negative transference, further intensifying it. The powerful force of envy is, in Klein's view, the primary source of patient resistance. By viewing resistance in this light, Klein shifted an analytic concept from its original libidinal meaning to an aggressive phenomenon. She felt that resistance to the awareness of libidinal drives, such as oedipal longings, did not represent as powerful an obstacle to treatment progress as did the patient's envy of the analyst.

Indeed, Klein viewed the resolution of envy as a major aspect of the analytic process, believing that all patients envy the analyst who represents the good breast and consequently have some degree of hostility to the analyst for being helpful. The analyst's task is to recognize and interpret this resistance, which relieves anxiety immediately but which itself eventually results in envy. Analysis tends to assume a cycle in which "good feeding" interpretations that relieve anxiety are followed by envy of the analyst/good breast for having this "good food" to offer, which leads to the need to spoil and increases resistance, which the analyst then interprets, thus offering more "good food." The good experiences of accurate interpretations will in each instance relieve anxiety and lead to the introjection of the good object. This side of the process must ultimately win out over envy if the analysis is to be successful. When the good object is successfully introjected, the patient is able to feel gratitude toward the analyst rather than simply envy. Gratitude reflects a strengthened introjection of the good object and allows the integration process to unfold. Just as in infancy the crucial factor in overcoming envy and aggressive wishes toward the breast is the introjection of the good breast, so too in treatment the good feeds, represented by interpretations have the potential to overcome envy, greed, and aggressiveness. Klein did not believe in the provision of a good therapeutic experience, as Guntrip (1969) did. Her theory of treatment was orthodox in its strict adherence to interpretation as the only appropriate analytic intervention. In Klein's view, the accurate interpretation represents the good feed that allows the patient to introject the analyst as a good object and eventually leads to ego integration.

If the patient's envy is excessive, resistance will be enacted in some way to defeat the help offered by the analyst. Every step of progress in the analysis is followed by an act designed to destroy it. Klein believed that excessive envy explained the need of many characterologically disturbed patients to devalue the therapeutic process, especially when it has been helpful. She was referring to patients who after helpful interpretation feel some degree of relief from anxiety and new hope and then attack the very interpretation that brought them relief. Klein (1957) described the ensuing therapeutic process with such a patient this way:

> His criticism may attach itself to minor points; the interpretation should have been given earlier; it was too long, and has disturbed the patient's associations; or it was too short, and this implies that he has not been sufficiently understood. The envious patient grudges the analyst the success of his work; and if he feels that the analyst and the help he is

giving have become spoilt and devalued by his envious criticism, he cannot introject him sufficiently as a good object nor accept his interpretations with real conviction and assimilate them . . . . The envious patient may also feel, because of guilt about devaluing the help given, that he is unworthy to benefit by analysis [p. 184].

The negative therapeutic reaction, in Klein's view, is not simply a matter of the patient feeling guilty; the patient envies the analyst and desires to scoop out the good food from the analyst and spoil it. Receiving anything good from the analyst is associated with the fantasied injury to him or her. To protect the good object, the patient does not tolerate being given to, and must sabotage any offer of help.

The treatment of the negative therapeutic reaction is illustrated by the analysis of a female patient who was convinced that her babyhood and early feeding had been unsatisfactory (Klein, 1957). One day the patient phoned to cancel two consecutive sessions because of shoulder pain. When she did come, she complained extensively of pain and of others' lack of interest in her. She felt a need for someone to cover her shoulder, make her feel warm, and then go away. It occurred to her that this must be how she felt as a baby when she wanted to be cared for and no one came. The patient reported a dream in which no one served her in a restaurant but a determined woman in front of her took two or three cakes and went away; the patient then took two or three cakes herself. According to Klein (1957), the patient's

grievance about the missed analytic sessions related to the unsatisfactory feeds and unhappiness in babyhood. The two cakes out of the "two or three" stood for the breast which she felt she had been twice deprived of by missing analytic sessions . . . . The fact that the woman was "determined" and that the patient followed her example in taking the cakes pointed both at her identification with the analyst and at projection of her own greed onto her . . . . The analyst who went away with the two or three *petit fours* stood not only for the breast which was withheld, but also for the breast which was going to *feed itself* [p. 205].

Klein pointed out to the patient that her frustration had "turned to envy," as the mother/analyst was suspected of enjoying herself while the patient was missing the analytic sessions. Klein's interpretation of the dream focused on the connection between the missed analytic sessions and the unsatisfactory breast experience, both of which made the patient feel envious and resentful. According to Klein, the patient had felt her mother "to be selfish and mean, feeding and loving herself, rather than her baby" (p. 205).

Klein reported that the interpretation of this dream resulted in a dramatic emotional shift in the patient, who felt a happiness and gratitude that made her feel as if she had had a perfectly satisfactory feed. The patient then related that her early feeding may have been better than she had thought, and for the first time she recognized her envy of the analyst and her desire to spoil both the analyst and the analysis. This session began a process of working through the shift from envy and the desire to spoil to gratitude and enjoyment. The dream interpretation illustrates Klein's technical principles in analyzing resistance and negative therapeutic reactions. The patient's envy of and hostility toward the analyst were interpreted and related to the early breast experience, and the interpretations themselves counteracted the aggressiveness by providing good feeds that resulted in the introjection of the "good analytic breast," leading to gratitude and enjoyment.

The interpretation of the negative transference and envy are no less significant in the analysis of depressive position dynamics of ambivalence toward whole objects (Klein, 1937, 1957). The primary difference between the analysis of dynamics in the depressive and paranoid positions is the focus on anxiety of damage to the object in the former position as opposed to fear of injury to the ego in the latter. In both cases the analytic process involves the gradual integration of love and aggression through the continued interpretation of the conflict between them.

Klein's approach to the treatment of fixation at the depressive position is illustrated in her discussion of a male patient who had not been fully aware of his destructive desires and guilt about them when he reported a dream about fishing (Klein, 1957). In the dream, the patient decided to put his fish in a basket to die rather than eat it. He was carrying the fish in a laundry basket when it turned into a beautiful baby with something green about it; he noticed that the baby's intestines were protruding because of the hook it had swallowed. The green color was associated with Klein's green books, and the patient stated that the fish stood for one of Klein's own books. In addition, Klein (1957) states, "the fish was not only my work and my baby but also stood for myself. My swallowing the hook, which meant having swallowed the bait, expressed his feeling that I had thought better of him than he deserved and not recognized that there were also very destructive parts of his self operative in relation to me" (p. 211). After the interpretation, the patient became deeply depressed as he was horrified to realize the depths of his destructive desires and envy. Klein interpreted this reaction as a response to a step toward integration.

The next night the patient dreamed of a pike, to which he associated whales and sharks although the pike was old and worn rather than dangerous. A suckerfish was on it, and the patient immediately pointed out that the suckerfish protects itself this way. Klein's (1957) analysis of the dream is as follows:

> The patient recognized that this explanation was a defence against the feeling that he was the suckerfish and I was the old and worn-out pike and was in that state because I had been so badly treated in the dream of the previous night, and because he felt I had been sucked dry by him. This had made me not only into an injured but also into a dangerous object. In other words, persecutory as well as depressive anxiety had come to the fore; the pike associated to whales and sharks showed the persecutory aspects, whereas its old and worn-out appearance expressed the patient's sense of guilt about the harm he felt he had been doing and was doing to me [p. 212].

The dream illustrates not only the patient's fear of having injured the analyst with his destructiveness and envy, but also a regressive reaction from depressive to persecutory anxiety, illustrating the mixture of depressive and persecutory anxiety often found in cases of depression. After the interpretation of the dream, the patient underwent an intense depression for several weeks during which his urge for reparation intensified. When he did emerge from his depression, the patient felt that his knowledge of himself increased to such an extent that he would never again see himself as he had in the past and that his tolerance of others had also improved. This step toward integration could not be sustained initially; the patient continually lapsed into depressive states, which were interpreted as guilt over injuring the analyst.

The analysis of the patient's guilt led to a realization regarding his need for reparation: "An overstrong identification with the object harmed in phantasy—originally the mother—had impaired his capacity for full enjoyment and thereby to some extent impoverished his life" (p. 213). Klein believed that the patient's early breast-feeding had not been completely satisfying because of his fear of exhausting and depriving the breast. Klein concluded that he had experienced guilt over envy of the breast too early, leading to persecutory anxiety, which explained his regressive response to the awareness of depressive anxiety. The interpretations of unconscious hostility, envy, and guilt focused on the analyst allowed the gradual integration of love and aggressiveness, resulting in an increase of gratitude and enjoyment and the eventual lifting of the depression.

This case demonstrates Klein's (1950) view of treatment goals and her criterion for a good psychoanalytic outcome: resolution of persecutory and depressive anxiety. Nowhere does Klein give any indication that treatment goals differ by diagnostic category; in her schema all patients seem to need to achieve the same goals. Differences among patients have to do with severity and the developmental phase of anxiety, not its content. Patients resolve their symptoms to the extent that persecutory and depressive anxieties are mastered in treatment, as indicated by the degree of introjection of the good object. Persecutory anxiety diminishes as the internalization of the good object mitigates the sense of danger from without, and depressive anxiety is assuaged as the fear of danger to the good object is reduced. As we have seen, for Klein these critical psychic shifts occur in response to good interpretations that reduce anxiety and foster the establishment of the good object within. The strengthening of the good object allows it to survive destructive impulses and contact with the bad object without suffering severe damage, thereby reducing the need for splitting and fostering whole object integration. Ultimately, Klein viewed the outcome of successful analytic treatment as the integration of the ego and whole objects.

CRITIQUE

Klein's views have been controversial from their inception and have stimulated so much intense criticism and debate within the psychoanalytic community that an appraisal of their strong and weak points is in order. After Klein developed the concept of the depressive position, her work came under intense attack from many traditional analysts. Glover (1945), the leader of the anti-Kleinian group, caustically criticized the "new metapsychology." Glover's hostile tone represented the atmosphere within the British Psychoanalytic Society at the time, where many traditional analysts felt Klein's views were highly speculative, even fantastical, and represented a departure from the foundation of psychoanalysis (for example, Waelder, 1937; A. Freud, 1927). These analysts were absolute in their rejection of Klein's views, resulting in a split between the Kleinian and anti-Kleinian forces within the British Psychoanalytic Society (Segal, 1980). It is only in recent years, as interest in object relations theories has intensified, that some Kleinian concepts have been given serious consideration beyond her group of devoted followers. Her theoretical system has been attacked on virtually every point, but the following five general criticisms are most compelling.

First, Klein has been widely criticized for "adultomorphism," that is, attributing to infants the mental processes of adults. Waelder (1937) was the first to set forth a thorough critique of the theory that infants have complex fantasy lives that include desires to injure, fear of retaliation, good and bad objects, and oedipal conflicts. Even if such fantasies are seen in the analysis of children as young as the third year, say anti-Kleinians, the assumption of their existence in the first year is unwarranted. Bibring (1947) pointed out that Kleinian theory assumes complex fantasied relationships among objects long before perception has developed to the point that such fantasies would be possible. This criticism by the anti-Kleinians seems well justified by research on infancy, which shows clearly that infants do not have the cognitive capacity to have the complex fantasy life Klein attributes to them (Lichtenberg, 1983, Stern, 1985). As a corollary to this criticism, Klein's belief that infants have knowledge of sexual intercourse is without basis; indeed, such knowledge is not possible given the cognitive equipment of infancy. Even children who do in fact witness the primal scene in the first few months of life have such a limited cognitive capability that it is impossible for them to fantasize that the father's penis is inside the mother and to have the wish to do the same themselves. Besides, even if one could argue that such cognitive capability exists in young infants, the evidence that they in fact have such fantasies is lacking.

The second major criticism of Klein's developmental theory is that she confuses psychopathological constellations with normal developmental process. She attributes the pathological reactions of paranoia, depression, mania, and obsessions to the normal infant, yet the only data she offers for this are her analyses of pathological children. Even if one agrees with her formulations of pathological mechanisms in these children, the vast research on infancy offers no evidence for the existence of these pathological constellations in normal infants (Stern, 1985). In Klein's defense, she was aware of this criticism and attempted to clarify her position by stating that the infant is not psychotic but has "psychotic-like" anxieties (Klein, 1946). While this clarification mitigates Klein's position somewhat, it does not resolve the problem; evidence that the normal infant has "psychotic-like" anxieties and complex defenses is unconvincing. From the fact that screaming infants are comforted, Klein (1952a) inferred that they feared attack from a persecutory object and were calmed when comforting allowed for the reestablishment of the good object. This "evidence" is insufficient for even the somewhat softened conclusion that children suffer "psychotic-like" anxieties. The fact that children scream does not warrant the conclusion that they feel persecuted, and their return to comfort does not imply the "re-establishment of the good object."

This critique points to difficulties inherent in Klein's concept of the aggressive drive, the third general area of difficulty with her system. Klein's use of the concept of aggression is far too loose: she interpreted infant distress as aggression, which she then equated with hatred, the desire to destroy, and sadism. Not only does distress not imply aggression, but even a legitimate aggressive response is not inherently hateful. As we will see in the discussion of Kernberg in chapter 5, joyful assertiveness is aggressive but not hateful. Sadistic wishes are pathological distortions of aggression and should not be equated with it. Klein did not make crucial distinctions between the infant's distress, joyful aggressive expressions, healthy assertiveness, and hateful forms of aggressiveness. Moreover, there is no basis for the assumption that aggression is a drive (as will be discussed further in chapter 5). Aggressive responses are not motivated by biological pressure for gratification, as are such drives as sex, hunger, and thirst (Scott, 1958). Klein based her developmental theory on a faulty, confused concept of aggression.

The fourth area of difficulty with Klein's theory involves the inconsistencies in her attempted distinction between the paranoid and depressive positions. Although many analysts have found the distinction to be generally useful, Klein's contention that destructive, sadistic desires exist in the paranoid position conflicts with her view that the desire to injure the object first appears in the depressive position. It may appear that Klein's view could be defended by reasoning that aggression in the depressive position is the first experience of intent to injure the loved object whereas the destructive desires of the paranoid position are directed toward the split-off bad object. However, the purported existence of envy in the paranoid position weakens this line of reasoning: envy is directed against the good object, and Klein's theory must somehow reconcile the envious desire in the paranoid position to damage the good object with the contention that the depressive position is defined by the first desire to injure the loved object.

The fifth major category of criticism of Klein's work is that her interpretive style involves unwarranted, even wild, inferential leaps that contradict sound analytic principles and lack evidential basis in the clinical material (Zetzel, 1956, 1964). Critics point to Klein's characteristic tendency to interpret children's play material as symbolic of the primal scene and other primitive fantasies without waiting for confirming associative material. The criticism applies also to adult analysis because, although Klein did not specifically advocate early interpretation in adult analysis, she used the same principles to deduce transference, the primal scene, and paranoid and depressive anxieties from symbolic material, deductions that sometimes lacked confirming associative data. Critics have argued that Klein ignored patients' needs for defenses and therefore the need to work through them gradually in order for the ego to be ready for the awareness of the unconscious material it had so staunchly resisted (Kernberg, 1972). Zetzel (1964) pointed out that interpretation implies a therapeutic alliance with part of the patient's ego, an alliance that allows the interpretive process to occur. Kernberg (1972) summarized these criticisms as the "ego-psychological critique" of Klein's work, because he felt Klein ignored one of the basic postulates of ego psychology, namely, that the ego and its defenses must be central to analysis before id interpretations can have a mutative effect.

As a corollary to the "ego-psychological critique" of Kleinian interpretive principles, critics (Kernberg, 1972) have suggested that Klein's early, deep interpretive style resulted in a lack of analytic process— the same material is addressed and interpreted at the same level from beginning to end. Klein herself acknowledged this persistence of interpretive themes in the case of Peter, but she apparently did not consider the lack of analytic process a problem. Geleerd (1963) found fault with Klein's analysis of Richard because the analysis never deepened; the same content was interpreted at the same level from first session to last. Geleerd pointed out that the result was a lack of discernible analytic progress.

Despite the serious flaws in Klein's views, she was able to explain a great deal of psychopathology by differentiating persecutory and depressive anxieties, demonstrating their role in a wide variety of psychopathological conditions, and illuminating the role of primitive defenses in neurosis and character pathology. Both Kleinians and non-Kleinian clinicians have found her notions of splitting, projective and introjective cycles, and the mechanisms of denial, omnipotence, and especially, projective identification to be of inestimable value in the treatment of severe character pathology. (Kernberg, 1975; Giovacchini, 1979; Ogden, 1982; Grotstein, 1986; Hughes, 1987). Projective identification has become widely used as a tool for the understanding of character pathology. In addition, a variety of symptoms and pathological patterns—such as food addictions, excessive object attachment, depression, and hypochondriasis—can be explained, at least in part, by Klein's understanding of depressive position dynamics, and the differentiation of these dynamics from paranoid anxiety provides the clinician with an effective tool for the separation of levels of pathology.

Further, Klein's view that ego and superego development are products of the internalization of object relations has been found useful by object relations theorists. We have already seen, in chapter 2, that Fairbairn and Guntrip used her concept of internal objects to develop their own conceptualizations of development and psychopathology and employed her concept of the depressive position to differentiate categories of psychopathology.

None of the aforementioned criticisms of Klein's views necessarily contradicts the object relations foundation of her view of development and psychopathology. One can agree with these major criticisms and continue to adhere to Klein's position that the crucial factor in early development is the initial object relationship and the relative balance of good and bad objects in this relationship. One need only change the Kleinian developmental timetable to the later phases of childhood, when the child has the cognitive and perceptual apparatus to perceive objects and their interrelationships, to escape the difficulties of adultomorphism while preserving Klein's object relations view of development and psychopathology. In this way, the substance of Klein's theory, that paranoid and depressive anxieties characterize the conflicts of early stages of development and that excessive conflict in these stages predisposes the ego to a pathological outcome later in development, is largely unaffected by the aforementioned criticisms. Klein's emphasis on object relations is consistent with the traditional psychoanalytic conception that conflicts and anxiety in each developmental phase leave the ego prone to some degree of fixation or regression that may result in pathology, but that these are also elements of the normal developmental processes does not necessarily include pathological elements. Finally, Klein's aggressive interpretive style has no inherent connection to her emphasis on object relations. Her view of development as consisting of good and bad internal object relations can as easily be applied clinically according to the technical precepts of developing an analytic relationship and sensitive interpretive timing. Indeed, Segal (1981) and Rosenfeld (1987) adapted Klein's theoretical concepts to a more cautiously interpretive analytic model. These and other modifications to Klein's basic theoretical postulates have been made by Klein's followers.

THE KLEINIANS

Despite the intense and frequent criticism with which her views were met by many analysts, Klein attracted a devoted group of followers who adopted most of her fundamental ideas. Her devotees modified and expanded many of her ideas, but they adhered to her basic concepts—the paranoid-schizoid and depressive positions,and the importance of the projective-introjective cycles, splitting in development and pathology—and a Kleinian school was born within the psychoanalytic movement (although it did take her theory in directions she probably did not anticipate). The most striking additions to Klein's thought among her followers fall into five general categories: (1) the expansion of the concept of projective identification; (2) the differentiation of clinical syndromes and their specific mechanisms and treatment approaches, based on Kleinian concepts; (3) the application of Kleinian technique to psychotic states; (4) the inclusion of noninterpretive techniques in treatment; and (5) the evolution of the treatment model to an emphasis on countertransference.

Projective identification has been used by the Kleinian school to reconceptualize the psychoanalytic theory of early development and psychopathology, as well as its principles of technique. The basic modifications in the concept have been its extension to an interpersonal process and elaboration beyond its defensive function (Segal, 1981; Rosenfeld, 1987). The predominant view among the Kleinians has been that the object must in fact experience the projection in order for an affect or unwanted part of the self to be successfully projected into it. The self gets rid of the distressing feeling by giving it to the other to feel. Whereas for Klein projective identification was a fantasy, it is for her followers an interpersonal process in which the object has the experience the self is not able to have. Rosenfeld (1987), for example, points out that projective identification is used by both infants and adults not only for defensive purposes but also for communication to let others experience one's feelings directly when words may not be direct or forceful enough. As we shall see in chapter 7, the concept of the patient communicating by having the analyst feel aspects of the self has become an important component of the interpersonal school of psychoanalysis.

For Bion (1959a, 1962), projective identification is a crucial component of the early child–mother interaction. The infant attempts to rid itself of distress by projecting it into the mother. In Bion's view the primary role of the mother in early infancy is to be a "container" for the frustration and pain the child's infantile ego is too fragile to contain. The mother not only contains the tension but also gives it back to the infant in a tolerable form. The mother's ability to soothe the infant in distress is dependent on her capacity to absorb the infant's tension and to allow the infant to internalize her as an object capable of tolerating the original anxiety (Segal, 1981). In this way the infant becomes capable of managing frustration and anxiety, thus acquiring a primary foundation of mental stability. That is to say, the mother's ability to allow the infant's projective identifications plays a crucial role in its eventual mental health.

The corollary of this view of early mothering is that if the mother is unable to contain the infant's distress, the child is left with overwhelming anxiety and is forced to deny reality. In extreme cases the denial leads to psychosis. According to Bion's (1961) particular way of formulating psychotic thought process, which is based on Klein's theory of the early projective and introjective processes and his own theory, thinking originates in a mating of a preconception and a frustration. If the infant expects a breast and none is forthcoming and if a minimal capacity for frustration exists, the thought "no breast" will be created to bridge the gulf between the want and the satisfying action. Bion (1962) calls this process "learning from experience." The development of thought, in this view, both depends on the capacity for frustration tolerance and increases it. If the mother cannot fulfill her function as container, the infant does not have enough frustration tolerance for thought development to occur (Bion, 1959a). Instead, the infant evades frustration by treating thoughts as bad objects that must be evacuated and by attacking the links between thoughts in an effort to deny reality. The result is a fragmenting of the thought process and eventual psychosis (Bion, 1957). Further, the infant is forced into a desperately excessive use of both projective identification and splitting in an effort to rid itself of frustrating experience; the outcome is forceful effort to enter the object, which results in psychotic delusions.

In Bion's (1957) view, even if the infant's attempts at projective identification are successful the object does not completely tolerate the anxiety, and when it is reintrojected it becomes attacking and starves the personality of all good qualities. If the infant's intolerance for frustration is too great—yet not enough for evasion—the outcome will be the use of omnipotence to avoid reality. In this case, omniscience becomes a substitute for learning from experience, and reality is denied, but thought does not become fragmented and the resulting personality organization is borderline rather than psychotic.

Rosenfeld (1965, 1983) adds a further component to the Kleinian view of psychosis: he points out that the psychotic not only needs desperately to project unwanted parts of the self into others but also introjects others just as forcefully into the self. Both processes result in the blurring of self–object boundaries, which the psychotic needs in order to defend against the awareness of separateness. Rosenfeld agreed with Bion that the mother must be a container for the infant's projective identifications, but he believed that the result of failed containment is excessive envy and aggressiveness and an intense need to defend against them. The blurring of self–object boundaries, according to Rosenfeld, is the psychotic defense against intolerable envy, aggressiveness, and the awareness of dependence.

Rosenfeld (1978) agreed with Bion that borderline psychopathology is attributable to a failure by the mother to introject the infant's projections. However, Rosenfeld put more emphasis on the resulting increase in envy and aggressiveness, which, he believed, disrupts the normal splitting process and thus causes prolonged states of confusion in which love and hate are undifferentiated. When strong affects are evoked, the child resorts to pathological splitting of ego and object into fragmented bits, a process leading to loss of the reality sense. In therapy, these patients, unlike psychotics, are able to maintain a sense of reality outside the transference and to have other relationships that do not evoke strong affects. However, the reality sense is always vulnerable to potential disruption by emotional contact or eruption of affect. Rosenfeld attributed the chaos of the borderline patient to the ease with which affect disrupts the reality sense.

Envy is defended against by attacking the dependent, libidinal self in an effort to destroy links to objects. The result is a primitive, attacking superego and idealization of the destructive, omnipotent self that disdains contact with objects. The child resorts to a fixated omnipotence in which reality is denied, yet the thought process is not totally disturbed, as it is in the psychotic solution of attacking thought itself. This formulation fits Bion's concept of the "in-between" childhood state in which the mother fails the infant's need for projective identification enough so that there is insufficient ability to tolerate frustration but not so much frustration that total evasion of it is necessary. Rosenfeld adds that since the failure of projective identification arrests development before the normal superego can develop, the attacks on the dependent part of the self substitute for normal superego development. Moreover, this primitive superego is projected onto others, leading to the persecutory fear that others are constantly critical and attacking.

Klein's followers have also delineated narcissistic pathology in a more precise way than Klein did herself. Klein (1946c) referred to narcissism in the context of the narcissistic object ties in schizoid mechanisms. Her followers used her concepts to formulate a view of narcissistic pathology as a syndrome in itself. According to both Segal (1983) and Rosenfeld (1971, 1978), the narcissistic character structure is a defense against envy and dependence.

Rosenfeld viewed narcissistic pathology, like borderline conditions, as a product of such excessive reliance on projection and projective identification that the self–object distinction becomes blurred. The difference between narcissism and borderline pathology is in the narcissistic patient's ability to utilize splitting effectively, that is, confusion is not a dominant component of the narcissistic personality. Rosenfeld saw the fusion of self and object in narcissistic states as a defense against the awareness of separateness, which stimulates envy, dependence, and frustration. The strength of this fusion is a function of the intensity of the destructive desire and envy that result from early frustration, failed projective identification in infancy, and constitutional disposition.

Rosenfeld (1971) differentiated libidinal and destructive narcissism: the former is the idealization of the self by the omnipotent introjection and projective identification of good objects while the latter refers to the idealization of the omnipotent destructive parts of the self that attack the libidinal self and libidinal object relationships that seek dependence ties. In narcissistic pathology the sense of humiliation regarding needs is so deep that the destructive narcissistic self wishes to dominate the entire personality and destroy the libidinal self in order to eliminate all possibility of dependence ties. Rosenfeld identified the dependent self as the sane part of the personality and felt that destructive narcissism is pathological. The clinician cannot usually discern the difference between the two types of narcissistic structure until the self-idealization is threatened by self-other awareness. At that point the eruption of envy and destructive desires leads to an attack by the destructive narcissistic self on the libidinal self, and the difference becomes clear as destructive omnipotence threatens to take over the entire personality; the patient now displays a superior, hostile posture, devaluing others and denying need for all objects.

Segal's (1983) formulation agrees with Rosenfeld's in viewing extended narcissism as a defense of withdrawal against envy and dependence. The difference in formulations is that in Segal's there is no role for libidinal narcissism. All prolonged narcissism, according to Segal, is based on excess aggression. The patient maintains a hostile, superior defensive structure to defend against envy and destructive desires; thus, envy is the crux of narcissistic pathology.

In both Segal's and Rosenfeld's conceptualizations of narcissism, Klein's concept of the pathogenicity of excessive envy is used to understand fixation in pathological narcissism, a syndrome not discussed by Klein herself. Narcissistic pathology, the borderline syndrome, and psychotic states are all syndromes that Klein did not delineate specifically, but that have been formulated by her followers in accordance with her theoretical concepts.

These views of Klein's followers have clear implications for treatment, the most controversial of which is the application of psychoanalytic treatment to psychotic conditions. While Klein treated only one psychotic patient, a five-year-old boy, her devotees carried out more systematically her view that such conditions are analytically accessible (Segal, 1980). Both Bion's and Rosenfeld's formulations of psychosis rely on the concepts of excessive aggressiveness and envy in the paranoid–schizoid position and the overreliance on projective identification. The clinical implication is that the analysis of envy, aggressiveness, and projective identification has the potential to resolve psychotic conditions. This view is the theoretical foundation for the treatment of psychosis among Kleinian analysts, each of whom emphasizes a different aspect of the process.

Rosenfeld (1987) emphasized the implications of the psychotic patient's reliance on projective identification for the transference, postulating that as soon as the patient enters the analyst's office he or she attempts to communicate by making the analyst feel unwanted parts of himself or herself. This is a mode of communication that is central to the psychotic patient, since verbal thought for such a person has not developed the meaning it has for the normal person. The analyst's first task is to understand the patient's nonverbal communications by accepting and understanding the patient's projections into him or her, since the mother's failure to do so in childhood is the presumed source of the psychosis. This therapeutic use of countertransference is a direct application of Bion's (1959, 1962) view that the mother must contain the infant's frustration for the ego development to proceed. The attitude of empathy and acceptance of the patient's unconscious communication by projective identification is considered to be as crucial to the success of the treatment as the accuracy of interpretations.

In Rosenfeld's view, psychotic patients also project their own use of projective identification onto the analyst and therefore fear the analyst will attempt to take over their personality: the belief that the analyst is forcefully intruding his or her feelings into them blurs self–object boundaries and leads to the formation of a psychotic transference. The resolution of the transference psychosis is the crux of the treatment. Before it can be analyzed, the analyst's task is to maintain the boundaries by continually sorting through the patient's projections into him or her to differentiate the patient's projections from his or her own feelings. A crucial component of the treatment is the analyst's holding the projective identifications and verbalizing them to himself or herself before an interpretation is made. In fact, Rosenfeld warned against interpreting too quickly, since premature interpretation will be felt by the patient as an expulsion from the analyst, and therefore as a repeat of early trauma. (Allowing for the unfolding of the transference constellation before interpretive work begins links Rosenfeld's technical views to Kohut's approach to the selfobject transference, as will be discussed in chapter 6.)

Rosenfeld went so far as to indicate that verbal interpretations can be harmful if they are made too quickly or are so persistent and rigid that they are experienced as assaults. However, he saw a crucial role for verbal interpretations made with tact, proper timing, and sensitivity to the patient's anxiety regarding awareness of the self–other distinction. If these conditions are fulfilled, the patient feels "held" by the interpretations in an almost physical sense. (Rosenfeld's concept of verbal and nonverbal "holding" is closer to Winnicott's notion of the analyst as the "holding environment," to be discussed in chapter 4, than to Klein's concept of early intervention.) While verbal interpretations play a crucial role in Rosenfeld's treatment model for the psychoses, their beneficial impact is a function of their ability to effect the positive therapeutic bond not experienced in the child–mother relationship. The resolution of the pathology still comes largely from the verbalization of unconscious material, but Rosenfeld's view of the treatment process includes recognition of an intense interpersonal process that is experienced but not interpreted verbally for some time. This conceptualization of the treatment process is based on the developmental view of psychosis as originating in the mother's failure to allow the child's affects inside her. According to Rosenfeld (1987), the psychotic patient needs to "find space inside the mother/analyst's body" more than he needs the breast (p. 278). The patient's needs for safety and acceptance must be provided for by the analyst's behavior in order for the child/patient to feel life. Only when the psychotic patient feels safe "inside" the analyst is it possible for verbal interpretations to have meaning.

One can see that Rosenfeld departed from Klein's principles of technique. He gave a prominent place in the treatment of psychosis to noninterpretive intervention, principally holding and verbalizing the patient's projectively identified affects. In fact, Rosenfeld believed that because the patient communicates nonverbally, the analyst satisfies many of the patient's needs by nonverbal behavior. Rosenfeld saw the mutative effect of the psychoanalytic treatment of psychosis as its ability to provide a satisfactory substitute for the unsuccessful mother–child relationship in the child's background whereas for Klein the curative factor is the same in the analysis of psychosis and neurosis, namely, making the unconscious conscious. This aspect of Rosenfeld's approach has a closer affinity to Winnicott's concept of holding and Kohut's use of empathy, as will become evident in chapters 4 and 6, than to Klein's principle of immediate interpretation.

Segal's (1981) view concurs with Rosenfeld's emphasis on the importance of containment of the patient's projective identifications, but she is closer to Klein in her view that interpretations of unconscious material and the transference should be made early in treatment at the point of greatest unconscious anxiety in order to establish contact with the patient's unconscious fantasy life. A fundamental principle of Segal's technique is the desirability of making a transference interpretation in the first session with all patients; Segal felt that such early intervention was of particular importance for psychotic patients, as they have an immediate need for anxiety relief. It needs to be underscored that Segal's early interpretations were based more on the patient's use of projective identification as a defense in the transference than on underlying aggressiveness, as was Klein's tendency. For example, in the first session with a schizophrenic patient, Segal interpreted that the girl had put all her "sickness" into the analyst as soon as she entered the room and then had experienced Segal as a sick and frightening person who would put the "sickness" back into her (Segal, 1981). Klein would likely have made a more developmental interpretation regarding early aggressiveness and anxiety. Nonetheless, Segal did interpret the primitive defense almost immediately, whereas Rosenfeld would have accepted the patient's projection into him, absorbing and thinking about it, rather than interpreting it in this first session. Like Klein, Segal (1981) saw the mutative effects of the analytic treatment of psychoses in the power of insight to integrate split-off parts of the ego, with persistent interpretation of projective identification, projection, and splitting due to excessive envy and aggressiveness leading ultimately to a reintegration of the ego split by these defenses.

Segal's (1981) approach to the treatment of the schizophrenic patient is illustrated by her analysis of Edward, who had typical schizophrenic symptoms: delusions of evil people taking over the world and auditory hallucinations. Her approach was to interpret the patient's feelings of being misunderstood and isolated and his fear of involving his analyst in his madness. Edward kept Segal as the one good, beneficent, unchanging figure in his life by withholding both love and hate. Although he treated her as if she were a matter of indifference to him, Edward was unceasingly demanding that she gratify him, a behavior she responded to by interpreting what he wanted and why he wanted it, but without gratifying the wish. According to Segal's report, by the sixth month of analysis, the treatment had the same focus as an analysis of neurosis: the understanding and working through of the patient's characteristic fantasies and defenses. The difference was that Edward's primary defenses were splitting—into the persecutory and idealized objects—and magical denial.

A good example of Segal's interpretive technique is found in a session when Edward reported a voice saying "dreams, dreams." When Segal interpreted that she had become the internal persecutor nagging him for dreams, Edward produced a dream from the preceding night that led to a confirmation of Segal's interpretation. In a part of the dream a white man was turning brown because of how he had been photographed. Segal interpreted the dream to mean that the analyst was making Edward evil, magically turning him into feces, as he believed he had done to his parents and to her, by wishing to watch her in sexual intercourse. According to Segal's interpretation of the material, Edward believed that she was retaliating by persecuting him with demands for dreams while he reprojected by filling her with feces, an act to which she responded by looking at him and thereby filling him with feces. In Edward's transferential projective and introjective cycles, he and his analyst were symbolically putting excrement into each other by looking at each other. In the following session, Edward felt much better. Segal (1981) concludes, "Obviously, he felt that he had projected the illness into me, so that he was free, but I became both the anxious and ill person and the external persecutor" (p. 114).

Segal indicated that after one year of analysis the patient's delusions had disappeared and that he was in contact with reality and was leading an apparently normal life; in fact, Edward was still preoccupied with fantasies of damage done to the earth, but he was responding to such fantasies with successful concrete action on environmental problems. Schizophrenic mechanisms continued to operate for a time, but they were interpreted until, as Segal reports, Edward became "free to accept a real good object, a real good experience and a real good hope of growing out of babyhood" (p. 117).

It can be seen from this case that despite the patient's obvious distress and deteriorated condition, Segal eschewed reassurance and support. Nonetheless, she departed from Klein, who would have offered immediate genetic interpretations of symptoms, by confining her early interventions to the patient's isolation, desire to be understood, conflicts around projective identification, and wish to and fear of driving the analyst mad. Segal's approach provides more of a sense of process from beginning to middle to end than one tends to find in the case material reported by Klein herself. We have seen that Rosenfeld was careful to wait and utilize noninterpretive containment before offering verbal interpretations of unconscious material. Since Segal is perhaps Klein's closest follower, it is safe to conclude that Klein's followers have tended to adapt her technical concepts to an analytic approach that times interpretations to the phase of the analytic process and moves gradually to deeper unconscious material. This case also illustrates the continuity of interpretive focus in the Kleinian tradition once the unconscious material was reached.

Similar features can be seen in the Kleinian approach to the treatment of borderline disorders. As we have seen, the Kleinians tend to view the pathogenesis of this disorder in the failure of the mother to contain the infant's projective identifications leading to the child's overdependence on projective identification, with the consequent loss of self to the other. The anxiety-driven reintrojection of the unwanted parts of the self forms the primitive superego (Rosenfeld, 1978). In the treatment situation this process repeats itself and becomes the transference psychosis, the resolution of which is the fundamental issue in the Kleinian treatment of borderline disorders. Patients believe the analyst is hypercritical and attacking, and they counterattack. According to Rosenfeld (1978), the borderline patient's intense projective–introjective cycles lead to confusion between patient and analyst. Borderline patients reverse roles, attacking the analyst for possessing the unwanted parts of the self. For example, in erotic transferences patients believe the analyst loves them. It is the analyst's task to accept, absorb, and put into words all such projections, as the mother failed to do in infancy. The analyst must continually search himself or herself to sort out all the patient's projective identifications in order to differentiate the patient's feelings from his or her own, which the patient cannot do. This task can be burdensome, making the treatment of the borderline emotionally draining for the analyst. Indeed, Rosenfeld viewed many of the frustrations and treatment impasses with such patients as results of the analyst's failure to see that his or her frustration with the patient is a communication from the patient that the latter has no other way of getting across. Only when analysts are able to use their own affective reactions in the formulation of interpretations can they effectively resolve the transference psychosis.

Rosenfeld (1978) provided a telling illustration of his technical recommendations with the borderline patient in an account of his treatment of a multitraumatized man who was in analysis for two and one-half years when he displayed a hostile posture and criticized Rosenfeld for being unceasingly critical of him. The attacks became so vituperative that Rosenfeld felt like a helpless child filled with futile rage. When the patient decided to leave treatment, Rosenfeld had him sit up and go over all his criticisms. In response, Rosenfeld "did not give any interpretations and adopted an entirely receptive, empathic, listening attitude to him. I also examined, as much as possible, my countertransference" (p. 219). The patient decided to stay in treatment, and it became clear to Rosenfeld that the patient had projected his perception of his mother, who could not "hold" him, onto his analyst and had turned the analyst into own severe, hypercritical superego. This interpretation began the resolution of the transference psychosis. When the patient went through a second bout of transference psychosis some time later, it did not last long because Rosenfeld was aware of the patient's need to project his primitive superego into him and to communicate by reversing roles and having the analyst feel as he had felt as a child. In this clinical illustration, too, one can see Klein's concepts of projective identification and the projective and introjective cycles as the core of the interpretive content, yet the emphasis on containment, empathy, and sensitivity is a critical component of the treatment representing a clear departure from Klein's principles of technique.

Klein's followers also have specific treatment recommendations for the analysis of narcissistic pathology. Rosenfeld's and Segal's treatment approaches follow directly from their formulations of pathological narcissism as a defense against envy and excessive aggressiveness. The crucial component of the treatment of pathological narcissism for both theorists is the interpretation of narcissistic withdrawal and the posture of superiority as massive character defenses against envy and the desire to destroy.

However, the treatment approaches of Rosenfeld and Segal diverge at this point. Rosenfeld (1971) tended to emphasize self–object fusion as a defense against the awareness of envy and destructiveness. He believed that in the treatment process the patient is inevitably forced to become aware that the analyst is a separate person; this realization results in the eruption of envy of the analyst and the wish to destroy him or her as the patient feels humiliated by the analyst's ability to help. The narcissistic patient becomes intent at this point on destroying the analysis, now equated with the destruction of the libidinal self of childhood dependency, the sane part of the personality. The analyst must make a persistent effort to interpret the dependent self in order to bring it in to contact with the analyst and, eventually, other positive objects; meanwhile, the destructive omnipotent self is interpreted in an effort to deflate it by exposing its infantile nature. When the libidinal self is contacted, the patient begins to form new, positive object contacts, which strengthen it and counteract the efforts of destructive omnipotence to dominate the personality. One can see that although Rosenfeld viewed pathological narcissism as a defense against envy and destructive desires, he felt that the mutative effects of the analytic process lie more in making contact with the split-off libidinal childhood self than in analyzing envy.

By way of contrast, Segal (1983) placed her treatment focus more exclusively on the analysis of envy. Following Klein closely, Segal conceptualized pathological narcissism as a withdrawal that is based on excessive use of projective identification and leads to fear of object contact. Her view was that as envy and destructive desires are analyzed, the need for narcissistic defense and the use of projective identification dissipate, and the patient can emerge from narcissistic withdrawal. As such patients make object contact, they can begin to grapple with depressive position conflicts, since both the positive and negative aspects of the transference can now be experienced. Segal disputed Rosenfeld's notion of a dependent libidinal self that must be contacted.

From the treatment principles advocated by Klein's followers in the analysis of psychotic, borderline, and narcissistic pathology, one can see a strong emphasis on projective identification, which they have modified to an interpersonal concept in forming analytic technique. Racker (1968) also made major contributions to this conceptual shift in modern Kleinian treatment by pointing out that the transference is revealed in the patient's attitude toward the analyst's interpretations. Racker contended that patients' attitudes toward the breast extend beyond envy and manifest themselves in a wide variety of reactions to interpretations, including indifference, frustration, hatred, guilt, greed, and fear of being controlled, among others. According to Racker, whatever manner the patient adopts in relation to the analyst's interpretations is a transference reaction reflecting the early attitude toward the breast. In turn, the analyst will have some type of reaction to the patient's response inasmuch as every element of transference is responded to with some type of countertransference reaction. The analyst's responsibility is to be aware of this law of the psychoanalytic process. Only awareness of countertransference responses can ensure that the analyst will not reenact the childhood interaction unwittingly. Patients' deepest conflicts can be resolved by analyzing their relationship with the analyst's interpretations if the analyst can become aware of his or her countertransference response.

Racker distinguished two types of countertransference based on two types of identification with the patient. The concordant identification is the analyst's direct identification with components of the patient's personality; it becomes the concordant countertransference. The complementary identification is the analyst's identification with an object of the patient's psyche, such as the patient's superego; this becomes the complementary countertransference. Both reactions are common in the analysis of all patients as the analyst becomes the critical superego of the patient. The complementary and concordant identifications indicate that the patient's transference is not simple projection, since the analyst identifies with an aspect of the patient. Grotstein (1986) carried this concept a step further with his view that all projection elicits a response in the object; that is, that there is no pure projection distinguishable from projective identification.

Even more crucial for the treatment process is Racker's distinction between countertransference thought and countertransference position. The former is any particular discrete response evoked by the patient, the latter a general attitude of the analyst's ego that interferes with the analytic posture. In Racker's view, the countertransference position is pathological because it threatens to lead to an acting-out response rather than an interpretive one. It is the analyst's responsibility to be continually vigilant of his or her responses to the patient to prevent such an acting out. Subtle behaviors by the analyst—such as the mind wandering—can be the acting out of a deeply unconscious countertransference position as much as more overt acting out in response to a frustrating and difficult patient can be.

A good illustration of Racker's use of the concept of countertransference is provided by his hypothetical description of the analysis of a patient suffering from a "neurosis of failure": the analyst's interpretations of the patient's need to fail and sabotage treatment have no impact, and the analyst feels angry and anxious over the possibility of failed treatment. The patient fears the analyst's aggressive response, which would be a reenactment of his childhood situation. According to Racker, this is the most crucial aspect of the treatment process. If the analyst acts under the threat of failure, he is dominated by his own archaic superego object and he colludes with the patient's pathology. However, if the analyst uses his frustration, fear of failure, and anger to understand the internal workings of the patient, he will interpret the transference-countertransference situation and take a step toward helping the patient out of his cycle of failure. Psychoanalysis, for Racker, is a continual working over of these apparent impasses and conflicts by using countertransference responses to understand and resolve pathological processes. Grotstein (1986) took a similar view of the process by pointing out that of all the responses an analyst can make in a given situation, countertransference will indicate which material is most "alive" for intervention.

Ogden (1982) employed a very similar analysis of the use of projective identification in the psychotherapeutic setting. In Ogden's formulation projective identification has three components: (1) the patient's projection into the analyst; (2) the therapist's awareness of the projected part of the self and the "metabolization" of it so that it loses the threat it possessed when in the patient; and (3) the therapist's "giving back" the unwanted part of the self to the patient in a way that makes the feelings tolerable to the patient. According to Ogden, this process is a critical component of all psychotherapy, especially with the regressed patient. One can easily discern in this treatment theory the developmental model of early mother–child interaction delineated by Segal and Bion.

It should be noted that Grotstein (1986) expanded the concepts of splitting and projective identification to all types of pathology and normality. Grotstein pointed out that these concepts help in the understanding not only of more severe pathology, but of neurotic cases as well. He adopted Segal's notion that when repression is at issue, an earlier split in the ego must have occurred. For Grotstein, the traditional psychoanalytic defenses, such as repression, intellectualization, and displacement, are not necessarily indicative of pathology; their dangerous potential arises from their use as instruments of splitting and projective identification. It is Grotstein's contention that unwanted parts of the self are expelled by these defensive maneuvers and that the goal of the treatment process is to find and explicate them in order to reintegrate the ego.

By way of summary, it can be seen that Klein's followers have continued her emphasis on the pathogenicity of aggressive object relations, envy, and the defenses against them, but by giving the concept of projective identification an interpersonal meaning, they have made significant changes in the Kleinian model of technique. The use of countertransference to provide an analytic relationship and as a vehicle for interpretation has played an increasingly prominent role in Kleinian analysis. This development has become the link between the Kleinian school and the interpersonal theory of psychoanalysis (which will be discussed in chapter 7). Bion (1959d) took this trend a step further with his application of projective identification to a model of group process. In individual psychoanalytic treatment one can see that the use of countertransference awareness has become a major instrument among Klein's followers in the achievement of ego integration, which remains the goal of Kleinian treatment.

The evolution of Kleinian technical principles has led to an increased focus on projective identification, in addition to splitting, as the primary modes of defense by which the ego rids itself of unwanted parts and weakens its cohesiveness. The goal of analytic treatment is to reintegrate the ego by uniting the parts split off by these defense mechanisms. Whereas for Klein ego integration was achieved exclusively by interpretation of the unconscious, her followers have put greater emphasis on the transference–countertransference interaction, including the analyst's management of countertransference responses. There are degrees of emphasis on the analyst's containment of countertransference feelings among Klein's followers, but even Segal, her most faithful devotee, gave a prominent place to the "holding" of projectively identified affects in the treatment of severely disturbed patients before interpretation could take place. In so doing, Segal, like many of Klein's other followers, endorsed a model of analytic process that includes the timing of interpretations on the basis of the evolution of the analytic relationship, a change in treatment that is tantamount to a revision of Klein's model of strict reliance on depth interpretation.

These modifications in technique, along with the recognition of the importance of early object relationships and recent spate of interest in character pathology, have led many psychoanalytic theoreticians and clinicians to adopt a more discerning and receptive attitude to some of Klein's views than was prevalent in the period when Glover attacked her work. The British "middle school" of object relations theorists, represented in this book by Fairbairn, Guntrip, and Winnicott, fits this category of psychoanalytic theorists who disagree with Klein's adultomorphic speculations on early infancy, pathologizing of development, and interpretive style but find her object relations concepts of great value in understanding and treating character pathology. We have already seen the Kleinian influence on the work of Fairbairn and Guntrip. Winnicott (1962b) was much more strongly influenced by Klein. He drew up an impressive list of what he felt were Klein's contributions to psychoanalytic theory while adapting Klein's object relations model to his own theory of early development and its impact on psychopathology. It is to his views that we now turn.

The Work of D. W. Winnicott

ALTHOUGH WINNICOTT'S EMPHASIS ON THE IMPORTANCE OF THE EARLY environment is widely acknowledged, his more specific ideas tend to be regarded as loosely connected, defying systematic organization: as disparate insights with little direct connection to each other. Greenberg and Mitchell (1983) present his ideas as relatively disconnected concepts, linked only by the fact that they all deal with object relations. Hughes (1987), also presents Winnicott's ideas as only vaguely related, and Grolnick (1990), a close devotee of Winnicott, sees his work as a conscious defiance of systematization and an embodiment of his notion of play.

While there is certainly a strong element of play and intuition in Winnicott's writing style, and perhaps in his therapeutic technique as well, the view taken here is that there is a system of thought in Winnicott's work that organizes all his ideas on development and psychopathology into a coherent whole. Although Winnicott did not present his thought in a clearly organized manner, being vague and even inconsistent at times, he espoused a consistent concept of development throughout his work, and his views on psychopathology and treatment emanate from this developmental scheme. If one can grasp the structure of his developmental theory, Winnicott's various clinical papers, which may appear disparate, can be seen as different aspects of a comprehensive view of development, psychopathology, and psychoanalytic therapy and the individual insights which appear intuitive and even whimsical, can be better understood as aspects of a comprehensive theory.

To further this view of his work, Winnicott's developmental theory will be presented first and his views on psychopathology will be taken up in the second part of the chapter as an outgrowth of the developmental theory. Of all the theories discussed in this book, Winnicott's views are most closely linked to a particular theory of development, and it is necessary to understand this theory in order to grasp his ideas on psychopathology and treatment. Winnicott often stated that his contribution to the psychoanalytic view of development lay entirely in his understanding of the preoedipal phases, although he often used his understanding of these early phases to suggest a deeper understanding of apparently neurotic disorders. Nonetheless, Winnicott's consistent view was that Freud's theory of the Oedipus complex explained neurotic disorders, which he considered interpersonal; but that the psychoanalytic theory of development needed to expand to the preoedipal phases for an understanding of psychological organization phases, which are at issue in more severe psychopathology and in regressions in neurotic disorders and that must be considered in the treatment of disorders that may appear neurotic but are refractory to traditional psychoanalytic interventions. Consequently, Winnicott set as his goal the understanding of the preoedipal phases of development and their role in psychopathology.

DEVELOPMENT

Winnicott's (1965) most general concepts are the "maturational process" and the "facilitating environment." According to Winnicott, every human organism is born with a drive, called the "maturational process," to develop in a given direction. This constitutional given cannot be changed, but it can be blocked if there is a failure of the "facilitating environment" that is required for the maturational process to take place. Maturational process and facilitating environment are two sides of one coin for Winnicott, as they are for Hartmann (1939). The environment need not be perfect, but it must be "good enough" for the maturational process to unfold. If it is not, development is blocked and emotional disorder is the likely outcome. For Winnicott, all symptoms are manifestations of arrests in development, or blocks in the maturational process.

More than any other psychoanalytic theorist, Winnicott emphasized the importance of the environment for the growth and development of the baby into a child. Since the baby cannot be thought of—much less perform its essential task of growing into a child and adult—without a maternal environment, the relationship of dependence between child and mother was the critical developmental axis in Winnicott's thought; that is, he conceived of development as phases of dependence of the child on the mother. Winnicott (1963a) described three phases of dependence: absolute, relative, and "toward independence." The "transition" phase between absolute and relative dependence, an important developmental milestone in his theory, is a subphase of the stage of relative dependence.

Although Winnicott wrote only one paper delineating clearly the three specific dependency phases, he continually referred to them and his work on development and psychopathology relies completely on them. On many occasions he referred to shifts in dependence as the critical features of development. Accordingly, the phases of dependence provide the framework for understanding his theory of development and psychopathology. By setting his various contributions into this context, their meaning becomes more comprehensible.

It should be noted that the last phase in Winnicott's schema, "toward independence," is given no more than a mention. He felt that this phase, equivalent to the oedipal stage, was well conceptualized and understood within the framework of classical psychoanalytic theory, and he did not attempt to contribute to this body of knowledge. The corpus of his work focused on the preoedipal stages of development, although the distinction between oedipal and preoedipal pathology is not so clear-cut: Winnicott believed that supposedly neurotic disorders often defend against more primitive issues and that even in neurotic conditions the possibility of regressive movement is very real. Nonetheless, Winnicott's contribution to the psychoanalytic theory of development, psychopathology, and treatment lies in the preoedipal phases of dependence. Given Winnicott's emphasis on early development and the interdependence of mother and child, each stage will be discussed from the viewpoint of both parties.

Absolute Dependence

Infant

In the first phase of development the infant is not aware of its dependence on the environment (Winnicott, 1963a). Because the infant cannot differentiate itself from the environment, there is no "me" or "not me." The mother, or maternal environment, provides for the infant's needs, but the infant has no awareness of the mother. According to Winnicott (1960a), the infant in this phase lives entirely in a magical world in which needs are met by their very existence. Reality has not yet entered the infant's experience. According to Winnicott, the infant's existence is so dependent on the mother that one cannot speak of a baby but only of "the environmental-individual setup." Winnicott (1952) described the situation this way: "There is no such thing as a baby. . . . if you show me a baby you certainly show me also someone caring for the baby, or at least a pram with someone's eyes and ears glued to it. One sees a 'nursing couple' " (p. 99).

There being no awareness of separateness, the infant–mother relationship exists at this phase on the basis of physical contact (Winnicott, 1963a). The infant is aware of the relationship only insofar as it feels touched, held, or caressed or experiences other physical contact. When such contact is withdrawn the loss of contact is felt, but separation from another person is not experienced. Winnicott (1952) emphasized here the lack of a "time factor." That is, the infant has no sense of continuity in self or other: it does not know that it exists or that the mother is real. Consequently, when there is separation, any physical contact will substitute for the lost contact. This primitive sense of existence is crucial for Winnicott's understanding of a variety of clinical conditions.

Because the sense of existence is so rudimentary, any disruption threatens the minimal sense of existence the infant is able to feel in this stage. As there is no self that could manage anxiety as a warning signal, all anxiety is experienced as annihilation anxiety (Winnicott, 1952, 1960a). Consequently, the infant in this phase lives on the brink of "unthinkable anxiety" (Winnicott, 1952). Since the lack of temporal sense gives the infant little belief in relief, annihilation anxiety can be quickly produced. As discussed in more detail later, environmental adaptation must be "near total" (Winnicott, 1956a) so that the small doses of reality are manageable and annihilation anxiety is fended off.

Signals do not exist in the phase of absolute dependence, according to Winnicott (1963a). Since the infant is unaware of separateness, it has no awareness of a person on whom it depends and cannot signal its needs. Thus, the caretaker must interpret the infant's behavior as communication even though the infant has no intention of communicating. The infant's needs must be met without any communication from the infant, and if the infant survives, some needs have apparently been met. Insofar as mentation is possible, needs appear to the infant to be satisfied by their very existence; they are experienced as bringing their own gratification. Thus, according to Winnicott (1945, 1960a), the infant in this phase lives in a magical world of omnipotence in which mentation produces gratification.

The first critical developmental task is the achievement of integration. Experience is "un-integrated" in this stage, as feelings, needs, and tension states are not experienced as belonging to a common whole (Winnicott, 1945, 1962). There is no "me" to hold together experiences, no sense that discrete experiences are linked and no time factor to connect discrete experiences. Here Winnicott is drawing on Glover's 1937 concept of "ego nuclei." Experiences are not linked together in time and are therefore not experienced as a "lived temporal unity."

According to Winnicott, they have no "unit status." Because experience is discrete rather than continuous, there is no "lived psychic reality" (Winnicott, 1945). The sense of temporal continuity is an achievement as experiences are gradually linked together into an integrated self.

It follows from the inability to differentiate "me" from "not me" that the infant is not yet able to experience itself as a person. This inability means there is a lack of "personalization" of experience; the infant's sensations, needs, and feelings are not personalized into "my experience." In Winnicott's words, experience is not yet "localized." "Personalization" is the second major developmental achievement, an outcome of successfully traversing the early phase of dependence.

From the infant's point of view, needs do not have to make a detour through reality to be met; thus there is no reality sense. The third primary task of absolute dependence is the gradual development of the sense of reality. As noted earlier, with each frustration, the infant experiences a bit of reality, and its "omnipotence" is pierced. Because "realization" is made possible by environmental failures (Winnicott, 1945), unsuccessful adaptation is as crucial to the infant's sense of reality as successful adaptation. Winnicott (1963d) points out that, "there is no question of perfection here. Perfection belongs to machines; what the infant needs is just what he usually gets, the care and attention of someone who is going on being herself" (pp. 87–88). The environmental adaptations and failures provide the infant with "doses" of reality in manageable portions: "The whole procedure of infant care has as its main characteristic a steady presentation of the world to the infant" (Winnicott, 1963a, p. 87). As the infant's needs are met, the nascent sense of self grows and frustrations become gradually more tolerable, resulting in the ability to feel a temporal sense. Gradually, reality and fantasy become distinguishable; however, there is still very little sense of reality in the phase of absolute dependence. Only with its passage into later dependence phases is the infant able to differentiate pure mentation, as in fantasy, from the experience of reality and thereby achieve "realization." (This conceptualization anticipated Kohut's, 1971 view, discussed in chapter 6, that maternal empathy and its failures are instrumental in the journey from archaic grandiosity and idealization to a realistic view of self and others.)

As there is no self–other distinction in the phase of absolute dependence, there are no objects yet for the infant (Winnicott, 1971). Insofar as one can speak of objects in the infant's awareness, they are experienced within the orbit of infantile omnipotence; that is, the infant feels they are under its complete control. One cannot yet speak of object usage, although there is a sense of "object relating" within the omnipotent sphere. In order to use an object, it must be seen as external to the self, and this awareness does not occur until the phase of relative dependence.

If there is no concept of an external object, what does the infant see when it looks at the mother? According to Winnicott (1971), the infant looks at the mother and sees itself. The mother is looking at the baby and "what she looks like is related to what she sees there" (p. 112). The mother performs a "mirror role" (but this function is not the same as Kohut's well-known concept of "mirroring," as shall be seen in chapter 6); that is, the mother functions as a mirror by giving back to the infant what it gives in its own look. The infant's first image of itself includes a connection with the mother; by the mother's look, the infant knows that it is seen.

Winnicott (1947, 1962, 1963b) adopted Freud's and Klein's view that aggression is inborn. Winnicott's views on the infant's aggression are somewhat confusing because he referred to both an innate aggressive drive and an "inherent aggressiveness in the love-impulse." Winnicott did make clear that in the early phase aggression is without intention, "pre-ruth." He pointed out that even in the womb, the baby kicks; aggression is originally "almost synonymous with activity" (Winnicott, 1950). The infant has no awareness that its aggressiveness can hurt the other. Aggression is inherent in the "love-impulse," so that when an infant is excited it "destroys." The excitement of instinctual gratification means an attack on the mother's body. Nonetheless, the infant does not know that the attack is visited on the same object whom it loves when not excited. As Winnicott (1945) wrote, "The normal child enjoys a ruthless relation to his mother, mostly showing in play, and he needs his mother because only she can be expected to tolerate his ruthless relation to her even in play, because this really hurts her and wears her out" (p. 154).

Winnicott's views on early aggression bear a similarity to those of Klein, by whom he was influenced, and yet they are decidedly different. As we saw in chapter 3, for Klein the aggressive and libidinal drives are directed toward different objects, since "good" and "bad" objects are split. For Winnicott, the drives are initially fused, since aggression is part of love, and the split is between excited states, which always include aggression, and quiescence. Splitting of good and bad objects is a defensive pathological reaction to the failure of the environment to hold the early aggression. If the environment is good enough, the infant has no awareness that its aggressiveness can injure and the aggression therefore remains a part of the "love impulse."

There comes a point at about six months of age when the infant becomes aware that it does not control gratification. This critical developmental step marks the beginning of the self–object distinction. The infant is now starting to see objects as outside the self, marking the entrance of the reality principle into the infant's life (Winnicott, 1971). According to classical psychoanalytic theory, the infant, out of frustration, has an aggressive response to the awareness of reality. Winnicott (1971) saw a more constitutive role for aggression—in the development of the infant's very sense of reality. He believed that the infant experiences its aggressiveness as expelling the object from the sphere of omnipotence. The object must be "destroyed," and only later, when it is "refound" as an external object in the phase of relative dependence, can it be "used." Thus, for Winnicott, aggression plays a crucial role in the development of the self, the sense of reality, and the recognition and use of objects.

To summarize the phase of absolute dependence from the viewpoint of the infant: the infant lives in a world of magical omnipotence in which there is no sense of self or reality, and no experience of objects. Experience is discrete, disconnected, fleeting, and outside of a "lived psychic reality." All these aspects of the absolute dependence phase are emphasized in Winnicott's work because he felt that they provide clues to the mystery of primitive psychopathology.

Mother

Winnicott (1956a) believed that the mother goes through a phase of "primary maternal preoccupation" beginning in the later stage of pregnancy, when she becomes emotionally focused on the soon-to-be-born child. This emotional preoccupation includes a natural adaptation to give up her previous life entirely or partially in order to meet the needs of the infant. All the preparations made for the coming child reflect a new state of mind, that Winnicott considered so extreme he would regard it as an illness if there were no baby.

The mother's absorption with the infant shortly before and for some time after birth allows the infant to bond without awareness of separateness and thereby makes possible the infant's experience of omnipotence. For the mother, normal activities are limited, and her emotional life is focused on the new baby.

Because the infant in the phase of absolute dependence cannot signal its needs, the mother must rely on empathy to meet them. Through her identification with the infant, based on her own experience of being mothered, the mother is able to know what the infant needs without being told or signaled. For Winnicott, empathy does not mean understanding verbal communications; it does not even mean grasping their affective undertones. It means knowing what the infant needs, even though the infant cannot communicate its needs. The empathic mother interprets her infant's behavior as a communication to her, even though the infant does not intend to communicate. The infant cries and the mother interprets the cry as a signal of hunger. The infant has not signaled, but its survival depends on the mother's ability to interpret its behavior as a signal. This definition of empathy is to be contrasted with Kohut's contemporary usage, described in chapter 6. Later, in the phase of relative dependence, communication between infant and mother enters their relationship, but in the phase of absolute dependence empathy through identification is the primary mode of adaptation the mother must make.

The mother need not adapt perfectly to the infant's needs, but the adaptation must be "good enough" to allow the infant the experience of omnipotence (Winnicott, 1960a); the infant is not yet ready for reality, and too early a confrontation with it would be dangerous. Adaptation by the mother must be "near absolute" so that the infant can live in its delusional world of omnipotence, however, it cannot and should not be perfect because environmental "failures" are necessary to prepare the way for the infant's descent into eventual reality.

The mother's provisions for the infant fall into two categories of maternal functions: the "object mother" and the "environmental mother" (Winnicott, 1963b). The object mother provides for the "object instinctual needs" by satisfying hunger, holding the infant, and keeping diapers clean. However, the object mother alone is insufficient. The infant has "ego needs" from the very beginning, and these are not met by the object mother. For example, the infant needs an environment in which air and water temperatures are relatively comfortable, the noise level is neither unstimulating nor assaultive, and there is visual stimulation that is interesting without being overwhelming. Most importantly, the environment must be relatively free of "impingements" that would interfere with emotional growth.

Winnicott placed great emphasis on ego needs because he felt that classical psychoanalytic developmental theory overemphasizes "object instinctual" needs while failing to recognize the importance of the early environment and overall maternal care in the growth of the ego. Because the phase of absolute dependence is subsumed under the oral phase in classical theory, emphasis is placed on the meeting of "object instinctual" needs. Winnicott pointed out that the primary developmental tasks of this phase—the development of "realization," personalization, and integration—are all ego needs and that it is possible for "object instinctual" needs, such as hunger, to be met adequately while developmental needs are not. Under such conditions the meeting of "object instinctual" needs does not lead to growth; it is only when the ego needs are met that object instinctual fulfillment promotes personality growth. For Winnicott, then, ego needs take precedence over object instinctual needs.

Winnicott's (1960a) general term for the role of the environmental mother in this phase is "holding," a term he described as follows:

> The term "holding" is used here to denote not only the actual physical holding of the infant, but also the total environmental provision prior to the concept of *living with*. In other words, it refers to a three-dimensional or space relationship with time gradually added.... It includes the management of experiences that are inherent in existence, such as the *completion* (and therefore the non-completion) of processes, processes which from the outside may seem to be purely physiological but which belong to infant psychology and take place in a psychological field, determined by the awareness and empathy of the mother [pp. 43–44].

The infant's needs and emotional states are "held" well enough by the good enough mother, who is able to contain whatever tension states occur by her empathy.

Because the only anxiety the infant experiences in this phase is annihilation anxiety, the mother must "hold" the anxiety and meet the infant's needs well enough to keep the infant from experiencing a sense of annihilation. To succeed in this preventive task, the maternal environment must protect the infant from impingements. According to Winnicott (1960a):

> The holding environment therefore has as its main function the reduction to a minimum of impingements to which the infant must react with resultant annihilation of personal being. Under favorable conditions the infant establishes a continuity of existence and then begins to develop the sophistication which makes it possible for impingements to be gathered into the area of omnipotence [p. 47].

The principal function of "holding," then, is keeping the infant sufficiently free of environmental impingement that it lives within its fantasy of omnipotence and continues to grow.

Included in the emotional states of the infant that must be "held" by the "environmental mother" is the infant's aggression (Winnicott, 1950). Recall that, according to Winnicott, the infant's erotic need has an inherent aggressive "pre-ruth" component. The infant's object instinctual need "destroys" by "attacking" the mother's body and the mother must be willing to absorb and hold such aggressive attacks. As we have seen, Winnicott (1971) believed that the destructive drive "pushed" the object outside the sphere of the infant's omnipotence, thus "objectifying" the object for the first time. It is crucial that the infant experience the object's survival of its destructive attacks; only then can the infant turn a "subjective object" into an "objective object." That is, only when the object survives the destructive attack can it be "used" by the infant. There is an inherent connection, for Winnicott, between the object's ability to survive the destructive attacks, the infant's growth out of omnipotence, and its ability to use an object. The mother's ability to hold the destructive attacks and not retaliate is critical to the infant's ability to perceive reality, see objects as "not me," and use objects as separate others for further growth.

If the environment is able to perform its functions well enough in this phase—that is, if it is able to prevent impingements; hold the infant's frustrations, thereby preventing annihilation anxiety; "hold" the aggression; and meet the infant's overall ego and id needs—the infant will begin to experience a sense of continuity of its various need states and a rudimentary sense of integration, personalization, and realization will occur. The inevitable environmental failures will force some degree of reality on the child, but these moments of brief recognition will not disturb infantile omnipotence because the holding has been "good enough" for the child to feel that its needs bring their own gratification. The growing child is then ready for what Winnicott sees as the first major developmental task in the formation of the self: the awareness of dependence.

Relative Dependence

Child

Many investigations of early development have noted that at six to eight months of age infants tend to become aware of their surroundings in a new way (Spitz, 1965; Mahler, 1975; Stern, 1980). They reach out to explore with their hands, especially the faces of caretakers, and they often do to the mother what the mother does to them (Mahler, 1975): they touch, soothe, caress, and stroke the mother's hair; some even offer the bottle to the mother. The infant for the first time differentiates clearly between mother and others and between familiar figures and strangers. Mahler (1975) called this newfound awareness "hatching," as the infant is now able to differentiate itself from the environment.

For Winnicott (1960a, 1963a), the critical aspect of this developmental shift is the child's awareness of its dependence on an object outside itself. It is by virtue of this awareness that the infant is said to move from absolute to relative dependence. The infant now becomes interested in exploring the object of dependence but also becomes anxious in separating from it. The first awareness of "me" versus "not me" is shown by the infant's reaching for objects, a new kind of play. "We can say at this stage a baby becomes able in his play to show that he can understand he has an inside, and that things come from outside" (Winnicott, 1945, p. 148). The infant recognizes that the environment is separate, "out there," and yet necessary to meet its needs. The infant becomes aware in a rudimentary way that its needs do not automatically entail their own gratification. This awareness of separation from the environment is the beginning of the sense of self—and, simultaneously, an experience of loss.

Winnicott (1963a) pointed out that infants now experience a new kind of anxiety: "When the mother is away for a moment beyond the time-span of his (or her) capacity to believe in her survival, anxiety appears, and this is the first sign that the infant knows" (p. 88). Spitz's research shows that around this time all infants experience both separation and stranger anxiety, with separation anxiety occurring about one month earlier. There are wide variations in degree, exact time of onset, and duration for both forms of anxiety, but Spitz was able to show, by slow-motion filming, that all infants experience both forms, in however mild or transient a form. This finding supports Winnicott's point that both anxiety reactions occur in response to the infant's awareness of its separateness from the maternal environment.

The infant attempts to preserve the attachment by identification with the mother. The infant's imitation of the mother which begins at this time, is conceptualized by Winnicott (1963a) as the first identification and as occurring in response to the newly discovered gulf between itself and its mother.

Relative dependence, for Winnicott, encompasses an extended developmental process from the breakdown of the omnipotence of the absolute dependence phase to the acceptance of reality and ambivalence toward whole objects. Included in this phase is a variety of developmental tasks, the first of which is to manage the anxiety of separation from the mother, the awareness that it cannot meet its own needs. To master this anxiety and bridge the transition to reality orientation, the infant utilizes a variety of possessions and experiences referred to by Winnicott as transitional phenomena, the "transitional object" being only one, albeit the best-known, example (Winnicott, 1951). Winnicott's concept of transitional phenomena is so widely discussed, so commonly oversimplified and misunderstood, and yet so important to his thought that it is worth considering in detail.

The essence of any transitional phenomenon, for Winnicott, is its function as an intermediary between the fantasied world of omnipotence in the absolute dependence phase and the acceptance of reality, which is the outcome of the phase of relative dependence. It is not commonly recognized that Winnicott (1951) distinguished three types of transitional phenomena. Initially, anything that is both "mine" and "not mine" is a transitional experience. Cooing serves this function; the infant emits the sound from within but hears it from without. The experience helps the infant differentiate "in" from "out" while providing a connection between them. Thumb sucking is a different type of transitional phenomenon, requiring organized control over the musculature; using the thumb is a developmental advance in that it begins the substitution of limited muscular control for the fantasy of omnipotent control. Thumb sucking indicates a willingness to yield the fantasy of omnipotence as the *exclusive* means of getting needs met and is a further step toward the acceptance of reality, even though the reality in this instance is a part of the infant's own body.

Some time after the thumb is used, the infant will draw from the realm of transitional phenomena a single object outside itself to which it becomes closely attached, its first "not me" possession. It is this possession that is called a transitional object. The infant knows that the stuffed animal, blanket, toy, or doll is outside of itself; therefore, it has relinquished to an even greater degree than with thumb sucking the fantasy of omnipotence of the absolute dependence phase. Not only does the use of the first possession substitute muscular control for omnipotent control, but the infant is now using something it knows not to be itself. The possession can be lost or misplaced, and it must be found. By using an object outside its omnipotent control and outside itself, the child has taken a further step toward reality acceptance:

> It is true that the piece of blanket (or whatever it is) is symbolical of some part-object, such as the breast. Nevertheless the point of it is not its symbolic value so much as its actuality. Its not being the breast (or the mother) is as important as the fact that it stands for the breast (or mother) [Winnicott, 1951 p. 233].

On the other hand, the transitional object is not a reality object. It is imbued with intense, powerful, personal meaning. Finding the object immediately reduces intense anxiety; sometimes anxiety can be soothed in no other way. The object is treated as though it were the mother, although the child knows that it is not. The paradox of the transitional object is that it is neither real nor delusional. It is *illusory*, an intermediate area of experience, lying between reality and fantasy (Winnicott, 1951, 1971; Barkin and Grolnick, 1970). According to Winnicott (1971), the transitional object begins the world of illusion and prepares the way for play in childhood. Child's play, according to Winnicott, is based on giving an illusory meaning to something real. The attributed meaning is known to be an illusion but is treated during the play as though it were not. Because the meaning must always be personal and unique to the individual, transitional phenomena and its later variant, play, are always creative. Winnicott felt that all child and adult creativity, as well as aesthetic experience, are transitional phenomena and that this intermediate area of experience must continue into adult life for creative and cultural living, which he identified with mental health.

The transitional object is a response to loss; for this reason, Winnicott (1971) believed that the transitional object is used as a "defense against depressive anxiety." Nonetheless, he felt that the importance of the transitional object lies in its *not* being the mother or the breast; that is, it indicates that the infant, through its ability to use a piece of the real world to fill an emotional need, is moving away from omnipotent fantasy and toward reality.

To realize its function fully, the transitional object must have certain features: the child must have complete ownership and dominance over it; it must contain intense feelings, both positive and negative; it must provide the experience of warmth and cuddling; and it must provide a feeling that it has a reality of its own. The assumption of dominance is critical so that the infant is not unduly frustrated, yet the object must have reality so that dominance is not confused with omnipotence. Having all these characteristics, the transitional object is able to be *used* as though it were the mother; it functions as though it were the mother, yet the infant knows and is reminded constantly by the object that it is not the mother.

Transitional objects help the infant ease the separation and stranger anxiety caused by awareness of dependence and separateness. Although these experiences are painful, they also betoken a developmental advance: the infant has moved from annihilation anxiety to anxiety of object loss. Episodes of stranger anxiety end when the mother returns, implying the existence of a maternal representation when she is not present. Stranger anxiety also implies a specific attachment to the mother as someone who has continuity in the infant's mind. Beginning with this attachment to the mother, the infant acquires a sense of the familiar. Experiences begin to connect with each other and the infant makes developmental advances it was incapable of in the phase of absolute dependence.

Primary among these new advances is the sense of "temporal integration" (Winnicott, 1962). Since continuity is now experienced, the previously discrete ego nuclei begin to link together and develop into a sense of temporal continuity, eventually leading to the achievement of the sense of integration. The infant now has the growing sense of itself as one person with a variety of experiences, rather than an awareness of only discrete experiences. This sense of continuity leads to a rudimentary sense of self.

Since experiences are now felt as belonging to a unit, a sense of "personalization" begins to develop. The growing child begins to experience what Winnicott calls a "lived psychic reality." The new sense of an "internal," a "me," is not solely a cognitive formulation. There is an "internal environment," since living now includes an "inside" and this is distinguishable from what is "outside." Whereas experience in the phase of absolute dependence simply occurs, in relative dependence experience begins to belong to "me," and it is in this phase that the child begins to use the word "me."

Personalization is closely linked to the third achievement in the development of the self in the phase of relative dependence: the growing sense of "realization." The infant has been "hatched" from the fantasy world of omnipotence into the realization that the environment is separate from the personalized self. The awareness of this distinction is the origin of the infant's sense of reality. In the fantasy of omnipotence, there is no sense of the reality of the world or of the self. As the infant gains a sense of personal reality, the awareness of the self–other distinction takes place and the world is experienced for the first time as having a reality apart from the infant's mentation. This awareness culminates in the sense of the self as a real person and the sense of the world as a separate reality. Both world and self are becoming "realized."

The infant now knows that its needs are met by a mother outside itself. The mother, as the medium for the fulfillment of the need, begins to represent reality to the child. In fact, Winnicott says, the mother "brings reality to the child" via her position between the need and its fulfillment. Every delay, every imperfect meeting of need, forces reality upon the infant who becomes aware that in order to have any control over the meeting of its needs, it must signal to its provider. The infant now intends to communicate. Whereas in the previous phase the infant cried and the mother interpreted the cry to mean hunger, now the infant cries to tell the mother of its hunger or, at a more advanced level of this phase, the child points to food. Now the mother need only understand communication; she does not have to create it. The child does not rely on the experience of need or wish to bring gratification; it relinquishes the magical control of pure mentation for the reality-based control of gesturing and communicating through word and deed.

Now that temporal integration begins to occur, the infant can "carry" experience from one contact to the next. As it begins to form a sense of a single person who meets its needs, the growing child begins to experience a relationship. And once the sense of the mother is maintained without her physical presence, an "ego-relatedness" takes place between mother and child. Out of this psychological way of relating, the object is internalized and a relationship is formed. According to Winnicott (1956d), the infant is now capable of a relationship based not on physical contact but on the psychological recognition of the other. The "ego relationship" between infant and mother is the key to the development of the infant's concept of the other as a separate person. In this sense, Winnicott (1956a) opposed the traditional analytic conception that recognition of others as separate from the self is a product of frustration: "From this angle the recognition of the mother as a person comes in a positive way, normally, and not out of the experience of the mother as the symbol of frustration" (p. 304).

The other side of ego relating is the development of the ego organization. "The first ego organization comes from the threats of annihilation which do not lead to annihilation and from which, repeatedly, there is *recovery*. Out of such experiences confidence in recovery begins to be something which leads to an ego and to an ego capacity for coping with frustration" (Winnicott, 1956a, p. 304). The infant develops an ego organization as he or she internalizes his ego-relatedness to the maternal environment that protects him outside of his awareness.

For the development of the capacity for such ego relatedness to take place, the infant must learn to be alone. First, the infant must be able to be alone in the presence of the mother, a paradox Winnicott noted, and even emphasized. By being alone in the presence of the mother, the infant experiences a relationship without physical contact or need gratification. The environmental mother is providing the child with an ego relationship, thereby allowing for her internalization. In

Winnicott's view, once the mother is internalized, the infant can be alone without her. Ego-relatedness and internalization imply and foster each other, and as they develop the temporal integration of the personality is strengthened (Winnicott, 1962).

At this point, "holding" has been replaced by "living with." The infant is developing a sense of self and the ability to communicate its needs to the mother. Recognition by the communicating infant that the mother is a separate person to whom communication must be made indicates that a relationship, a "living with," is beginning to form. The physical correlate of this shift from "holding" to "living with" is the difference between the mother holding the child in her arms and the child slipping off her lap, crawling away, and appealing to the mother when help is needed. However, the defining feature of the shift is not so much physical growth as the infant's recognition of the mother as a separate person to whom it communicates and with whom it begins to form a relationship (Winnicott, 1960a).

With the development of the temporal unity of the personality, the growing child links experiences and begins to perceive that the "object mother" whom it "destroys" when excited is the same as the "environmental mother" whom it loves when quiescent. This integration of objects creates a special problem, as the infant is now aware that it can injure the object of its love (Winnicott, 1963b). The infant has shifted from the "ruthlessness" of object instinctual attacks on the mother's body to awareness that it has been attacking the mother who cares for it.

Although this formulation calls to mind Klein's "depressive position," Winnicott (196b3) preferred the expression "stage of concern." In Winnicott's formulation, the child's concern is rooted in its belief that it can injure the mother with its aggressiveness but this concern need not lead to depression, nor even "depressive anxiety." Like Klein, Winnicott believed that guilt originates with the experience of object integration (in opposition to Freud, 1923 who dated guilt from the oedipal phase). The realization that the child has hated or even been angry at the same person who is loved and depended on produces anxiety over injuring the object, and this anxiety inevitably leads to guilt (Winnicott, 1954a). However, for Winnicott, unlike Klein, the development and vicissitudes of guilt may lead either to a healthy concern for others or to depressive anxiety, depending on the environmental reaction to the child's aggression.

The mother's reaction to her child's aggression will be discussed in detail in the next section; here we note that the crucial experience from the infant's viewpoint is that its aggression neither injures nor destroys its mother. If the infant sees that its mother survives and accepts its aggressiveness, it is able to believe in the value of its aggression, which can then remain connected with the "erotic impulse." Instead of linking aggressiveness with destruction, the infant believes its aggression promotes a connection to the maternal love object: "On the erotic side there is both satisfaction-seeking and object-seeking, and on the aggressive side, there is a complex of anger employing muscle erotism, and of hate, which involves the retention of a good object-imago for comparison" (Winnicott, 1963b, p. 74). The child is now able to experience love and hate, positive and negative feelings, to the same mother without fear of injury or destruction. Guilt, in the sense of concern for others, is felt, but it facilitates rather than blocks the maturational process by leading to altruism and ethical responsibility. In Winnicott's view, the experience of ambivalence toward whole objects is the origin of the adult desire to contribute to family and community.

The experience of love and hate toward the same object makes a crucial contribution to self development. First, the mother is perceived as a whole object, which furthers the "me"–"not me" distinction. According to Winnicott (1963b), as the infant experiences ambivalence, "the infant is beginning to relate himself to objects that are less and less subjective phenomena, and more and more objectively perceived 'not-me' elements" (p. 75). Secondly, the child's experience of self is enhanced: as the mother becomes a whole object, "inner psychic reality...becomes a real thing to the infant, who now feels that personal richness resides within the self. This personal richness develops out of the simultaneous love–hate experience which implies the achievement of ambivalence, the enrichment and refinement of which leads to the emergence of concern" (p. 75).

The fantasy of injuring the loved object is, according to Winnicott, the first experience of agency. In this regard, Winnicott continued to follow Klein. In the phase of absolute dependence the infant is helpless and experiences itself as a victim of attack; in the phase of relative dependence the infant experiences itself as an agent of aggressive attack. The successful completion of this phase results in a sense of responsibility and the capacity for guilt, with minimal anxiety over aggressiveness. The sense of agency and of its corollary, responsibility, culminate in the initial sense of an active self able to control life events.

If all goes well, toward the end of the phase of relative dependence the child has an integrated sense of self as continuing over time and differentiated from others. The child is now at the whole object level, able to contain ambivalence and therefore able to maintain relationships with others. A child whose development has proceeded to this point has the capacity for ambivalence required for entry into the oedipal phase.

The Mother

The entire developmental process through the phase of relative dependence depends on the "good enough" maternal environment. Both the "object mother" and "environmental mother" must make shifts in their adaptations in accordance with the child's developing sense of self. In the phase of absolute dependence the mother made a near-total adaptation to "hold" the infant; now the mother must begin to develop her own growing independence in order to "live with" the child. According to Winnicott (1960a), one of the mother's primary tasks in this phase is to "allow" the child to communicate and then to respond to the communication. She responds less out of empathy and more out of an understanding of the child's communication: "there is a very subtle distinction between the mother's understanding of her infant's need based on empathy, and her change over to an understanding based on something in the infant or small child that indicates need" (p. 51).

The mother who continually utilizes maternal empathy after the infant has begun to recognize the self–other distinction is fostering a continued sense of omnipotence in the infant at the expense of its growing need for a sense of self and movement toward reality. The mother must begin to develop a sense of independence from the infant corresponding to its movement away from her so that the infant can begin to relinquish the fantasy of omnipotence in favor of reality, develop a sense of self, and form a relationship to a separate other. The mother's increasingly imperfect adaptation allows the child to experience gradually the delays and imperfections of reality. Her "failures" are critical in "bringing reality to the child" (Winnicott, 1956a). She allows "real-ization" by meeting needs imperfectly and by her own need to become more independent. The mother's near-perfect adaptation now becomes an environmental impingement, just as inability to adapt was an impingement in the previous phase (Winnicott, 1960a).

Along with her growing independence, the mother must develop a different type of relationship with the child. She must give "ego support" to the child's growing need for independence both by providing a safe, protected environment, and by allowing the child to explore, manipulate the environment, and to play without interference while continuing a relationship with the child. According to Winnicott (1958), since the child needs a relationship without dependence on physical contact, the mother must offer such an "ego relationship" in which emotional contact is provided without instinctual gratification.

We saw earlier that Winnicott emphasized the importance of the child's being alone in the presence of the mother in the development of the sense of self. The mother's role in the development of the capacity to be alone is to offer an ego relationship in which she is not threatened by the child's being alone in her presence and she does not withdraw. She must allow herself to be ignored. Her presence, experienced by the child, provides an ego relationship that can now be internalized.

The mother's willingness to allow the child to be alone in her presence is one special aspect of her provision of "ego coverage" (Winnicott, 1960a). This creation of a safe, protective environment, relatively free from major disturbances, allows the child to "go on being" and fosters spontaneous ego growth (Winnicott, 1963b). If the child must be concerned about disturbances, its emotional focus is diverted from natural growth and development to reactions to the environment. Such impingements and the child's reactions to them lead to preoedipal psychopathology.

Toward Independence

Once the child has an integrated sense of self and has internalized whole objects, it is prepared for movement Winnicott calls "toward independence," synonymous with the oedipal phase of development. He proffered no contribution to the classical psychoanalytic literature on the oedipal period and, in fact, wrote little regarding the phase of "toward independence," as he felt his contribution to psychoanalytic thought was in his ideas about the earlier phases. Winnicott's relatively sparse comments regarding the phase "toward independence" are summarized briefly to provide closure to his developmental theory.

As the child moves toward independence, its sense of self relies even less on physical needs and sensations than in the previous phase. Now that the child has a sense of "an internal environment" it not only is able to be alone but often seeks to be alone.

Winnicott adopted the classic analytic position that the child is now able to manage three-party relationships. This developmental step has the same meaning for Winnicott that it has in classic psychoanalytic theory: the child can now move beyond an independent relationship with each parent to an awareness that the parents have a relationship with each other from which the child is excluded. In Winnicott's formulation, as in classical theory, ambivalence toward the parents and their relationship is crucial to the resolution of the oedipal phase. Winnicott believed that the child's developed self and ability to experience ambivalence allowed movement from the child's "living with" each parent to child, mother, and father "living together." The child becomes part of a network of others, able to relate to others as part of a family or other unit.

The mother must proceed with her movement toward a more independent life. The child now fits into her life rather than being the almost exclusive focus of her life as in the previous phases. The mother's achievement of independence while maintaining her relationship with the child and meeting such dependency needs as the child has allows the child to experience living together in the family unit. The mother is now able to reinvest in the relationship with the father in a more focused way. She may return to work, have other children, begin a new career, or engage in other activities, new or old.

PSYCHOPATHOLOGY AND TREATMENT

All that has been said thus far regarding preoedipal development assumes the presence of a "good enough mother" who provides a "facilitating environment." What happens if the maternal environment is not "good enough" and impingements occur? Winnicott's answer is that the effects of environmental failure depend on the developmental phase and the type of impingement. Although Winnicott did not set forth a comprehensive system of psychopathology, he did conceptualize impingements and their effects sufficiently so that one can discern in his work a theory of clinical syndromes and their causes. It should be noted that he believed certain specific impingements and their sequelae in a preoedipal phase could lead either to a clinical syndrome or to a more transient manifestation in a higher level neurosis. Because this difference was not systematized in his work, it has never been clear why certain impingements eventuate in relatively fixed syndromes in some cases and transient manifestations in others.

Winnicott's view of psychopathology follows his developmental scheme so closely that he felt the words *patient* and *baby* could be used interchangeably. All psychopathology, in Winnicott's view, results from an insufficiently facilitating environment, that causes the infant or child to react to environmental impingement, and thus arrests the maturational process. Impingements in the phase of absolute dependence potentially result in the most disabling forms of emotional disorder because they interfere with the most basic psychological structures. In the phase of relative dependence impingements may create character pathology whereas oedipal phase impingements are the source of neurosis.

Psychopathology and Absolute Dependence

Winnicott (1952) called impingements in the phase of absolute dependence "privation" because needs are not met. "Deprivation," which signifies that something that was given is subsequently taken away, applies to the phase of relative dependence. In the phase of absolute dependence, if the satisfaction of environmental and object needs is not "good enough," the child cannot focus on "going on being." If maternal empathy is lacking, omnipotent fantasies are assaulted by reality before the child is ready to relinquish them and accept reality. The child becomes aware that needs are not met by their existence and is forced into a premature awareness of self–object differentiation. This premature awareness interrupts the development of integration, personalization, and realization. All forms of psychopathology originating in the phase of absolute dependence result from this dynamic.

Premature awareness of the self–other distinction results in the eruption of annihilation anxiety, an "unimaginable terror" or fear of falling apart, akin to the anxiety of falling endlessly through the air (Winnicott, 1952). "Maternal failures produce phases of reaction to impingement and these reactions interrupt the 'going on being' of the infant. An excess of this reacting produces not frustration but a *threat of annihilation*. This in my view is a very real primitive anxiety, long antedating any anxiety that includes the word death in its description" (Winnicott, 1956, p. 303). This state is so terrifying that it must be defended against by whatever means are possible, and the only defense the infant has are omnipotent fantasies. Thus, the infant creates omnipotent fantasies to protect itself from annihilation anxiety (Winnicott, 1952), and these fantasies cannot be gradually relinquished in favor of reality. A prisoner of fantasied omnipotence, the infant protects itself against any incursion of reality into its private world; indeed, when reality threatens to intrude, it must be reinterpreted according to the child's omnipotent fantasies, or "brought into the sphere of omnipotence."

This distortion of reality by infantile omnipotence is the essence of

Winnicott's concept of the developmental origins of psychosis. He did not deny the possibility of constitutional factors in psychosis, but he believed that impingements play a crucial role by producing annihilation anxiety and the omnipotent defenses against it. Fixated in the omnipotent defense, the ego cannot become integrated, and indeed all developmental tasks suffer as the child's investment is focused on protecting itself via omnipotent defenses. "The focus is on the shell, not the kernel" (Winnicott, 1960a). Since all tension states threaten to become annihilation anxiety, frustration and disappointment tend to be denied and "magically" relieved, fixating the personality at the level of magical thought. Any assault from reality threatens to pierce the fragile defense and must be reinterpreted in line with the fantasied omnipotence. Thus, the growing child is driven further from reality and nearer to the outbreak of psychosis.

These dynamics are illustrated in Winnicott's case of Miss X (Winnicott, 1963d), a schizoid patient who had the habit of covering herself with a rug in her treatment sessions. In a Tuesday session that Winnicott reported, Miss. X spent her time covered with the rug and said very little; although neither she nor Winnicott was anxious, nothing much happened. Toward the end of the hour on Wednesday, she pointed out that the Tuesday session had been crucial because she had gone through a difficulty that had blocked her previous analysis. That analyst had not allowed her quietude, and Miss X initially felt that the Tuesday hour signified the failure of her analysis with Winnicott. However, during the session she realized, according to Winnicott, that this analysis "was not going to fail in the usual way, and that she would go ahead and take all the risks and let feelings develop, and perhaps suffer deeply. In this way she found this Tuesday hour extremely satisfying, and she felt grateful" (p. 237). The case of Miss X demonstrated to Winnicott that what patients like her need is for the analyst to "know and tell them what they fear. They themselves know all the time, but the thing is that the analyst must know and say it" (p. 237). The patient pointed out that she needed Winnicott to "take over" her omnipotence so that she could "with relief break down, break up, and experience the worse degree of disintegration or sense of annihilation" (p. 237). In the Thursday session the patient showed the first indications of ambivalence in her relationship with Winnicott, a significant step forward.

Winnicott believed that this vignette illustrated why the analyst must meet the patient's need for omnipotence in treating borderline cases. Once the patient felt that she was understood without having to signal her needs to Winnicott, she was able to "let go" of her omnipotence, surrender her minimal sense of self to him, and begin the process of developing a real sense of self. As the omnipotent defense was relinquished, the patient experienced the annihilation anxiety that had been hidden underneath it. In Winnicott's view, Miss X, while not clinically psychotic, had psychotic needs because of her reliance on the omnipotent defense to protect against annihilation anxiety.

Winnicott applied a similar analysis to states of "depersonalization" and "derealization." Both conditions result from impingement in the phase of absolute dependence (Winnicott, 1962). Winnicott equated such states with the eruption of an underlying lack of personalization or underdeveloped sense of reality. In the case of "depersonalization" episodes, even though a presumably normal or neurotic personality may have grown around the deficit, the underlying sense of having a "lived psychic reality" is shaky; there is never a definite sense of experience as belonging to oneself. Similarly, Winnicott understood "derealization" experiences as the surfacing of an underlying uncertainty about the relationship of the self to reality. Both states are symptomatic of damaged self development due to impingement in the phase of absolute dependence, even though the personality may appear relatively healthy.

The omnipotent defense need not lead to a psychotic personality organization (Winnicott, 1960a). The result seems to depend on the severity of the impingement. If the self is completely unintegrated the likelihood of a psychotic outcome is great, but if the self has achieved some degree of integration there may be a stable omnipotent defense that is in continual conflict with reality but does not lead to a full-blown psychosis. In these cases conflict and tension are "brought into the sphere of omnipotence" (Winnicott, 1960a). Borderline and narcissistic personality disorders fit Winnicott's concept of trauma in the phase of absolute dependence with arrest at the level of omnipotent defense.

Patients at this level have expectations of people and their therapist that reflect their omnipotent world of absolute dependence. They typically expect the therapist to fulfill all manner of needs and desires. There is no sense of others, including the therapist, as having lives of their own, or even feelings of their own. We saw in the case of Miss X that she needed the analyst to know her fears without being told. Patients' demands that the therapist bring them home, give them money, reduce their fees, and hold and caress them, are all, for Winnicott, manifestations of the omnipotence resulting from impingements in the phase of absolute dependence. Patients expressing such demands are trying desperately to blur any awareness of others as separate.

Because such patients have no awareness of the other as separate from the self, they are pre-ruth, unable to discern that their rage can injure the other and consequently feel no guilt for "injuring" other people. When such patients react angrily to threats to their omnipotence, they can rage, insult, threaten, and even become physically violent without guilt. From the ego psychological viewpoint, this indifference to hurting others reflects a superego lacuna, a gap in the structure of the psyche. While Winnicott would not disagree that there is such a deficit, in his view, this apparent coldheartedness stems from fixation at the phase of absolute dependence, before the capacity for concern has a chance to develop.

The therapist's role is to attempt within the therapeutic context to meet as much as possible the patient's previously unmet need for life within the sphere of omnipotence (Winnicott, 1954c). The therapist attempts to understand the patient's behavior as communication even when the patient does not know he or she is communicating. To achieve this goal, the therapist uses the empathy of the "good enough mother," who relies on identification with the baby to meet uncommunicated needs. Because psychopathology at this stage is due to premature interference in the delusional omnipotent world of absolute dependence, Winnicott (1954c, 1960a) believed that the therapist should offer the patient, insofar as possible, the opportunity to return to this world. Such patients need to feel what they should have felt as a baby: dependence without awareness, the omnipotent feeling that needs are met magically without communicating them. The therapist's sensitivity to this need and effort to meet it, when possible, return the patient to the point of ego arrest, from which the maturational process can be unblocked.

This principle is illustrated by Winnicott's (1954b) discussion of a schizoid-depressed patient who was not generally regressed but who lapsed into momentary withdrawal states. In one session the patient had the fantasy of curling up and rolling over the back of the couch. A few weeks later when he asked Winnicott for advice and Winnicott did not comply, the patient withdrew and felt the desire to curl up. Winnicott interpreted that the patient's throwing himself around and curling up implied the "existence of a medium" (p. 256). Soon after, the patient had a dream of discarding a shield, which Winnicott interpreted as a symbol of his unneeded defense now that he (Winnicott) had proven himself a suitable medium for the patient at the moment of regression: "It appears that *through my immediately putting a medium around his withdrawn self I had converted his withdrawal into a regression,* and so had enabled him to use this experience constructively" (p. 257).

Understanding the patient's need for a lap to curl up on, Winnicott provided an "analytic lap." Considerable therapeutic progress followed these events. The patient gained a clear understanding of the analyst's role, resulting in his management of reality situations at home and work in a new way. Additionally, he began to feel concern for his mother.

This vignette illustrates Winnicott's idea that patients who are not generally regressed often need moments of regression to return to primitive parts of the self that are fixated in the phase of absolute dependence. This patient needed to return to dependence without awareness in order to advance to ambivalence and the confrontation of reality situations in his life. By understanding his need for a "medium," a "lap" to curl up in, Winnicott met his need for a brief return to absolute dependence in order to allow movement into relative dependence.

This approach highlights Winnicott's view of psychotherapy as adaptation to need. Winnicott (1959) made clear that he was giving up his traditional view of psychotherapy as the making of "clever" interpretations in favor of a view of psychotherapy as the analyst's adaptation to the patient's unmet needs. The therapist's role is to assess the point of developmental arrest in each patient and then to make an adaptation to the arrested need. Verbalization is only one way this may happen, but for preoedipal disorders words are often not suited to the task.

A good example of Winnicott's principle of adaptation to regressive needs in a functional patient is the case of a 47-year-old woman who had made a seemingly positive adjustment to the world, was earning a living, and was well liked (Winnicott, 1949, 1954b). Despite these outward signs of health, she felt completely dissatisfied with her life, having never felt in contact with herself. A classical analysis had not affected this core belief. Winnicott (1949) described her treatment as follows:

> With me it soon became apparent that this patient must make a very severe regression or else give up the struggle. I therefore followed the regressive tendency, letting it take the patient wherever it led; eventually the regression reached the limit of the patient's need, and since then there has been a natural progression with the true self instead of a false self in action. . . . In the course of the two years of analysis with me the patient has repeatedly regressed to an early stage which was certainly prenatal [p. 249].

In this patient's previous analysis she had hysterically thrown herself off the couch. Winnicott interpreted this behavior as her unconscious need to relive the birth process. In her treatment with Winnicott she relived the birth experience over and over again. The patient experienced the anxiety of having her head crushed; she managed this anxiety by identifying with the crushing mechanism, obtaining gratification from the fantasy of destroying her head, which no longer felt like part of the self. The patient "had to accept annihilation," which was experienced as a giving in, and "eventually the appropriate word was 'a not knowing' "(p. 250). The acceptance of "not knowing" gave the patient tremendous relief and was, as Winnicott put it, "transformed into the analyst knows, that is to say, behaves reliably in active adaptation to the patient's needs" (p. 250).

In Winnicott's view, this case illustrates a functional patient's need for regression to absolute dependence and the analyst's role of making an "active adaptation" to this need. Winnicott understood the patient's throwing herself off the couch as a need to relive the birth process, but he did not believe the treatment could progress solely by this understanding. He used his formulation to help the patient relive the birth process and, thereby, to experience the annihilation she had been defending against with her superficial adaptation to reality. The key to the therapeutic process was, according to Winnicott, her ultimate willingness to "give herself over" to the analyst—that is to say, to accept absolute dependence—so that she could begin to form a true sense of self. Thus, Winnicott conceptualized the analyst's role as one of managing the patient's dependency needs rather than providing interpretations; the analyst uses his understanding to adapt to the patient's need to regress to absolute dependence and annihilation, from which point the patient is able to move forward.

Winnicott's use of general management in severely regressed patients is also illustrated in his treatment of the analyst Margaret Little. In her description of her analysis with Winnicott, Little (1985) pointed out that Winnicott made few interpretations, preferring to manage her regression primarily in nonverbal fashion. In the first session Little lay silent, curled up tight under a blanket; Winnicott said nothing until the end of the hour, when he commented, "I don't know, but I have the feeling that you are shutting me out for some reason" (p. 20). Some weeks later Little was seized with spasms of terror, and Winnicott, who believed she was reliving her birth and said as much, let her cling to him until they passed. In many sessions Little lay inert under the blanket and Winnicott held her hands tightly in his. Little described Winnicott as generally "holding" her, taking full responsibility, including management of her life when necessary. For example, once he was concerned about her ability to withstand his vacation, so he arranged, without her knowing, for a friend to invite her to Switzerland. On another occasion, he hospitalized her while he was away, and during a period when she could not reach her analytic sessions he came to her house.

It is clear from Little's description of her analysis with Winnicott that he attempted to meet the needs of her state of absolute dependence by overall management of her care. He did make interpretations, but they were not as important as his adaptation to her regressed state. Winnicott attempted to function like the "good enough" mother of an infant in the phase of absolute dependence. As Little began to do more for herself, he "de-adapted" just as the mother does when the infant reaches the phase of relative dependence.

Winnicott (1963c) believed interpretations were effective only when they adapted to the patient's needs. He reported an example of such an interpretation in the treatment of a woman who had recently changed her analytic schedule from once to five times per week when Winnicott announced his impending month-long vacation. Before the announcement she had a dream in which a tortoise with a soft shell was killed to relieve its misery; the dream indicated to Winnicott that she had come to treatment for relief of her suicidal tendency. After the vacation announcement the patient became physically ill, and Winnicott linked the illness with his impending departure. The vacation reenacted traumatic events of the patient's childhood. Winnicott wrote, "[The patient felt] as if I were holding her and then became preoccupied with some other matter so that she felt *annihilated*" (p. 250). Winnicott then interpreted to the patient that by killing herself she would gain control over the annihilation associated with feeling dependent and vulnerable. Further, he pointed out that the illness was a physical localization of her urge to die. This interpretation relieved the patient's feeling of helplessness, and she was able to allow Winnicott to go on vacation. Winnicott described his understanding of the effectiveness of his interpretation as follows:

> One can only assume that understanding in a deep way and interpreting at the right moment is a form of reliable adaptation. In this case, for instance, the patient became able to cope with my absence because she felt (at one level) that she was now not being annihilated, but in a positive way was being kept in existence by having a reality as the object of my concern. A little later on, in more complete dependence, the verbal interpretation will not be enough, or may be dispensed with [p. 250].

Winnicott's interpretation turned a potentially traumatic repetition into a new, positive experience. The value of interpretation, for Winnicott, lies in the meeting of a childhood need, in this case, the need to be recognized within a dependent relationship. (As we will see in chapter 6, Kohut too held that the effectiveness of interpretations lies in the type of experience they provide, rather than in the accretion of knowledge, although his conceptualization of their impact differs from Winnicott's.)

Winnicott did not believe that the therapist will always be successful in understanding and meeting the patient's need. The therapist's failures are inevitable, just as the mother's adaptation to her child is never perfect.

Just as the mother's failures help the infant achieve a sense of reality by forcing the infant out of the delusional world of omnipotence, so too do the therapist's failures in adaptation force the patient to see, however briefly, that the therapist is not under his or her omnipotent control (Winnicott, 1963b). The patient's recognition of the therapist's limitations is equivalent to the mother's "bringing reality to the child." It is as important in the former case as in the latter that too large a "dose" of reality not be given too soon. The therapeutic process of adaptation and failure, if not so severe as to be traumatic, aids in the development of the patient's sense of time and the continuity of experience. Like the mother, the therapist bears the greatest burden of synchrony with needs deriving from the absolute dependence phase. Just as failures in environmental adaptation become more bearable and can be born for a longer period once the baby develops a temporal sense, so too is there more leeway for therapist error with later developmental issues. In short, the therapist's role is the same as the mother's: to meet the needs as well as possible and then gradually bring the patient/child into reality by a process of adaptation, failure, and repair that allows reality to be experienced in manageable doses.

Critical to the success of the therapeutic process is the therapist's willingness to acknowledge "failure." Winnicott felt that an exclusive reliance on interpretation of the patient's reaction to the therapist's failures does a disservice to the patient because it does not use the mistake to help the patient achieve a sense of reality. Any patient disrupted by the therapist's error must have at least some residual fantasied omnipotence not fully brought into the reality sense; for this reason, acknowledgment of failure is a therapeutic necessity. The therapist's willingness to admit error acknowledges his or her limits and brings to the patient the reality of the therapist as a person, thus, for that moment, breaking through infantile fantasized omnipotence. Just as the infant gradually learns reality through failure and frustration, so too must the patient be gradually "brought to reality" by the failures of the therapist and their realistic acknowledgment.

Winnicott (1951) also believed that the origins of fetishism were to be found in the absolute dependence phase. Like Freud, he felt that such attachments to objects were encapsulated psychoses, based on denial of reality. Whereas Freud believed the basis of the fetishistic attachment was a sexual denial, Winnicott believed the psychotic attachment had a presexual origin. Unlike the child, who knows that the transitional object is not the mother, the fetishist believes the fetishistic object to *be* the longed-for object. According to Winnicott, the fetish originates in an impingement in this phase, which forces the infant out of its delusional world and into reality before the ego is ready. To defend against this premature awareness of reality, the fetishistic object is brought into the "sphere of omnipotence" where the magical wish for the need to bring its own gratification is satisfied. Such an object is not used as a transitional object is, that is, to shift from omnipotent control to limited control, but enables the child/patient to stay within the orbit of omnipotent control; because it must always be available to satisfy magical desires it cannot be given up. Whereas the transitional object is known to be outside omnipotent control but is treated as though it were not, the fetishistic object is not experienced as outside. It is "pretransitional," and therefore the attachment to it is delusional as opposed to illusional.

The treatment for fetishism follows the same principles as therapy for any symptom originating in the absolute dependence phase. The therapist's role is not to try to teach the patient reality by interpreting the attachment to the object as unrealistic. Even if the interpretations are thoughtful, in-depth, and accurate, words cannot alter omnipotent defenses needed to protect against annihilation anxiety; words have little meaning to the patient who needs to be in the orbit of infantile omnipotence.

The most benign outcome of impingement in the phase of absolute dependence is "ego distortion in terms of true and false self" (Winnicott, 1960b). If impingement is not too severe and some integration of self has occurred, the child may be able to defend itself by environmental compliance. That is, the child attempts to provide the environment with what seems to be expected. In order to protect the minimal sense of "true self," the environment is offered a personality. The defense protects the buried "true self" from contact with the environment and in so doing forfeits feelings, the very sense of aliveness. The surface personality looks normal and is taken by the world as the real personality. However, it does not feel real to the patient, whose principal feelings are boredom, restlessness, and emptiness. This malaise results from a lack of connection to inner experience. "Authenticity" is a crucial category for Winnicott, designating the healthy personality governed by the true self. Living inauthentically is a defensive reaction, a distorting of the ego to protect all "real" feelings from environmental contact. Unlike cases in which the unintegrated personality is predisposed to psychosis, in cases of ego distortion a self exists, even if only in a nascent state, but its buried under a constructed "normal" personality.

We have already seen an example of this split between the true and false selves in the case of the 47-year-old woman who seemed to have effected a normal adaptation but felt disconnected from herself. The patient's personality and life had been built around mental functioning; she lived in her head and was disconnected with the rest of herself. Consequently, she had no sense of self until Winnicott followed her regressive need to absolute dependence, entailing fear of annihilation, the "limit of her need." When the patient reached this point of the treatment, she reached the buried true self, and for the first time felt connected with herself.

Winnicott felt that such constructed false selves are more common than is usually recognized even by psychoanalysts and that they tend to be analyzed as though they were real. He mentioned cases of patients previously analyzed along classical lines where the patients' "nonexistence" had to be recognized before therapeutic movement could begin (Winnicott, 1954c, 1960b). To analyze wishes, conflicts, and oedipal issues in such cases is meaningless because the patient does not feel real. The patient only feels communicated with when his or her fundamental nonexistence is recognized; only at that point can the analysis have a meaningful beginning. Winnicott (1960b) reported a case of a male patient who had had an extensive previous analysis.

> My work really started with him when I made it clear to him that I recognized his non-existence. He made the remark that over the years all the good work done with him had been futile because it had been done on the basis that he existed, whereas he had only existed falsely. When I had said that I recognized his non-existence he felt that he had been communicated with for the first time. What he meant was that his True Self that had been hidden away from infancy had now been in communication with his analyst in the only way which was not dangerous. This is typical of the way in which this concept affects psycho-analytic work [p. 151].

The very feeling of unreality is the analytic issue, and the analyst's task is to point out the unreality of the false self until the true self can begin to emerge. Insofar as it helps to get beneath the false self, defense interpretation is useful, but when it treats the false self as though it were real, it is destructive to treatment. The analyst's task is to make contact with the true self, as Winnicott did in this case by pointing out the patient's nonexistence.

Psychopathology and Relative Dependence

We have seen that as children move into relative dependence by becoming aware of the mother as a separate person, they begin to internalize the mother and develop a sense of self as continuous and integrated. Impingement in this phase occurs to a *developing* self—not to an unintegrated self, as in absolute dependence, nor to a fully integrated self, as in the oedipal phase. Having achieved some degree of internalization, the infant experiences impingement as deprivation, a loss of something that was there, as opposed to the "privation" of impingement in absolute dependence.

According to Winnicott, if mothering has been good enough until some point in the phase of relative dependence and then fails significantly without repair, the child will seek to regain what has been lost. Efforts to regain the lost object gain expression in the various symptoms of character disorders and borderline cases. One typical reaction is to attempt to replace maternal deprivation by taking objects. Winnicott (1956b) understood child and adolescent stealing as efforts to regain the lost mother by laying claim to the world. Children attempt to steal back what was stolen from them. In Winnicott's view, such behavior reflects a belief based on an unconscious memory of gratification that there is something of value to be found. Because an attempt to find the object is really an effort to "re-find" it, reflecting deprivation of something once possessed, Winnicott considered stealing a positive indicator.

If the environment understands the effort to re-find in the act of stealing, the behavior can be halted. For example, Winnicott (1963d) reported the case of an 8-year-old boy who had been caught stealing. When Winnicott interpreted to him that he was searching for the "good mother" from the time before she conceived his younger sibling, the delinquency ceased. In some cases the treatment must go beyond interpretation by meeting dependency needs antedating the deprivation. For example, a 13-year-old boy was not only slashing sheets but also stealing at school and getting into other serious trouble. Winnicott arranged to have him "mentally nursed" at home while he underwent a period of regression from which he spontaneously emerged. The boy ceased his delinquency and eventually returned to school. In Winnicott's view, the "mental nursing" provided the boy with the "good mother" for whom he had been searching, thus obviating his need to steal. In both cases the therapeutic environment adapted to the patient's need for the gratification that was once obtained and then lost. When this need was met, the search for the lost object ceased.

Some patients attempt to re-find the lost object through direct physical gratification, which leads to addictions involving food, drugs, and alcohol as well as to sexual promiscuity (Winnicott, 1951). Winnicott believed that such addictions are similar to transitional phenomena because they represent the mother and yet are recognized as not being the mother. Unlike the child's transitional possessions, addictions are not given up naturally because they are a regressive response to deprivation, an effort to regain an earlier relationship with the mother before deprivation. Consequently, rather than moving the developmental process forward, addictions tend to remain fixated.

Some babies suffer impingement in the phase of relative dependence not from an object taken away prematurely, but from a maternal environment unable to shift from the "near-absolute" adaptation of absolute dependence to the lesser degree of adaptation necessary for the next phase (Winnicott, 1960a). In such an environment the mother-infant "set-up" continues to be based on object instinctual excitement rather than fostering the development of an "ego relationship." The growing infant has a continual need for contact, to know it is in a relationship, and thus lacks the capacity to be alone (Winnicott, 1958). While the infant is differentiated enough to have a relationship, it is not able to maintain a sense of the other without physical presence. The infant has enough of a "lived psychic reality" to feel alive and whole when in the presence of the mother but not enough to feel alive and whole in her absence. Patients fixated at this level cannot be alone without feeling lonely and desperate for physical contact to regain the feeling of life and reality. Such patients become addicted to others, either through excessive dependence or a need for sexual contact; that is, they use people for the same purpose other patients use food, drugs, or alcohol.

Because the inability to be alone is created when the child is not allowed "to be alone" in the mother's presence, patients who cannot be alone need to have the experience with the therapist they should have had with the mother: they need to be alone in the presence of the therapist (Winnicott, 1958). If the therapist insists on verbal intervention, the patient is denied this critical therapeutic experience. The therapist's role is to be a presence without intruding on the patient's need to be alone—which will usually be manifested when the patient chooses to be silent. Silence in such patients is not to be interpreted as resistance but as the patient's effort to unblock the effects of not having been allowed to be alone and resume self-development by the formation of an ego relationship. The therapist's silence offers the patient a sense of connection without physical contact so that the patient can internalize the therapist as a good object. Once the therapist is internalized, the patient is able to be alone without the anxiety of losing a sense of existence.

Winnicott's (1971) treatment of the patient who lacks the capacity to be alone is illustrated by his rather detailed description of a session with a patient who found, after a six-year analysis of five sessions per week, that she needed sessions of indefinite length. To accommodate this need, Winnicott saw her once a week for three hours, later reduced to two hours. In the session described by Winnicott, the patient said very little for the first half hour during which she either sat on a chair or on the floor or walked around the office. She then commented that she was unable to be herself, that she was "not really looking," and that there was "just a mess inside, just a crash" (p. 58). After about one hour, with her head on a cushion, she mentioned a dream of a girl bringing pictures that showed no improvement; once again she commented that she did not feel a "me." She was mostly silent for the next half hour and then said, "Just drifting like clouds" (p. 59). She began to talk about being of no consequence and of attempting to feel that she mattered by conforming to what was expected of her. She then mentioned with surprise that a girl sent her a postcard. Winnicott commented, "As if you mattered to her. But you don't matter to her or anyone" (p. 59). The patient commented that she had not made contact with Winnicott all day.

Winnicott noted that after two hours the patient for the first time "seemed to be in the room with [him]" (p. 60). It was a makeup session and she said she was glad Winnicott knew she needed the time. The remark was made as though it were her first comment to Winnicott that day. The patient began to look back on the session but could not remember what she had said. At this point, Winnicott made his first interpretation: "All sorts of things happen and they wither. This is the myriad deaths you have died. But if someone is there, someone who can give you back what has happened, then the details dealt with in this way become part of you, and do not die" (p. 61). When a little later the patient expressed the feeling that she had come to meet someone who did not appear, Winnicott began to make links between her comments and to reflect back what she was saying. At one point, the patient realized that she had interrupted Winnicott, indicating her acceptance of his existence. They went on to discuss how talking to herself did not help her feel a sense of existence unless it was a continuation of talk reflected back to her by another. The patient commented, "I've been trying to show you *me being alone.*" She talked of her use of mirrors to search for herself, and Winnicott pointed out that it was *she* who was searching. Winnicott reported that by the next session the patient had forgotten this session and they took two hours to reach this same point again. In the second session the patient asked a question and said with deep feeling that "one could postulate a ME from the question, as from the searching" (p. 64).

This session clearly reveals Winnicott's technique, but the important point in the present context is his willingness to allow the patient to be alone in his presence. He made no effort to get her to talk and asked no questions. Allowing her to be alone until she made contact with him. By beginning to "come into the room" and recognize his existence, she began to form an ego relationship, thus initiating the development of the capacity to be alone, a crucial step in her self development. The fact that this patient could not take this step without Winnicott's presence and attention to her behavior illustrates a crucial point in Winnicott's theory of technique. Winnicott's task was to "hold" the situation by linking the various moments of the session and giving them back to her. He performed the function of self integration by giving her self back to her in coherent form. It was Winnicott's belief that he was performing the task of ego organization, which the parents had failed to perform in the patient's childhood. This belief was borne out in the next session when the patient recognized herself as existing in her question.

It is not that Winnicott believed that silence could not be resistance as it is viewed in classical psychoanalytic theory. Rather, he believed that it has different meanings depending on the developmental level of the patient and the stage of the treatment process. In a neurotic patient anxious about intense affects, silence is a resistance. For the preoedipal patient trying to develop the capacity to be alone, silence is a developmental advance toward the creation of the self via an ego relationship. Illumination of the therapist's responsibility to adapt to this need is one more way in which Winnicott that felt his studies of preoedipal disorders expanded psychoanalytic theory and technique without questioning its relevance to neurotic disorders.

Confusion results because neurotic patients, too, may have some arrest in the phase of relative, or even absolute, dependence. Although these issues would be more transitory in such cases, they may still require intervention geared to the preoedipal disturbance at those "regressive moments." If one such moment involves an unresolved need to be alone, silence may emerge with the unconscious purpose of affording the patient the experience of aloneness with a mother who will tolerate being ignored. In this situation, requests for free association or interpretations of resistance will interfere with the patient's developmental need to be alone and will reenact the behavior of the mother who intruded with contact and stifled the child's need to form an ego relationship. Whether verbal intervention is used in any individual situation depends on the assessment of the patient's developmental level.

Many borderline personality disorders fit Winnicott's (1960, 1963a) concept of trauma in the phase of relative dependence. Winnicott viewed the overwhelming dependence ties and acting out so characteristic of such patients as efforts to "lay claim" to something in the world, to use people or things as transitional objects in an effort to regain a lost maternal bond. Borderline patients often create burdensome countertransference strain because of the demands and expectations they place on the therapist. Common clinical terms used to describe this phenomenon include "entitlement," "lack of boundaries," and "unrealistic expectations." As we shall see when we consider Kernberg's work in chapter 5, treatment recommendations for such patients often involve limit setting and confrontation with reality (Kernberg, 1975). Masterson (1976) also subscribes to this approach.

In Winnicott's view, all such recommendations ignore the developmental meaning of the patient's behavior. He believed that since the patient's expectations and demands are an effort to lay claim to an object once possessed but now lost the therapeutic task is to adapt as much as possible to the patient's longing for a gratifying object. By so doing, the therapist places himself in the position of a transitional object—to be used as a symbol for maternal gratification and discarded when no longer needed. According to Winnicott, this type of adaptation unblocks the arrested maturational process.

The case of Miss X discussed earlier illustrates the meaning of the borderline patient's "claim" to others (Winnicott, 1963e). Recall that in one session Miss X regressed to a desire to have Winnicott know her needs without any communication from her, thus reflecting her omnipotence. In the next session, she became greedy and expressed the desire to "eat" Winnicott. They discussed the "compulsive element" in her appetite and its manifestation in her relationship with Winnicott, and it became clear that there was a "compulsive greed in her antisocial tendency" (p. 238). The meeting of her regressed need from the phase of absolute dependence had clearly led to a movement toward relative dependence. She now recognized Winnicott as an object upon whom she was dependent and claimed him as her own. This movement was also manifested in a new ambivalence toward Winnicott.

The borderline patient, according to Winnicott (1960a), lives in the "intermediate area" of infancy when the child goes back and forth between merger and separation. During merger, the mother/therapist is expected to know the infant's/patient's needs without being told even at those times when the infant/patient has a need to feel separate; yet such maternal empathy is also felt as a stifling assault on the need to separate. Therefore, the patient's "claims" on the therapist are contradictory; moreover, they oscillate quickly and contain no signal about which need is being expressed at any given moment. The therapist inevitably feels intruded upon, confused, dejected that he or she cannot do anything right, and, ultimately, enraged at the patient. The twofold therapeutic task is to understand that the ricocheting behaviors are symptomatic of a developmental process arrested in the transitional phase and to meet the need for a transitional object to unblock the arrested maturational process. Limit setting from this point of view misses the patient's transitional level of development. If such patients respond to limit setting, they are only conforming to the expectations of the therapist.

Such conformity can have no emotional meaning to them and their need for the lost object can only be buried. Limit setting not only means lost therapeutic opportunity, according to Winnicott, but is antitherapeutic in that the patient's desperate effort to signal for help is quashed. The therapist must present himself or herself as an object to be merged with and separated from, as needed, just as the transitional object must be available for comforting when it is needed, only to be forgotten about at other times.

Insofar as interpretation is useful for borderline patients, it tends to emphasize the patient's unconscious object seeking and the way the patient needs to use objects. However, Winnicott seemed not to rely heavily on interpretation in borderline and other preoedipal cases. Rather, he stressed the importance of "using" the therapist as an object. (In Winnicott's, 1971, writings this expression refers to the way an object is employed to aid the developmental process; it does not imply an exploitative motive.) As we saw, in the phase of absolute dependence there is no use of an object because there is no awareness of objects. It is only when the child "expels" objects out of its sphere of omnipotence, beginning with transitional possessions, that it learns to "use objects." To be used as a transitional object the therapist must withstand an intense variety of feelings, be there when needed and forgotten when not needed.

For the patient to use the therapist in this way the therapeutic space must be formless so that the patient can create meaning out of it. The therapist must be careful to avoid imposing preconceived categories on the patient so that the patient can regress to a blank space and create a new object endowed with personally created meaning, just as the child creates its transitional object. If the therapist does not interfere by making intrusive, premature interpretations or otherwise imposing meanings on the therapeutic space, the patient is able to use it to create his or her own meaning. This process is crucial to shifting the analytic process from interpretation of the past to creation of new meaning. According to Winnicott, creativity plays a major role in all effective analyses because only through creativity can one give one's own meaning to reality, that is, enter the process that forms the self. In normal development the transitional object is used for this purpose; in analytic treatment the analytic space functions in an analogous way by facilitating creation of personal meaning. This principle holds true to some degree for all analytic treatment, but it is especially significant for the borderline patient, whose emotional development is arrested at the transitional phase. For such a patient there is no internalized maternal image; the primary transference issue is this absence rather than the repetition of an existing maternal image, as seen in higher level disorders. Consequently, the creation of a new object in the absent space is a major outcome of successful treatment.

The creation of meaning out of formlessness is illustrated in the three-hour analytic session described earlier. Winnicott made no effort to get the patient to talk or free-associate. He allowed her to use the session as she saw fit. This atmosphere is what Winnicott means by the "formlessness" from which the patient is able to create personal meaning. In the session in question, the patient eventually created a sense of herself and Winnicott that felt real and meaningful to her. Recall also that this process was made possible by Winnicott's reflecting back "bits" of the patient in coherent form. This mirroring function of the analyst makes the creation of self possible as the patient moves from the sense of being an absence to that of being a newly created presence.

This movement from absence to presence is also illustrated by

Winnicott's (1971) treatment of a middle-aged woman who tended to lapse into dissociated states. The patient felt that nothing had significance for her, that she did not exist in her own right, and that all her activities were meaningless. In the analysis she realized that no one in her childhood had recognized her need for formlessness and that she had been molded into forms for others, none of which had meaning to her. As she reached this realization, she became intensely angry. At the next session she expressed fear that Winnicott would interpret recent constructive changes in her life as evidence of therapeutic progress. For example, in describing how she had cleaned up messes that had been neglected for months, she expressed the suspicion that Winnicott had somehow prearranged this change. Winnicott pointed out to her that he had to be careful not to show any pleasure in her activities lest she feel he had fit her into a pattern. The patient asked what the previous session had been about, and Winnicott described it as formless. She said that she was feeling tired and realized she could sleep in the session. This thought allowed her to imagine being healthy, and she had the idea that she "might be able to be in charge of [herself]" (p. 36). Eventually she arrived at the conclusion that in illness she was certain of what to expect but in health she had the anxiety of uncertainty. Winnicott felt that a great deal had been accomplished, but he did not allow himself to become pleased.

This case demonstrates Winnicott's ability to let the therapeutic space be used as material for the creation of a transitional object. The patient's anger had a profound impact on her because it spontaneously erupted out of the formlessness of the therapeutic space. Winnicott believed that if he had interpreted her anger toward childhood figures, the interpretation, although correct, would not have belonged to her and therefore would have impinged on her need to possess her experiences as her own. In fact, he referred to such premature interpretations as "stealing" from the patient. One of Winnicott's cardinal therapeutic principles is that therapeutic effectiveness is greatly enhanced if the patients themselves make the interpretation, because in the process they take a step in the creation of the self.

Winnicott (1971) summarized the use of therapeutic space for the creation of the self this way:

> The searching can come only from desultory formless functioning, or perhaps from rudimentary playing, as if in a neutral zone. It is only here, in this unintegrated state of the personality, that that which we described as creative can appear. This if reflected back, *but only if reflected back*, becomes part of the organized individual personality, and

eventually this in summation makes the individual to be, to be found; and eventually enables himself or herself to postulate the existence of the self.

This gives us our indication for therapeutic procedure—to afford opportunity for formless experience, and for creative impulses, motor and sensory, which are the stuff of playing. And on the basis of playing is built the whole of man's experiential existence [p. 64].

The patient's need to use the therapist as a transitional object makes the countertransference an especially difficult issue with such patients. Winnicott (1960c) defined countertransference as disturbance in the therapist's observational stance. As the patient demands compliance with expectations that the therapist function as a transitional object, the therapist experiences a countertransference strain. Such patients are demanding that the therapist yield the professional analytic attitude, and they become enraged whenever they feel the therapist has not complied with their expectation. This strain makes working with such patients more emotionally draining than the psychotherapy of neurotic patients, and a major component of the therapeutic work is the management of these very difficult countertransference feelings. According to Winnicott, countertransference feelings—which range from anger, disruption, and feeling threatened to love and affection—must be felt by the therapist. The danger lies not in having countertransference feelings but in repressing them, for repression can lead to countertransference acting out. The containment of these intense feelings imposes a burden on the therapist as heavy as the mother's when she manages her infant's distress. Further, since the best therapeutic approach is often to remain silent, the therapist is denied even the outlet of interpretation. The therapist's absorption and management of personal feelings must be outside the patient's awareness, just as the mother bears the strain of nurturing the baby outside its awareness.

According to Winnicott (1960c), it is an inevitable part of the treatment of borderline patients that they will "break through the barriers that [are] called the analyst's technique and professional attitude, and force a direct relationship of a primitive kind, even to the extent of merging" (p. 164). Borderline patients require and even force the needed primitive relationship, and therapists have no choice but to alter their professional attitude. Winnicott believed that in most cases patient and therapist will develop the needed relationship in an orderly way and will "recover from it" in a similar fashion. Adaptation to the borderline patient's need for a regressive relationship is the crux of the therapeutic effort for such a patient.

A special countertransference problem is created by patients who need the therapist to hate them (Winnicott, 1947). According to Winnicott, in psychotic and borderline cases the therapist will inevitably "hate" the patient at some point during the treatment process. This feeling may also occur in the analysis of neurotics, but hate can be kept latent in those cases much more easily. Thorough awareness of hate is required in the treatment of some severely disturbed patients because the therapist's hatred is a crucial aspect of the patient's pathology. For example, Winnicott (1947) found an obsessional patient loathsome for years. When the patient became lovable, Winnicott realized that his unlikableness had been a symptom. It was a major advance in his treatment when Winnicott was able to tell him that he had hated him but that he had been too ill to be told. Winnicott referred to this type of hatred as "objective"; he believed that the analyst is not only justified in feeling it but also that he *must* feel it in order to treat the patient effectively.

Winnicott believed that the mother hates the baby no matter how deep her love, long before the baby is able to hate her. As we have seen, the growing child has a developmental need to integrate love and hate (Winnicott, 1963b); the infant must learn to hate the mother without the feeling of destruction. For Winnicott, infants learn to hate their mother from the mother's hatred of them; it follows that primitive patients can only learn to hate if the therapist first hates them. Much of borderline patients' abusive behavior is designed unconsciously to evoke the therapist's hate so that they can experience their own hatred of the therapist. Patients are then in a position to integrate love and hate of the therapist/mother.

The inability to integrate aggressiveness and love is a problem found in a variety of character-disordered patients (Winnicott, 1963a). Particular forms of impingement in the phase of relative dependence may have interfered with the child's ability to integrate aggressiveness with love for the mother. If the mother does not survive, the child is left with the unconscious interpretation that its aggression killed the mother. In this situation, unresolved guilt over aggressiveness is inevitable and will result in one of several forms of defensive reaction. More commonly, the mother may physically survive but be unable to contain the child's aggression. If she is made unduly anxious by it, the child will become anxious over its own aggressiveness and will disavow the aggressive component of its personality. The child is then unable to fuse its love and anger, and this "defusion of the instincts" splits off aggressiveness from the rest of the personality.

For Winnicott, full object instinctual gratification and excitement require the integration of aggression, a "fusion" of the two impulses. In addition, because the constructive ability to pursue realistic goals is based on the "aggressive impulse," the absence of aggression blocks the achievement of these goals. Regardless of the specific pathological reaction that results from the inhibition of aggressiveness, its inhibition means that a primary source of motivation and zest for life has been squeezed out of the personality, resulting in its weakening and a major loss of opportunity for fulfillment.

Various defensive maneuvers may be used to wall off aggression, all of which rob the personality of its aggressive component. Perhaps the most widely discussed defense against aggression is its splitting from the erotic impulse (e.g., Grotstein, 1986). As we will see in the next chapter, Kernberg (1975) views this defensive maneuver as a pathognomonic feature of the borderline personality disorder. For Winnicott, splitting is characteristic of any condition in which depressive anxiety causes aggression to be kept separate from objects of dependence and love. Patients who must maintain this split are forced to deploy aggression toward other objects, leading to a continual search for "bad objects" toward whom aggression can be directed. Conversely, dependent relationships must be kept conflict free, with any disturbance in them being experienced as a threat. This constellation of object relationships means that enemies must always be found and maintained and that love relationships will lack intensity and full excitement, since all aggression has been removed from the erotic impulse.

A more benign defense against aggression is reaction formation, whereby the child turns all aggressiveness into its opposite, is unable to experience aggression toward an object, and is unable to deploy aggression in the pursuit of life goals or ambitions. Since any conflict with others must be denied, the patient denies a great deal of reality to keep all relationships consistently positive. Further, when an aggressive response is needed for self-protection, the individual, having a general character inhibition, is unable to provide it. This formulation applies to patients typically described as passive or inadequate. It was Winnicott's (1950) belief that if aggressiveness is not integrated into the personality in the phase of relative dependence, the constructive goal-related pursuits of the individual are severely compromised and the result is passivity and inadequacy.

This principle is exemplified by a patient who was given to frequent destructive outbursts (Winnicott, 1963b). He began an analytic hour by expressing the wish that his analysis would be of value to the world. During this session the patient achieved a new awareness of his envy of Winnicott for being a good analyst; he also wished to thank Winnicott for meeting his needs.When Winnicott linked his destructive urge with his view of Winnicott as a good analyst the patient agreed but was relieved that Winnicott had not interpreted his wish to contribute to the world through his analysis as a defense against his wish to destroy in response to the initial remark. Winnicott (1963b) explained:

> He had to reach to the destructive urge before I acknowledged the repa-ration, and he had to reach it in his own time and in his own way. No doubt it was his capacity to have an idea of ultimately contributing that was making it possible for him to get into more intimate contact with his destructiveness. But constructive effort is false and meaningless unless, as he said, one has first reached to the destruction [pp. 80–81].

In Winnicott's view, the destructive and constructive urges are inextricably connected. Patients who cannot "reach to" their aggres-sion cannot make use of constructive energies; their zest for life is crippled. The therapeutic task with such patients is to help them find their destructive urge. As this clinical vignette demonstrates, patients find meaning in constructive desires and making contributions only after they fully experience their destructive impulses.

If the child is unable to "repair" the fantasized injury to the loved object, there is no opportunity to resolve guilt over aggressive feelings (Winnicott, 1963b). Like the character-inhibited patient, the depressive is anxious over aggression and unable to use it constructively. The dif-ference is that the depressed patient, crippled by guilt, directs aggres-sion against the self. The typical depressive symptoms of self-hatred and self-accusations are understood by Winnicott, as by Klein, as manifestations of guilt over the intention to injure the loved object. In its extreme form this dynamic results in "implosion," with rage being directed with uncontrolled fury at the self in order to protect the loved object (Winnicott, 1950). These patients run the greatest risk of suicide.

"Introversion" is also a regressive response to the failure of the environment to contain aggression in the phase of relative depen-dence (Winnicott, 1950). This defensive maneuver also involves a type of split, but in this case the good is kept within and all bad feelings are projected onto external objects. A persistent pattern of such projection defends against aggressiveness and provides relief from the guilt but fills the world with persecutors, with the result that withdrawal is then used as a defense against the world of hostile objects. The child may attempt a recovery from introversion by attacking the persecutors.

In Winnicott's view, this "acting out" is a healthy sign, but if it is misunderstood by the environment as a negative behavior, it will easily disappear, with the child lapsing back to introversion. In the extreme form of this pattern, the true self is hidden away, and a false self is created to hide it. In this way, conflicts over aggression can lead to true self–false self pathology.

As we have seen, Winnicott (1950) believed that aggressiveness plays so crucial a role in the development of the self that if it is disavowed the growing child will not feel real. To gain a feeling of reality, outlets are sought for the obstacles that provide an opportunity for an aggressive reaction. This is Winnicott's understanding of chronically aggressive patients. Since the feeling of reality only lasts as long as the expression of aggressiveness, such patients must continuously do battle; they seek opposition over and over again, even over seemingly inconsequential events, in a desperate struggle to feel real by aggressively opposing the environment. To an observer this type of patient may appear to be hostile or to have difficulty controlling aggressive impulses, but in Winnicott's view, the patient is attempting to achieve a sense of reality. The therapeutic task is to understand this meaning of the seemingly hostile behavior.

The traditional ego-psychological view of excessively aggressive patients is that they lack drive control regulation owing to defective ego structures. (In chapter 5 we will see that Kernberg put forward such a view.) In opposition to this approach, Winnicott saw a self-defining meaning in rageful behavior. The clinical implication of Winnicott's formulation that extremely aggressive patients are attempting to achieve a feeling of reality and a sense of self is that such patients need to be able to express their rage in the treatment setting. Expression of aggression must be permitted for a variety of reasons: First, the therapeutic environment must not repeat the mistake of the early caregivers by reacting negatively to aggressiveness; if therapists react by blocking aggressive outbursts, they risk colluding in the reenactment of the original trauma. Second, patients gain such sense of themselves as they have by the expression of aggressiveness; a negative reaction from the therapist robs such patients of their fragile sense of self and leads to still more desperate efforts to achieve selfhood. Finally, and most importantly, the hoped-for outcome of such expression is the fusion of aggressiveness with the erotic drive, from which it was originally de-fused as a reaction to trauma. In short, Winnicott felt that since excessive hostility is due to the failure of the early environment to contain the aggressive impulse, thus splitting it from the rest of the personality, the task of the therapeutic setting is to "contain" aggressiveness in order to reintegrate aggression into the personality. Containing the expression of aggressiveness is an example of the therapist's facilitating the resumption of the blocked maturational process by acting as a "good enough" mother.

Patients who need objects for their aggression may desperately attempt to "re-fuse" the erotic impulse with the aggressive drive (Winnicott, 1950). In such patients the erotic impulse, instead of being imbued with aggression, subserves aggression. In Winnicott's view, both sadism and masochism may be understood in this way. The origin of sadism lies in the need of the individual to feel real through ruthless, destructive attacks on others that are exciting by virtue of their fusion with the erotic impulse. To achieve this feeling, the object must not be simply a "bad object" suitable for attack but the recipient of erotic feelings. If the ruthless attacks are turned toward the self, masochism results.

How far was Winnicott willing to go in allowing the expression of the aggressive impulse? Little (1985) reported that Winnicott only rarely attempted control over her many aggressive outbursts. He forbade them verbally only when he felt that she was in danger—and he was not always successful. He held her hands—to contain her anxiety, not to control her aggressive outbursts. In one session, Little smashed and trampled a vase; Winnicott's response was to leave the room and return toward the end of the session. At the next session he had a new vase. The incident was neither interpreted nor discussed at any point; the only comment Winnicott made to her was that she had broken something valuable to him. He took quick preventive action only to protect Little. In one session, she intended to rush out of the office and drive away recklessly. Winnicott took her car keys until the end of the session. These incidents demonstrate that Winnicott allowed Little a full range of aggressive expression within the limit of assuring her safety. The protective measures he took strengthened the safety of the holding environment until her destructive urge could be integrated into her personality.

Winnicott's approach of allowing the expression of the aggressive impulse holds for all pathological reactions to aggressiveness. His treatment goal for splitting, reaction formation, and depression was to bring the aggressive impulse back into "fusion" with the erotic desire from which it was defused by environmental failure. The healthy personality has most of the aggressive impulse fused with the erotic drive, and the consequent ability to contain ambivalent feelings to whole objects and to enjoy healthy love relationships (Winnicott, 1950). Even in health there is always an aggressive component "left over" seeking obstacles for expression, but such aggressive expression is experienced joyfully as "appropriate opposition" is sought. In order for the patient to arrive at this level of development, the therapist must find the split-off or hidden aggression and allow its fullest possible expression in the safe environment of the treatment setting. Only when the aggression is allowed such full expression can it be fused with the erotic drive and integrated into the personality.

Aggression expressed outside the treatment setting was seen by Winnicott as a reaction to the environmental failure of the therapy, that is, as evidence that the patient found the setting unsafe for aggression. He deemphasized the role of interpretation here, as he did in the treatment of all preoedipal disorders. Since the treatment objective is to correct an early environmental failure, therapeutic action occurs by virtue of the provision of a safe environment for the expression of the aggressive impulse and its fusion with the erotic drive.

The phase of relative dependence marks the beginning of maternal expectations and thus gives rise to yet another potential source of pathology: the mother demands that the child be gratifying to her, the child must learn to adjust what it feels in order to please her. In this way, the mother molds such a child to please her at the expense of the child's own feelings. Once again, the "kernel" has been sacrificed to the "shell," and false-self pathology results. The child's aggression is a major feature of this syndrome: if the child's aggressiveness is threatening to the mother, the child must defend against its expression in order to allay her anxiety. If the mother is threatened by strong affect in general, the child must bury all its feelings, which is to say, its nascent personality. The result is a feeling of nonreality, leaving life empty. Such a patient appears to be treatable by traditional analysis, but treatment only begins when the true self is uncovered.

SUMMARY

Winnicott's theory of psychopathology and treatment is a direct outgrowth of his concept of development as a series of phases of dependence that must be overcome to arrive at a healthy, independent adult life. He saw all preoedipal forms of psychopathology as environmentally induced arrests in the movement from absolute dependence toward independence, that is, from omnipotence to reality. Treatment has to do with locating the developmental arrest and providing the appropriate environmental response. For patients with preoedipal psychopathology and for neurotic patients in moments of regression, psychotherapeutic action involves the provision of a therapeutic atmosphere in which patients have the developmental experiences they were denied in the preoedipal phase. The analytic process is used, but it is modified according to the developmental issue alive in the treatment at any given moment.

Winnicott proposed a hierarchy of values different from those in the traditional concept of psychoanalytic therapy. His fundamental premise is that psychoanalytic therapy is like the mother's role in development: its essence is adaptation to need. Just as the mother must understand the child's developmental level to provide for its needs, so too must the psychoanalytic therapist gear interventions to the patient's level of dependence and the associated developmental blocks. Interpretations are used insofar as they fit the developmental need, but adaptation is often the more appropriate modality. For example, if the patient is unable to integrate aggression with the erotic drive because of an early arrest in the experience of aggressiveness, the therapist's role is to help bring aggression into the patient's affection for the him or her so that the two impulses are "re-fused."

According to Winnicott, interpretations are most profitable when understanding meets the developmental need, but even neurotic patients frequently require other types of intervention. The traditional model sees interpretation as the only mode of therapeutic action; thus any need the patient appears to evince must be interpreted (Brenner, 1979; Gill, 1981). From this viewpoint, if the aggressive and erotic impulses are unintegrated, walled-off aggression would be interpreted, making the patient more aware of his or her aggressiveness within the transference. The developmental level of the conflict would also be interpreted to the patient, but any other response would violate the theoretical framework. By challenging the primacy of interpretation, Winnicott proposed a new, more developmentally grounded, model for psychoanalytic therapy. According to this alternative model, psychoanalytic therapy is the application of a developmental understanding of psychopathology, based on environmental failures encountered in phases of dependence, by means of the therapist's active adaptation to the patient's childhood needs as they become manifest in the therapeutic setting.

Winnicott's thought bears a clear similarity to Guntrip's view of the analytic process as offering a new beginning if the patient could reach the most regressed portion of the psyche. The difference is that Winnicott's more specific concept of development enabled him to gear treatment to the specific needs of individual patients, and thereby avoid the homogenization of pathology that we observed in Guntrip's work.

As we will see in chapter 6, Winnicott's thought anticipated certain features of Kohut's self psychology. Both theorists emphasized the relationship between self and object as the key to development, both recognized the importance of unrealistic expectations in early development, and both saw the development of the reality sense as a function of gradual environmental failure. In the clinical arena, Winnicott and Kohut were both sensitive to the importance of allowing patients illusions of self-aggrandizement until they were ready for the "descent" into reality. However, Kohut's developmental scheme, formulations of pathology, and treatment approach have certain essential differences from Winnicott's, as will be discussed in chapter 6.

Winnicott's view of psychoanalytic treatment is not to be confused with Franz Alexander's "corrective emotional experience." Alexander (1950) artificially constructed situations to induce certain experiences he thought would be therapeutic for the patient. Winnicott was opposed to artificiality in the treatment process, believing that action is therapeutic precisely because it adapts to a spontaneously expressed need of the patient and that the art of therapy lies in the ability to assess which developmental need is being manifested and determining how to meet it. For the "false self" patient, artificial contrivances are even more dangerous, since they fit into and buttress existing defenses.

The result of therapeutic adaptation to spontaneously expressed needs is an analytic space in which the patient creates a new self. It is insufficient, in Winnicott's view, to overcome the past. Indeed, it is probably not possible to overcome the past totally until new experience is integrated into the psyche.

Clearly, in many clinical situations Winnicott would assess and intervene differently from the manner prescribed by the traditional psychoanalytic approach. Perhaps more than any other psychoanalytic theorist, he based his interventions on the mother–infant relationship. In this sense, he is the most purely object relational of all analytic theorists.

CRITIQUE

Winnicott's theory is the most thorough, detailed, and consistent version of the developmental arrest form of object relations theories. The conceptualization of development in terms of phases of dependence has considerable observational and empirical support (e.g., Spitz, 1965; Mahler, 1975; Stern, 1980). Also impressive are the results Winnicott frequently reported in his discussion of clinical cases. He made many theoretical contributions, but perhaps his most lasting contribution is his belief that meaning can be sought in even the most bizarre clinical material.

There are, however, certain conceptual ambiguities in Winnicott's thought. First, the role of interpretation is not clear. If psychoanalysis is adaptation to need, it is not clear why the process should ever consist of interpretation. Winnicott's answer is that interpretation is an adaptation for some patients at certain times in the treatment. The difficulty lies in understanding how interpretation could ever be an adaptation to a developmental need. The child, after all, does not require interpretation. The logic of Winnicott's view of the analytic process as adaptation to arrested developmental needs would seem to obviate interpretation. Since Winnicott clearly did not draw this conclusion, the conceptual integration of interpretation in his treatment model is an enduring problem.

Second, it is not clear exactly what adaptation to a developmental need means. One cannot reverse time and begin the developmental process anew. Regression is not a return to an earlier fixation point, but the simulation of such a return (Bettelheim, 1972). It seems somewhat mysterious that periods of regression in the consulting office, often brief, could constitute the meeting of a developmental need. Winnicott seemed to feel that the patient could "re-live" episodes and even patterns in the analytic setting. But one may question whether such re-living can actually occur and, even if it can, how exactly one would know if and when it was occurring.

Beyond the problem of conceptualizing the re-living of earlier episodes in general is the validity of certain inferences Winnicott tended to make regarding the content of the re-living. This tendency to make inferential leaps is most striking in Winnicott's not infrequent interpretation that patients were re-living the birth process. For example, when Little was seized with terror during a therapy hour, Winnicott told her that she was re-living her birth. Such an inference is, to say the least, highly speculative, and one wonders on what basis it is justified. Further, such an interpretation requires the assumption that the patient remembers the birth experience, if not verbally, then somatically. This assumption, too, is highly questionable.

In short, there are conceptual difficulties with Winnicott's theory. Nonetheless, one cannot fail to be impressed with his clinical results, at least for some patients. To achieve these results, he stretched the concept of psychoanalysis considerably—his critics would say he distorted it beyond recognition. In fact, it is debatable whether his treatment approach ought to be called psychoanalysis. But more important than the label is the effectiveness of his treatment strategy. Winnicott found a way to reach some very disturbed patients, and this fact cannot be dismissed lightly. He exercised considerable influence on a number of analysts who attempted to apply some of his concepts in their own work. So whether or not Winnicott's work deserves to be labeled psychoanalysis, it has given many analysts useful technical principles and the courage to employ them in the treatment of severely disturbed patients. We conclude this chapter with a brief consideration of the work of some of Winnicott's closest followers.

THE "WINNICOTTIANS"

Winnicott's followers have tended to emphasize three primary aspects of his work: (1) the application of psychoanalytic therapy to severe emotional disorder; (2) the use of the psychoanalytic setting in this type of treatment; and (3) the role of the therapist and his countertransference in the analytic process, especially in working with severe pathology.

Khan (1963) believed that Winnicott contributed greatly to the understanding of psychopathology with his concept of environmental impingement. In Khan's view, Winnicott added a critical dimension to pathogenesis that is captured in the concept of the "cumulative trauma." The primary maternal function is to operate as a protective shield to keep impingements from interfering with ego development. In agreement with Winnicott, Khan believed that the infant needs a period of omnipotence before it can adapt to reality. The protective shield allows the child to have this illusion, but if there is a breach in it, trauma will accumulate silently as the child is forced into awareness of the environment before the ego is ready to manage reality awareness.

Children subjected to such cumulative trauma will be forced to adapt to the environment by the formation of a false self, and the development of psychological capacity will be arrested. The result is an inability to use symbolism (Khan, 1962). Such children utilize action to discharge tension states because they cannot use psychological means, such as language. The arrested psyche with little capacity for symbolism and covered by a false-self organization is Khan's description of the borderline personality disorder.

In Khan's view, the proper treatment approach is to recognize the acting out of such patients as their only means of communication and to tolerate it. The therapist acts as the protective shield so that the patient can eventually tolerate the inner panic defended against in the acting out (Khan, 1964). The analyst operates as an auxiliary ego, "holding" the situation until the patient can internalize the analyst as a new object. The relationship with the analyst is not a transference in the sense that the analyst is an object for the patient but the result of the process is that the analyst *becomes* an object. Such patients, lacking the ability to use symbols, communicate by what they make the analyst feel, often conveyed in silence (Khan, 1963). Consequently, the primary analytic instrument is the countertransference, and the analyst's task is to pay close attention to his reactions to the patient (Khan, 1960). The patient conveys an early primitive object relationship, and the feelings of the analyst may correspond either to the patient's early experience or to the experience of the object. This emphasis on the countertransference for understanding pathology and reversal of roles in the transference–countertransference enactment is the link between Khan's Winnicottian approach and the Kleinian school.

In Khan's view, Winnicott's concept of illusion, the transitional space between reality and fantasy, describes accurately the psychoanalytic space Freud created with his discovery of "cure by language" (Khan, 1971). Psychoanalysis creates an area of illusion so that symbolic discourse can take place. The borderline patient is unable to use this space and infuses it with action. The goal of treatment for such a patient is to gain the ability to utilize the analytic space through symbolic discourse. Since patients who possess symbolic capacity use the analytic space to create a new sense of self, the analyst also functions for these higher level patients as a vehicle for new self experience. In Khan's view, Freud's genius was in creating a setting in which new forms of self experience could be created, and Winnicott's brilliance lay in his ability to see Freud's work in this way.

Margaret Little, whose analysis with Winnicott has been described, also applied Winnicott's insights to severely disturbed patients. Little (1981) drew a critical distinction between transference neurosis and the delusional transference. Like Khan, she believed that the former is a relationship based on symbolism whereas the latter is an undifferentiated state in which words have little meaning. In Little's view, borderline and psychotic patients, who form delusional transferences, lack integration of psyche and soma. Such patients exist on the action level; they *must* act because their somatic existence is disconnected from the linguistic, or psychological, level. Consequently, they cannot use interpretations but require the presentation of reality, and the delusional transference must be broken up before interpretations are useful.

Little advocated two primary deviations from classical technique to dissolve the delusional transference so that interpretations could be employed. Like Khan, she believed that the use of the countertransference was critical to the treatment of severely disturbed patients who communicate experience by evoking feelings in the analyst. Little felt that in the countertransference lies the key to understanding. The aim of treatment in severe character pathology is not to understand the symbolic meaning of verbal communication, as it is with neurotic patients, but to understand the meaning of the analyst's reactions to the patient. In Little's view, if these patients are to let go of their transference delusions, the analyst must, at the appropriate point in treatment, let them know his or her feelings and reactions. This communication constitutes Little's first deviation from classical technique and its purpose is to help the patient differentiate reality from fantasy. Often the patient's perceptions of the analyst are accurate, and the patient needs to know this to appreciate the parents' real irrationality. Also, gaining knowledge of how the analyst feels can shock the patient into reality.

Little's second deviation from classical technique is her occasional use of physical intervention to help the patient dissolve the delusional transference. If Little felt there was no other way to "present reality" to the patient, she would make body contact, usually by reaching over and touching the patient. The purpose of this maneuver was to help the patient differentiate self from other. For example, Little put her hand on the ankle of a female patient who felt entrapped and let her push it away; the patient felt free, and this event marked the beginning of her sense of differentiation.

The breakup of the delusional transference, in Little's view, is similar to awakening from a dream. The patient must be confronted with reality, and the analyst's "personhood" and presence is the reality with which the patient must be confronted. It is up to each therapist to find the way to use his or her own reality to break up the delusional transference. Once it is dissolved, the patient advances to a symbolic level and can make use of interpretations.

For Little's technique to be effective, the analyst must respond from within, as a real person. Little not only saw the countertransference as a crucial component of the analytic process but also broadened the concept to embrace the analyst's total response to the patient. Although she agreed with Winnicott that there is an "objective" countertransference consisting of the analyst's reactions evoked by the patient, she also believed that the countertransference could not be limited to such feelings. The treatment of character-disordered patients, the group in which Little included most of her patients, required, in her view, a commitment from the analyst to go as far "into the patient's illness" as possible. Deprived patients must be given to before they can give, and what analysts can give is limited by who they are as a people. The patient's deepest needs cannot really be met; analysts can only offer themselves with their realistic strengths and limitations. However, these very limitations are not drawbacks but assets, since they make the reality of the analyst known to the patient.

In Little's case of Frieda, seven years of transference interpretations had no meaning until the patient's friend died and, Little expressed her feelings of sorrow, distress and pain for the patient in her grief. This open acknowledgement of feelings was the turning point of the analysis, since the patient felt for the first time that the analyst was "a real person" and not "counterfeit" like her parents. Thereafter, transference interpretations began to have meaning to her. It was Little's contention that if she had not genuinely felt distress and pain on hearing of the friend's death, her expression of feelings would not have been effective.

André Green is the other major contributor to psychoanalysis whose views grow out of Winnicott's thought. Green (1978) pointed out that psychoanalysis has refound subjectivity in object relations theory. He noted that in Freud's metapsychology the object is linked to the drive, not the subject. In object relations theories, however, the complement of the object is not the ego but the self, making the subject as an experiencing person the central focus of the analytic process. In Green's (1978) view, Winnicott made several lasting contributions to psychoanalysis: (1) he made psychoanalytic theory applicable to borderline personality disorders, which, Green felt are the paradigmatic cases of our time; (2) he put the countertransference in the center, not the periphery, of the treatment process; (3) he gave theoretical focus to the psychoanalytic setting; and (4) he made the patient's experience, rather than theoretical schematizing, his primary concern.

According to Green, Winnicott recognized that a crucial aspect of development is the evolution of the child's sense of the object from the "subjective object" to the "objective object" and that the role of the mother is crucial in this process. Borderline and other severe character pathology is characterized by arrest in the transitional phase between the delusion of the "subjective object" and the recognition of objective reality (Green, 1975). The implication for treatment of such patients is the use of the "analytic space" for the creation of a new object. The analyst is a participant in this endeavor, since the new object is created out of the therapeutic interaction, just as early objects in normal development are created out of the mother–child relationship. In Green's view, Winnicott made a seminal contribution with his reconceptualization of the role of the analyst from detached observer to a participant in the process. The aim of treatment is to make the "analytic object," which is created out of the therapeutic interaction, usable by the patient in the analyst's absence. In Green's view, among all psychoanalytical theoreticians, only Winnicott conceptualized the analytic setting as potential space for the creation of a new object and this concept describes the analytic process and its goals for today's patient more accurately than does Freud's notion of the blank screen on which templates from the past are projected.

The pathology of the borderline personality disorder is conceptualized by Green (1977, 1978) as an absence. While neurosis may be usefully conceptualized in terms of conflictual mental representations, the key feature of the borderline personality is the very lack of object representation, resulting in a blankness, a lack of self development. According to Green, treatment of such a patient cannot be focused upon "dis-covery" because no object is to be found. In Green's view, it was Winnicott's unique contribution to understand that the conceptualization of transference as repetition of early object relations is not applicable to character pathology. Rather, the essence of treatment must be the transformation of absence into potentiality by the creation of the "analytic object." Green believes the future of psychoanalysis rests in this conceptualization because it applies to the most typical cases now seen in treatment.

Green (1975) agreed with Little that the split between psyche and soma makes borderline patients unable to use symbols. Such borderline patients communicate either by action, acting out, or somatization, and the therapeutic challenge is to translate this type of language into verbalization. In Green's (1977) view, the primary tool in this process is the countertransference. His view, in agreement with Little's, is that therapists must use the feelings induced in them by borderline patients as the key to understanding. The other primary technical instrument used by Green is the analytic setting, which, if properly employed, can become a metaphor for maternal care. Since the provision of a "good enough" environment is believed to facilitate the use of symbols, Green, like Little, supported variations in technique for the purpose of fostering the use of symbolization. In the analyst's efforts to use himself or herself to facilitate symbolization, analyst and patient alike will come upon the analyst's own limitations, but in Green's view, these limitations are a crucial part of the treatment, as they aid patients in their journey toward the recognition of reality.

Green's views have much in common with those of Little and, to a lesser extent, of Khan. All three Winnicottians see Winnicott's lasting contribution as his reconceptualization of the analytic process as the unblocking of early developmental arrest by the creation of a new object and its corollary, a new self. Analysis becomes an experience with a new person that allows for the transcendence of old perceptions, patterns of relating, and defenses.

Thus, Winnicott and his followers shift Freud's model of a detached scientist observing and providing insight to a model of two selves in interaction. Both participants in the exercise are affected, and both are undoubtedly changed. The outcome is successful if the patient becomes a new person, experiencing himself or herself and others in new and richer ways.

CHAPTER 5

The Work of Otto Kernberg

OTTO KERNBERG'S CONCEPTUAL FRAMEWORK IS CHARACTERIZED BY A BLEND of object relations theory and ego psychology. Kernberg (1972) wrote a thorough critique of the Kleinian school, emphasizing its violation of ego psychological principles of theory and technique and suggesting that Klein's object relations approach to development and psychopathology be integrated with the findings of ego psychology. Kernberg's work may be looked upon as an effort to achieve the goal he outlined in that critique. As we shall see, Kernberg utilizes Klein's theoretical tools in his conceptualization of severe personality disorders, but he makes major modifications in Klein's theory of development and does not adhere to Klein's principles of technique, preferring to focus interpretation on specific types and levels of defense as described in ego psychology.

Kernberg offered several major criticisms of Klein's views, three of which were discussed in chapter 3; namely, Klein's adultomorphism, her pathologizing of development, and her assaultive interpretive approach. In addition, Kernberg attacked Klein for failing to appreciate the importance of diagnosis and the need to adapt treatment to the type and severity of the disorder and for her disregard of environmental factors, neglect of psychological structure, conceptualism of defensive organization and developmental process, and ambiguity in terminology. Despite all the weaknesses he finds in Kleinian theory, Kernberg accepts the importance of early object relationships, aggression, envy, splitting, and the projective–introjective processes in both early development and the pathogenesis of character pathology. Kernberg also adopts Klein's view of the defensive constellations against aggression and envy and her notion of early superego formation.

The other major influence on Kernberg's object relations psychology was Edith Jacobson. From Jacobson, Kernberg (1980) takes the concept of ego development as a product of object relationships. As discussed in chapter 1, in Jacobson's (1964) view, life begins with an initial undifferentiated phase, out of which object-representations of the self and objects gradually become differentiated in the second phase, although they are still split between "all good" and "all bad." The third phase involves the integration of the self- and object images to form psychic structure and affects become intrapsychic regulators by means of their investment in representations of the self and objects. Similarly, Jacobson believed that the superego was formed from the integration of the initially split bad-object images with the ego-ideal and parental prohibitions. Kernberg builds on Jacobson's developmental integration of object relations theory and ego psychology to construct his general theory of psychopathology.

Kernberg (1980) was also influenced by Mahler's theory that after the child emerges from the symbiotic phase, it enters the separation-individuation process, which ends in the oedipal phase (Mahler et al., 1975). Kernberg's view concurs with Mahler's formulation that pre-oedipal development includes a gradual process of separating from the maternal figure and individuation of the sense of self and that these issues influence oedipal development. However, Kernberg's view of severe character pathology tends to emphasize Klein's concept of splitting more than Mahler's subphases of the separation-individuation process.

METAPSYCHOLOGY

Although Kernberg, like Klein, adheres to the dual-drive theory, the primary motivational system for Kernberg consists of inborn affect dispositions. All gratifying and frustrating experiences stimulate affect, which is initially pleasure and unpleasure. Early affect states are organized in this very rudimentary way, but as perceptual and cognitive elaboration increases, affective states become increasingly more complex and their discharge function becomes less important. Since the child's experiences with the environment trigger its affective states, the affect is always embedded within a relationship between self- and object images, however rudimentary they may be. These object relations units are stored as "affective memory." The experiential store of psychological experience upon which the psyche is constructed consists, therefore, of object relations units, each of which consists of a self- and object image and a connecting affective link.

Kernberg (1976) makes an effort to integrate psychoanalytic drive theory with the modern concept of instinct, pointing out that the trend in both ethology and neuropsychology is away from the view of instincts as given responses to specific environmental circumstance and toward a concept of instincts as "organizations which, through learning, integrate various inborn patterns ('building blocks') into flexible, overall plans"(p. 86). He notes that Freud differentiated the biological *Instinkte* from *Trieb*, or drive, which lies on the borderline between the biological and the psychological. Instincts are discrete, self-preservative behavioral responses called upon when necessary. Drives are cyclical, initially physiological stimulations to action that motivate behavior for their gratification and therefore give rise to wishes, their psychological expression. Freud's *Trieb* is, for Kernberg, an organized system built on the initially discrete "instinctive components," or "building blocks," that are "released" by the mother–child interaction. Kernberg's concept that drive develops in the context of the mother–child relationship is similar to Loewald's (1971) view. Kernberg argues that the innate, instinctive components gradually develop into the drive organization as pleasure becomes a component of libidinal object relations units and "unpleasure" evolves into aggressive object relations units. In accordance with this shift, affects change their function as they and the developing drive system become more complex; at first organizers of the instinctive components, affects become "signals" of the drive organization.

One can see from these conceptualizations that for Kernberg drives are not inborn motivational units, as they are for Klein. Affective dispositions and instinctive, behavioral "building blocks" are inborn, but the drive organization is conceptualized as an outcome of developmental experience that begins as undifferentiated object relations units and develops gradually into more complex object relationships. In its psychological form, a drive is represented by a wish for an object. Given this, one might conclude that object relationships replace both drives and affects as the primary motivational system in Kernberg's theory. This is just the conclusion drawn by Fairbairn and Guntrip (see chapter 2). Kernberg, however, chooses not to view object seeking as primary.

Kernberg (1976) offers three reasons for his opposing Fairbairn's and Guntrip's replacement of drive theory by an object-seeking model. First, the Fairbairn-Guntrip view ignores the importance of the aggressive drive, which seeks not to attach to an object but to eliminate it. Second, the organization of the psyche into "good" and "bad" object images is more important than the fact that the contradictory affects are directed to the same object. Finally, making object striving primary ignores qualitative shifts in the drives during crucial developmental advances, such as the transformation of libido into the genital organization in the oedipal phase; that is, the striving for the breast is not the same as genital wishes, a difference that Kernberg believes is abolished by the primacy that Fairbairn and Guntrip place on object seeking. For these reasons, Kernberg's view differs from those of Fairbairn and Guntrip and maintains the primacy of drives in development; Kernberg views affect, not the object relationship, as the primary motivator of the psyche. It should be emphasized, however, that since affects are always experienced within an object relationship, in Kernberg's formulation, the two are difficult to differentiate.

Like Klein, Kernberg (1976) assumes that positive early experience leads to libidinal object relationships and negative experience results in aggressive object relationships. Unlike Klein, but in accordance with Jacobson, he believes that the development of these object relationships results in the structure of the ego, which determines the health or pathology of the personality. As opposed to classical ego psychology, which views ego structure as a product of drives and their vicissitudes, Kernberg's theory emphasizes that ego structure results from object relations units, which also determine the drive organization. Development, for Kernberg, consists of a series of internalizations of object relations units and the defenses against them. The dynamic unconscious, therefore, consists of object relations units defended against, and hence made unconscious, by either primitive early defenses or more advanced later defenses. Whereas for Klein and her followers psychological structure is tantamount to object relations fantasies, for Kernberg, as for mainstream theorists, there is a clear distinction between fantasy and structure: the object relationship leads to psychic structure but is not equivalent to it.

The internalization of object relationships is of three types in Kernberg's (1976) scheme. The most primitive form of internalization is introjection. Whole interactions with the environment are taken into the psyche and reproduced with the corresponding self- and object image and affective coloring. In the next phase the child begins to identify with the parent as the developing ego takes in the role aspect of social interaction. In Kernberg's view, the child's imitation of the mother and the performance of roles constitute the first identifications and the intermediate level of internalization. The highest level of internalization in this scheme falls under the rubric of ego identity, which Kernberg (1976) defines as "the overall organization of identifications and introjections under the guiding principle of the synthetic function of the ego" (p. 32). These three modes of psychological growth and organization occur in developmental sequence and we shall now turn to this development view of the internalization of object relations.

DEVELOPMENT

Kernberg (1976) divides development into five stages. In the first month (Stage 1), the normal undifferentiated self–object representation is built. From the second month until about the sixth to eighth month (Stage 2), self- and object images become differentiated. Also, the consolidation of the "good" self- and object representations occurs in response to pleasurable, positive mother–child interactions. Simultaneously, all negative experiences become organized into "bad" self- and object representations. These two separate object relations units constitute the first introjections. The good self- and object representations become invested with libido whereas the bad self- and object representations are invested with aggression. Initially, these two kinds of object relations units are separate because of the physiological inability of the primitive ego structure to integrate them. Beginning at about the third to fourth month the ego actively splits the two kinds of self- and object images apart in order to protect the "good" self- and object images from the destructiveness of the bad images. At this point splitting becomes the primary defense of the developing ego. This stage encompasses Mahler's symbiotic phase, in which self and object are not yet distinguished, and her differentiation subphase of the separation-individuation process. Kernberg collapses the two phases in his developmental schema because he believes that in the differentiation subphase refusion of self- and object images takes place frequently.

The third stage begins with the differentiation of self- and object images within the good and bad object relations units and ends with the integration of both good and bad self-images and good and bad object images. It begins at about six to eight months and lasts until 18 to 36 months, when the integration of self- and object images results in object constance. At the beginning of this phase re-fusion of self- and object images still can happen under stress, but during this phase ego boundaries are sufficiently well established that they are maintained even under stressful conditions. In this schema, just before or during the third year the child begins to integrate good and bad images in both his self- and object representations. By the end of this phase, good and bad self-representations are consolidated into an integrated self-concept, and good and bad object images form total object representations.

Stage 4 extends throughout the oedipal period and is characterized by the solidification of libidinally and aggressively invested self-images into "a definite self system" and good and bad object images into "total object representations." Ego, id, and superego become differentiated as defined psychological structures. While one can see Kleinian influence in Kernberg's emphasis on early splitting and the development of self and object integration, in contrast to Klein, Kernberg believes that the integration of self- and object representations in this phase means that repression replaces splitting as the primary defensive organization, thus allowing for the division of the psyche into ego, superego, and id. Whereas for the Kleinians repression is pathological only if it is related to unresolved splitting, for Kernberg the appearance of repression involves the establishment of a new defensive organization that can be pathogenic in itself. Negative introjects are no longer split off into a separate ego organization but are repressed within a unitary psychological structure. It is only at this point that psychological structure is formed and an ego organization can be meaningfully spoken of. In this way, Kernberg integrates Klein's object relations theory with the ego psychological emphasis on structure. In Kernberg's formulation, ego identity is established in this phase as a result of the integration of self- and object representations.

According to Kernberg, the integration of self- and object images gives rise to ideal self-representation and ideal object representations. Following Jacobson, Kernberg believes that these ideal representations must be integrated with the earlier fantastical, sadistic superego forerunners. Under optimal circumstances the consolidation of these sadistic, attacking superego precursors with the new ideal-representations and with realistic parental prohibitions leads to the superego as an independent psychic agency.

The final stage of development, Stage 5 in Kernberg's formulation, is the consolidation of ego and superego integration. As the superego becomes consolidated, its sharp distinction from the ego decreases and the superego is gradually integrated into the personality. The integration of the superego reciprocally fosters ego identity, which also continues to develop and solidify through effective relations with others, which are in turn made possible by the already achieved integration of the psyche. The modulation of object images in the previous phase allows for satisfying relations with external objects, which, in turn, help solidify both self- and object images. If all goes well in this phase, relationships with the world continue to solidify the integrated self- and object images and with them, the integration of ego and superego.

In Kernberg's developmental scheme two key steps are crucial to avoiding the development of severe psychopathology. First, self–object differentiation must take place. The failure of this psychic reorganization corresponds to the psychotic potential of the developing personality. When self–object boundaries become established, the psyche is defined as separate from the environment, but the psychological organization continues to be defined by splitting and its related defenses. The second crucial developmental step is the shift from splitting to self- and object-integration, which, for Kernberg, is equivalent to the shift from a split ego to an integrated ego that organizes defenses around repression. Failure to achieve this developmental milestone results in ego weakness and severe character pathology. Once repression and related defenses replace splitting as the primary organizer of the psyche, the ego is integrated and neurosis is the worst possible outcome.

PSYCHOPATHOLOGY

These stages of development, for Kernberg (1976), demarcate the developmental issues of the major categories of psychopathology. Fixation in the first stage results in the failure to develop the undifferentiated self–object image and inability to form a symbiotic bond with the maternal figure. The resulting pathology is autistic psychosis. Personality arrest in the second stage is reflected in the lack of differentiation of self–object boundaries; the child never emerges from, or regresses to, the symbiotic phase, when self- and object-representations were merged. Here Kernberg places adult schizophrenia, psychotic depression, and childhood symbiotic psychosis. Although Kernberg mentions these disorders in the context of his overall theory of development and pathology, he does not discuss pathological fixations in Stages 1 or 2 and offers no contribution to their understanding and treatment. Kernberg makes the disorders originating in Stage 3 the focus of his theory of psychopathology.

Kernberg proposes a classification of character pathology based on the developmental shift from splitting to repression. "Low level" character disorders are those organized around splitting and related defenses. Character pathology at this level has its fixation point in Stage 3, as positive and negative self- and object-representations have not been integrated. There is so little superego integration that superego "nuclei" tend to be projected, resulting in paranoia as a major character trait in these patients. According to Kernberg, since their character traits are "instinctually infiltrated," such patients tend to be impulsive. Because splitting is the primary organizer of the psyche, there is little ego integration or object constancy. Kernberg includes in such low level character pathology the borderline personality organization, many narcissistic personalities, sexual deviancy, hypomanic disorders; most infantile personalities; antisocial, impulse-ridden, "as if," and inadequate personalities; and prepsychotic character disorders. In all these character disorders, which share the use of splitting and related defenses, pathology is defined by the failure to develop the integrated object relationships out of which an integrated ego and superego emerge.

In the intermediate and higher level character disorders, where the integration of self- and object representations has been achieved and object relationships are stable, pathology results from conflict between ego and superego structures.

In the intermediate level of character pathology Kernberg places all character disorders that primarily utilize repression, but that use some lower level defenses such as splitting as well. At this level the superego is severe, but it is not well integrated; that is, the harsh sadistic superego exists alongside the primitive ego ideal. Intermediate level character patterns involve fewer inhibitions and more impulsivity than higher level character disorders and some degree of splitting. Kernberg includes in this category passive–aggressive, sadomasochistic, infantile, and many narcissistic personalities. In all these personality disorders the defenses organized around repression are used, but not exclusively. The clear separation of instinct and defense characteristic of pathology in the high level character disorders is lacking here because the ego structure is neither as well organized nor as stable. Kernberg believes psychoanalysis is the treatment of choice for these disorders but acknowledges that the treatment will be lengthy and difficult and may involve modifications in some cases.

Character pathology organized around repression and related defenses, such as suppression, isolation of affect, and intellectualization, is high level pathology because the ego has an organization that clearly separates defense and drive. Character defenses at this level tend to be phobias, inhibitions, and reaction formation. Kernberg includes in this category hysterical, obsessive–compulsive, and depressive–masochistic personality types. Here, character pathology has advanced beyond Stage 3 in his schema to the structuralization of the ego. The superego has become consolidated as a separate psychic agency, but it is not integrated into the ego. Consequently, its severity inhibits affects and personality development in general. The result is an organized ego that can function but at the cost of diminished emotional gratification, at best, or severe depression and complete inability to experience satisfaction, at worst. Because conflicts take place within an organized psyche, the treatment of choice for the highest level of character pathology is psychoanalysis.

It should be noted that narcissistic personalities are placed at different levels of Kernberg's schema, resulting in some confusion regarding his categorization of these cases. Pathological narcissism is placed on a spectrum ranging from Stage 3 to 4. Kernberg categorizes most narcissistic cases in Stage 4, with regression to Stage 3. He views these cases as fluctuating between the two stages, since the majority of narcissistic personalities are not completely fixated in Stage 3 like patients with borderline personality organization, but have not advanced to complete self- and object integration.

It can be seen from this discussion that Kernberg's classification of character pathology has direct treatment implications. The decision to conduct psychoanalysis proper or expressive psychotherapy depends on the diagnosis of character pathology. Since these treatments have distinct attributes, diagnosis, for Kernberg, is a task of considerable importance. Consistent with his structural understanding of personality and pathology, Kernberg focuses his diagnostic approach on the organization of object relationships. The patient's psychological structure is reflected in the degree of identity integration, characteristic defenses, and capacity for reality testing. The interviewer seeks to determine if the patient is dominated by introjection, has some degree of identification, or has achieved ego identity. The diagnostician is especially attuned to the determination of whether self–object differentiation has occurred and, if so, whether the defenses are organized around splitting or if a significant degree of ego and object integration has been achieved. To accomplish these goals, the interviewer has three diagnostic tasks: he must explore the patient's subjective world, observe the patient–interviewer interaction, and observe his or her own reactions.

The content of the interview is initially conducted along the lines of the standard assessment interview, but when symptoms appear during the interview, Kernberg (1984) recommends that the interviewer utilize the three therapeutic techniques: clarification, confrontation, and interpretation. Clarification is the request for explanation of what is unclear or contradictory at the conscious or preconscious level. In confrontation, the interviewer directs the patient's attention to information he or she has presented that is contradictory and to the presence of conflictual functioning and relates these observations to other areas of the patient's life and functioning. Interpretation is the offering of possible unconscious motivations for the perceived areas of conflict. In this process the interviewer builds up a view of the patient's self- and object images that allows a placement of the patient into one of the three broad categories of personality organization or, if the patient is character disordered, into one of the subgroups of character pathology.

The value of Kernberg's comprehensive diagnostic system and conceptualization of development and psychopathology lies in the application of his object relations/ego psychology integration to severe personality disorders, especially the borderline and narcissistic organizations. Like Jacobson (1964) and Mahler (1975), Kernberg applies a psychoanalytic approach to the "intermediary" area of developmental experience between merger and the formation of psychic structure, an area that he feels accounts for pathology between psychosis and neurosis. In this way, Kernberg contributes to what Stone (1954) referred to as the "widening scope of psychoanalysis."

The Borderline Personality Organization

Borderline pathology, according to Kernberg (1975), is in essence the failure to resolve the critical task of Stage 3 to integrate good and bad self- and object images. Borderline patients, in this view, have not been able to blend these two types of images into an integrated self-concept or whole-object representations. Either because of inborn excessive aggressiveness and inability to tolerate frustration or because of severe trauma in this phase leading to excessive aggressiveness, the good self- and object representations are continually threatened by bad representations of both types resulting in splitting the good and bad self- and object representations. The integration of the ego, which leads to the tripartite division organized around repression as the principal defense, does not develop, and the result is general ego weakness, as the ego structure necessary to manage tensions and conflicts between drives, superego strictures, and the environment is missing. Rather than the structured ego that is the normal outcome of Stage 3, one sees a fixation at the primitive defensive organization of the splitting phase, including projection, projective identification, and introjection.

This primitive defensive organization can result in fusion of self- and object images in close relationships, leading to transient psychotic episodes. Nonetheless, reality testing remains intact in other situations, since self- and object images have become differentiated in the previous phase. This defensive constellation organized around splitting and the tendency to fuse in close relationships while reality boundaries are maintained in other situations defines the borderline personality organization in Kernberg's view. He believes that most cases falling within this category require psychoanalytic therapy with parameters in order to control severe, frequently psychotic transference regressions. In his more recent writing Kernberg has expressed more optimism regarding unmodified psychoanalytic treatment for at least some borderline patients (Kernberg, 1984).

Kernberg (1975) enumerates the following as typical symptoms and character patterns of the disorder (although no single symptom is pathognomonic): chronic, diffuse anxiety; polysymptomatic neurosis; polymorphous perverse sexual trends; paranoia; schizoid personality; hypomanic and cyclothymic personality; infantile, "as if," antisocial, and narcissistic personalities; and impulse neuroses (Kernberg, 1975). Some combination of these symptoms is present in all borderline personality organizations, resulting in the chaotic, confusing, disorganized clinical presentations so characteristic of these patients. The presenting features suggest a diagnosis of borderline personality organization, but in place of the *DSM-III* approach to diagnosis by the enumeration of symptoms, which has no apparent relevance to treatment, Kernberg (1984) proposes an assessment of the psychological structure of the patient, which he believes has direct treatment implications. The manifest symptoms, some of which will appear in every borderline personality, are, in his view, a product of an ego structure that is not simply defective but is based on pathological internalized object relations and the use of splitting as an active defense to keep apart good and bad object representations. Thus, Kernberg uses this fixation point to explain virtually all the symptoms and character features typically found in the borderline personality organization.

Kernberg's structural analysis of the borderline personality organization includes four structural indicators: "non-specific manifestations of ego weakness," splitting, a shift toward primary-process thinking, and pathology of internalized object relationships. Kernberg attributes the nonspecific manifestations of ego weakness to the split between libidinal and aggressive self- and object images that prevents the integration of the ego structure necessary for the management of anxiety and impulse. Here Kernberg invokes Hartmann's (1939) concept (discussed in chapter 1), that libido neutralizes aggressiveness and integrates it into psychic structure. When the two drive organizations are split, the ego cannot be structuralized and lacks the ability to manage anxiety and impulse. Since the specific defense mechanisms of borderline pathology—splitting, primitive idealization, denial, devaluation, and omnipotence—are organized around splitting object relationships, this second structural indicator is tantamount to the characteristic object relationships of the disorder. Kernberg attributes the "shift

toward primary process thinking" primarily to the pathology of internalized object relationships and the "reactivation" of splitting and
related defenses, which, as we have seen, is pathology of internalized
object relationships; thus, this structural indicator is a product of
regression in object relationships. The fourth structural indicator,
pathology of internalized object relationships, is tantamount to splitting. Thus, Kernberg's four structural characteristics of the borderline
personality organization are all attributable to splitting good and bad
self- and object images and its consequences.

Splitting is illustrated by Kernberg's brief description of Miss A
(Kernberg et al., 1988). The patient viewed the therapist in two distinct ways: as a strict parent and as a loving, tolerant person. When
the therapist was seen as the harsh object, Miss A experienced herself as depreciated and hated herself and her body. When the therapist was a positive, caring object-representation, she felt caressed
and loved and felt free to express her wishes to exhibit her body.
Each object image was linked to its corresponding self-image by an
affective state, but the two self- and object image units were not
experienced by the patient as belonging to the same self or object.
This separation of the two disparate views of self and object is the
clinical manifestation of the use of splitting as a defense. Miss A's
feelings of fear of the object and her self-depreciation and hatred
were too extreme to be connected to the positive feelings she also
had about the therapist and herself; she feared that she would be
damaged, if not destroyed, by the contact.

The conclusion to be drawn from this account of the borderline personality organization is that the chaos and confusion of the presenting
clinical picture is not simply an indication of an ego defect. Ego psychologists have tended to view the deficits seen in the borderline personality solely as "weaknesses" in the structure of the psyche. While
Kernberg fully recognizes the defects in the ego of the borderline
patient, he considers them to be an outcome of the active use of splitting to keep "good" and "bad" self- and object images apart. In other
words, what appears to be chaos betokens an active defensive process.
In this sense, Kernberg, like Winnicott, is a critic of the purely ego-
psychological approach to severe character pathology, as he believes
the description of ego defects does not provide a sufficient explanation
for the structural organization of the psyche.

In Kernberg's view other characteristic defense mechanisms of the
borderline personality are products of the split-ego organization.
Because the good object representation is unable to withstand contact
with the bad object representation, it must be free from all negative

features and all aggressiveness, so that it easily becomes an unrealistic, all-powerful, all-good object image. Kernberg (1975) differentiates this "primitive idealization" from later idealizations based on reaction formation that are motivated by the need to defend against aggressiveness. Primitive idealization involves no aggressiveness, consciously or unconsciously; it is a "primitive fantasy structure in which there is no real regard for the ideal object, but a simple need for it as a protection against a surrounding world of dangerous objects" (p. 30).

Another consequence of split self- and object images is that the patient is left with excessively aggressive images of both types, unmitigated by positive contact. The pain of these images leads to the need to project them; consequently, paranoid trends are strong in the borderline patient. The immediate consequence of the projection is fear of retaliation from the now dangerous "external" object that contains the projected aggressiveness. Kernberg calls this an "early form" of projection. Since the projection tends to be unsuccessful owing to the weak ego boundaries, borderline patients utilize projective identification by identifying with the object onto whom their aggressiveness has been projected, exacerbating the fear of their own projected aggressiveness. To protect themselves, these patients attempt to control the object in order to avoid attack, further weakening ego boundaries. In close affective relationships patients alternate self- and object images so quickly and intensely that reality testing becomes lost and regression to psychosis may occur within the context of these relationships while reality boundaries are maintained in all other situations. This is why loss of self–object boundaries is common in these patients' close relationships. This type of projection is to be contrasted with its forms, found in neurotic pathology, in which ego boundaries are delineated so that there is no need to control the projected affects and projective identification is unnecessary. As shall be seen later, the loss of reality boundaries in borderline patients has critical implications for the transference of these patients.

Borderline patients use denial to maintain splitting, since they must be able to "mutually deny" two areas of consciousness. Denial may manifest itself as a simple disregard of entire areas of subjective experience or as actual denial that they exist. If pressed, patients may be able to acknowledge that what they experience now contradicts what they felt and said previously, but the denied sector of the personality has no emotional relevance.

The final defenses Kernberg lists as characteristic of the borderline personality organization are omnipotence and devaluation. Again, Kernberg (1975) acknowledges that these defenses are also "intimately linked to splitting" (p. 33). The identification with the all good self-image easily results in a sense of omnipotence, or grandiosity. In a subgroup of borderline patients, to be discussed in the next section, the fusion of self-concept, ego-ideal, and ideal object results in the narcissistic personality structure. However, in all borderline patients, the tendency to feel omnipotent is strong, since the patients identify with the all good self-image to protect against the painful all bad self-image fraught with self-hatred and insecurity. The omnipotence defense also protects against persecutory anxiety, since the patient lives in continual fear of persecutory objects owing to the projection of oral rage.

Devaluation of the object is another major defense against persecutory anxiety, as the patient attempts to keep the object from appearing dangerous. The aforementioned "primitive idealization" also serves this function by endowing the object with magical qualities. The patient appears to submit to a "magical," idealized figure but, according to Kernberg, treats the object ruthlessly, exploiting it only for protection and gratification. When the object can no longer serve these functions, it is easily devalued and rejected. However, devaluation is not simply a response to the idealized object's failures in this regard: it is a defense against the need for and fear of the object. Because the patient still needs the protection of idealization, a cycle of idealization and devaluation ensues. The patient's grandiosity fits both sides of the cycle, as it is gratified by identification with a magical, idealized figure and also allows for haughty devaluation of objects no longer deemed necessary for protection or gratification.

From the brief discussion of the characteristic defenses of the borderline personality organization it can be seen that they all follow from the predominance of splitting in the organization of the psyche. The separation of all good and all bad self- and object images leads to primitive idealization of the all good object image, fantasied omnipotence in the all good self-image, the use of denial to keep the oppositely valenced images apart, projection and projective identification to get rid of the all bad self-image, and devaluation to protect against the persecutory object filled with projected aggressiveness.

The typical constellation of defenses seen in the borderline personality organization is found in the case of Miss B, who had great difficulty committing to treatment and had a history of failed relationships (Kernberg, et al., 1988). This patient went to great lengths to be able to begin treatment with her therapist, whom she considered the only person who could help her. However, no sooner had she obtained entry into treatment than she began to devalue him as "provincial," intellectually inadequate, lacking in sophistication, and without sufficient self-assurance. At one point she seriously considered moving to San Francisco to live with a man whom she believed to be far more sophisticated than the therapist. In response to this devaluation, which was delivered in a superficially friendly manner, the therapist felt dejected, devalued, and despairing of the treatment until he realized that Miss B was wreaking her vengeance on the therapist for what she presumed was his feeling of superiority when she was so desperate to be accepted into therapy with him. Further, since her mother adopted toward her the same attitude of quiet superiority and subtle devaluation that made the patient feel stupid, inferior, despairing, and incapable of living up to expectations, the patient was evoking in the therapist the same sense of inadequacy and despair she had been made to feel. Her image of the therapist as provincial, unattractive, and intellectually slow was Miss B's self-image when she felt criticized by her mother. When the therapist pointed this out, "she now reverted to a dependent relationship with the therapist, practically without transition, while projecting the haughty, derogatory aspects of herself as identified with mother onto the man from San Francisco" (Kernberg et al., 1988).

Idealization was Miss B's initial defense until the relationship with the therapist became a reality, at which point she shifted quickly to devaluation to protect herself. This led to her primary defense of projective identification: Miss B attempted to rid herself of her infantile, negative self-image by projecting it into the therapist, whom she attempted to control with subtle denigration. As she did so, she became her aloof, haughty mother, adopting an omnipotent posture while devaluing the therapist. When this dynamic was shown to her, she quickly shifted roles once again, becoming dependent on the therapist—and presumably reverting to idealization to some degree, as the man from San Francisco suddenly became the object of her devaluation defense. Miss B showed no awareness of the shift nor of the existence of conflict among her disparate ego states. Kernberg points out that this quick oscillation and lack of awareness indicates the existence of split object relations units, the pathognomonic indicator of the borderline personality organization. This brief description of the case of Miss B shows in condensed fashion many of the characteristic defenses of the borderline personality organization. In the section on treatment, we will have occasion to return to this case to demonstrate the technique Kernberg advocates for the resolution of borderline defensive operations.

The superego pathology of borderline patients is a direct product of the defensive organization. Because the self-image is split between all good and all bad, there is no opportunity for superego integration. As we saw in the discussion of development, in Kernberg's view, normal superego integration results from the integration of the sadistic, highly fantastical superego forerunners with the ideal object-representations and with normal parental prohibitions as the split self- and object-representations are integrated into the ego structure. However, if the splitting process becomes entrenched as a defensive organization, instead of this integration into realistic self-regulating capacity, the internal prohibitions of the psyche are left to the primitive, sadistic self-attacks of the splitting stage. The ideal object-representations become condensed into the sadistic superego forerunners, and no realistic parental prohibitions are integrated into this primitive structure. This is what happens in the borderline personality organization, as Kernberg conceives it. Such patients can control themselves only with harsh self-attacks, which explains their intensely negative self-devaluation. To defend themselves against the pain of these self-attacks, borderline patients identify with their ideal self-image and resort to grandiosity, feeling themselves to be above normal human strictures. The result is an oscillation between grandiosity and self-flagellation in lieu of realistic values and prohibitions.

In Kernberg's's view, because the oral rage embedded in aggressive object relationships is dissociated from libidinal object relationships and not neutralized by libido, excessive oral aggressiveness is the fundamental problem of the borderline patient. Again, one can see the clear Kleinian influence in Kernberg's thinking. Kernberg believes that in any given case there may be a constitutionally excessive aggressive drive, or inability to tolerate frustration, extreme environmental frustration, or some combination of these issues. Whichever possibility may apply in an individual case, the result is extreme oral rage that must be managed by primitive defenses, thereby arresting further development, including the genital organization of the libido. In one case described by Kernberg (1975) the patient screamed so loudly at her therapist during their interviews that she was heard throughout the building. The therapist was so shaken by her rage that he sometimes was "virtually trembling" after he saw her. On one occasion he saw her by chance after a session and was shocked to see her relaxed and smiling; the hospital personnel confirmed that she was relaxed with other staff members. The intensity of the patient's rage split off from other object relations is characteristic of the borderline personality organization, according to Kernberg.

All these characteristics of the borderline personality organization have direct application to the treatment process. However, before we proceed to draw out those clinical implications, we turn to Kernberg's understanding of the narcissistic personality, the other form of severe character pathology to which he directs a great deal of attention.

The Narcissistic Personality Organization

As we have seen, Kernberg (1976) traces the origin of the narcissistic personality to either Stage 3 or Stage 4 of his developmental scheme. He views the narcissistic personality as the use of a pathological grandiose self to defend against splitting and other primitive defenses of the underlying borderline personality organization. Kernberg's acknowledgment that there is a subgroup of these patients who function on an overt borderline level lends confusion to his seemingly clear statement that the narcissistic personality is simply a more superficially adapted borderline patient. Further, since the borderline personality originates in Stage 3 of his developmental scheme, the existence of some narcissistic personalities in Stage 4 would seem to imply that not all have an underlying borderline personality organization. It is clear that Kernberg believes that pathological narcissism encompasses a range of disturbances whose overt functioning ranges from borderline organization to higher level character pathology.

At the highest level of narcissistic pathology are patients who have unusual talents, skills, or attributes through which they derive abundant gratification from external sources. Such patients come for treatment because of serious neurotic symptoms or interpersonal difficulties and have a good prognosis with psychoanalysis but may have difficulty engaging in treatment initially. The second subtype consists of most narcissistic personality disorders; Kernberg believes these patients also have a good prognosis with psychoanalysis proper. The third subtype is the category of patients who exist on an "overt borderline" level. These patients are more chaotic than other narcissistic personalities. They are distinguishable from other borderline patients by their frequent outbursts of narcissistic rage and by their inability to depend on others, in contrast to the excessive clinging of most borderline patients. A subgroup of this subtype includes patients who have strong antisocial tendencies and hence a poorer prognosis. This subgroup shades into the fourth subtype: patients suffering from "malignant narcissism" who have virtually no structured superego and consequently, have the poorest prognosis of all.

In Kernberg's (1975, 1984) view, narcissistic personalities are differentiated from other borderline patients by their fusion of the ideal self, ideal object, and self-image, resulting in a grandiose self that compensates for ego weakness so that the inability to manage tension states is not readily apparent. This pathological construction allows for better social adaptation than is characteristic of other borderline personalities. Thus, the aforementioned nonspecific manifestations of ego weakness are not seen in most narcissistic personalities. The degree of success of this defense varies from well-integrated character pathology to cases of overt borderline functioning in which the grandiose self has not compensated well for the primitive defensive organization.

Because they have no realistic self-concept, these patients show an exaggerated degree of self-reference. They need to be loved and admired; to bolster the grandiose self, they actively seek continual attention and admiration from the world. If they do not receive this self-affirmation, they tend to feel bored and restless; the need for continual bolstering by the environment is a telltale indicator that a presumably positive self-concept is a defense against underlying personality structure built upon splitting. The self-images of these patients, like those of all borderlines, are split between all good and all bad. They differ from other borderline patients in that the all good self-image has become integrated as a stable structure. When the environment does not affirm the grandiose self, the negative devaluing self-image appears. Consequently, grandiosity and self-devaluation tend to alternate in consciousness, each split from the other.

This combination of grandiosity and need for affirmation is illustrated by Kernberg's (1984) case of Mr. T, a social rehabilitation professional who entered analysis for help in his relations with women, inability to empathize, and general boredom, irritability, and dissatisfaction with life. In the early phase of analysis Mr. T was finely attuned to every move Kernberg made and was angered whenever a detail of the material was forgotten. He complained that his girlfriend was exploiting him, but he was dominant and exploitive in his relationship with her, expecting her to guess his moods and respond to his needs without his telling her what they were. Although he adopted the posture of a helpless little boy exploited by powerful, aggressive figures both outside the analysis (for example, with women) and within it, Mr. T was, in fact, hostile and exploitive in both spheres. He consistently denigrated Kernberg and summarily dismissed interpretations with which he disagreed—when he agreed with an interpretation, he acted as though he already knew it. He frequently reacted to interpretations by attacking Kernberg for trying to make him feel guilty. When his response to interpretations was analyzed, he expressed the belief that when Kernberg's comments were accurate, they implied a "grandiose triumph" over him. Nonetheless, Kernberg frequently felt helpless, as though he were paralyzed by the patient. During a protracted period of the treatment, the patient "confided" Kernberg's shortcomings to people who were hostile toward Kernberg and extracted information from them that he considered damaging to his analyst. At first he mentioned none of this in his analysis. When he finally did admit to this pattern of behavior, he acknowledged a sense of power and excitement in feeling that he could control and manipulate his analyst. This feeling turned out to be an identification with his sadistic, controlling mother, the core of his pathological grandiose self.

The case of Mr. T illustrates typically narcissistic split self-images; he was either sadistic and ruthless, dominating others or the inadequate, helpless little boy feeling exploited. Mr. T was more conscious of the latter, but the analysis revealed that this negative childhood self-image hid his grandiose identification with his sadistic mother. Once the grandiose self was revealed, the patient alternated between the two self-images, with Kernberg being the other pole of the object relations unit. When the patient was the grandiose, sadistic mother, Kernberg was the helpless little boy; when the patient experienced himself as the latter, he felt that Kernberg was the ruthless, exploitive mother.

The degree to which the environment denies these needs for continual affirmation is the degree of difficulty the grandiose self has in serving its function of effecting a stable organization that allows for smooth surface adaptation. Thus, the stability of the grandiose-self organization is much enhanced in narcissistic patients who possess some type of special talent, skill, or attribute that brings narcissistic supplies from the environment. The clinician can be surprised by the depth of regression when such patients lose narcissistic bolstering from the environment or regress within the treatment setting in response to the analyst's failure to affirm their superiority. Nonetheless, Kernberg considers such patients to have the best prognosis of all narcissistic patients.

Because of their continual need to "feed" the grandiose self, the object relationships of these patients tend to be exploitive. Others are valued for their ability to enhance the feeling of superiority and devalued when they do not serve this function. Consequently, there is little warmth or depth to the personality or to interpersonal relationships. The organization of the personality by the grandiose self dictates cold, exploitive, even arrogant attitudes toward others. In the narcissistic patient, the omnipotence defense becomes the organizing force of the personality, with others being devalued because they represent a threat to the grandiose self. However, if objects enhance the grandiose self, grandiosity will be projected onto them, resulting in idealization.

Kernberg is careful to differentiate the narcissistic personality from other character pathology with narcissistic defenses. He believes that the term *narcissistic* is overused because clinicians do not make the distinction between narcissistic defense and the narcissistic personality organization. Indeed, Kernberg points out that there are three levels of narcissistic defense. At the first level all defenses serve to protect self-esteem to some degree; this characteristic of all neurosis is easily distinguishable from the narcissistic personality organization. At the second level are the many narcissistic defenses in character disorders to protect and enhance self-esteem. For example, the hysteric may be flirtatious and seductive to defend against penis envy. Her desire to be thought of as beautiful and seductive serves to enhance her self-esteem, but the defense is directed against penis envy. When she is not viewed as beautiful or her overtures are not responded to, she does not crumble because her self-concept is not fused with her ideal of being the beautiful seductress. Further, her relationships continue to include warmth even when she is not responded to as she wishes to be. At the third level is the narcissistic personality structure in which libidinal investment in the self is equated with ideal qualities. A woman with a narcissistic personality who desires to affirm her grandiose self by being recognized as beautiful and seductive cannot tolerate being viewed in any other way. When her overtures are not responded to, she flies into a rage or attacks herself, and objects that do not affirm the pathological grandiose self are devalued as worthless. Consequently, the warmth and depth that are found in the hysterical personality structure are absent.

There is a subgroup of narcissistic personalities for whom the grandiose self does not allow for smooth social functioning. Such patients display the same "non-specific manifestations of ego weakness" as other borderline patients, with the same resulting chaos and displays of oral rage. In addition, these patients are narcissistically demanding and are given to frequent outbursts of narcissistic rage when their need for adulation is not met. Kernberg considers them a risk for treatment, especially if they have antisocial tendencies.

Because the grandiose self is a condensation of the ego ideal with the ideal self and the self-concept, narcissistic personalities tend to have even less integration of early sadistic superego forerunners with realistic parental prohibitions and the benign, loving ego-ideal and ideal-object images than is true for most borderline patients. That is to say, the ideal-self image tends to be absorbed into the pathological grandiose self. Consequently, in lieu of some degree of realistic, integrated superego, some narcissistic personalities have an almost total continuance of the early fantastical sadistic self-attacks. This primitive superego forerunner tends to be projected onto objects, accounting for the paranoia seen so frequently in these patients. Consequently, sociopathic tendencies are frequently stronger in narcissistic personalities than in other borderline patients. According to Kernberg, sociopathy lies at the severe end of the narcissistic continuum, making the degree of sociopathy a major prognostic indicator for narcissistic patients. Narcissistic personalities with some degree of concern for their effects on others have a better prognosis than those who do not.

In its most extreme form, this process results in what Kernberg (1984) calls "malignant narcissism." In these cases the idealized object images that are normally integrated into the superego, are completely absorbed into the pathological grandiose self. In Kernberg's (1984) view, idealized object images are absorbed to some degree in all narcissistic personalities; however, in most cases, "a remnant of idealized superego precursors remains outside the pathological grandiose self" (p. 297), permitting some superego functioning. However, since no such remnants exist in cases of malignant narcissism, ideal self-images and ideal object images become a part of the grandiose self, with the result that the sadistic superego forerunners express unmitigated aggression and the grandiose self now contains all the aggression within itself. Kernberg (1984) summarizes: "The pathological grandiose and sadistic self replaces the sadistic precursors of the superego, absorbs all aggression, and transforms what would otherwise be sadistic superego components into an abnormal self structure that then militates against the internalization of later, more realistic superego components" (p. 298).

These unneutralized, highly sadistic, cruel, punitive self-attacks are projected onto objects, resulting in a paranoid personality structure as an alternative to self-directed sadism. As the patient can now become the victim of humiliating and exploitive attacks by the object, he or she will at times revert to sadism and attack objects to protect against perceived persecution. This dynamic of projection and attack is Kernberg's formulation of the frequent paranoid transference regressions seen in cases of malignant narcissism.

Because the grandiose self is condensed with sadism, these patients have a tendency to obtain sadistic glee from feeling victorious over others, even when their own existence is at risk. Consequently, such patients lie at the most severe end of the spectrum of narcissistic pathology and their prognosis tends to be poor. According to

Kernberg, they are willing to self-destruct to feel the joy of triumph over the analyst and to render the analyst impotent.

Kernberg is not definitive regarding the reasons for the pathological fusion of the ideal self, ideal object, and self concept in narcissistic personalities. He attributes the formation of the grandiose self to excessive oral aggressiveness, but cannot offer a decisive account of why some borderline patients are able to construct such a narcissistic defense, while others are not, but he does believe that certain familial patterns are apparent in the histories of these patients. Kernberg's (1975) clinical experience suggests that there is usually one chronically cold parental figure who is indifferent and spitefully aggressive. This cold aggressiveness leads to an increase of oral aggression in the child, which exacerbates envy and hatred. The envy is defended against by inciting envy in others. Again, the special quality or talent plays a key role. Kernberg insists that such patients tend to have some realistic attribute that does incite envy and admiration in others. Further, he contends that this special quality was used by at least one parental figure to achieve compensatory admiration. Consequently, the patient tends to play a special role in the family, such as "the family genius," which serves to form a nucleus for the grandiose defense against oral rage. Kernberg fully acknowledges that he cannot definitively explain narcissistic pathology by this family pattern, but he does believe that once the grandiose self is formed as the stable defensive configuration, a cycle of self-admiration and devaluation of others takes place.

It is in his discussion of narcissistic pathology that Kernberg's Kleinian influence is most apparent. He assigns a primary pathogenic role to excessive aggressiveness and envy and the defenses against them in the formation of the pathological grandiose self (Kernberg, 1975). In his view, the intensity of envy and hatred lead to an inability to depend on others for fear of inciting oral rage and envy. Such patients feel forced to adopt the posture of arrogant, callous indifference and haughty devaluation of others as if to proclaim their lack of need for others. Consequently, such patients must spoil all they receive from others to defend against envy of them. Any gratification from another is an acknowledgment of dependence, an intolerable feeling to the narcissistic patient. One can see in this analysis Klein's (1975) formulation that the need to defend against dependence and object contact is rooted in envy and defended by devaluation and omnipotence. Even closer to Kernberg's view is Rosenfeld's (1971) concept of the grandiose self as a pathologically aggressive structure that defends against the libidinal, dependent self. The result of the inability to receive from others is an empty, hungry self that envies others all the more. According to Kernberg, the empty, hungry, enraged self is the deepest level of the self-concept of the narcissistic personality disorder, but it may only appear at the end of treatment, if the grandiose self defense has been successful.

These dynamics are illustrated in the case of Mr. T, discussed earlier, who either accepted interpretations as though he had already had the insight himself or summarily dismissed them. Nonetheless, he often used Kernberg's interpretations in his own work. Kernberg concluded that the patient was unable to depend on him for psychological exploration and instead "extracted interpretations" and put them to his own use. Kernberg (1984) points out that when these reactions were explored, "it emerged that Mr. T was protecting himself against intense feelings of envy of me by utilizing for his own purposes whatever he saw as new and good coming from me" (p. 214). The patient's inability to depend on Kernberg was rooted in his need to defend against envy, a need so strong that Mr. T was willing to deny himself the value of his analysis to satisfy it.

Nonetheless, narcissistic patients will idealize others who they feel possess what they lack. The idealization should not be mistaken for genuine admiration and appreciation; rather it is a projection of the grandiose self onto an object who is perceived to possess wished-for qualities. Such objects are not, therefore, experienced as who they are; they represent the patient's self. If such objects fail to serve the narcissistic purpose, by disappointing the patient or losing some admired quality, they are easily given up and frequently devalued, reflecting the lack of real attachment. Thus, idealization does not help narcissistic patients achieve any genuine gratification from the object; even idealized relationships leave them empty. Such patients have no capacity for empathy, and cannot experience depression, or mourn loss of objects; they can only feel lack of narcissistic gratification.

Kernberg (1975) illustrates his view of the idealization typical of the narcissistic patient in his description of the analysis of a professional colleague who believed his analyst to possess perfect technique and who gradually formed an image of him as an absolutely self-assured, incorruptible, perfectionistic technician who was cold and distant but masterful and reliable. It turned out that the patient was preparing to switch to an analyst in another city in case he found any flaw in his current analyst. The patient presented to his own patients the same qualities he ascribed to his analyst, evincing a cold, distant, intellectually precise approach of which he was quite proud. He became extremely disappointed whenever the analyst did not conform to his self-image; he felt threatened by the independence of the analyst. It is

Kernberg's view that such an idealization showed neither concern for nor real attachment to the analyst, as the patient expected to control the analyst and was quite prepared to dismiss him summarily at the first indication of a flaw. In addition, Kernberg points out that the idealization was a projection of the patient's grandiose self: the analyst was seen as possessing the same characteristics as the patient and no other qualities were tolerated. In Kernberg's view this exploitive idealization is quite different from a genuine appreciation of admired qualities in another.

Kernberg is careful to differentiate the idealization characteristic of the narcissistic patient from other forms of idealization. The typical borderline patient's idealization is of the primitive type discussed earlier, in which others, including the analyst, are seen as all good to protect against contamination by the persecutory object, which is dangerous by virtue of projected oral aggressiveness. In less primitive character pathology, by contrast, idealization is a defense against ambivalence and guilt over aggressiveness; thus genuinely loving feelings are part of the relationship. At a still higher level of idealization, the object is viewed in accordance with higher level values and superego functions. This type of idealization is characteristic of falling in love. All three types of idealization differ from the projection of the grandiose self, the idealization characteristic of narcissistic patients.

It should be noted that all pathological forms of idealization are defensive constructions; they differ only according to the level of conflict against which they defend. This view sets Kernberg's formulation of idealization in clear opposition to Kohut's (1971) concept that idealization in the narcissistic personality is a response to developmental arrest (as will be discussed in chapter 6).

Kernberg's view of idealization in the narcissistic personality is an application of Klein's concept of projective identification: the object stands for the self and must therefore be controlled so as to fit the projection. This is not a merger in Kernberg's view; the object must be *like* the patient, not merged with the patient. Consistent with his developmental approach, Kernberg considers true merger to exist only in psychotic states. He feels that the terms *merger* and *symbiosis* are too loosely used, and (as we will see in chapter 6) this is one of the major points of disagreement between Kernberg and Kohut. In narcissistic pathology, Kernberg believes that since self–object boundaries are maintained, there is no true confusion between the experience of the self and the object. The object is not fused with the self, it represents the self and must conform to this representation. Because most people do not fit the projection, interpersonal relations tend to fail, resulting in an exacerbation of emptiness that leads to a self-perpetuating cycle of rage and envy, frustration, emptiness, more rage and envy, devaluation, and a sense of impotence.

According to Kernberg, then, most patients with narcissistic pathology are accessible to psychoanalytic treatment but require intervention unique to their pathology, as do other borderline patients. We now turn to the specific type of psychoanalytic treatment Kernberg recommends for both borderline patients and narcissistic personalities.

TREATMENT

Kernberg (1980) divides psychotherapy into three categories: unmodified psychoanalysis, or psychoanalysis proper, psychoanalytic psychotherapy, which he calls expressive psychotherapy, and supportive psychotherapy. As we have seen, Kernberg recommends psychoanalysis for the neurotic personality organization and for most narcissistic personalities and expressive psychotherapy for severe character pathology, such as the borderline personality organization. He also advocates psychoanalytic psychotherapy for milder neurotic cases in which the unmodified psychoanalysis is not necessary. Interestingly, Kernberg believes that for the latter group, supportive measures can be included in the treatment because they do not confuse the patient. For severe character pathology, however, inherent ego weakness renders the patient too vulnerable to the gratifications of supportive techniques and confuses the patient about the role of the therapist and the purpose of treatment. Further, since supportive therapy cannot strengthen the ego structure, this form of treatment leaves the ego deficient whereas expressive psychotherapy strengthens the weak ego and can thereby result in appreciable improvement. In this sense Kernberg opposes the orthodox view that the more severe the pathology, the more supportive the treatment should be. His contention is that severe character pathology requires a psychoanalytic approach to undo the primitive defenses and help the patient advance to higher level ego structures.

Kernberg adopts Gill's (1954) tripartite definition of psychoanalysis: the position of technical neutrality, the use of interpretation, and the systematic analysis of the transference. Accordingly, he defines psychoanalytic psychotherapy as treatment that modifies one or more of these principles. As discussed earlier, Kernberg (1980) views interpretation, clarification, and confrontation as the three primary psychotherapeutic techniques. Psychoanalysis proper uses predominantly or exclusively interpretation, whereas psychoanalytic psychotherapy utilizes a mixture of interpretation, clarification, and confrontation. Transference interpretation is used in psychoanalytic psychotherapy as a primary tool but not as systematically as in psychoanalysis proper; rather, the therapist selectively chooses to work on some resistances while supporting others. The therapist attempts to maintain technical neutrality in psychoanalytical psychotherapy, but it is expected that this will not always be possible with more severe psychopathology. The more the therapist is able to employ the three principles of Gill's tripartite definition of psychoanalysis, the more closely the treatment approximates psychoanalysis proper; the more the therapist must deviate from these principles, the more closely the treatment approximates supportive psychotherapy. The latter utilizes very little if any interpretation and relies instead on clarification, abreaction, suggestion, and manipulation.

Treatment of the Neurotic Personality Organization

Although Kernberg (1980) has focused his work on the understanding and treatment of severe psychopathology, he applies his object relations theory to a general concept of psychoanalytic treatment that embraces all levels of psychopathology. His object relations approach to development and psychological structure leads him to reconceptualize the therapeutic action of psychoanalysis. He points out that since both drives and defenses are always expressed through object relationships, intrapsychic conflict in neurotic cases involves object relations units. Therefore, the psychoanalysis of neurosis involves the breakdown of the ego and superego structures into their constituent object relations components and the rebuilding of these structures with a new integration of object relationships.

The therapeutic action of psychoanalysis in Kernberg's view is not so much in making drive derivatives conscious as in making conscious the object relationship building blocks of the psyche and reintegrating them. Kernberg (1988) believes that his reconceptualization of the psychoanalytic process helps the analyst gain insight into material frequently obscured by the classical model. Since the psyche is formed from the internalization of object relations units, not objects per se, the patient forms an interpersonal relationship with the analyst based on identification with either self or object, with the analyst perceived as the other pole of the object relationship. In Kernberg's (1988) object relations model the analyst is alert to the fact that patients will not only enact themselves as their childhood selves, with the analyst as the parental figure, but will also enact the parental figure, with the analyst as the childhood self. Often the analytic material appears not to make sense because the patient is enacting an internalized object relations unit with the roles reversed. Kernberg believes that this object relations perspective on psychoanalysis broadens the therapeutic armamentarium of the analyst.

For the neurotic personality organization, the analytic process results in the breakdown of the ego and superego structures into their constituent object relations units. As a result, the analysis leads to the emergence of splitting and the rapid cycling of self- and object images in a manner similar to treatment process with the borderline patient. At this point in the analysis of the neurotic personality, the treatment setting becomes the focus and sudden shifts in the enacted self- and object images give a chaotic, confusing feel to the analytic regression. Consequently, the analyst may feel tempted to believe that the patient is not analyzable and yield analytic neutrality. However, Kernberg points out that since the cause of the chaos is the regression to splitting, the appropriate analytic intervention is the interpretation of the splitting. No extraanalytic measures are necessary if the analyst is able to perceive the part object relations units enacted in the analytic regression.

The best clue to understanding the enacted object relation is the affective atmosphere generated by the patient and felt by the analyst. Kernberg defines the countertransference as the totality of the therapist's affective responses to the patient, and he views countertransference reactions on a continuum from those that come mostly from the therapist to responses that come primarily from the patient. Kernberg believes, like Winnicott (see chapter 4), that countertransference reactions should be neither repressed nor split off, but used as a source of information about the patient. In general, Kernberg feels that the more severely character disordered patients and neurotic patients in moments of analytic regression tend to elicit more intense emotional reactions from therapists than do patients with higher level disorders. Nonetheless, even in the more routine periods of the analysis of neurotic disorders, the countertransference can be a valuable clue to understanding the currently enacted object relationship.

While countertransference is useful during any part of an analysis, it is Kernberg's contention that the countertransference is an especially good indicator of analytic regression. Chaotic, intense, quickly oscillating countertransference reactions are likely to indicate a regression in the patient that may go unnoticed if the countertransference is not attended to. By regarding the countertransference in this way, Kernberg is applying Racker's (1968) notion of "concordant" countertransference to the treatment of the neurotic patient. (Here again one sees the impact of the Kleinian movement on Kernberg's thinking.) He finds projective identification and especially Racker's concepts of complementary and concordant countertransference to be of special importance in the treatment of these patients and suggests that the analyst pay close attention to their affective responses to the patient and rather than act on them, use their understanding of the enacted object relationship to inform their interpretations.

One can see from this approach to analytic regression that Kernberg opposes the view that analysts need at certain points in the treatment to offer themselves as a "real" person or to become more "human," an approach that considers the therapeutic action of analysis to lie in the patient's internalization of the analyst's "maternal function." Kernberg (1980) is critical of Fairbairn and Guntrip for adopting this approach. Kernberg makes a clear distinction between maternal empathy and analytic empathy: the latter includes the analyst's understanding of the patient's dissociated and repressed material, acting out, and nonverbal interaction with the analyst and thus involves a great deal more than the maternal empathy. Kernberg correspondingly feels that identification of the therapeutic action of psychoanalysis with the internalization of the mothering function is misleading and misses the unique value of psychoanalysis. He believes that empathy is a crucial ingredient of the analytic process—but as a prerequisite of interpretation, not a substitute for it. The analytic resolution of conflict is served by interpretation of the dynamic unconscious and by the integration of the revealed part-object relations units that compose the personality, not by the offering of a personal relationship that violates technical neutrality.

Kernberg's concept of the analytic treatment of the neurotic personality organization is an application of his object relations model of personality structure and psychopathology within the context of the three cardinal principles of psychoanalysis. Unlike Fairbairn, Guntrip, and Winnicott, Kernberg does not believe that the principles of psychoanalysis need to be modified, but he does believe that they must be applied in a manner somewhat different from that suggested by the classical model of psychoanalysis. Kernberg's model focuses on making conscious object relationships that are enacted in the transference paradigm and on using of countertransference as a primary tool to achieve understanding, rather than on making conscious drive derivatives through defense analysis. Thus, his contribution to psychoanalysis is both a reconceptualization of the classical view of the aims of the analytic process and a counterpoint to the radical departures in analytic technique suggested by other object relations interpretations of psychoanalysis.

Kernberg's (1980) approach to the analytic treatment of a neurotic case can be seen in the psychoanalysis of a professional man in his forties who entered analysis for help with his chronic marital conflicts, severe work inhibition, and occasional sexual impotence. The patient was potent with prostitutes and achieved sadistic sexual gratification with them. He feared and depreciated his father, who was a prominent man. His mother submitted to the father but was constantly complaining, guilt-evoking, and hypochondriacal. The patient presented in the analysis as shamefully submitting to his wife who imposed restrictions on him and his work. He devalued Kernberg and kept him analytically impotent with his nagging protests about treatment and his amused reactions to interpretations that seemed as if they were prods accompanied by the message, "You can do better than that." When Kernberg realized how impotent he felt, he interpreted to the patient that he was enacting his nagging wife while projecting into Kernberg his self-image of impotence and helplessness. The patient then began to view Kernberg as forceful, as someone who would not put up with a wife's constant complaints, and, indeed, Kernberg felt a sudden sense of power. This was understood as an enactment by the patient with Kernberg as his powerful, brutal father forcing him into homosexual submission. Kernberg went on to point out that the patient's search for prostitutes and his fear of competing with the analyst/father lest he lose his masculinity were defenses against the temptation to submit. The patient responded to these interpretations by becoming depressed over opportunities lost because of his neurotic fears. He realized for the first time that part of the reason he and his wife did not have children was his inability to assert himself against her reluctance. In response to this painful realization, Kernberg felt a strong sense of empathy and positive concern for the patient.

This brief vignette from the analysis of a neurotic patient involved three phases of object relations enactments. In the first phase the therapist was the projected self-representation of the patient, impotent in response to the sadistic mother/wife. In the second phase the therapist was the powerful, brutal father and the patient was the helpless, fearful child. In the third phase Kernberg felt empathy for the patient's self experience. Thus the analysis involved the continual interpretation of enacted object relationships. Further, Kernberg's ability to understand the object relationship enactments was critical to his awareness of his changing countertransference feelings. This vignette, although brief, illustrates Kernberg's reconceptualization of the therapeutic action of psychoanalysis as the uncovering of internalized object relations units by the understanding of transference–countertransference interactions.

Despite his reconceptualization of the psychoanalytic process, Kernberg's primary efforts have been focused not on the psychoanalysis of neurotic personalities but on expressive psychotherapy for borderline and narcissistic personalities, and it is to his contributions in this area that we now turn.

Treatment of the Borderline Personality Organization

Kernberg's recommendations for the psychotherapy of the borderline personality organization follow closely his conceptualization of the pathology. Because the fundamental pathogenic issue is excessive oral aggressiveness split off from libidinal object relations, the critical transference development is excessive oral aggressiveness directed to the therapist. The negative transference tends to become the treatment focus as the early pathogenic object relationships are activated. Patients project their intense aggressiveness onto the therapist, who quickly comes to represent a hated figure of the past. Because the intense oral aggression interferes with the therapeutic alliance, both in its direct and projected forms, it must be addressed immediately. It is one of Kernberg's cardinal technical principles that the negative transference must be interpreted quickly and forcefully with the borderline patient. If the therapist chooses to ignore the negative transference, there is no chance to disrupt the projective–introjective cycles and no opportunity to build the therapeutic alliance, a prerequisite for the observing ego. In Kernberg's view, the consistent interpretation of the negative transference is necessary for the development of the patient's observing ego, and the enhancement of the observing ego helps in the disruption of the projective–introjective cycles.

While Kernberg advocates early, forceful interpretation of the negative transference to build the observing ego, he recognizes that some degree of preexisting alliance must be present for transference interpretations to be effective. He resolves this problem by pointing out that there are some modulated, positive feelings toward the therapist that are not part of the idealizing defense. One of his treatment principles for the borderline patient is that these feelings should not be interpreted because they aid in the development of the therapeutic alliance. Thus, while treatment involves confrontation of the negative transference, the more "modulated" aspects of the positive transference are not interpreted but utilized to advance the therapeutic process.

Interpretation of the negative transference may seem obvious when it is acted out, but in some cases the negative transference is not clearly seen. Kernberg distinguishes between the manifest and latent negative transference in the borderline patient. In the latter case the patient maintains a presumably friendly, albeit superficial, attitude toward the therapist, devoid of signs of aggressiveness, while splitting off his or her negative object relations from the treatment situation. If the therapist accepts the patient's superficial, detached presentation, the relationship comes to be based on a denial of the negative transference, a denial that fosters the fundamental pathology. The therapeutic intervention is to interpret the split-off negative transference in order to bring the patient's aggression into the analytic relationship. Kernberg fully acknowledges in cases of this type that therapeutic interventions generate anxiety. However, he feels this anxiety indicates therapeutic progress since it reflects the entry of aggressiveness into the transference and allows for the resolution of splitting.

Kernberg's (1975) approach to splitting in borderline patients who maintain a detached, superficial attitude to the therapist is illustrated in the case of a female patient suffering from drug and alcohol addiction. The patient made considerable progress in the hospital and seemed to make a good adjustment after discharge, but her attitude in outpatient psychotherapy was shallow and "conventionally friendly." After some months of sobriety, she became drunk, depressed, and suicidal and required rehospitalization. She kept this episode from her therapist, who found out about it only after she was rehospitalized. After discharge, she denied all transference and emotional implications of the episode, despite her memory of anger and depression during it. At this point the therapist began a long effort to correlate the patient's detached attitude in treatment with her alcoholic crisis. After two more episodes of this type it became clear that "she was experiencing the therapist as the cold, distant, hostile father who had refused to rescue her from an even more rejecting, aggressive mother" (p. 95). Kernberg summarizes the situation this way:

> The patient felt that if she really expressed to the psychotherapist-father how much she needed him and loved him, she would destroy him with the intensity of her anger over having been frustrated so much for so long. The solution was to keep what she felt was the best possible relationship of detached friendliness with the therapist, while splitting off her search for love . . . and her protest against father in alcoholic

episodes during which rage and depression were completely dissociated emotionally from both the therapist and her boyfriends [p. 95].

Kernberg's central point is that it was necessary for the therapist to introduce all this material into the transference through a systematic confrontation with the patient's effort to split off her aggressiveness toward the therapist. This type of intervention—confronting of the "friendly" relationship toward the therapist with the negative transference—aims at the "undoing" of splitting. Kernberg acknowledges that in this case the therapist's interventions increased the patient's anxiety to the point that she became even more distrustful and angry, reverting to her old alcoholic patterns; he acknowledges further that interpretation did not suffice to control this behavior and that there was another hospitalization. Nonetheless, he contends that although the patient appears to have done worse "from a superficial point of view," the therapist felt that "for the first time he was dealing with a 'real' person" (p. 96).

Object relations are split into part self- and part object image units, and the primary goal of the treatment of the borderline patient is to integrate these part object relations units into whole self- and whole object images. To accomplish this task the therapist must identify and label the split-off self- and object images. For example, when Miss B, described earlier, devalued her therapist, she was enacting her mother's sadistic attitude toward her and evoking in the therapist the feelings she had experienced in response to her mother's criticisms. Her other primary object relations enactment was of a helpless child dependent on and submissive to the mother. In fulfilling the therapeutic task of identifying the roles patients enact for both themselves and their therapists and then pointing out the conflict between them, Miss B's therapist interpreted her haughty devaluation as an enactment of herself as her mother while projecting into the therapist the feelings she had when her mother criticized her. When Miss B immediately became dependent on the therapist and projected her haughty grandiosity onto her boyfriend, the therapist interpreted this new object relations constellation. In Kernberg's view, the therapist must continually search for the object relations unit enacted at each phase of the treatment, label for the patient the self- and object images enacted, and identify the connecting affective link. Additionally, the therapist must point out the existence of contradictory self- and object images and their connection in order to bring them together into integrated whole object representations.

This case illustrates the primary role of the countertransference in the understanding of the enacted object relationships in the treatment of the borderline patient. The therapist understood Miss B's enactment of the haughty mother and the attacked, helpless child object relationship when he realized that he was feeling the victimized helplessness that the patient felt in response to her mother's criticisms. This countertransference response was the primary clue in unlocking the mystery of the interaction, and Kernberg believes this is typically the case with borderline patients because of the dominant use of projective identification. That is, the patient tends to communicate by projecting feelings into the therapist, rather than by verbalizing. In formulating transference interpretations to borderline patients, the first task for therapists is to sort out and understand their own affective responses. Only after therapists have differentiated their affective responses to the patient are they in a position to identify the actors in the drama that is being enacted with the patient.

This task is rendered difficult by the fact that the patient shifts so rapidly between different object relations units. The rapid reversal of self- and object images is illustrated by events in a therapy session of an 18-year-old girl who initially spoke in a deeply emotional manner about matters that concerned her very much and then suddenly became bland and indifferent regarding these same issues (Kernberg, 1975). Kernberg tried repeatedly to explore this material with the patient but eventually gave up in frustration. When he ceased his active effort, the patient suddenly became insistent that he give her advice about a reality situation. As the patient became more demanding, Kernberg felt distant and impatient with her. He then realized that in the first part of the session she had enacted her mother as a distant, aloof, cold person while he was her self-image as a demanding, frustrated child. In the later part of the session Kernberg had become the rejecting mother and the patient was the needy, demanding, frustrated child. When Kernberg realized these mother–child roles were being played out, he was able to formulate an interpretation. It needs to be underscored that Kernberg was able to grasp the meaning of the patient's sudden behavioral shift when he realized that he felt distant and impatient with her and was subsequently able to connect these feelings with the behavior of her indifferent mother. In Kernberg's view, by paying close attention to their emotional reactions to patients, therapists will frequently be able to link the borderline patient's presumably impulsive, chaotic behavior with a crucial self–object unit from the patient's past.

Once the therapist has been able to interpret the currently operating object relationship, special attention is paid to the patient's response to this interpretation. Kernberg believes the patient's reaction to the awareness of the enacted object relationship will frequently reveal an additional component of the object relationship structure of the personality. For example, when the therapist interpreted to Miss B that she was enacting her mother while putting her therapist in the position of her childhood self, she responded by reverting to her previously dependent relationship on the therapist and projecting her haughty, sadistic object image onto her boyfriend. In Kernberg's view, a frequent response to the interpretation of an object relationship is role reversal of the same object relationship. However, other responses are possible, including the intensification of the same object relationship with the same role enactment. If the patient's response to the interpretation of the object relationship unit reflects a different aspect of the object relationship structure of the patient, an interpretation of this newly enacted object relationship should be made.

Eventually, the patient's response to the therapist's insistence on interpreting splitting is to use one or more of the primitive defenses characteristic of the borderline personality organization. As we have seen, all these defenses are designed to foster the splitting process. When the dominant use of splitting is threatened by the therapist's systematic interpretations, the patient resorts to other primitive defenses—projection, projective identification, primitive idealization, omnipotence, denial, and devaluation—in a desperate effort to keep apart the good and bad self- and object images. The therapeutic task is to interpret these defenses as systematically as splitting is interpreted. Only when these defenses are resolved is the patient able to relinquish splitting as the primary organizing principle of the psyche.

Kernberg advocates limit setting, clarification of ego and object boundaries, and confronting patients with their own aggressiveness when they direct their excessive oral aggressiveness at the therapist. Similarly, he believes primitive idealization should be treated by confronting patients with their unrealistically exaggerated positive feelings and inquiring as to their origin. The point of the investigation is to show patients that their idealization defends against their persecutory fears of the therapist, which in turn are a projection of their oral aggressiveness. Kernberg acknowledges that patients will attempt to maintain their idealized perception of the therapist and that the unrealistic nature of their transference perception must be confronted over and over again. Only when the idealization is pierced will patients' paranoid fears and primitive aggressiveness become manifest.

Denial, omnipotence, and devaluation are all addressed similarly. In Kernberg's view, denial can be directed against sectors of subjective or external reality. In either case patients are confronted with the reality of the oral aggressiveness that they prefer to deny. Omnipotence and devaluation are often not apparent, and the therapist interprets these attitudes to the patient to make conscious the use of the defenses before confronting the reasons for their existence. All these defenses must be systematically undone for the ego to become integrated and develop higher level defenses. This undoing requires a combination of clarification, confrontation, interpretation, and limit setting.

A good illustration of Kernberg's approach to the defenses of the borderline patient is provided by his account of the treatment of an obese patient who believed that she had a right to eat whatever she pleased and that she was still entitled to be "admired, pampered, and loved" (Kernberg, 1975, p. 102). She felt entitled to come for therapy at any time she wished, and to behave as she chose, including leaving cigarette ashes all over the furniture in the therapist's office. "It was only after the therapist made very clear to her that there were definite limits to what he would tolerate, that she became quite angry, expressing more openly the derogatory thoughts about the therapist that complemented her own feelings of greatness" (p. 102). The patient's conscious inferiority feelings had until this point masked her omnipotence. The therapist's confrontation of the patient's entitled behavior made conscious her feelings of greatness, which had been operating as an omnipotent defense. That type of intervention Kernberg believes, must be consistently applied to "undo" the defense. While Kernberg does not say what was defended against in his reporting of this vignette, he makes clear that omnipotence is characteristically used against awareness of oral aggressiveness and threatening dependency needs.

To summarize, Kernberg believes that for the integration of split object relationships his treatment principles gain expression in a series of therapeutic steps (Kernberg et al., 1988). Because of the chaos of rapidly shifting self- and object image enactments, the first step for therapists is the exploration of their countertransference. Once therapists understand the role or roles they are being given to enact by the patient, they are able to identify the self- and object images enacted in the transference. In the third step, the therapist interprets the transference paradigm by "naming" these split object relations. Fourth, the therapist pays special attention to the patient's response to the interpretation of the object relations enactment and interprets this response if it involves a shift to a new dyad. Finally, the interpretation of splitting will eventually result in the appearance of one or more of the primitive defenses characteristic of the borderline personality, and this too must be interpreted systematically to resolve splitting definitively.

The integration of split object relations units in a borderline patient treated by expressive psychotherapy is illustrated in the case of Miss L, a Latin American artist in her twenties, who sought help for a severe sexual inhibition, although her diagnosis was borderline personality organization with severe depression and schizoid tendencies (Kernberg, 1984). Miss L's sexual fantasies involved the mutilation of her and her partner's genitals during sexual intercourse. Her initial transference paradigm was organized around her desire for the therapist to rape and kill her during sexual intercourse. Her second major transference involved a view of herself as a dependent child, with the therapist seen as a motherly father from whom she could receive warmth, protection, and love if she could suck his penis. It became clear to Kernberg that Miss L's sexual inhibition was a result of her inability to separate the two transference constellations, an inability that lead to her fear that her hatred and love would come together and that she would destroy her only potential source of love, warmth, and protection. Later in treatment Miss L's fear of orgasm was connected to a fear of "uncontrollable wetness" and a fear that her personality would dissolve into impersonal fragments. Kernberg summarizes the situation:

> The predominance of splitting mechanisms, the fear of conflicts related to severe oral frustration, and the regressive dangers of the oedipal situation all blocked sexual excitement and orgasm. At a still later time Miss L was able to fantasize more elaborate sexual experiences with men, the therapist in particular, which centered upon letting herself go and urinating during orgasm and which expressed her longings for dependency and sexual gratification in more synthetic ways [p. 109].

Kernberg notes that after this development Miss L began to date more and engaged in petting. However, a negative therapeutic reaction ensued when Miss L became aware of a primitive, sadistic superego that prohibited further improvement in her relations with men. She now submitted to this primitive superego which appeared to be a condensation of the "hated and hateful pregenital mother with the feared oedipal rival" (p. 109). After working through this primitive superego, Miss L was able to establish a sexual relationship with an appropriate object.

In Kernberg's view, this case shows the resolution of pathology in a borderline personality organization by the integration of the two primary split object relations units enacted in the transference. The major therapeutic shift occurred when Miss L became aware that her hatred, death wishes, and fear of destruction involved the same person toward whom she looked for the fulfillment of her needs for love, warmth, and protection. The recognition that she had both sets of feelings toward the same man resulted in the integration of her view of men and the capacity to open herself to her genital longings. After her dependency longings became manifest, Miss L began to describe in more detail her sexual fantasies and her tolerance of genital longings increased. At that point Miss L began to have sexual experiences with men; concurrently she became more productive at work.

The persistent search for the object relations role enactments is to be found in the case of Miss N, who presented with a borderline personality organization with obsessive and schizoid features (Kernberg, 1984). In the first period of treatment, the transference paradigm involved a masochistic search for a warm, giving, but sadistically powerful father. Then Miss N shifted to a preoedipal mother transference and accused the therapist of being cold and rejecting. This paradigm alternated with her view of Kernberg as a sexually exciting, powerful, dangerous man. When her fear of her sexual longings for the therapist/father were interpreted, she regressed markedly. Miss N let the therapist know that he must say only "perfect and precise things that would immediately and clearly reflect how she was feeling and would reassure her [he] was with her" (Kernberg, 1984, p. 129). (As we will see in chapter 6, Kohut, 1971, referred to this need as the "mirror transference.") During this period Kernberg only pointed out to the patient how frightened she was of his overpowering her with his comments and that he understood her need for him to understand without her having to tell him. In response to this limited interpretive stance, the patient appreciably improved, but when Kernberg attempted to explore the two types of transference, no progress was made. Eventually, Kernberg interpreted that Miss N had two alternating views of him: in one he was a warm, receptive mother, in the other the sexually tempting, dangerous father figure. Miss N then revealed that when Kernberg was active she saw him as "harsh, masculine, and invasive." When he listened more passively, he was "soft, feminine, and somewhat depressed." After Kernberg interpreted this transference paradigm as her effort to avoid the conflict between her need for a nurturing mother who forbade sex with the father and the need to be a receptive woman to a masculine man, the treatment continued to advance toward oedipal conflicts.

This case demonstrates Kernberg's technique of integrating object relations in the transference. Even though at a major point in the treatment Kernberg felt compelled not to interpret actively, he eventually was able to interpret Miss N's need to place him in the passive role he had been playing in that phase of the treatment. A cardinal tenet of Kernberg's approach to the psychotherapy of the borderline patient is that the therapist must continually reflect on the role enactments between patient and therapist to understand the interaction, especially when the treatment appears not to be progressing. Miss N's putting Kernberg in a passive role was an enactment of a crucial component of the treatment, not an interference with it. When Kernberg discerned what role he was playing and interpreted that to the patient, the treatment was able to progress.

Despite Kernberg's adherence to interpretive principles, he believes that interpretation is almost never sufficient for most borderline patients. As we have seen, Kernberg believes that the borderline patients lose self–object boundaries when the projective–introjective cycles become intense and quickly alternate. Consequently, when the transference intensifies, it may become psychotic, but the reality sense is maintained in other situations because the patient has fundamentally intact self–object boundaries. This is Kernberg's concept of the transference psychosis. To resolve it, parameters must be used. The therapist clarifies the distinction between the patient and himself or herself and limits the acting out of the negative transference. The characteristic development of transference psychosis is another reason for the employment of noninterpretive intervention and contraindicates psychoanalysis proper.

The addictive case referred to earlier illustrates the use of parameters in Kernberg's treatment approach to the borderline patient. The intense negative transference was interpreted, but it was also limited by the use of the hospital. This is a good illustration of why Kernberg does not believe in psychoanalysis proper for these patients. The acting out of the negative transference tends to become so extreme that extra-interpretive means are frequently necessary to control it so that the treatment process can take place. Even in the case of patients who act out the negative transference directly in the treatment setting, the therapist must often set limits on what will be tolerated. This is not simply protection for the patient and therapist. In Kernberg's view, the limit setting is necessary for the development of the observing ego and helps the patient reestablish reality boundaries. Limit setting extends to the acting out of the patient's intense oral aggressiveness, which, in Kernberg's view, is "instinctually gratifying." (Here Kernberg applies his belief in the drive component of his object relations model directly to his technical approach. Since he views aggressiveness as a drive, it follows that the persistent oral rage attacks of borderline patients, if allowed to continue, provide drive gratification.) From Kernberg's point of view, as long as the patient's repetitive behavior brings instinctual gratification, working through is not possible; thus, the setting of parameters becomes critical to the treatment process.

It should be noted that all interpretations cited that were aimed at resolving oral aggressiveness and undoing defenses have focused on the here-and-now transference. Kernberg believes that genetic constructions should be avoided during the greatest part of the treatment of the borderline patient. Owing to the fragility of the ego organization of such patients, such interventions tend to foster confusion between past and present, fantasy and reality. Since the purpose of the treatment is to help secure the patient's distinction between perception and reality, Kernberg believes interpretations should be focused on the patient's interpretation of here-and-now reality. According to Kernberg, during most of the treatment the origins of the patient's distorted perceptions should be included in the intervention only when aspects of the past are conscious; in this case, the connection of the patient's transference perceptions with past history can help the patient make the distinction between reality and perception. Genetic reconstructions in the usual sense of making conscious the unconscious past are recommended only after the reality sense is more fully developed near the conclusion of treatment.

By way of summary, one can see that Kernberg elucidates nine cardinal principles for the treatment of all borderline patients, whatever the particular character disorder may be. First, the negative transference must be made a major treatment focus, whether its manifestation is latent or manifest. Second, the therapeutic alliance/observing ego must be built via a combination of negative transference analysis and noninterpretation of the modulated positive aspects of the patient's relationship to the therapist. Third, and most important, the split object relations units must be systematically integrated by identifying and labeling them for the patient and then pointing out the conflict between them. Fourth, special attention must be paid to the countertransference for the identification of these split object relations units. Fifth, attention is focused on the patient's responses to interpretations of the enacted object relationships. Sixth, all related defenses must be systematically "undone" by persistent interpretation. Seventh, to resolve the acting out of the negative transference, and to help foster reality testing and the observing ego, parameters must be employed to prevent "instinctual gratification" of aggressiveness in the treatment sessions. Eighth, the transference psychosis must be managed by clarification of reality as well as by parameters to reestablish self–object boundaries. Ninth, the transference analysis must be limited to here-and-now interpretations, with genetic reconstructions left to the end of treatment, if they are used at all.

These principles define Kernberg's approach, built on the work of Klein and ego psychology, to the treatment of the borderline patient. Kernberg's treatment recommendations are a consistent application of his belief that severe character pathology should be treated by modified psychoanalytic psychotherapy. However, there is one subgroup of borderline patients who he feels can manage and benefit from unmodified psychoanalysis: the narcissistic subgroup of borderline patients.

Treatment of the Narcissistic Personality Organization

Kernberg takes the view that because narcissistic personalities are able to utilize the grandiose-self defense, the danger of regression and psychosis and therefore the need for parameters, is not as great, as with other borderline patients. On the other hand, because the grandiose self appears to be so effective, it is even more difficult to resolve than other borderline defenses. For both these reasons, Kernberg (1975, 1984) advocates unmodified psychoanalysis, the aim of which is the revelation and undoing of the grandiose self. For the subgroup of narcissistic personalities who present overt borderline personality organization, psychoanalytic psychotherapy is the treatment of choice, as it is for most borderline patients.

The grandiose self is a stubborn, effective defense and must be consistently interpreted with a view to revealing the oral rage and persecutory anxiety that lie beneath it. As discussed earlier, the grandiose self will be projected onto the analyst, and this idealization is also to be treated as a defense against rage and the paranoid fear of the therapist. Critical to Kernberg's treatment recommendations is the idea that the grandiose self and idealization that must be undone by interpretation. As we will see in chapter 6, Kernberg criticizes Kohut for recommending the acceptance of idealization without interpretation. To Kernberg, this is supportive psychotherapy because it bolsters defenses rather than undoing them; for him a psychoanalytic approach must be directed at the unearthing and resolution of the oral aggressiveness, persecutory anxiety, hunger for objects, and fear of dependence that underlie the grandiose-self and idealization defenses.

According to Kernberg, narcissistic patients present other special clinical problems. Their excessive inability to depend on others, even when idealization is prominent, result in special resistances. Narcissistic patients have more difficulty than other borderline patients in receiving help, since help tends to elicit envy. The analyst's interpretations tend to be devalued or ignored, rather than used for insight. Consequently, they tend to spend countless sessions, sometimes for prolonged periods, either overtly devaluing the analyst or trivializing the process by keeping it superficial and giving it little importance. Kernberg's approach to these narcissistic resistances is to interpret them as defenses against envy, rage, and the anxiety of dependence. Although Kernberg acknowledges that the resolution of these resistances takes a long time, he is opposed to allowing them to be enacted without interpretations, as he feels that only a systematic interpretive stance can eventually lead to their undoing.

Kernberg's treatment of narcissistic resistances is illustrated in his discussion of a patient who fell in love with a woman whom he idealized as beautiful, warm, and gifted. After they married, he became bored with and indifferent toward her. In the analysis he became aware that he treated his analyst in a similar manner and depreciated all he offered in order to defend against his hatred and envy of him. Subsequently, he became aware of his hatred of his wife for possessing all he lacked. After this awareness, he responded to his wife's expressions of love for the first time. "His awareness of his aggressive disqualification of her and his analyst, and his increasing ability to tolerate his hatred without having to defend against it by destroying his awareness of other people, made both his wife and his analyst 'come alive' as real people" (Kernberg, 1975, pp. 237–238). This vignette demonstrates Kernberg's approach of interpreting the narcissistic patient's devaluation of the analyst and resistance to receiving help as a defense against envy and aggressiveness.

The use of the grandiose self as a defense against receiving help from the analyst constitutes the primary narcissistic resistance and tends to become the focal point of the treatment. Because the grandiose self is so well organized, even if the patient responds initially to the analyst's interpretation of the resistance, he or she will quickly revert to the defense. In Kernberg's view, the treatment process tends to become a repetitive cycle involving the analyst's interpretations of the patient's resistances, the patient's response and subsequent resurrection of the narcissistic defense, and the analyst's interpretation of the renewed defense. The following case illustrates this focal conflict in the treatment of the narcissistic patient (Kernberg, 1975).

The patient complained ceaselessly of monotony and boredom in the sessions and insisted that treatment was hopeless; meanwhile, his outside life seemed to be going well. Kernberg pointed out that to the patient his criticism of analysis was an indirect devaluation of Kernberg as the provider of useless treatment. While the patient initially denied this, he later admitted to Kernberg that he blamed him for the failure of the analysis and was surprised to find himself so pleased to continue his treatment with him. At that point Kernberg was able to interpret that the patient had, in fact, been quite satisfied to view him as worthless while achieving success in life. In response to this interpretation the patient became extremely anxious, feared that Kernberg hated him, and developed paranoid fantasies of Kernberg wreaking vengeance upon him. Kernberg interpreted that it was precisely this fear of attack that lay behind the patient's need to reassure himself that he was not in analysis by repeatedly proclaiming that nothing of significance was occurring in the sessions. The patient expressed admiration that Kernberg had not been derailed by his continual assertions that analysis was a failure. Kernberg (1975) then describes the crux of the ensuing process this way:

> At the next moment, however, he thought that I was very clever, and that I knew how to use "typical analytic tricks" to keep 'one up' over patients. He then thought that he himself would try to use a similar technique with people who might try to depreciate him. I then pointed out that as soon as he received a "good" interpretation, and found himself helped, he also felt guilty over his attacks on me, and then again envious of my "goodness." Therefore, he had to "steal" my interpretations for his own use with others, devaluating me in the process, in order to avoid acknowledging that I had anything good left as well as to avoid the obligation of feeling grateful. The patient became quite anxious for a moment and then went completely "blank." He came in the next session with a bland denial of the emotional relevance of what had developed in the session before, and once again the same cycle started all over, with repetitive declarations of his boredom and the ineffectiveness of analysis [p. 245].

Kernberg believes that the process illustrated in this case is a reflection of the narcissistic patient's inability to depend on the analyst. Kernberg's continual interpretations of the patient's need to devalue the analytic process were geared to making conscious the patient's fear of acknowledging his need for the analyst because of his rage and envy of him. As soon as the patient would begin to feel he had received something useful from Kernberg, he became anxious and then dissipated the anxiety by devaluing Kernberg and his offerings.

It is the analyst's task to persist in the interpretation of these seemingly endless complaints and not be driven by them into collusion with the patient by concluding that the patient is untreatable. While many analysts believe that a patient who remains superficial and seemingly uninvolved in treatment for a prolonged period of time is unable to develop a transference and is untreatable, Kernberg's view is that the narcissistic patient is in fact expressing an intense transference based on "devaluation, depreciation, and spoiling." Consequently, the interpretation of the negative transference is even more crucial in the treatment of the narcissistic personality than in the treatment of other borderline patients.

The most extreme form of narcissistic resistance is found in patients who suffer from "malignant narcissism" (Kernberg, 1984). As discussed earlier, the psychological organization of such patients tends to be consumed by efforts to defeat others; hence they make triumph over the analyst's efforts their primary treatment goal. Their sadism is so gratified by such a "victory" that they are willing to lie and may even become dangerously destructive and self-destructive in order to achieve such a "triumph." Such patients self-mutilate and even make serious suicide attempts in order to feel the exhilaration of defeating the analyst. The first technical priority with such a patient is to confront and limit both destructive and self-destructive behavior; otherwise, the treatment cannot proceed. The second priority is to confront and interpret, if possible, the patient's lying, for this too renders treatment impossible. Kernberg acknowledges that once a firm stand is taken against lying, the patient will frequently regress to a paranoid transference. Nonetheless, in Kernberg's view, the analyst must be able to withstand and work through this development because the alternative is unworkable.

If these two threats to the treatment can be controlled, the treatment of malignant narcissism proceeds to the major dynamic issues: the patient's envy of and inability to depend on the analyst. These are typical transference issues for most narcissistic patients, but in cases of malignant narcissism they have a special quality: such patients have a need to destroy the analyst psychologically. They attempt to defeat the analyst's interpretations and to rob him of his most valued possessions, whether intellectual or physical. They set out to defeat the analyst whenever the treatment threatens to progress. When the analytic work finally seems to be going well after endless complaints of the lack of progress, such a patient will suddenly dismiss it all with an attitude of triumph. Kernberg attributes the intensity of this desire to defeat the analyst to the patient's envy of the analyst's nurturing qualities and to his or her freedom from the same pathology that enslaves the patient. The analyst's task is to interpret both the unconscious need to defeat the analyst and the envy that motivates it. It is also crucial that the analyst not submit to the grandiose self but instead take a firm stand on reality by interpreting the patient's distortions, even though the patient will become enraged and may act out in ways that threaten to terminate the treatment. Kernberg does not agree with Winnicott (1954b) and his followers (for example, Khan, 1960), who, as we saw in chapter 4, advocate tolerance of paranoid regressive episodes. In Kernberg's view, the analyst's firm stance and persistent interpretation of transference distortions reestablishes the analytic framework and eventually allows patients to acknowledge the unreasonable nature of their aggressiveness, resulting in guilt and concern for others. At that point the establishment of more normal object relations and superego structures begins to take place.

Because the patient treats the analyst as an extension of the self, consideration of the countertransference is even more crucial in the treatment of the typical narcissistic patient than in that of most borderline patients. In Kernberg's view, when a narcissistic patient consistently devalues the treatment process the analyst's emotional response is a good indicator of the patient's hidden intention. In the clinical vignette described earlier, Kernberg's feeling of being devalued as useless and silly was the clue to his interpretation that the patient's intention was to make him feel worthless. The most difficult and typical countertransference is the analyst's feeling of being controlled and devalued. The danger, in Kernberg's view, is in analysts acting out their countertransference anger by rejecting the patient in retaliation for the rejection they experience. Although analysts cannot always assume that everything they experience is a reflection of the patient's current issues, Kernberg does point out that because narcissistic patients treat the analyst as an extension of themselves, the countertransference does tend to be much closer to the patient's affective life than is normally the case. While other sources of data must always be used, the countertransference tends to be a more significant indicator with narcissistic personalities than with most other patients.

Confrontation with the rage, envy, and fear of dependence underlying the grandiose self, if pursued persistently, eventually leads to the eruption of these highly anxiety-provoking affects (Kernberg, 1975). The result is an upsurge of hatred and its projection, leading to an intense negative transference. The pathological internalized object relationships that the grandiose self split off from awareness now become activated in the transference. The analyst becomes the sadistic parental object, but to defend against this awareness the patient re-idealizes the analyst. In this phase of treatment of the narcissistic personality, the patient's identification will rapidly alternate among the idealized self- and object images and the negative self- and object images while the analyst is perceived as the complementary representation (Kernberg, 1984). For example, the patient may identify with the infantile, victimized self while the analyst is experienced as the sadistic mother, or the patient may assume the role of the idealized father and see the analyst as an empty and greedy child, longing for him. These split-off object relations units had been hidden under the grandiose self and now appear in response to its interpretation. In Kernberg's view, this development can take as long as three years to appear and should be seen by the fifth year if the grandiose self is analytically resolvable. In this advanced stage of the psychoanalysis of the narcissistic personality, the treatment appears to be much like that of other borderline patients. The focus is on the interpretation of the quickly shifting, intense split object relations units.

Eventually, as the negative transference and oral rage are worked through, patients are forced to become aware that the hated, feared mother/analyst is a projection of their oral rage and is the same as the idealized, longed-for mother/analyst whom they wish to be rescued by (Kernberg, 1975). Kernberg agrees with Klein (1937) that the treatment of splitting involves the resolution of the depression resulting from the awareness that the hated object is the loved object. This realization ushers in a crucial period of treatment. Patients now feel guilty and despairing for having hated the analyst/mother whom they also love and long for. The guilt results in depression and may be strong enough to elicit suicidal ideation. It is crucial that analysts be alert to the context and reasons for the depression. If they are not, the depression may be mistakenly viewed as regression, rather than progression. Kernberg sees depression as not only a positive movement in therapy but also a significant structural shift, as the patient is able to experience true guilt for the first time and mourning can now take place. It is critical that the analyst understand that new psychological structure is being formed and interpret the patient's depression as guilt over having injured, even if only in fantasy, the object of love and dependence.

That the patient can now experience this depression reflects three crucial therapeutic transformations. First, the ability to experience ambivalence indicates movement to the level of whole object integration. Because whole-object integration is the necessary condition for the formation of the structured tripartite ego, the resolution of guilt and ambivalence results in the development of the ego-superego-id structure of the psyche. Second, the analyst is experienced as a separate, independent person for the first time, allowing the patient to show genuine interest in others as separate, "real" people. Third, and perhaps most important, the resolution of the narcissistic resistances results in normal infantile narcissism and now dependence on the analyst. Interpretations can now be used for understanding, as opposed to being "stolen" greedily as magical "food" or rejected to defend against envy. A benign cycle takes place in which the utilization of interpretations leads to an internal richness that replaces emptiness and gradually alleviates envy.

The best description Kernberg (1975) provides of the treatment process with the narcissistic patient is the analysis of an architect in his late thirties. For the first three years of analysis the patient showed the typical narcissistic paradigm. He initially idealized the analyst and then shifted to a continual oscillation between grandiosity and idealization. The interpretation of these narcissistic defenses led initially to the revelation of intense envy and competitiveness and later to oscillation between "oral demandingness and anger to longing for a dependency on a loving, protective father–mother image, and strong guilt feelings for his attacks on the analyst" (p. 304).

This transference paradigm shifted to a more stable dependence on a loving father image, and it was only at this time, after three years of analysis, that the patient came to depend on the analyst as a real person. He now began to miss him on weekends and separations and for the first time felt depression and mourning in his relationship with the analyst. The patient reacted to this phase by withdrawal and feelings of emptiness, and the sessions appeared to revert to the previous stage of narcissistic resistances. However, the material was replete with references to the patient's sadistic, withholding mother, and he became aware that he was identified with her while he treated the analyst as his infantile self. The interpretation of this new transference paradigm brought about a further deepening of the realistic dependence on the analyst. Kernberg described the ensuing process this way:

> The patient now saw [the analyst] as a protective, loving father toward whom he could turn for the gratification of his dependent childhood needs; and he now felt he could abandon himself to the analytic situation. . . . Now, for the first time, the patient became aware of how his entire attitude toward the analyst had been influenced by his basic conviction that no real relationship would ever occur between him and the psychoanalyst. . . . A year later the full development of oedipal conflicts

emerged in the transference, and the analysis acquired features of the usual resistances and manifestations of these conflicts [p. 305].

This vignette shows how a prolonged period of narcissistic resistance was eventually "undone" by persistent interpretation of the grandiose self and idealization defenses. The result was an eruption of oral rage and envy that was worked through by interpretation, and followed by the crucial stage of object integration to which the patient responded by narcissistic withdrawal. Even though this stage appeared to erase the treatment gains, it was a temporary regression stimulated by the anxiety of ambivalence toward the analyst/mother whole object. Depression and mourning were signs of forward movement. The fact that interpretation quickly moved the process forward indicates that progress had taken place. At that point the dependence on the analyst took root allowing the patient to experience his own emotional needs as well as those of his family. This case illustrates Kernberg's view that when the patient is able to depend on the analyst, the narcissistic defenses have been resolved and the analysis moves to a neurotic level.

By way of summary, it can be seen that Kernberg's view of the treatment of the narcissistic personality eventually becomes similar to the treatment of other borderline patients. The most striking difference is the prolonged period of time devoted to the interpreting and working through of the narcissistic resistances that precedes the revelation of the borderline dynamics of pathological internalized object relationships. The other major difference is the prominence of the envy that emerges in the pathological constellation. This envy leads to especially difficult resistances and regressive swings as the patient is unable to depend on the analyst and is therefore resistant to accepting interpretations. Because both these factors make the defenses of narcissistic patients especially difficult to resolve, Kernberg prefers psychoanalysis proper for these patients whenever possible to give the best possible chance for the resolution of the narcissistic resistances.

SUMMARY AND CRITIQUE

Kernberg has created the most comprehensive object relations theory of development, psychopathology, and treatment yet developed. His approach is a systematic application of both object relations and ego psychology developmental theory to pathology and treatment. He has been able to enhance the value of the Kleinian object relations model and its understanding of defense mechanisms without falling into the most serious errors of the Kleinian school (see chapter 3). No other theorist has succeeded so well in synthesizing the work of Jacobson, Mahler, and Klein and in integrating object relations theory with the structural concepts and technical principles of ego psychology. Further, Kernberg has developed an object relations model of treatment consistent with the technical requirements of traditional psychoanalytic therapy. In this respect, his thought stands in opposition to the work of Fairbairn, Guntrip, and Winnicott, all of whom ultimately recommended modification of the classical analytic stance in the interests of becoming more of a real person to the patient. At this point, a critical assessment of Kernberg's work is in order. Three categories of difficulty with Kernberg's views will be discussed.

First, there are conceptual problems with some of Kernberg's distinctions between psychopathological conditions and their clinical implications. Foremost among these difficulties is confusion surrounding his conceptualization of a subgroup of narcissistic patients who function on the overt borderline level. By Kernberg's definition, narcissistic personalities are borderline patients who use a grandiose-self defense to conceal the underlying personality organization. The conceptualization of a subgroup for which this is not true contradicts Kernberg's own definition of narcissistic personality organization. Kernberg contends that patients in this subgroup, despite overt borderline functioning, are narcissistic personalities because of the predominance of envy and the presence of a narcissistic personality structure, although its functioning is ineffective. However, these criteria change Kernberg's definition of the narcissistic personality organization and make this subgroup virtually impossible to distinguish from other borderline patients who use omnipotence as a defense. Further, since psychoanalysis is not recommended for this group—sometimes not even expressive psychotherapy—its inclusion in the category of narcissistic patients is even more dubious.

Perhaps more significantly, there is a problem with Kernberg's recommendation of psychoanalysis proper for narcissistic patients and expressive psychotherapy for other borderline patients. The latter are deemed too weak in ego strength and boundaries to withstand psychoanalysis, yet psychoanalysis is recommended for the narcissistic patient, who is said to have an underlying borderline personality organization. If narcissistic patients are really borderline personalities, their weak ego structure should contraindicate psychoanalysis for them as for other borderline patients. Kernberg's contention is that when the grandiose-self defense is worked through in treatment, the underlying borderline personality organization becomes manifest.

According to Kernberg's conceptualization of treatment, expressive psychotherapy should be the treatment of choice at that point. Kernberg's rationale for recommending psychoanalysis for the narcissistic patient is that only the most intensive form of treatment can hope to dissolve narcissistic defenses. While this may be so, it does not address the contradiction inherent in the assertion that psychoanalysis can be effective in the treatment of the now-apparent ego weaknesses of the narcissistic patient's underlying borderline personality organization whereas it is not considered effective with other borderline patients.

These considerations lead to a general problem with Kernberg's concept of applying different treatments to different of levels of personality organization. The neurotic personality organization is considered appropriate for psychoanalysis proper, unlike severe character pathology, which requires the integration of split object relations. However, as we have seen, Kernberg views psychoanalysis as a process of breaking down the personality into its component object relations units, and then reintegrating them into a new structure. Given this concept of the analytic process, the difference between the treatment of neurosis and severe character pathology lies primarily in the setting of limits. Yet, as we saw, many borderline personalities do not require the setting of limits. Treatment approaches that Kernberg presents as clearly different are more alike than he believes. The similarity of treatment approaches is underscored by the neurotic patient discussed earlier who showed no more simultaneous awareness of different object relations units than do most borderline patients. The analytic process for the neurotic patient involved undergoing different phases in the enactment of split-off object relations units, a process that is difficult to distinguish from the treatment of the borderline patient who does not act out severely. The common occurrence of this process in the treatment of neurotics led Grotstein (1986) to conclude that splitting is ubiquitous rather than a particular mechanism of severe psychopathology (see chapter 3). Kernberg presents his categories of patients and treatments as discrete groupings, whereas the differences seem to be of degree and not kind, and the criteria for making the distinctions are much less clear than Kernberg contends.

The second questionable aspect of Kernberg's theory is his adherence to the concept of drive. In Kernberg's view, a drive can only be expressed through an object relationship. The embeddedness of drives in object relations raises the question of why the concept of drive should be retained at all. The primary reason Kernberg gives for maintaining the drive concept is that a pure object relations model denies the importance of the aggressive drive, which seeks not to obtain an object but to eliminate it. But, is aggressiveness a drive? As mentioned earlier, Kernberg distinguishes between an instinctive response as an inborn, discrete self-preservative behavior, and a drive. By definition, a drive is a cyclical biological impulse that motivates behavior to achieve gratification. Kernberg uses the concept in this sense when he contends that the aggressively acting-out patient is receiving "instinctual gratification." As pointed out in the critique of Klein (see chapter 3), sex, warmth, hunger, and thirst all fit this model, but aggression does not have such a biological rhythm (Scott, 1958). Aggression *does* fit the model of an instinctive response, as it is an innate disposition that is evoked when circumstances warrant. However, to conclude from this that it is a drive seeking gratification is to disregard Kernberg's own distinction between instinctive response and drive. The evidence that aggression does not operate as a drive appears to eliminate Kernberg's only justification for differentiating his theory from a pure object relations model.

Similarly, Kernberg treatment strategy does not justify postulating an aggressive drive. Kernberg applies this concept to both the setting of treatment parameters and the interpretive process. One need not, however, assume that aggression is "instinctually gratifying" in order to justify limiting destructive behavior. It is sufficient that the behavior is harmful. Kernberg (1975) provides two clinical illustrations of limiting "instinctual gratification." One case was the patient mentioned earlier who screamed at her therapist interminably although she was calm and relaxed outside the sessions. The therapist limited her behavior, thus creating more conflict outside the sessions and an increase of anxiety. One can understand the material as easily from a purely object relations point of view: the patient may have been enacting a split object relationship from her past with reversed roles so that she was the abusive parental figure and the therapist was placed in the role of the victimized child/patient. Having achieved mastery over the childhood abuser/therapist, she was then able to relate normally to other people. When the therapist prevented the enactment of this relationship, the sense of mastery over trauma was taken away and the need to enact it infiltrated other relationships. While one cannot make a definitive formulation from the material presented in Kernberg's vignette, it is sufficient for the present purpose to note that it can be understood without the assumption of drive gratification.

In another case Kernberg presents as an illustration of limiting "instinctual gratification," the patient angrily demanded an increase in hours. When interpretation was to no avail, the therapist refused to increase the hours and made a change in the patient's behavior a condition for the continuation of the treatment. The patient's behavior changed markedly in a few days, and he admitted that he had enjoyed his expression of anger. The positive response to limit setting contradicts a drive interpretation of the patient's behavior. According to the postulates of psychoanalysis, if the expression of a drive is blocked, frustration will be experienced and the drive derivative will seek expression in an indirect, pathological form. Apparently this did not happen in this case. Furthermore, the satisfaction experienced by the aggressive expression does not imply "instinctual gratification": enactment of an object relationship can be enjoyed for any number of reasons, depending on its meaning to the patient.

Kernberg applies the concept of an aggressive drive to the interpretive process in his recommendation that the therapist focus on the negative transference. We have seen that he attributes the abusive, hostile acting out of the borderline patient toward the therapist to "excessive aggressiveness." However, in Kernberg's view, as drives are expressed only through object relationships, the negative transference is the enactment of a split object relationship, and the therapist's task is to discover and label it. The conceptualization of the aggressive object relationship as a drive does not add to the interpretation and could potentially misdirect it. To give but one example: when Miss A devalued her therapist as "provincial," intellectually inadequate, unsophisticated, and lacking in self-assurance, she was enacting her mother's superior, devaluing attitude toward her as a child and causing the therapist to feel the sense of inadequacy and despair she had felt. Kernberg interpreted this transference paradigm as an enactment of her internalized mother–child object relationship. To equate this transference enactment with an aggressive drive does not contribute to the interpretation, and to interpret the patient's hostility as the acting out of excessive aggressiveness would be to miss its object relations significance. To Kernberg's credit, he does not suggest the latter but proposes the object relations interpretation. However, having done so, he obviates the need to invoke aggression as a drive.

A related problem with Kernberg's concept of the aggressive drive is his failure to distinguish between aggression and hate. When Kernberg develops his view that the earliest object relationships are divided into the libidinal and aggressive object relations units, he identifies libido with love and aggression with hate. However, aggression is an energetic expression that can occur in a variety of affective contexts such as joy, excitement, mastery, assertiveness, or hate. The degree to which aggression is manifested as hate is often the degree to which it tends toward the pathological. As we will see in chapter 6, Kohut (1977) makes the distinction between the healthy assertiveness of the normal child and the pathological rage of the narcissistic personality disorder. The baby in distress is clearly in pain, and Kernberg is quite justified in presuming that such states of "unpleasure" or pain are in marked contrast to the infant's pleasurable states. However, it is an unjustified inference to conclude that the infant feels "hatred" whenever it feels pain. Hatred appears later, when the child is able to target an object of its frustration. Aggressive acting out of hateful feelings is one type of expression of aggression, the most negative form it can take.

To identify the intense hatred and destructive expressions of the borderline patient with childhood aggression is to equate pathology with normal childhood, a mistake Kernberg accuses Kohut of making with the latter's concepts of grandiosity and idealization. While Kernberg (1975) criticizes Kohut for failing to distinguish normal and pathological idealization, Kernberg appears to have made a similar error in equating hatred and aggression. The abusive, destructive hostility of the borderline personality organization is not an excess of joyful aggressive assertiveness; it is a different psychological phenomenon. Thus, excess aggression of people who are assertive in the achievement of life and work goals is qualitatively different from the hostility of the borderline patient. The aggression of the borderline patient is pathological not because of its quantity but because of its hateful, destructive quality. To view hateful, destructive aggressiveness as somehow primary, and healthy assertiveness as a sublimation of the hateful state is to pathologize human motivation in ways that are not consonant with recent developmental research into infancy and childhood (Lichtenburg, 1983, 1989).

Stern's (1985) compilation of the evidence from infant research leads to the conclusion that the notions of hatred and "bad" are symbolic forms beyond the ken of the infant. Stern points out that the infant has four to six feedings each day with varying degrees of pleasure and that the infant's cognitive ability enables it to discern face and breast across these varied tones of pleasure more easily than it is able to organize experiences into pleasure and unpleasure and then conceptualize these states as "good" and "bad." It is perhaps unnecessary to state that hatred requires still one more inferential step. The evidence from infant research indicates that "good," "bad," and "hatred" are later conceptualizations that are possible only after speech has developed. Stern does suggest however, that infant research allows one to infer that infants experience pleasure and unpleasure in the early phase and that these experiences will be clustered around their "hedonic tone." However, he points out that the infant has many such "working models of mother" and that there is no basis for giving primacy to categorization according to hedonic tone. Stern concludes that splitting is not a normal state of infancy but a later construction that lends itself to pathological conditions.

Given that aggression does not evince the biological rhythm of drives, that drives in Kernberg's view "find expression" only through object relationships, and, finally, that the presumption of aggression as a drive seems clinically unnecessary and confusing, Kernberg's object relations model does not require the retention of a drive concept. It does not fit Kernberg's metapsychology and theory of personality development, and it renders his clinical theory needlessly confusing. In fact, the drive concept simply risks interfering with the consistent application of his object relations model of treatment. The only purported application of the concept is to explain limit setting, which, we have seen, can be explained without a drive concept. Even at the oedipal level, Kernberg's approach is to analyze the constituent object relations that compose the psychological organization. It is the apparent irrelevance of the drive concept to the object relations view of psychoanalytic treatment that led Greenberg and Mitchell to conclude that Kernberg was being "political" in his retention of the drives (Greenberg and Mitchell, 1983).

This discussion of the drives leads to a third cluster of questions regarding Kernberg's treatment principles for pathological aggression. His primary postulate of confronting the patient with split-off aggression to "undo" the splitting process is not sustained by his own clinical illustrations. In the clinical vignettes he offers to demonstrate this technique, the patient frequently regresses. In one case illustration of "undoing" splitting discussed earlier, the therapist confronted the patient with her alcoholic binges and the patient needed to be rehospitalized. The therapist felt he was dealing with a "real person" for the first time—and may well have been. However, given the patient's reaction, this feeling on the part of the therapist does not demonstrate the effectiveness of the technique; follow-up data confirming the expected long-term beneficial results are necessary. While Kernberg is convinced of the importance of "undoing" splitting by confrontation in such cases, the clinical vignettes he reports do not justify his certainty. The fact that the patients often become more symptomatic may well be a product of ill-timed or misconceived interpretation. For example, if the aforementioned patient was drinking for a reason other than anger at the therapist, she may well have regressed in response to feeling misunderstood.

To support his claim for the effectiveness of his method, Kernberg often refers to the findings of the Menninger Research Project on Psychotherapy and Psychoanalysis (Kernberg et al., 1972). This impressive research project is one of the few well-controlled studies of psychotherapy with severely disturbed patients, and its findings provide no evidence relevant to the validity of Kernberg's approach to excessive aggression or aggressively fueled defense mechanisms. More significantly, the study is not as supportive of Kernberg's claim that expressive psychotherapy is the treatment of choice for borderline patients as he seems to imply. The Menninger study only compared supportive psychotherapy to psychoanalysis proper; there was no group receiving expressive psychotherapy. The basic findings were that patients with low initial ego strength (borderlines) did poorly in both treatment modalities and patients with high initial ego strength did well in both modalities. In both groups, patients receiving psychoanalysis did better than patients receiving supportive psychotherapy. However, there were some patients in the latter group who received "supportive-expressive" psychotherapy, and the low initial ego strength group did better with this modality than either of the others. Kernberg deduces from this finding that these poorly functioning patients require a special type of treatment: modified psychoanalysis. It needs to be underscored that no group in the study was given this type of treatment. Kernberg's conclusion is an inference from the data, not an outgrowth of it. While he recognized that he was making such an inference, he pointed to his clinical data to support his claim for modified psychoanalysis (Kernberg et al., 1972). But, as noted, his clinical data are wanting. It must be concluded that despite the impressive, consistent system Kernberg advocates for the treatment of the borderline patient, the clinical and research data he offers in support of it do not justify such confidence.

While Kernberg's approach to the undoing of splitting and the handling of the negative transference is not convincing, he provides better evidence for his overall strategy of labeling split object relationships and integrating them via interpretation. For example, when Miss L's two primary transference paradigms—the wish to be raped and killed and the infantile dependence—were brought together, she began her improvement. This integration was achieved by interpretation rather than an undoing by confrontation, and the mutative effects of the interpretive process are impressive. Three points are relevant in the present context. First, the pathology in this case lay not in excessive aggressiveness but in the splitting of two conflictual object relations units. This fact would seem to belie Kernberg's claim that splitting is always a product of excessive oral aggressiveness and that the latter is the root of pathology in the borderline personality organization. Second, the splitting of Miss L's object relations units cannot be conceptualized as a split between good and bad. Both object relationships had positive and negative qualities, and both were fraught with conflict. In fact, very few of Kernberg's clinical illustrations of splitting can be readily formulated as good and bad. Miss L represents the more typical borderline patient who splits between two highly conflicted object relationships, each of which is threatened by the other. Third, this case, like others without acting out of excess aggressiveness, was managed by interpretation alone and showed great improvement.

The same principles apply to Miss N, the patient who saw Kernberg as either a harsh, dangerous masculine figure or a soft, slightly depressed feminine figure. Despite Kernberg's attempts to fit these transference paradigms into his "all good" and "all bad" scheme, both object relations units had good and bad qualities. They were split apart, but not organized by good and bad. In this case, like the case of Miss L, there was no indication of "excessive aggressiveness" and no discussion of acting-out a negative transference. In cases of this type—in which object relations units are split, but not into good and bad—Kernberg seems to apply his interpretive principles of object relationship enactment most clearly and consistently, and one can most easily see therapeutic benefit. There are some patients, such as Miss B, whose splitting is organized around good and bad, but they appear to be but one variant of split ego organization.

In summary, Kernberg's clinical illustrations fit his concept of object relationships as the root of the borderline personality organization but not his equation of splitting with good and bad. In the cases discussed, one can see that the pathological splitting process involves complex object relations units that are split apart for a variety of reasons. It would be a major oversimplification to reduce the pathology to excess aggressiveness. The splitting process in both Miss N and Miss A was not motivated by excess aggressiveness but by the need to keep apart perceptions of self and object that were too confusing and difficult to integrate.

Finally, it should be noted that this critique of the drive component of Kernberg's thought is not meant to suggest that his theory of the analytic process is implicitly social or interpersonal. The current school of interpersonal psychoanalysis, discussed in chapter 7 and represented by such theorists as Gill and Mitchell, conceptualizes the

analytic process as interpersonal in the sense that patient and therapist are engaged in a mutual relationship in which each party continually e nacts and reenacts roles (Gill, 1983; Greenberg and Mitchell,
1983; Mitchell, 1988). For Kernberg, role enactments are a playing out
of the patient's drama. The therapist's behavior will often fit a prescribed role, but the interaction follows from a script written by the
patient's unconscious. Kernberg has managed to create a conceptualization of psychoanalytic treatment that takes into full consideration
the enactment of role relations between patient and therapist without
becoming an interpersonal alternative to the psychoanalytic process of
an analyst analyzing a patient.

CHAPTER 6

The Work of Heinz Kohut

HEINZ KOHUT BEGAN HIS MAJOR THEORETICAL INNOVATIONS IN PSYCHO-analysis with the effort to fill what he, much like Kernberg, felt was a void in the psychoanalytic theory of psychopathology between the structural neuroses and the psychoses. Initially, he applied his self-psychological theory to the narcissistic disorders, which he felt were the primary syndromes lying between these two classes of pathology, and accepted the drive-ego model for the neuroses. This concept of self psychology became known as self psychology "in the narrow sense." Eventually, Kohut expanded his theoretical viewpoint to self psychology "in the broad sense," which included his reconceptualiza-tion of the neuroses as well as the therapeutic action of psychoanaly-sis. This shift entailed considerable conceptual change that Kohut did not always acknowledge. For this reason his work can be confusing and lends itself to different interpretations. While Kohut never altered his initial views of narcissistic pathology, he broadened his theoretical constructs to envelop all of psychoanalytic theory. His new theory, self psychology, became the second major school within the frame-work of psychoanalysis. Adherents of self psychology differ as to whether their model is an object relations theory. For example, Wolf (1988) views self psychology as an intrapsychic theory and eschews its categorization as object relations, whereas Bacal and Newman (1990) conceive of self psychology as a variant of object relations theory. Self psychology is classified as an object relations theory here because it views development and psychopathology as rooted in the internaliza-tion of objects and thus fits the definition of object relations theory as presented in chapter 1.

Kohut (1959, 1982) viewed psychoanalysis as the science of com-plex mental states. He pointed out that any science is defined by the method it uses to gather its data. Psychoanalysis, as the psychology of complex mental states, uses empathy and introspection. Kohut defined empathy as vicarious introspection, the means by which we understand others' communications. It is our ability to adopt the

247

stance of others from their viewpoint that allows us to understand them. The knowledge we gain by looking at the world through the lens of others constitutes psychological knowledge. Whereas the natural sciences gather their data by observation, acquiring knowledge of the physical world through the senses, psychological knowledge is won by empathy and introspection. We understand other people not by observing their behavior but by empathizing with their psychological states. Knowledge gathered by extrospection is not psychoanalytic data and cannot inform psychoanalysis as science or therapeutic procedure. From a theoretical point of view, Kohut hoped to delimit the type of concept admissible in psychoanalytic discourse. He advocated the elimination of concepts such as dependence from psychoanalytic consideration because he felt that such concepts could be either biological or sociological but never psychological (Kohut, 1982). By defining psychoanalysis as the science of empathy and introspection he hoped to found it as a pure psychology, independent of biology or any other discipline. The implication for treatment is that free association is replaced by empathic immersion in the patient's psychological world as the primary investigative tool (Kohut, 1959, 1977, p. 303).

In accordance with his emphasis on empathy and introspection, Kohut (1984) distinguished "experience near" from "experience distant" theory: theory based on the empathic grasp of what patients experience at any particular time is experience near whereas theory that uses an external frame of reference is experience distant. That is, considering certain behaviors normal or abnormal is an experience-distant approach, whereas grasping empathically the meaning of the behavior is an experience-near approach. The central point of Kohut's therapeutic prescription is that the analyst must always be attuned to the experience near, the meaning of the behavior, even though his empathic understanding has to be informed by experience-distant guidelines of normality. Kohut believed that classical psychoanalytic theory had become too removed from patients' experience and that psychoanalytic theory must return to its roots in patients' subjective experience.

Because Kohut's views shifted dramatically, and were continually evolving, even immediately prior to his death in 1981, his work is best approached historically. Consequently, after a brief account of his developmental views, which provides the conceptual framework for his general theory of psychopathology, his formulations of narcissistic pathology will be discussed in detail. We will then examine their expansion into self psychology as a global theory that now forms the basis of a separate psychoanalytic school.

DEVELOPMENT

Kohut (1966, 1971) accepted Freud's (1914) theory that the initial stages of infancy are autoerotism and primary narcissism, which is defined by the libidinal investment of the self, and that the infant emerges from the latter stage when it recognizes that its source of supplies comes from outside itself. At this point, says Kohut, following Freud, much of the narcissism from the stage of primary narcissism is now invested in the parental figure, resulting in the idealization of the object. In the resolution of the oedipal complex, the parental figure is internalized to form the superego-ego ideal structure. Thus, the personality structure is a result of the reinternalization of primary narcissism after a "deflection" through the idealized parental object. Up to this point, Kohut follows Freud.

According to Kohut (1977), the earliest phase of infancy is a prepsychological stage characterized by physiological needs and tension states without awareness. However, he believed that one could justifiably view even this early prepsychological state as a self *in statu nascendi* because the infant is treated as though it were a self. The empathic maternal environment responds to the baby as a virtual self, and so begins the process of self formation. Even the first maternal contact begins the process that will result in the birth of the self. Thus, ministrations of the maternal environment constitute the first "selfobject" in the infant's experience. By this term Kohut refers to the object as fulfilling a necessary (that is, psychologically life-sustaining) function that the self is unable to perform for itself. (Initially Kohut hyphenated this term, but since he eliminated the hyphen in all his later work and his followers have continued this usage, the hyphen will be eliminated here as well.)

The early maternal environment provides the child's first experience of empathy; by means of empathy the mother of the neonate knows the child's psychological states and responds to them. Empathy, the tool by which we know others, is also the origin of psychological life in Kohut's (1977) view: without the empathic mother responding to the infant as though it already had a self, the infant would not develop a sense of self. The child is born with innate potentials, and the environment responds selectively to them, thereby channeling innate givens into a "nuclear self." In short, the birth of the self is a function of maternal empathy mobilizing the child's constitutional endowment.

Psychological life begins with emergence from primary narcissism and is stimulated by the inevitable failure of the parents to satisfy perfectly the child's narcissistic needs. According to Kohut (1971), the child now becomes aware of its vulnerability and attempts to recapture the lost bliss of the narcissistic state in two ways. First, the child effects a renewed libidinal investment in the self, which Kohut originally called the "narcissistic self" and later changed to the "grandiose self." This self has grandiose and exhibitionistic needs, but since it is too weak and vulnerable to satisfy them itself, it requires an object for confirmation. A crucial function of the parental object in this phase is to "mirror" the vulnerable, grandiose self. The parent who mirrors the child's need for admiration and approval is performing a necessary function and thereby bolstering the child's sense of self. The child who receives such mirroring does not view the parent as an autonomous individual but as a means for strengthening its sense of self; this is why Kohut terms such parental behavior a "selfobject" function.

Some of the narcissistic libido is invested in the idealization of the parent, which results in what Kohut called the "idealized parental imago." Attachment to this imago provides an additional source of narcissistic gratification. The child oscillates between recognition of the parent as "other" and resubmergence into a primitive merger state. Out of this oscillation, the idealized parental imago is established. In supplying this narcissistic function the parent once more is viewed not as an individual in his or her own right but as a means by which the child can achieve an enhanced sense of well-being. Availability for idealization, then, is the second selfobject function performed by the parent in the first years of life. The grandiose self and the idealized parental imago are the transformations of primary narcissism that form the archaic self in the preoedipal phase. While Kohut recognized that either parent may be involved in mirroring the grandiose self or allowing idealization, he did believe that one could roughly equate the mother with the mirroring function and the father with the need to idealize.

Gradually, as further disappointments in the parent are recognized, the idealized parental imago is given up. Every blemish on the idealized parental imago leads to its internalization until the ego ideal is firmly established within the psyche. The process by which this occurs is an almost imperceptible yielding of the idealized parental imago and its transformation into psychological structure, the ego ideal. Kohut calls this process "transmuting internalization," a term he applies to any internalization process that results in new psychological structure. In this case the idealized parental imago is transformed into ideals that the child hopes to realize.

Kohut follows Freud in seeing superego structure as the result of oedipal loss. However, unlike Freud, he sees the idealization of the superego as resulting not from its content but from its genesis in primary narcissism. According to Kohut (1966):

> That the original narcissism has passed through a cherished object before its reinternalization and that the narcissistic investment itself has been raised to the new developmental level of idealization account for the unique emotional importance of our standards, values, and ideals insofar as they are part of the superego [p. 434].

Thus, the internalization of the idealized parental imago results in the formation of the ego ideal, this new drive-regulating structure also imparts vitality to the superego, which becomes idealized, life in general now incorporates goals worth striving for. The end result of this process is an internalized set of ideals, cherished because of their connection to lost primary narcissism. These ideals form, in Kohut's terminology, one "pole" of the self.

The distinction between the process of superego formation and the ego ideal implies a difference between the development of narcissism and the development of object libido. Postulating these two separate lines of development was critical for Kohut; it allowed him to account for discrepancies between narcissistic equilibrium and superego formation. Kohut disputed Freud's U-tube analogy of narcissism in which the more narcissistic cathexes are "sent out" to objects the less love is available for oneself. He pointed out that love for the object does not decrease self-esteem but, rather, enhances it. In the present context it is unnecessary to summarize his argument; it suffices to note that, for Kohut, narcissistic libido and object libido underlie separate developmental processes. Narcissistic cathexes that are invested in the idealized parental imago result in the drive-neutralizing capacity of the psyche and in the idealization of the superego whereas object cathexes result in superego formation. The implication of this distinction is that the superego can be formed without being idealized; in such a case, superego structure is present but has little meaning to the personality. We will see the value of this distinction in Kohut's extensive discussion of patients with narcissistic personality disorders who have integrated but inadequately idealized superegos.

The archaic infantile grandiosity has a different fate. It too is gradually relinquished as parental responses inevitably fail to satisfy the child's grandiose needs. As the grandiose-exhibitionistic needs are optimally frustrated, they become transformed into realistic ambitions, forming the other pole of the self structure. Ideals and ambitions constitute the "bipolar self." In Kohut's view, ambitions push the individual but they are not loved as ideals are. Narcissistic libido becomes transformed from infantile, archaic grandiosity to realistic ambitions; these ambitions drive individuals to achieve their loved ideals. Between ambitions and ideals lie the individual's innate talents and skills. Ambitions and ideals must be sufficiently realistic so that they are within reach of one's talents, and the latter must be adequate to achieve ambitions and fulfill ideals. Consequently, Kohut conceives of talent as a "tension arc" between the ambitions and ideals that makes their achievement possible. In normal development the infantile grandiose self and idealized parental imago are transformed into realistic ambitions and loved ideals so that a cohesive, vital, harmonious self is capable of achieving a fulfilling life by realizing its ideals and ambitions with its available talents.

Kohut's views on the Oedipus complex changed decisively during the course of his theoretical development. In his early work Kohut (1971) accepted the classical psychoanalytic view of the Oedipus complex as the crucial developmental phase for the pathogenesis of the structural neuroses. At that point, he confined his contribution to the delineation of narcissism between the phase of primary narcissism and the oedipal period. His contention was that once the narcissistic phase was overcome by the relinquishment of archaic selfobjects and the emergence of an independent self, the child entered the oedipal phase with the typical sexual and aggressive conflicts described by classical psychoanalytic theory.

In his second book Kohut (1977) showed indications of shifting away from strict adherence to the classical position, but he did not delineate a clear alternative view. In subsequent publications, most notably in his third book, it became clear that Kohut (1984) no longer viewed the oedipal phase as a qualitatively different developmental period characterized by drive, as opposed to narcissistic, conflicts. In this revised developmental scheme, once the self is firm, vital, and harmonious, it is ready to address the issues of the oedipal phase but does not necessarily engage an Oedipus complex. The oedipal phase involves phase-appropriate affectionate and assertive feelings toward the parents; the Oedipus complex is the pathological outcome of unresolved conflicts in the oedipal phase. The phase is universal, the complex is not. The child who has formed a strong sense of self via the internalization of the preoedipal selfobjects, according to Kohut, joyfully enters the oedipal phase. If the parental objects are empathic with the affectionate feelings for the opposite-sex parent and the assertive feelings toward the same-sex parent and if they respond with pride and affection of their own, the child will be able to integrate affectionate and assertive strivings into its self structure. The integration of these affects enhances the ability of the self to achieve its ambitions and ideals.

Departing from classical theory, Kohut (1984) ultimately contended that sexual and hostile feelings in this phase are neither ubiquitous nor healthy but, instead, a product of pathogenic parental responses. According to Kohut, the drives are not inborn; disposition to affection and assertiveness is inborn, but these feelings only become transformed into lust or hostility under pathogenic conditions. The normal outcome of the oedipal phase, in Kohut's view, is not the acquisition of mastery over the drives, but the ability of the self to achieve its ambitions and fulfill its ideals. The key variable is neither the strength of the drives nor their prohibition but the empathy of the selfobject milieu.

The place of the oedipal phase in Kohut's final theory of development is very different from the decisive role it plays in classical psychoanalytic theory for the ultimate health of the personality. In Kohut's scheme previous phases are more crucial because if the self is strong, vital, and harmonious on entering the oedipal phase, the failure of the oedipal selfobjects can only impede the self's achievement of its goals; it cannot weaken self structure.

It is clear that drives do not play a major role in normal development in Kohut's scheme. The crucial variable is the development of the self, which is a product of the responses of the selfobjects of childhood to the narcissistic needs of the child. If the self is cohesive and vital there are no isolated lustful longings or hostile wishes. In the healthy self, according to Kohut, both affectionate and assertive feelings are experienced joyfully. To the extent that the self is defective, affection becomes split off into lust, and self-assertion "breaks down" into hostility. In his view, sexual and hostile wishes are not inborn drives that must be tamed to achieve psychological organization; rather, the dispositions toward affection and assertion are inborn, and hostility and lust are pathological products of their distortion. The fate of affection and assertion is determined by the strength of the self which, as we have seen, is a function of the responses of the crucial selfobjects. If the selfobject responses are empathic, phase- appropriate, and optimally frustrating, sexual feelings are the healthy outgrowth of affectionate feelings and aggression is the joyful expression of self-assertion. If the responses of the selfobjects are not empathic but are excessively frustrating or stimulating, either in the preoedipal or oedipal phases, self-development is arrested and pathology ensues. We now turn to the variety of pathological outcomes of faulty selfobject responses.

PSYCHOPATHOLOGY

Kohut's views on psychopathology grew out of his developmental theory. Since the crucial aspect of emotional development is the self and since its well-being depends on selfobject responsiveness, the crucial factor in psychopathology is disturbance in the self–selfobject relationship. If the selfobject responses are not optimally frustrating, that is, if they are excessively frustrating or stimulating, the vulnerable childhood self is threatened and will be forced to erect defenses to protect itself. Kohut calls this threat "disintegration anxiety," the fear of loss of self. The fear of loss of sense of who one is, according to Kohut, is the deepest form of human anxiety; it underlies all pathology. Because disintegration anxiety is so intolerable, the self will always choose to protect itself, no matter what the cost. Kohut called this the "principle of the primacy of self-preservation." Protection of the self has greater motivational power than any type of libidinal or other gratification, and its failure is feared more than death. Consequently, threats to the self call forth strong defenses that protect the weak childhood self but, in so doing, block its further development. All psychopathology, in Kohut's view, ultimately results from arrested self development and, therefore implies failure of the selfobject milieu. Differences in pathology are due to the severity and developmental stage of the selfobject failure and to the secondary conflicts that follow from such failures. With these concepts Kohut replaced the conflict-defense model with a model of pathology based on blockages in the development of the self. While a detailed comparison with Winnicott's theory is not possible here, it should be noted that Kohut's view of pathology as arrested development strikingly parallels Winnicott's concept of pathology as blocked maturational process.

Throughout his theoretical writings, Kohut (1971, 1984) maintained that there are three categories of psychopathology: the psychoses, narcissistic pathology, and the structural neuroses. The first category consists of "prepsychological states" operating at the level of primary narcissism. In Kohut's (1984) view, psychotics are arrested prior to the awareness of selfobjects, that is, prior to psychological life, and so fail to achieve a cohesive self, cannot use selfobjects or form transferences and are not analytically accessible. Such patients, in short, lack a self. This does not seem to be a remarkable point of view—except that Kohut included in this category borderline patients. While he acknowledged that his clinical experience with such patients was limited, he insisted that they are psychotic, once deeming them "really schizophrenic" (Kohut, 1971), and he differentiated them from other psychotic patients only by their ability to defend against their psychosis. Since patients in this category are not psychologically accessible, Kohut does not advocate psychoanalytic treatment for them and purports to offer no therapeutic contribution to this type of pathology.

In Kohut's second category of psychopathology are patients who form a cohesive self that is enfeebled, lacking in vitality, and easily threatened. Kohut believed that this group of patients suffers from narcissistic disorders. In these cases the self has developed to the point of cohesion; however, owing to failures in the parental selfobjects, the development of this nuclear self is arrested and it becomes prone to temporary fragmentation.

The highest level of pathology in Kohut's scheme consists of the structural neuroses. Unlike narcissistic patients, neurotic patients have a strong sense of self. They suffer not from an enfeebled self but from the inability to complete the achievement of goals. In Kohut's view, a neurosis is not a defect in the self structure, but a product of the frustration of a self that has not been allowed to complete its "nuclear program."

Since Kohut purported to make no contribution to the understanding of psychotic states and focused primarily on narcissistic pathology, the discussion of his theory of psychopathology will begin with his views on the latter.

Narcissistic Disorders

Kohut's views on pathological narcissism emanate directly from his developmental theory. Narcissistic personality and behavior disorders both result from faulty selfobject responses to the narcissistic needs of the growing child between the phase of primary narcissism and the oedipal phase. If there is a consistent lack of optimal frustration in this phase, the child is faced with the humiliation of its grandiose-exhibitionistic needs or a longing for idealization and erects staunch defenses against them. The result is arrest in the development of the grandiose-exhibitionistic self and/or of the idealized parental imago. The selfobject failure with respect to the needs of the grandiose self stems from a lack of sufficient mirroring; selfobject failure with respect to the idealized parental imago is due to the unavailability of suitable idealizable objects. If there is a deficit in either the grandiose self or the idealized object, an attempt will be made to erect compensatory structures by strengthening the other pole of the self to compensate for the defective pole. If this effort at compensation is not effective because of selfobject failure in the second pole, defenses will be used to the exclusion of compensatory structures, self development will be arrested, and the self structure will be defective. In Kohut's view, only the concurrence of both types of selfobject failure leads to narcissistic fixation. However, each case of narcissistic personality or behavior disorder tends to be characterized by a predominant defect in one of the two poles of the self, depending on whether the greater trauma lies in faulty mirroring or in the unavailability of the idealized parental imago, although the other pole is sufficiently damaged that compensatory structures cannot make good the defect.

As we have seen, in Kohut's view, the self structure is formed from the transmuting internalization of the grandiose self and the idealized parental imago. If either or both become arrested, the self is unable to develop completely and remains weak, lacking in vitality, and disharmonious. Instead of realistic ambition, there will be arrested grandiosity; instead of tension regulation and the idealization of the superego, there will be continuing dependency on idealized figures. In either situation, transmuting internalization has either not taken place or has been incomplete. It may be said that all narcissistic pathology, in Kohut's view, results from the failure of transmuting internalization in the narcissistic phase of childhood. In accordance with Kohut's presentation of narcissistic pathology, we will consider the failures of idealization first.

Any premature disruption in the idealized parental imago deprives the child of the opportunity to come to see gradually the realistic qualities of the parent. This is most pronounced in cases of early parent loss, but it applies to any forced relinquishment of the idealized imago before the psyche is able to cope with it. According to Kohut, the most potent pathogenic factor in this situation is the child's loss of the opportunity to see the parent realistically, with the result that the early idealization endures. The perception of the parent continues in fantasy instead of being modified by reality, and the child is not able to use the gradual disillusionment in the fantasied parent to build psychic structure. Consequently, the idealized parental imago is either repressed or split off. In either case, it endures without modification by reality in the psyche of the child. The absence of transmuting internalization results in a deficit in psychological structure.

Trauma with respect to the idealized parental imago may occur in a variety of ways. The parent may be so unavailable that the child is deprived of the opportunity to idealize the parent, or the idealization may occur but be prematurely disrupted, such as by parental

withdrawal or loss of the parent. Whatever the source of defect in idealization, the result is a gap in psychic structure and a continual need
to fill this gap. Individuals who suffer from disturbances in the idealized parental imago have a continual hunger for objects; the object is
not sought for its own qualities but to make good an internal defect.
This use of the object is the distinguishing feature of narcissistic disturbance as opposed to the idealization characteristic of the neurotic
patient. The latter will exaggerate positive qualities, but the object is
separate and perceived as a complete person, even if viewed in an
exaggeratedly positive fashion. According to Kohut, the object hunger
of the patient suffering from disturbance in the earlier idealized
parental imago has no conception of the object as a separate person,
since the object is being used to fill a gap in the self.

In accordance with his view of the dual function of the idealized
parental imago to control drives and idealize the superego, Kohut
defined three separate levels of disturbance in the transmuting internalization of the idealized parental imago. The very earliest level is
the most disruptive since it leaves a gap in the psyche: only a minimal
formation of psychological structure has taken place and therefore diffuse narcissistic vulnerability results. Later disruptions in the idealized parental imago lead to deficiencies in one of the two functions of
the idealized parental imago. If the disturbance occurs after a greater
degree of structure has formed, the gap in the fabric of the psyche
leads to a deficit in neutralizing capacity and the ability to control the
drives. If the idealized parental imago is traumatically disrupted upon
entry into the oedipal phase, the result is a failure in the idealization
of the superego. In this case, the superego may be well formed as a
result of the vicissitudes of object-libidinal strivings, but compliance
with its demands will provide little joy. Lacking gratification from the
adherence to its own internalized values, the child attempts to restore
narcissistic balance by the admiration of external figures. Such an
"idealization" is not the appreciation of admirable qualities but a
desperate effort to achieve narcissistic balance by filling a gap in the
psyche.

A good clinical illustration of Kohut's (1971) understanding of narcissistic pathology originating in disturbance of early idealization is
his discussion of Mr. A. The patient presented with a complaint of
homosexual preoccupation. Although he had never had a homosexual
experience, Mr. A did have occasional sexual fantasies of controlling
and dominating powerful men. During the analysis it became clear
that far more crippling than these fantasies were his tendency to feel
depressed and lethargic and his exquisite sensitivity. The transference

consisted of two primary demands: that the analyst share the patient's values and that he confirm "through a warm glow" that the patient had lived up to the analyst's standards. When the patient did not feel this glow from the analyst, his behavior, no matter how moral, felt empty and trite. In the course of the analysis Kohut found the patient to suffer from exquisite and diffuse narcissistic vulnerability. He was easily injured by any imperfection in the analyst's ability to achieve complete and immediate understanding of him.

In his effort to understand Mr. A's pathology Kohut first focused on the patient's mother. He believed that his present-day behavior justified the inference that she was a "deeply disturbed" woman who easily disintegrated under pressure. Kohut (1971) concluded: "It may thus be assumed that the patient suffered many disappointments in the mother's phase-appropriately required omniscient empathy and power during the first year of his life and that the shallowness and unpredictability of his mother's responses to him must have led to his broad insecurity and narcissistic vulnerability" (p. 61). This lack of empathic attunement by the mother left the child with early narcissistic fixations because his infantile grandiosity had insufficient opportunity to become transformed into "drive-regulating structures."

In Kohut's view, even more important to the patient's pathology than his traumatic disappointment in the mother's lack of empathy was the lack of sufficient opportunity to idealize the father. This in itself may not have been pathogenic except that the boy suffered a second traumatic loss of idealization. The father had been a successful businessman in Europe before World War II, and the family, being Jewish, was forced to flee the Nazis, resulting in the loss of the family business and financial status. Before that time the father and son had been close and the boy had greatly admired his father. According to family lore, the father had often taken his young son to the workplace and had discussed the business with him. When the family emigrated to the United States, the father tried many times to reestablish his business, often with great hope for success, only to be disappointed on every occasion. Thus, Mr. A as a boy had suffered repeated disappointments "in the power and efficacy of his father just when he had (re-)established him as a figure of protective strength and efficiency" (Kohut, 1971, p. 58). Thus, the father, onto whom all the patient's needs for attachment to an idealized figure were placed, disappointed his son traumatically.

Kohut concluded from this pattern of traumatic disappointment that no transmuting internalization of the idealized parental imago had taken place. In Kohut's view, this failure resulted in a gap in the psyche where the idealization of the superego would normally be. Here Kohut applied his distinction between narcissistic and object-libidinal development. According to Kohut, since the object-libidinal attachment to the father was undisturbed, the superego was well formed. However, since the idealization of the father did not result in the transmuting internalization of the idealized parental imago, no narcissistic investment in the superego—the heir of the relationship with the father—took place. The patient had an intact superego, but since there was no narcissistic investment in it, compliance with it gave him no pleasure.

Lacking idealization of his superego, Mr. A needed the analyst both to share his values and to "confirm with a warm glow" that he had lived up to the analyst's standards in order to feel any meaning in the achievement of his life goals. In addition, Mr. A continued to seek replacements for the lost father of his early years by soliciting the counsel and approval of men whom he considered superiors or elders, despite his considerable level of success. When he felt their approbation was not forthcoming, he felt enervated and lost enthusiasm; it was only when he felt they expressed interest in and approval of him that he felt complete and whole. In Kohut's view, it is typical of the relationships formed by patients who have suffered traumatic disappointments in the idealized parental imago that older persons are sought out to fill the gap in the psyche left by the traumatic disappointment in the idealized parental figure.

Kohut attributed Mr. A's homosexual fantasies to the sexualization of the narcissistic disturbance. The fantasies involved his dominating and enslaving physically strong men, were not always orgastic, and sometimes did not even involve masturbation. On occasion, Mr. A achieved orgasm with the fantasy of masturbating a strong, powerful man and draining him of his power. Kohut interpreted these fantasies as the sexualization of Mr. A's need for the approval of older men. According to Kohut's formulation, Mr. A's sexual attraction to powerful men was correlated with his demands for the analyst's approval. Further, the fantasies of draining powerful men were manifestations of Mr. A's need for psychological structure. He sexualized his need for a strong, firm psyche, which was in contradistinction to his own sense of enfeeblement. This sexualization took place, in Kohut's view, because the early narcissistic disturbance damaged the neutralizing capacity of the psyche; as a result, the drives were not well regulated. This lack of neutralizing capacity and the gaps in the psyche created by premature and traumatic disappointment in the hypercathected idealized paternal imago resulted in a narcissistic disturbance that was characterized by homosexual fantasies; sensitivity to injury, resulting in frequent depression; and the constant emotional dependence on approval from older men.

Kohut understood Mr. A's homosexual fantasies, frequent bouts of lethargy and depression, and his chronic lack of self-esteem as emanating from the gap in his psyche left by the too-early, too-abrupt loss of the idealized father. He also included in his formulation of this case a consideration of the mother's lack of empathy, which he presumed led to the special importance the idealization of the father assumed. Further, the lack of maternal empathy meant that the mother could not be turned to in order to compensate for the disturbance in the idealized parental imago. The case of Mr. A is a good illustration of Kohut's views on the pathological results of trauma to the idealizing parental imago: Kohut accounted for all Mr. A's symptoms by the inability to idealize the superego and from the absence of drive-regulating structures.

Having discussed Kohut's views on disturbances in the child's need for idealization, we now turn to the pathological effects of arrest in the other narcissistic structure, the grandiose self. If there is a defect in the parental capacity to mirror the child's grandiosity, the child's narcissistic-exhibitionistic needs are frustrated and are then either split off or repressed, leading to the arrest of the grandiose self rather than to its modification by reality (Kohut, 1971). Whether the grandiose self is split off or repressed, the result is a split in the psyche; the child's grandiosity remains out of touch with the reality-based self, rather than becoming gradually integrated into it.

If the grandiose self is repressed, the result is general psychological impoverishment, including low self-esteem, vague depression, and lack of initiative. If the grandiose self is split off, the psyche then has a structure that relates to reality and a grandiose self that functions but is walled off, without contact with the rest of the psyche. The split-off grandiosity is manifested in a boastful, superior attitude, sometimes with cold arrogance. Kohut (1971) calls this a "vertical split," which he differentiates from the "horizontal split" caused by repression. Since the narcissistic cathexes are invested in this split-off grandiosity, the more realistically oriented part of the self is robbed of self-esteem. Consequently, the conscious feelings tend to be lethargy, depression, and emptiness, similar to the symptomatic manifestation of repressed grandiosity. The difference is that in vertically split off grandiosity the psychological impoverishment coexists with the arrogant, haughty, superior attitude. In addition, the empty, lethargic self represses the vulnerable nuclear self to protect it from feared injury. As a result, the usual structure of pathological narcissism includes both a vertical split between grandiosity and the reality-oriented empty self and a horizontal split in which the depleted self represses the vulnerable nuclear self with its unfulfilled narcissistic longings.

Whether the grandiosity is split off or repressed, the psyche is robbed of its primary source of self-esteem. Without this supply of narcissistically invested libido, self-esteem is minimal, and the child will develop a hypersensitivity to criticism and lack of approval. When deficits or limitations of any type are apparent, the personality reacts with shame or rage. There is no solid source of self-esteem with which to combat injuries, whether real or apparent. It is not simply that such patients were not mirrored and so do not value themselves. In Kohut's view, the lack of mirroring results in the need to protect the infantile grandiosity with a massive defense so that the personality is deprived of its source of self-esteem. The archaic grandiosity does not become transformed into realistic self-esteem, and the resulting personality is characterized by both archaic grandiosity, with the need to be mirrored constantly, and a poverty of self-esteem. The arrested grandiosity is walled off from the rest of the psyche, robbing it of its most important source of self-esteem, and thereby leaving it vulnerable to narcissistic injury. This formulation is Kohut's explanation of the apparent contradiction that patients suffering from pathological narcissism are grandiose, feeling superior to others, and yet are so vulnerable that they have an exquisite sensitivity to slights.

One can see that Kohut's view of pathological narcissism is clearly in conflict with Kernberg's conception of the disorder (discussed in chapter 5). The principal difference is that in Kernberg's view, the grandiose self and primitive idealization are both defenses, pathological constructions to protect against oral rage, envy, dependence, emptiness, and paranoia. For Kohut, pathological narcissism, whether due to a fixation of grandiosity or idealization, is a developmental arrest; the longings of the patient are "phase appropriate" for the narcissistic stage of development. As we shall see in the next section, this difference leads Kohut to a sharply different treatment approach.

The vertical and horizontal splits means that the grandiose-exhibitionistic needs of the self are unable to find expression. Consequently, there is a buildup of tension due to the dammed-up exhibitionism. In Kohut's view, typical expressions of this unconscious exhibitionism are hypochondriasis, a propensity to shame, and self-consciousness. These symptoms are all the products of excessively repressed or split-off exhibitionism that overtaxes the capacity of the psyche, and all three are common to narcissistic personality disorders. Unable to contain the push for the expression of the exhibitionistic-grandiose needs, the psyche expresses its tension somatically, resulting in hypochondriacal symptoms. The tendency to feel shame comes from the lack of self-esteem in the realistic portion of the psyche: any limitation is experienced as a revelation of the inadequacy of the self. Similarly, the constant fear of being exposed gives rise to continual self-consciousness. These symptoms tend to characterize the narcissistic personality disorder whose deficit lies primarily in the arrest of the grandiose self.

Nonetheless, one can find similar symptoms in many neurotic patients. Kohut warns that one cannot make a diagnosis of narcissistic pathology on the basis of symptoms. It is not the hypochondriasis, self-consciousness, or shame in and of themselves that warrant the diagnosis of narcissistic pathology. The decisive pathognomonic feature is the source of the symptoms, the split-off grandiosity. The key to whether the presenting symptoms are due to walled-off grandiosity is quality of the object relationships. If the patient treats others only to suit his or her own purpose, one can safely conclude that the underlying pathology is narcissistic, which means that any of the symptoms being discussed is a product of split-off grandiosity. If others are treated as full persons in their own right, the symptoms are most likely due to a structural neurosis.

In addition to shame, the other major reaction of the narcissistically vulnerable patient to disappointment and injury is narcissistic rage. In Kohut's (1972) view, aggression is most destructive not when it is impulsive but when it results from narcissistic injury. The threat to the self and the sense of shame lead to a need to inflict injury on the perpetrator, and the revenge motive knows no rest until the injury is repaired by satisfaction of the need to avenge the wrong. In Kohut's view, this compulsion to repair injury by inflicting it differentiates narcissistic rage from other forms of aggression. Because the motive is repair of narcissistic injury, the rage and revenge show no regard for reasonable human limitation in their implacable need to eradicate the injury. The irrational pursuit of revenge and repair reflects the narcissistic motivation of the aggression. Other types of aggression, such as competitive hostility, do not include the compulsive need to avenge injury. Patients suffering from arrested archaic grandiosity are easily injured and are prone to bouts of rage whenever their expectations for mirroring are not met. For this reason, narcissistic patients are given to chronic rage attacks. Indeed, the same holds for patients suffering from arrested development of the idealized parental imago. When the need for idealization is frustrated, the self is threatened and the patient will become enraged and seek revenge on the source of the threat.

In accordance with his theory of development, Kohut (1971) delineates three levels at which the grandiose self may become arrested. At the lowest level so little psychological structure has taken place that others are experienced as part of the mind or body of the grandiose self. If a greater degree of self development has occurred, others are perceived as like the self but not a part of the self. If development is arrested closer to the oedipal phase, others are experienced as separate but are significant only insofar as they fulfill the needs of the grandiose self for admiration and mirroring. At all three levels, others are experienced as selfobjects; that is, they exist, from the point of view of the patient, only insofar as they meet a narcissistic need at one of these levels. In short, the other is not recognized as a separate person. When narcissistic needs are not fulfilled at any of these levels, the self is threatened and the patient feels a profound sense of shame or rage or both.

Kohut's (1968) view of arrested grandiosity is illustrated by Miss F, who sought analysis because she was unable to be intimate and felt "different from other people and isolated" (p. 503). In the analysis it became clear without apparent cause that she was given to abrupt changes between anxious excitement and elation, when she experienced herself as "precious" and consequently felt superior to others, and states of emotional depletion. In the analysis Miss F demanded that the analyst repeat to her what she said but not go beyond it. When Kohut complied, she became calm and content, but when he either remained silent or attempted to add to her comments, she became enraged, feeling misunderstood and undermined. During her childhood her mother had been depressed during the narcissistic phase, and Kohut concluded that her grandiosity had not been mirrored, resulting in the splitting off of the grandiose self from the rest of the personality. Consequently, Miss F attempted to use others for the narcissistic echo she missed in childhood. Kohut began to see that he was not a separate, autonomous person to her but a function. In her view, Kohut's role was to fill the gap in her psyche by mirroring her comments. When he did so, she felt the elation of having her grandiosity, her "preciousness," confirmed; when he did not, she felt the depletion of unfulfilled grandiose-exhibitionistic needs. This constellation, in Kohut's view, is characteristic of narcissistic personality disorders. The arrest of the grandiose self results in depletion of the psyche and a need for others to approve of and confirm the grandiosity in order to fill the deficit in the self. Miss F's isolation and inability to be intimate were a direct result of her perception of others not as whole persons but as impersonal functions for the completion of her self.

These same dynamics of arrest in the grandiose self and idealizing parental imago apply to narcissistic behavioral disorders. The difference is that in the narcissistic personality disorders the weakness in the self results in symptoms such as hypochondriasis, depression, and lethargy; in the narcissistic behavioral disorders the patient attempts to fill the narcissistic deficit with action, such as delinquency, perversions, or addictions (Kohut and Wolf, 1978). Both are disorders of the self in that the self is enfeebled and lacking in cohesiveness and vitality, but in one case the weakness in the self is directly expressed in symptoms whereas in the other the patient takes action to fill the gap so that the weakness of the self is not experienced. Although Kohut included delinquency in his list of narcissistic behavioral disorders, his discussion of the dynamics of this type of narcissistic pathology was confined to addictions and perversions. We will approach the addictions first, focusing on drugs and eating disorders, and then use the fetish as an example of his understanding of perversions.

Kohut (1971) viewed drug addiction as a self disorder in which the drug is used to fill the missing gap in the psyche. According to Kohut, the mother of the addict failed to perform her tension-regulating and other functions, resulting in a traumatic disappointment in the idealizing selfobject. Consequently, the child is robbed of the opportunity to internalize the object gradually to form psychological structure. The addict uses the drug not so much as a substitute for what was not given, such as love or food, but to fill the gap left by the missing idealized object. Whereas patients with narcissistic personality disorder attempt to form idealizing attachments to people to fill the gap in their psyche, drug addicts, representing a form of narcissistic behavioral disorder, use the drug in a desperate effort to achieve the same goal.

Kohut (1977) viewed eating disorders in a similar fashion. He did not believe that pathological overeating is a result of strong oral drives or fixation at the oral level. In his view, the child needs a "food-giving selfobject." If the environment does not meet this need, the child does not feel responded to as a whole self and regresses to intensified, fragmented pleasure-seeking oral stimulation. The result is an addiction to food. Pathological eating is a good illustration of Kohut's belief that the drives intensify and become fragmented in response to disruptions in the self. The selfobject failures traumatize the grandiose self and lead the child away from its center of initiative and toward pleasure seeking to feel whole and real. Overeating is an effort to experience the feeling of wholeness without relying on a failed and untrustworthy human environment.

Kohut applied a similar analysis to fetishes. In his view, the fetish is a substitute selfobject that patients use to attempt to receive the soothing they did not get from the mother. Faulty maternal empathy leaves the grandiose self unresponded to, and the child regresses to "archaic pleasure gains" in response. The child finds a substitute that will provide the soothing merger feeling he or she could not obtain from the human environment. The fetish is not so much a substitute for food or love as a desperate effort to fill a defect in the self; the fetishistic object substitutes for the missing admiration and approval needed for the nourishment of the grandiose self.

Kohut's (1977) understanding of the fetish is illustrated by the case of Mr. U, a brilliant but relatively unsuccessful college professor who received little enjoyment from his work and entered analysis to eliminate his need for certain fetishistic objects, such as nylon stockings and underwear. His previous analyses had focused on castration anxiety and denial. Kohut, however, believed the fetish was related to Mr. U's "oddly empathic, unpredictable, emotionally shallow mother" (p. 55) who would become overly involved with him, caressing him and meeting his wishes, and then suddenly withdraw and become unresponsive. Kohut believed that Mr. U withdrew from the unpredictability of his mother to the soothing touch of objects, which eventually developed into the fetish. The father was self-absorbed, and all the patient's efforts to be close were rebuffed. According to Kohut, the boy was deprived of the opportunity to idealize an object and gradually relinquish it. The lack of internalization of an idealized object left him without internalized ideals and solid self-esteem. He felt either inadequate to achieve lofty ideals or superior to worthless goals, resulting in abrupt and severe shifts in self-esteem. In a desperate effort to boost his feeling of self-worth, the patient intensified his attachment to the mother-fetish. This case is a good illustration of Kohut's views of the fetish and of narcissistic behavioral disorders in general. Whereas a narcissistic personality disorder would demand attunement and admiration and become ashamed or enraged at not receiving it, Mr. U attempted to achieve his sought-for merger through his attachment to the fetish.

As can be seen from this discussion, Kohut was able to explain a wide range of pathology by failures in the self–selfobject relationship and the resultant arrest in development of the self. He explained symptoms and disorders in the character disorder range on the basis of failure in narcissistic development. Symptom syndromes, such as depression and hypochondria, and behavioral syndromes, such as perversions, addictions, and delinquencies, were all explained as

manifestations of a depleted self. The question of Kohut's understanding
of neurosis now arises, and it is to this subject that we now turn.

The Structural Neuroses

Kohut's position on the structural neuroses shifted in accordance
with the causal role he attributed to the Oedipus complex. When
Kohut limited his theoretical contribution to narcissistic disorders,
he believed that the development of the self was completed before
the oedipal phase, resulting in the separation of self from object. In
this view, the child has moved from the selfobject phase, in which
objects serve functions for the self, to the oedipal phase, in which
others are seen as separate, autonomous objects who become the target of aggressive and sexual feelings. Thus, in this formulation, narcissistic disorders are products of faulty self development, and
conflict, occurring in the oedipal phase, is responsible for structural
neurosis. That is, in his early theory Kohut attributed neurosis to
unresolved oedipal conflict. However, Kohut changed his view of
the importance of the oedipal phase as he developed a broader view
of self psychology. The logical consequence of this shift was a modification of his views of the dynamics of structural neurosis. Kohut
(1984) came to see oedipal conflicts as a product of a weak, defective
self. If the parents are threatened by the child's assertiveness or
affection and respond with competitive hostility or overstimulation,
the child experiences a traumatic disappointment in the oedipal selfobjects, and the development of the assertive, affectionate self is
arrested. The joyful affectionate and assertive feelings become intensified and are split off from the core of the self and transformed into
gross sexuality or hostility. It is in this way that the oedipal phase
becomes pathological, and it is to this pathological constellation that
Kohut gives the name Oedipus complex.

In Kohut's view, the primary fear of the girl in the oedipal phase
is a seductive father or a hostile mother; the boy fears a seductive
mother and hostile father. If these fears are realized, selfobjects
become threatening rather than empathic and the self begins to disin-
tegrate; to protect itself from spreading anxiety, the child isolates the
drives from the rest of the self. At this point, affection becomes sexuality and assertiveness hostility. These sexual and hostile responses,
according to Kohut, always serve to protect threats to the self. The
nuclear self, in his view, includes affectionate and assertive feelings,
but if these feelings are threatened by traumatic selfobjects, it will protect itself by isolating these positive feelings and transforming them

into sexuality and hostility. Since the isolation of the drives protects from a threat to the self, the Oedipus complex is ultimately an effort to defend against "disintegration anxiety."

Kohut (1984) does acknowledge that since the same-sex parent is now hated and feared, the child will feel a threat from its rival, which boys experience as castration anxiety. Kohut does not discount the phenomenon of castration anxiety, but in his view castration anxiety is not a cause of symptoms, but symptomatic of a threatened self. Just as the hostility to the same-sex parent is self-protective, so too is its sequel, castration anxiety: the focus on loss of the penis defends against the far more threatening loss of the integrity of the self. According to Kohut (1971), classical analytic theory does not analyze castration anxiety to its root; the biological bias of classical theory leads it to the assumuption that castration anxiety is psychological bedrock, but this focal anxiety always masks a far more frightening anxiety, the threat to the integrity of the self. In Kohut's view, psychological bedrock is the cohesiveness of the self and the deepest anxiety is any threat to the integrity of the self.

In Kohut's reformulation of the oedipal phase, the Oedipus complex is a pathological product of faulty selfobject responses to the oedipal-age child. Since oedipal conflicts result from a defect in the self, we are left with the question of whether one can do away completely with the concept of structural neurosis and instead adopt the view that all neuroses are really narcissistic personality disorders. Kohut (1984) rejected this conclusion and, in fact, in his last work defended the concept of structural neurosis, including the term *transference neurosis*, but he distinguished between the structural weakness of the self and the developmental failures that lead to those weaknesses. If such weaknesses occur in the preoedipal phase, they lead either to perversions and addictions, as in narcissistic behavioral disorders, or to the symptoms of an enfeebled self, as in narcissistic personality disorders. If they occur in the oedipal phase, they lead to intensification and isolation of the drives; the drive fragments must be defended against, and neurosis is the outcome.

According to Kohut's final view, both pathological narcissism and neurosis are the product of faulty selfobjects, resulting in defects in the self. They differ in the developmental phase in which the self defect occurs and therefore in the resulting symptoms. In pathological narcissism the nuclear self is enfeebled, lacking in vitality, and disharmonious; in structural neurosis the nuclear self is unable to reach its goals not only because its development has been arrested by the lack of mirroring response by the selfobjects of the oedipal phase but also because its energies become absorbed by these oedipal conflicts, so that it is unable to realize its ambitions and ideals.

Kohut (1984) illustrated the self-psychological approach to the neuroses in his discussion of agoraphobia. According to the classical view, the agoraphobic woman cannot leave the house because of the incestuous wish that is displaced onto the males she might see on the street. According to Kohut's reformulation, the faulty selfobject milieu in the oedipal phase is the primary cause of the disorder. This is so for two reasons. First, the failure of the paternal selfobject to respond appreciatively to the little girl's affection and assertiveness as she enters the oedipal phase results in the breakdown of the self and the conversion of these positive attitudes into lust and hostility; that is, the advent of the Oedipus complex results in the disintegration of normal affection for the father and its conversion to sexual fantasies. Second, the faulty maternal selfobject results in failure to internalize self-soothing functions, a failure that leads to the tendency for anxiety to become converted into disintegration anxiety. The patient has developed no self-soothing functions and therefore cannot leave the house without a maternal figure to soothe her; leaving the house alone threatens an outbreak of disintegration anxiety. Kohut (1984) concluded that "the addictionlike need for an accompanying woman is not to be viewed as a defensive maneuver but as a manifestation of the primary disorder: the structural defect of which both the unconscious oedipal fantasy and the conscious need for a female companion are symptoms" (p. 30).

In Kohut's view, agoraphobia is illustrative of the pathogenicity of faulty self–selfobject relationships. Moreover, neuroses, each with its own specific dynamics, involve the failure of the oedipal selfobjects, and it is this failure that results in the breakdown of the self with the threat of disintegration anxiety and the onset of the pathogenic Oedipus complex. The neurotic symptom, then, is an effort to bind disintegration anxiety; thus, in each neurosis the intensity of the drives is symptom, not cause. Thus, we see that Kohut does give the oedipal phase an intermediary role in the onset of neurosis. Once the selfobject milieu fails in the oedipal phase, the weakened self engages the Oedipus complex, with the ensuing conflicts around lust for the opposite-sex parent and hatred for the same-sex parent, resulting in neurotic symptoms, but, for Kohut, the primary cause of these symptoms remains the defect in the oedipal self that results from faulty selfobjects.

With this view of neurosis, Kohut (1984) adopted the view that all psychopathology is based on disturbance in the structure of the self. As we have seen, his initial position was that severe pathology involves defects in the self whereas structural neuroses result from conflicts that arise after the complete formation of the self; then, as he began to expand self psychology, he ultimately concluded that incomplete self development is the primary cause of neurotic pathology, too. We have seen that Kohut maintained a distinction between pathological narcissism and neurosis despite his belief that all psychopathology consists of defects in the structure of the self. Does this view of neurosis as self-pathology mean that the drive–ego model of the structural neuroses can be dispensed with in favor of the self-psychological view? Kohut (1984) himself raised this question and stated that he could not give a definitive answer although in the future the answer might well be in the affirmative. However, this tentativeness is in apparent conflict with his analysis of neurosis as self pathology, and his views on oedipal dynamics and the role of the drives. If neurosis involves a primary defect in the self, then it is a form of self pathology and it follows logically that its treatment, to be discussed shortly, would follow the guidelines of self psychology. In Kohut's scheme no primary causal role is attributed to the drives or to the Oedipus complex; thus, the drive–ego model has, in fact, been replaced by the self psychology model (despite Kohut's unwillingness to acknowledge this). Indeed, we saw an example of this in Kohut's discussion of agoraphobia, in which he delineated the self-psychological view of this neurosis: he indicated clearly his view that self psychology offers an alternative to the drive–ego way of understanding the disorder.

At this point it becomes clear that Kohut has broadened self psychology into a model for understanding all pathology, thereby replacing the traditional emphasis on the vicissitudes of the drives and defenses against them with an emphasis on the structure of the self. According to Kohut, pathology is arrested development, not conflict within the self, and defenses are efforts at self-preservation that play no causal role in pathology. The source of all pathology is not conflicting forces within the self but developmental arrest rooted in failures in the selfobject environment. The relationship between self and selfobject is the crucial variable for understanding such failures and how they eventuate in psychopathology. This new psychoanalytic paradigm of psychopathology has clear and far-reaching implications for treatment, and it is to these implications that we now turn.

TREATMENT

Having reformulated psychopathology as developmental arrest due to selfobject failure, Kohut viewed the psychoanalytic process as the means by which the arrested self is able to complete its development with a new selfobject experience. This process consists of the therapeutic mobilization of the arrested self, the use of the analyst as the selfobject that was missing in development, and the transmuting internalization of this selfobject into psychological structure. The analytic process is based not on the interpretation of defense to uncover drive wishes but on the overcoming of developmental arrest. The analytic situation, if not disrupted with premature interpretations or analytic "moralism," allows the spontaneous therapeutic mobilization of the arrested self (Kohut, 1971). The analyst empathically immerses himself or herself in the patient's experiential world through accurate and well-timed interpretations. This analytic empathy allows the analyst to be used as a selfobject. Thus, interpretations are key to the analytic process not because of the knowledge they provide but because they convey empathic attunement with the patient's experiential world. Failures in the analyst's empathy are disruptive to the self–selfobject relationship but also provide opportunities for the transmuting internalization of the selfobject into psychological structure.

Kohut divided the interpretive process into two phases. In the understanding phase, the analyst grasps the meaning of the patient's behavior and communication. For example, if a patient feels disrupted by the analyst's approaching vacation, the analyst's connection of the patient's affective state with the interruption in treatment demonstrates his or her understanding to the patient. In the explanatory phase, the analyst looks for the genetic-dynamic determinants of what has been understood. To continue our example, the analyst's explanatory communication to the patient might correlate the patient's reaction to the vacation with a childhood experience and its current influence. In Kohut's view, understanding must always precede explanation. Kohut felt that classical analysts tend to rush too quickly to explain without first understanding. The understanding phase conveys the analyst's empathy, making possible the reexperience of the developmental arrest, which sets the stage for the transmuting internalization that did not take place in childhood. To explain without understanding is to demonstrate a lack of empathy with the patient's experience and therefore to re-create the empathic rupture of childhood rather than help to repair it. Understanding is a crucial component of the empathy needed for the analytic completion of the developmental process; for some patients it may consume a great deal of the analysis. As a corollary to this two-phase view of the analytic process, Kohut (1984) advocated interpretation of transference first, with genetic reconstruction to be employed only after the transference is understood.

Since Kohut viewed borderline and psychotic conditions as syndromes in which no self has developed and therefore as inaccessible to analytic intervention, he professed to offer no contribution to the treatment of those forms of psychopathology. He initially offered his specific treatment views within self psychology in the narrow sense by focusing on understanding narcissistic disorders while he still believed in the application of the drive–ego model to neuroses. Eventually, as self psychology expanded beyond the borders of narcissistic pathology, Kohut broadened his goals to include a reconceptualization of the psychoanalytic process, and at that point his theoretical shift away from traditional analytic theory began to have relevance to the neuroses. In accordance with the development of Kohut's thought, we will first discuss Kohut's conception of treatment for narcissistic disorders and then consider his revised model of psychoanalysis, as he ultimately elaborated it, and at that point, his views on the treatment of neurotic pathology will be discussed.

Narcissistic Disorders

Since the causes of narcissistic disorders lie in arrests in the development of the bipolar self, the transferences of these patients will be formed along the axis of either the grandiose self or the idealized parental imago, depending on which pole of the self was more damaged. While Kohut fully acknowledged that some patients move between these two types of transference, he believed that the predominant transference paradigm will coalesce at one pole of the self and that at any one time one of these two types of transference will be in operation. Patients who suffer primarily from an arrest in grandiosity will eventually form a mirror transference based on the archaic need to have their grandiosity mirrored. Patients whose primary defect is the arrested need to idealize a parent will form an idealizing transference.

In Kohut's view, the analytic setting provides the conditions for narcissistic patients to form one of the two types of selfobject transference, which will form spontaneously if allowed to do so. In Kohut's formulation, as in the classical model, transferences are believed to be mobilized by the regressive features of the analytic setting. The analyst's task in the first phase of treatment is not to interpret the transference but to allow it to unfold. Any educational measure designed to "tame" a selfobject transference runs the risk of forcing it to be submerged under a wall of defenses to protect the patient's narcissistic vulnerability. Premature interpretation has the same potential danger, as the infantile self is vulnerable and interpretation is likely to injure it. The crucial technical principle in the understanding phase of the analysis, which may last for an extended period, is that the analyst's task is to accept the selfobject transference and understand it as a "phase-appropriate" development. The unmet childhood needs are now seeking gratification from the analyst, and the analyst's attitude should be to welcome this as the therapeutic activation of the childhood self that was not allowed to complete its development. This view is a direct application of Kohut's belief that narcissistic transferences represent arrested development of the self.

The acceptance of the phase appropriateness of the selfobject transference should not be confused with its gratification. Kohut was quite clear and consistent that efforts to gratify the patient's narcissistic longings are in error because they do not allow for "optimal frustration," which, as we shall see, is the crux of the therapeutic action of the analytic treatment of narcissistic pathology. Attempts at gratification may impede the therapeutic activation of the transference, just as rejecting responses may. Consequently, the analyst, in Kohut's view, should foster the development of the selfobject transference but not gratify it. In this way, the infantile self in its fullest form is most likely to become therapeutically activated.

The only interpretations Kohut considers appropriate in this phase of the treatment are geared toward removing defenses against the narcissistic transference. Some patients attempt to protect themselves against narcissistic vulnerability by disavowing or denying their needs for mirroring or idealization. In that case, the analyst interprets the defenses in order to foster the development of the narcissistic transference. However, once the transference has been mobilized, the analyst allows its continuance without interpretation. In this phase, interpretation must be in the service of fostering the development of the narcissistic transference, not in resolving it. The implication is that analysts must understand and accept that they are a selfobject for the patient. They may well experience a narcissistic injury at being "used" in the service of the patient's self development, as opposed to being allowed to fulfill their professional ideal as they conceive it. The analyst's ability to contain this countertransference reaction is a crucial component of the process and is a major aspect of some variants of self psychology, as will be discussed later.

These treatment principles apply equally to both types of narcissistic transference. All further treatment recommendations are specific to the type of narcissistic deficit mobilized in the transference. In accordance with Kohut's presentation, we will discuss the idealizing transference first and then the mirror transference.

In the idealizing transference the patient uses the analyst to fill the gap in the psyche by accepting the analyst either as a drive regulator or as an external figure to complete the idealization of the superego. In either case, the attachment to the analyst becomes essential to the functioning of the patient's self. By means of this attachment the patient is able to function, but the fact that an external figure is needed indicates that the self is defective. The distinguishing feature of the narcissistic, as opposed to the neurotic, idealizing transference is the utilization of the analyst as a selfobject to make good the self's functional deficits. The neurotic patient idealizes by exaggerating positive qualities of the analyst who is seen and treated as a separate person, that is, an object, rather than a selfobject. The narcissistic patient who forms an idealizing transference uses the analyst to achieve narcissistic equilibrium and therefore treats the analyst as a part of the self, rather than as a separate person.

There are three types of idealizing transference corresponding to the levels of rupture in the idealized parental imago. If the trauma was very early, the patient's diffuse narcissistic vulnerability results in a global use of the analyst to achieve narcissistic balance. The idealizing transference in this case is the sole means of the patient's self-esteem regulation; without it the psyche is vulnerable to narcissistic injury of almost any type with minimal provocation. If the trauma was somewhat later, the idealization of the analyst is used to perform the neutralizing function missing from the patient's psychological structure. In this case drive wishes and impulses, normally controlled by the idealization of the superego, are controlled by the idealization of the analyst. If the phase of trauma to the idealized parental imago was later still, patients do not idealize their superego but instead search for external figures who will approve of and admire their values. The analyst becomes such a figure for the patient, and this use of the analyst defines the highest level of idealizing transference.

Kohut illustrated his view of the function of the idealizing transference and his principles of its treatment in his discussion of Mr. A who suffered from lethargy, depression, a diffuse sensitivity to narcissistic injury, and a preoccupation with homosexual fantasies of draining men of their power. When he received approval from men he functioned well, but when confirmatory responses were not forthcoming he felt at first depleted and depressed and then became cold and haughty. The transference consisted primarily of two demands: that the analyst share the patient's values and that he confirm "with a warm glow" that the patient had lived up to them. When Mr. A felt that his wishes were gratified, he felt whole and full of energy. When he did not feel that the analyst shared his values or that the analyst felt he was living up to them, Mr. A felt disappointed and depleted; lost his zest; and eventually withdrew into a cold, haughty attitude toward the analyst. The transference was thus characterized by "reactive swings toward a hypercathexis of the grandiose self" (Kohut, 1971, p. 68). At these times the patient became emotionally cold, adopted grandiose schemes, and was hypochondriacally preoccupied.

Some of the interpretive work involved the drawing of parallels between Mr. A's demand for approval of his values by the analyst and his fantasies of pursuing powerful men; between his reactive grandiosity and the "princely young men" by whom he was sexually stimulated; and between the orgiastic experience of gaining strength in fantasy by draining it from strong men and his need to acquire psychological functions to fill the gap in his psyche. The homosexual fantasies were ultimately interpreted as the sexualization of his need to gain strength from an idealized figure. That is, Mr. A achieved narcissistic balance by sexualizing his need for idealization. Kohut (1971) contends that "the direct interpretation of the content of the sexual fantasies is not an optimal approach in the analysis of such cases, and that it should at first be demonstrated to such patients that the sexualization of their defects and needs serves a specific psychoeconomic function, i.e., it is a means for the discharge of intense narcissistic tensions" (p. 72). Kohut questioned the value of entering into the retrospective investigation of sexual content even after this function is shown to patients as they are already beyond the sexualization of their conflicts at that point.

The case of Mr. A demonstrates the value of addressing the defect in idealization in a case of presumed sexual dysfunction. Once the narcissistic tensions were dealt with via the idealization need, Mr. A's homosexual preoccupations abated. What appeared to be a sexual problem was, in fact, according to Kohut, a case of severe narcissistic imbalance due to the defect in the idealized paternal imago; thus, the therapeutic action of the case involved interpretation of the narcissistic defect rather than a direct discussion of the "sexual problem." The patient had attempted to fill the gap in his psyche with his fellatio fantasies, but they provided only temporary relief and had to be repeated continually. Kohut (1977) pointed out that "the successful filling in of the structural void could, however, ultimately be achieved in a nonsexual way via working through in the analysis" (p. 127). Similarly, when new structures were laid down by the internalization of the analyst, Mr. A's self-esteem solidified and his other symptoms abated.

The transference, then, consisted of the patient's use of the analyst to fill a gap in the self, in this case the idealizing imago; the analyst's task was to allow this process to occur and later to interpret the narcissistic defect that the transference was filling. The working through of the patient's use of the analyst in this way constituted a resolution of the narcissistic pathology, and the symptoms were relieved as this occurred.

This use of the analyst implies that any disappointments in the idealization during treatment will be threats to the cohesion of the self. Such disappointments will inevitably occur, and Kohut differentiates between major and minor "failures" of the analyst. The latter include day-to-day failures such as misunderstanding, not being perfectly in tune with the patient, changing appointment times, or beginning a session a few minutes late. Major "failures" are vacations or extended interruptions of any type. Both types of failure, or disappointment, disrupt the patient's narcissistic equilibrium because the patient's self-esteem is based on his or her attachment to the idealized object. While the rupture may seem trivial to an external observer, it is traumatic to the patient because it interferes with narcissistic equilibrium, which is delicately balanced on the idealization. Once the idealization is disturbed, the self loses its self-esteem and power, resulting in disintegration anxiety. The consequence is a collapse of the self, which will manifest itself as lethargy, a sense of worthlessness, and a feeling of powerlessness.

Such disappointments in the idealization of the analyst are not only inevitable but are, according to Kohut (1971), an essential part of the therapeutic action with the narcissistic patient who forms an idealizing transference. Since the collapse experienced by the self requires interpretation to be repaired, it is at the point of disruptive disappointments in the idealization that interpretive work begins in earnest. The analyst's role is to discover the cause of the patient's sense of disruption and renewed symptoms. By empathic understanding of the patient's iatrogenic symptoms, the idealization is restored, as the patient now feels understood by the analyst. However, the reestablishment of the idealization is never totally complete: each disappointment in the analyst leads to a microscopic bit of internalization of the functions provided by the idealized figure, and each such bit adds to the analysand's investment in his or her own set of standards. It is this bit-by-bit cycle of idealization, disappointment, interpretation, and restoration with microscopic internalization that is the essence of the structure-building process with such patients. To put this another way, the essence of the therapeutic action of the analytic treatment of the idealizing transference is the transmuting internalization of the self-sustaining functions of the idealized analyst into a structure of ideals and values. In this way, according to Kohut, the analytic process completes a developmental process that was arrested in childhood.

It is crucial in Kohut's view that the interpretations of the patient's intense disappointments in the analyst are stated in a way that puts the focus on the analyst's "failure." Since the transference replicates the patient's functional reliance on the parental selfobjects, it follows that the patient's disappointments in the analyst are a replica of the failures of the selfobjects of childhood. If the interpretation focuses on the patient to the exclusion of the "failure" of the analyst, there is real danger of repeating the childhood trauma by "blaming" the patient for the "failure" of the parent/analyst. According to Kohut, the analyst must recognize that although the precipitant of the patient's disappointment may seem trivial, from the patient's point of view the analyst has failed. The adoption of this stance is an empathic attunement with the patient because it accepts the latter's point of view as valid. Once patients see that the analyst accepts their point of view, they are able to re-idealize the analyst. Again, each time this occurs, a bit of the former idealization has, via transmuting internalization, become internalized into a bit of psychological structure.

This process is illustrated in the reaction of Mr. G to Kohut's (1971) announcement of a vacation. The patient responded by withdrawal from idealization to a "primitive form of grandiose self." However, Mr. G was reacting not to the separation itself but to Kohut's defensive and unempathic tone of voice in making the announcement. Kohut fully acknowledged that he had thought primarily of bracing himself against the "coming storm" when telling the patient of his absence:

It was in reaction to this attitude that the patient had experienced a traumatic disappointment in my empathic capacity which he had previously idealized as limitless, and no progress was made until I could offer my understanding and thus again enable the patient to recathect the idealized selfobject [pp. 93–94).

This vignette demonstrates Kohut's principle that the interpretation of such disillusionments must include full acknowledgment by analysts of the role they play in evoking the response. More critically, it demonstrates the ease with which patients suffering from narcissistic deficits are injured by seemingly minor slights, such as the defensive tone of voice in which Kohut announced his vacation to Mr. G. In Kohut's view, the therapeutic action of the idealizing transference consists of a myriad of such disappointments coupled with empathic, interpretive responses of the analyst that repair the idealization, as occurred in the case of Mr. G when Kohut realized that his voice tone was the source of the patient's injury. It was Kohut's empathic understanding of the patient's reaction to his tone of voice that turned the patient's regressive reaction into a therapeutic process. Mr. G could then not only restore his idealization but also accept that Kohut's empathy was not limitless, thereby allowing a bit of transmuting internalization to take place.

The working-through process of the idealizing transference occurs primarily by the interpretation of its disruption. Resolution is possible because, according to Kohut (1984), interpretation itself provides the optimal frustration required for the structure building that was missed in childhood. The empathy of the interpretation provides the patient with a needed developmental experience, but the fact that it is interpretation rather than gratification is also frustrating. In the vignette of Mr. G's reaction to Kohut's vacation, Kohut's empathy consisted of his understanding of the patient's reaction to his voice tone, but Kohut did not attempt to gratify the patient by apologizing for his empathic lapse, or by canceling his trip. Overindulgence stifles growth by failing to provide the stimulus of frustration. This explains more fully Kohut's position on reassurance or any other form of gratification by the analyst. Kohut viewed such behavior as contraindicated because it does not provide the optimal frustration necessary for growth to occur. Only interpretation has the proper mixture of empathy and frustration to allow the transmuting internalization process that was arrested in childhood to become completed.

The structure built from the transmuting internalization of the idealized analyst imago becomes the ideals of the patient. The patient now has values and principles worth striving for because the idealization formerly invested in the analyst as an external figure is now focused on the values and principles held by the patient. The narcissistic libido formerly invested in the external figure of the analyst is now devoted to a part of the patient's own psyche. Once this process is completed, the patient's ideals have been sufficiently strengthened to function effectively as an integral pole of the self. The superego not only exists but is held dear and becomes meaningful for the achievement of the patient's life goals. If the patient had suffered from a more primitive rupture in the effort to idealize the parent, the internalization of a solid set of ideals now helps to achieve a narcissistic balance from the inside, which heretofore was achievable only from the attachment to an external figure. If the trauma was to the middle level of idealization, the internalized set of ideals helps to create the neutralizing capacity that had been missing. Whatever the level of the trauma in the early idealization of the parental figure, the transmuting internalization of the idealized analyst results in a set of ideals and values that are solid and meaningful and that function as an integral part of the self.

Kohut illustrated his concept of the resolution of the idealizing transference in his discussion of Mr. X. Like Mr. A, this patient presented with a presumed sexual dysfunction. Mr. X masturbated with homosexual fantasies but had had no sexual experience of any type when he came to treatment at age 22. Like Mr. A, he was socially isolated and lonely. His mother was enmeshed with him and fostered a depreciatory attitude toward the father. The patient wished to join the ministry and had a clear identification with Jesus Christ. His mother emphasized to him the story of the baby Jesus and his mother. However, Mr. X could not join the ministry, as was his wish, because he had sexualized his relationship with religion. He had homosexual fantasies of his pastor, and his most powerful masturbatory fantasy was of crossing his penis with that of the priest at the moment of receiving Holy Communion:

> At the moment of climactic ejaculation the patient's preoccupation with a powerful man's penis, with oral incorporation, and with the acquisition of idealized strength found an almost artistically perfect expression in his sexualized imagery about the consummation of the most profoundly significant symbolic act of the Christian ritual [Kohut, 1977, p. 201].

In the first phase of the analysis of Mr. X, the transference consisted of the patient's grandiosity, as expressed in his arrogant behavior and his identification with Jesus Christ. As the vertical split between his grandiosity and his empty self broke down, it became clear that the latter was more authentically his and the grandiosity an appendage of his mother's self. After the vertical barrier was removed, the analysis shifted to the second phase of making conscious "the unconscious structures" that were defended by his lethargy and emptiness. The longings that lay buried were depicted initially in the following daydream: The patient is driving his car while the engine sputters and eventually stops working completely. He realizes he has run out of gas. He is unable to obtain help from passersby but remembers that he stashed away a gallon of gasoline in his trunk under a pile of junk. He pours the gas into his tank as the daydream ends. It developed in the analysis that on occasion Mr. X had taken long walks with his father during which his father told him stories of his hunting skill and success. At these times he greatly admired his father as a teacher and guide, but the pair never spoke of these walks afterward, and they remained isolated in Mr. X's life. Kohut interpreted the gasoline fantasy as the patient's expression of his need to be helped to find his nuclear self, which was formed on the basis of his idealized relationship with his father but long ago buried.

The second phase of the analysis consisted of making conscious this idealization of the father and its manifestation in the idealizing transference, which became the central transference theme of the analysis. Once the idealizing transference became established, the focus of the analysis became "(a) merger with the paternal ideal, (b) de-idealization and transmuting internalization of the idealized omnipotent selfobject, and (c) integration of the ideals with the other constituents of the self and with the rest of the personality" (Kohut, 1977, p. 217). As these ideals became integrated into the self, the structural defect was filled and the erotized enactments gave way. The homosexual fantasies were a temporary means to attempt to fill the defect in the self left by the burial of the idealized parental imago. The analytic process replaced the need for the fantasies by activating the idealization in the transference and working it through. In this way, Mr. X reactivated the real childhood relationship with his father. Kohut (1977) concluded as follows:

> It was with the aid of the analytic work focused on the sector of his person-ality that harbored the need to complete the internalization of the idealized father imago and to integrate the paternal ideal, after the analysis had shifted away from preoccupation with Mr. X.'s overt grandiosity, that struc-tures began to be built, that a firming of the formerly isolated, unconscious self could take place through gradual transmuting internalization [p. 218].

Kohut viewed the case of Mr. X as a demonstration of the treatment of a patient with narcissistic personality disorder and a predominantly idealizing transference structured with the typical combination of vertical and horizontal splits. It should be noted that Mr. X's grandios-ity was manifest long before the need for idealization but that the lat-ter, deeply repressed, was more crucial for the therapeutic process. It was the transmuting internalization of the activated need for the ide-alized father that led to the formation of new psychological structure. This fact also illustrates Kohut's (1977) principle that in narcissistic pathology the goal of treatment is to strengthen one pole of the self enough that the self is able to function. Once Mr. X's idealization pole was sufficiently strengthened, his homosexual preoccupations abated; and at that point he had the psychological organization necessary to function socially and harmoniously. Having illustrated the therapeutic process with regard to the idealizing transference, we now turn to the process of structure formation resulting from the therapeutic transformation of the mirror transference.

In Kohut's view, the manifestation of the grandiose self in treatment leads to a mirror transference. Kohut referred to both a mirror transference in the broad sense and a mirror transference in the narrow sense, although some of his followers have recommended that it be given a single usage (Wolf, 1988). In Kohut's terminology, mirror transference in the broad sense refers to the needs of the grandiose self in relation to the analyst at any of its three levels. In its most primitive form, the patient seeks a merger, as the boundaries of the grandiose self extend to include the analyst; in the merger transference, such patients expect to have the same degree of control over the analyst as they do over the parts of their own body or mind. In the intermediate form of mirror transference the analyst is expected to share the same characteristics and attitudes as the patient; Kohut calls this form of mirror transference the "twinship transference." The highest level is the mirror transference in the narrow sense, or the mirror transference proper, which includes the need of the grandiose self for the analyst to confirm its value by giving approval and admiration.

In all three forms the analysis becomes focused on and organized around the needs of the grandiose self to be confirmed and admired. In an analogous manner to the idealizing transference, the analyst as an external figure is providing the narcissistic function that patients cannot provide for themselves. In this way, patients experience self cohesion via their attachment to the analyst. The analysis therapeutically activates the archaic childhood grandiosity, and the analyst sustains it by fulfilling the selfobject function not provided by the parents in childhood.

Does this mean that the analyst should mirror the patient by providing the approval and admiration that were not received in childhood? Kohut's answer to this question is an unequivocal no. Any such effort by the analyst would gratify the patient's childhood longing rather than help resolve it. This is a common misunderstanding of Kohut's approach; therapists frequently speak of "mirroring the patient" as though the provision of admiration and approval were a component of Kohut's treatment approach (Wolf, 1988). The analyst's role is to foster the emergence of the archaic grandiose self but not to gratify it. Patients form a mirror transference, but the role of analysts is no more to mirror than their role in the idealizing transference is to make themselves idealizable. Patients feel mirrored by the analyst's empathic understanding, and to the extent that they do not, their reactions are interpreted. It is the interpretation of frustrated needs for mirroring that becomes the heart of the therapeutic action. This process should not be disturbed by the provision of artificial gratifications.

The same principle applies here as in the case of the idealizing transference: the point of the therapeutic activation of the grandiose self in the form of the mirror transference is to relinquish it gradually and thereby transform the grandiose self via transmuting internalization into psychological structure. As is true of the idealizing transference, this transformation can only occur if the analyst provides optimal frustration. In his early work, Kohut (1971) attributed optimal frustration to the inevitable failures in the analyst's empathy. Later, Kohut (1984) pointed out that even accurate interpretations, although they provide understanding, are inherently optimally frustrating because they do not gratify directly the unmet needs of childhood. According to this later view, the patient always wants more than the interpretation provides. Since the analyst's empathy with the needs of the grandiose self is not tantamount to the meeting of those needs, analytic empathy is the means for the transformation of archaic grandiosity into new psychological structure.

Kohut's view is that the mirror transference, like the idealizing transference, will spontaneously establish itself if given the opportunity by the analyst. The analyst's role early in treatment is not to interpret the patient's grandiose-exhibitionistic needs and is certainly not to interfere with them in any way. Any educational measure designed to tame the patient's grandiosity by labeling it "entitlement" or any other pejorative will injure the fragile grandiose self and may lead to its repression. The analyst's role is to accept the mirror transference and the patient's tendency to use him or her as a selfobject as the expression of a developmentally appropriate need.

The therapeutic mobilization of the mirror transference is represented by the analysis of Miss F, whom Kohut (1968) treated when he was still operating within the traditional analytic framework; indeed, some have given this case the pivotal role in changing Kohut's theoretical orientation from ego psychology to self psychology (Ornstein, 1978). During prolonged phases of the analysis of Miss F, sessions developed a repetitive pattern. In the initial part of the session the analysis seemed to be progressing smoothly: the patient appeared to free associate easily and to be engaging in self-analysis. However, Kohut (1968) eventually made a significant observation:

> I came to the crucial recognition that the patient demanded a specific response to her communications and that she completely rejected any other. Unlike the analysand during periods of genuine self-analysis, Miss F could not tolerate the analyst's silence; at approximately the midpoint of the sessions, she suddenly became angry at me for being silent [p. 504].

When Kohut summarized what she said Miss F felt calm, but if he went even slightly beyond her comments she became enraged and accused Kohut of ruining the analysis. Kohut eventually came to view this pattern as the emergence of the patient's grandiose self and its concomitant need for mirroring. In this mirror transference the patient did not view the analyst as a separate person but as a functional part of her grandiose self. In the patient's view, the analyst's role was to admire and echo her.

According to Kohut, the treatment took the proper course when he realized that this mirror transference was Miss F's attempt to integrate her archaic grandiosity with the rest of her personality. Miss F's presumed self-analysis masked her need to be echoed and admired. In Kohut's view, the effort to use the analyst in this way is not a "resistance" but the spontaneous mobilization of a phase-appropriate developmental need. The patient's "narcissistic demands" were her effort to complete the arrested development of her self. The use of the analyst to mirror her was her effort to achieve in the analysis what was missing from her childhood: a functional reliance on a selfobject to strengthen the developing self. For the crucial issues to be mobilized in the transference, the analyst had only to avoid interfering with their spontaneous appearance.

The case of Miss F also illustrates Kohut's approach to defense and resistance, which will be discussed further later. As can be seen from this case, Kohut's belief that narcissistic pathology consists of arrested self development leads to an appreciation of the patient's need to form the selfobject transference rather than to receive interpretations of resistance. Miss F was not "resisting," in Kohut's view, but attempting to get her thwarted childhood needs met. The patient's demands represent a positive move and must be interpreted as such by the analyst for the full mobilization of the transference. To have interpreted Miss F's demands as resistance would have been a technical error and would have risked the resubmergence of her efforts to resume self-development.

In Kohut's view, there are two additional advantages to the analyst's acceptance of the phase appropriateness of the mirror transference: it eliminates iatrogenic anger, which tends to result from a critical therapeutic attitude, and it stimulates childhood memories of thwarted narcissistic needs. Both advantages are demonstrated in the case of Mr. Z (Kohut, 1979). This is Kohut's only published case of two complete analyses of the same patient, one from the traditional perspective and the other from the viewpoint of self psychology. Mr. Z was socially isolated—had no girlfriends, he had only a single male friend—and lived with his widowed mother. He sought analysis after his only friend found a girlfriend and distanced himself from him. The patient's only sexual involvement was masochistic masturbatory fantasies in which he was a slave to domineering women. In the first analysis Mr. Z demanded that the analyst be under his "exclusive control"; Kohut interpreted that he wanted to be "admired and catered to by a doting mother who . . . devoted her total attention to the patient" (p. 5). The patient responded to this interpretation with explosive rage. Indeed, the first one and one-half years of the analysis were consumed with Mr. Z's rage at Kohut, which subsided only after Kohut made the comment, "Of course it hurts when one is not given what one assumes to be one's due" (p. 5). After the patient calmed down, the analysis entered the second phase, which was dominated by the Oedipus complex, as Kohut then understood it. The analysis centered upon Mr. Z's castration anxiety, his masturbatory fantasies, his fantasies of the phallic woman, his witnessing of the primal scene, and a homosexual relationship with an adult man when the patient was 11 years old.

Although Kohut felt the analysis had been a success, the patient contacted him five years later because his relationships were still emotionally shallow; he received no joy from sex; and he did not enjoy work, although he was successful. In the second analysis the patient once again demanded "perfect empathy," became enraged at the slightest misunderstandings, and adopted an attitude similar to the first phase of the first analysis. The difference was Kohut's (1979) attitude: "I looked upon it as an analytically valuable replica of a childhood condition that was being revived in the analysis" (p. 12). This time there were no complaints of being misunderstood and no rage reaction from the patient. Instead, there appeared a stream of childhood memories that had been absent from the first analysis. "This phase of the analysis revived the conditions of the period when, in early childhood, he had been alone with his mother, who was ready to provide him with the bliss of narcissistic fulfillment at all times" (p. 12). Kohut now viewed the patient's demands as his struggle to disentangle himself from the mother, a noxious selfobject who had later become psychotic.

As a result of these memories, a whole new sector of the patient's personality—the arrested development of the self—opened itself for analysis. The patient's traumatic disappointment in his father; his life-long yearning for an idealized, strong replacement; his need to break away from the merger with his delusional mother—these were the elements that occupied the center of the second analysis. Kohut viewed the dramatic shift in the analytic material as the result of his acceptance of the phase appropriateness of the patient's narcissistic demands and his willingness to take them seriously rather than attempt to get rid of them by interpretation. He concluded that his interpretive approach toward the patient's narcissistic demands in the first analysis had conveyed a moralistic, disapproving stance and had led to Mr. Z's compliance with his theory, just as the patient had complied earlier with his mother's delusions. When Kohut shifted toward understanding the patient's demands, Mr. Z was able to open his analysis to his childhood longings for the idealized father and to his merger with the delusional mother, from which he could now dare to free himself.

Kohut recommended that grandiosity not be interpreted when its functioning is smooth because the analyst is serving as the mirroring selfobject needed to achieve self-cohesion. However, just as with the idealizing transference, this function will inevitably be disrupted by major and minor "failures" in analytic empathy. In analogous fashion to the analysis of an idealizing transference, the therapeutic action begins when the selfobject fails. As discussed earlier, such empathic failure is most commonly seen in seemingly minor events when the analyst misunderstands a communication or fails in any way to be perfectly in tune with the patient. Major failures include vacations or other interruptions of the treatment. Any of these events will be experienced as an injury and will disturb the patient's narcissistic equilibrium. The trauma here is loss of the mirroring function on which the cohesiveness of the self depends. The threat to the self gives rise to disintegration anxiety, and the patient's response to the empathic failure will be either shame or rage followed by a regressive reaction. Patients who feel shamed by the revelation of a defect may become depleted and show signs of depression and lack of energy or may become preoccuped with bodily tensions, resulting in hypochondriacal symptoms. Or the patient may become enraged at the "offense," resulting in intense and fragmented rage and often a need for vengeance (Kohut, 1972).

A good example of a regressive reaction to the analyst's vacation by a patient with a mirror transference is the case of Mr. K (Kohut, 1971). After a brief period of idealization, this patient formed a merger/twinship transference in which the importance of the analyst lay in his function as an extension of the patient, and at times in being like the patient. Whenever the analyst went on vacation, Mr. K felt empty, withdrawn, and depressed. In addition, his dreams shifted strikingly from people imagery to machines, electrical wiring, and, often, spinning wheels. Mr. K was not aware of having an affective reaction to the impending separation from the analyst. However, it developed in the analysis that the machine imagery and especially the spinning wheels represented parts of the body and that the impending separations had given rise to a regression to hypochondriacal preoccupations. This regressive reaction was analogous to the patient's investment in his body when as a child he was faced with narcissistic trauma. For example, at age three, his brother was born and his mother, unable to cope with more than one child at a time, abandoned the patient emotionally. He turned to his father, but the mother's interference and the father's inability to tolerate idealization made this solution impossible. The boy attempted to discharge his narcissistic tension by engaging in physical activities. When the analyst announced a vacation, Mr. K regressed to bodily preoccupations in order to discharge the narcissistic tension created by the impending absence of the selfobject who served the mirroring function. It should be emphasized that Mr. K did not miss the analyst as a person. Rather, he felt a loss of a self function, a part of his self, a loss that led to narcissistic tension. Mr. K attempted to resolve the tension through bodily means, and this was represented in the dreams by machine imagery.

Whether the patient becomes ashamed or enraged, the analyst's task is to discover the source of the injury and interpret it. Just as with the idealizing transference, the active interpretative work begins with the disruptions to the patient's narcissistic balance due to disturbances in the selfobject transference. The analyst's role is both to uncover the source of injury and interpret its phase appropriateness. That is, the historical source of the narcissistic deficit must be shown to patients so that they can see that the analyst accepts their reaction as an understandable response to an unmet childhood need. The dual function of discovering the source of injury and understanding its developmental context is the essence of the explanatory component of interpretation.

Kohut's understanding of the meaning of the mobilization of grandiosity in the treatment situation is in clear opposition to Kernberg's treatment approach. For Kernberg, as we saw in chapter 5, the grandiose self is a pathological, defensive construction, whereas for Kohut it is a normal, phase-appropriate developmental step that has become arrested due to trauma. Therefore, while Kernberg recommends immediate interpretation of grandiosity as a defense, Kohut's therapeutic approach is to allow the full development of the grandiose self and to appreciate the appropriateness of its reemergence in view of the developmental context in which the patient was traumatized. In Kohut's view, this technical approach provides the empathy that was not received in childhood and that is now needed in adulthood to resolve the childhood trauma. From this perspective, Kernberg's approach of interpreting the grandiose self as a defense would serve only to bury the patient's frustrated longings, which need to be therapeutically activated to be resolved.

The empathic response of the analyst allows the mobilization of the patient's grandiose self within the mirror transference. The treatment process becomes a continual cycle of mirror transference, disruption, interpretation, and restoration of the mirror transference. Each time the cycle occurs, a bit of the grandiose self becomes transformed into a structure of realistic self via transmuting internalization. In this way, the nuclear self becomes invested with narcissistic libido. If the analyst continues to respond empathically, the patient is gradually able to transform the grandiose self into realistic ambitions and a healthy sense of self-esteem, both of which are now invested with the positive self-enhancing feeling that initially inhered in the grandiose self. As ambitions become realistic and solid, new psychic structure is formed and one pole of the self is strengthened.

Despite his copious clinical illustrations, Kohut did not provide detailed descriptions of the working-through process of the mirror transference, that is, the process of transformation of archaic grandiosity into realistic ambition. The best such description is probably the case of Mr. I, a patient who was treated by one of Kohut's colleagues (Goldberg, 1978). This young man sought analysis because he felt that he was too preoccupied with his unhappiness and the lack of direction in his life to perform well on his job. He had difficulty reading or sitting still long enough to complete his work projects. It became clear that he had a frenetic lifestyle that included addictive masturbation, preoccupation with one-night sexual exploits, and sitting on the toilet frequently and for prolonged periods. He had to date frequently but was unable to form and maintain a relationship.

Mr. I immediately settled down in the analysis, and his sexual obsessions subsided. He became quickly connected to the analyst, toward whom he felt like a "splat on a wall." He became preoccupied in the analysis with his desire that the analyst be excited by him, and he wished the analyst to witness his every act. He expressed the wish for extra-long sessions and once verbalized the wish that the analyst would take one month just to listen to him. Mr. I took all this as evidence of his "addiction" to the analysis. He felt that the analyst was a powerful figure who provided him with a stable, safe anchor, and he began to feel that the analyst was "perfectly in tune" with him. The analyst's response to him became the most significant issue in his life, even though he hated his dependence on the analyst. Before the analyst's first vacation Mr. I had a strong reaction and developed homosexual fears. During the vacation Mr. I assumed a gross identification with the analyst, treating his girlfriend with the kindness, understanding, and tact he himself felt from the analyst, but had not heretofore shown to her. The patient was quite excited that he and the analyst "hit it off" after the vacation, and at that point his masturbation, desperate need for dates, and prolonged toilet sitting all markedly declined.

The first phase of Mr. I's analysis, a period during which he married, focused on the idealizing transference, but our focus in this discussion is on the process of resolution of the mirror transference. After the idealizing transference had been worked through, Mr. I began to discuss the possibility of termination, although this was partly forced by an impending job change. The anticipation of termination led to the establishment of a mirror transference as Mr. I developed an intensification of his sensitivity to separation and to the analyst's response to him. He became consumed by the topic of separations; weekends, vacations, and termination were the primary issues in the analytic sessions. During a Christmas vacation, Mr. I felt "disconnected," drab, and colorless. The analyst commented on the positive aspect of this response and how it meant that he was able to keep himself calm without the analyst, although he eventually "overshot the mark and then began to feel the emptiness and monotony" (Goldberg, 1978, p. 82). The patient was so moved by this remark that he felt like crying, and the analyst commented that he was overstimulated by the experience of feeling understood after not having been understood for so long. The patient was also struck by the truth of this remark and felt moved once again. The impact of this understanding was enduring. Mr. I had the impulse to tell the analyst to "cut it out" but later realized that he could now react without falling apart.

Over the next weekend Mr. I dreamed that he put gas in his car but could not shut it off and that it spilled over. The dream was interpreted as the patient's sensitivity to the analyst's interventions. The patient responded by verbalizing his fear that termination meant flying off into space and that his "equipment" would not function and he would crash. The analyst pointed out that whenever Mr. I felt his landing instruments or the analyst's radar were defective, he feared "losing contact with ground control."

The next day the patient reported "a dramatic change," which indicated to him that the analyst's sensitivity must have been just right. He also had an elated response to a talk by a senior executive at his firm, feeling that the implication was that "father and son should work together." He felt that the previous day's session had indicated that the analyst's "radar" and "ground control" were functioning well and that he was not going to crash land. Mr. I went on to say, "[I need] a base of operations, a relationship to give meaning to all my activities. I don't need as much as I used to from somebody else. But if I don't get it I feel let down, sick, and futile" (p. 85). The analyst did no more than agree, and when over the next few sessions the patient was frequently silent, the analyst was also. Mr. I felt the silences were accomplishments, as it had taken him three years of analysis to be able to be silent.

This process seemed to result in a dramatic shift in Mr. I. He told the analyst, "[I will] take this unit, you and me, put it in a capsule, and bury it somewhere deep inside me—it will always be there and give me self-confidence and consistency" (p. 87). By this comment, the patient seemed to be concretely representing his ability to take in the analyst and his mirroring function and make them a part of his own psychic structure. Soon after, he began to discuss a specific termination date. He then reported that he no longer needed to sit on the toilet for long periods of time. He realized that the prolonged toilet sitting had been one more way of getting pleasure and excitement and that he no longer felt the need for this. When he had a birthday during this period, he described feeling a lack of "fanfare" no "bands playing" and reminisced about the difficulty in giving up the desires of the past and putting the analysis into the past. When the analyst next went on vacation, the patient had a good experience which was represented in a dream that he hugged a boy who had epilepsy and who suffered no seizures if hugged. The interpretation was that the patient was both the boy and himself in the dream, that is, that he could now soothe himself. At this time Mr. I and his wife gave a party, and he felt no need for special attention; this incident made him recall how desperately he had needed attention at the beginning of the analysis.

When Mr. I did set a definite termination date for two months after the party, he became depressed and scared that the ending would be "too much." Although he felt that there were no further content issues left in his analysis, he was frightened that without the analysis his stability was at risk. The patient became highly sensitive once again to the analyst's interventions. He told the analyst that he needed him to listen again and not say too much. He felt that he could now say anything and felt more "equal" to the analyst. Toward the end of the analysis, Mr. I dreamed of a man who swallowed a clarinet that played from inside him. He felt that he was taking the analyst with him, whole. The analyst pointed out that he would have to digest the analyst and that the music came from inside him. In the last few weeks of the analysis, Mr. I reviewed his accomplishments in the treatment. He believed that the "underlying force" was the stability of the analytic relationship and that this had allowed him to transfer his ties to others. He felt that he was different "every minute of the day" and that he now could do for himself what the analyst had done for him.

This case illustrates the working-through process of the mirror transference according to the principles of self psychology. The patient's functioning depended on the stability of the analytic relationship, specifically, the mirror transference. All the disruptive analytic experiences were part of the transmuting internalization process, which changed the narcissistic need, in this case to be mirrored, into psychological structure in the form of realistic ambition. Early on in the analysis, the analyst replaced the masturbation and sexual addictions. By the end of the analysis, Mr. I no longer needed the analyst to soothe him, reduce his tension, or perform any other function. The transmuting internalization process had been completed.

The therapeutic action in the analysis of the grandiose self, as in that of the idealized parental imago, is a combination of acceptance and even welcoming of the archaic, repressed, or split-off self and the interpretation of the narcissistic injuries it receives once it has become activated in the transference. In this way, the analytic process allows the arrested self to resume development by transforming archaic grandiosity into mature self structure with realistic self-esteem. Does this view of the analytic process apply only to narcissistic disorders or is it to be taken as a new model for psychoanalytic treatment in general? To address this question, we must understand Kohut's view of the self-psychological treatment of the structural neuroses.

Treatment of the Structural Neuroses

Kohut's view of neurosis as a disorder of the self leads us to consider the implications of self psychology for the treatment of neurotic conditions. First, self psychology reformulates as narcissistic disorders those cases that are viewed as oedipal neuroses in the classical model. We have seen that Kohut believed that the drive–ego model led analysts to view oedipal conflicts and drives as psychological bedrock when, in fact, deeper anxieties and issues frequently lay beneath them. Although cases with clear oedipal issues tend to be diagnosed as neurotic disorders just as in the classical model, the emphasis of self psychology on threats to self cohesion and on disintegration anxiety implies a tendency to see oedipal material as a manifestation of a defective self. This means that Kohut diagnosed many cases as narcissistic disorders that appeared to be oedipal neuroses and focused the treatment on the resolution of the selfobject transference rather than on an oedipal drive-dominated transference.

The case of Mr. Z illustrates this implication of self psychology. Recall that in Mr. Z's first analysis he was treated as a neurotic case, his demands were treated as resistances, and his treatment focused on his fantasies of the phallic woman, castration anxiety, masturbatory fantasies, and his witnessing of the primal scene. His homosexual preoccupations were interpreted as a regression from the oedipal competition with his father and the resulting castration anxiety. In the second analysis the same symptoms were interpreted as products of the patient's inability to feel alive. His stimulating masturbatory fantasies counteracted his feeling of deadness and replicated his childhood masturbation, which he used to soothe his joyless, depressed childhood. In the second analysis Kohut understood Mr. Z's homosexual relationship with the older man in childhood and his adult homosexual interest as his yearning for a relationship with an idealized father figure. Kohut concluded that competition with the father and castration anxiety had no appreciable causative role in the homosexual masturbatory fantasies and interest. He interpreted all the oedipal material, including fantasies of the phallic woman and castration anxiety, as products of the patient's desperate effort to escape internal "deadness" and feel alive by stimulating himself.

In the second analysis Mr. Z's demands for "perfect empathy" were viewed not as a resistance but as a desperate effort to fill a gap in his self structure, that is, as evidence of a narcissistic deficit. Consequently, his longings and demands were accepted and understood as developmentally phase appropriate. The result was a spate of material about the patient's mother's domination of him, including her preoccupation with his feces, possessions, and skin blemishes. This material had not appeared in the first analysis; it developed in accordance with the patient's longing for an idealized figure, which he found in the analyst. In the second analysis, the oedipal issues and masturbatory fantasies of strong women were not prominent analytic material and became resolved once the self developed a more stable structure. This is typical of the way Kohut regarded oedipal conflicts and what classical analysts would call drive-related issues. He tended to focus on the selfobject transference and felt the drive issues would abate once the self was strengthened.

As we have seen, Kohut rejected the view that all structural neuroses may be reformulated as narcissistic disorders and maintained a belief in the value of the diagnosis of structural neurosis in certain cases, presumably fewer than would be so designated by classical analysts. This brings us to the clinical implications of self psychology for cases that fit the diagnosis of structural neurosis.

Because Kohut (1984) viewed structural neuroses as products of arrested development due to faulty self–selfobject relationships in the oedipal phase, he felt that it was necessary for the analytic situation to engage the thwarted needs of this phase. Just as narcissistic patients must bring forth their archaic narcissistic configurations, so too must neurotic patients mobilize the needs with which they entered the oedipal phase. If the treatment situation is to mobilize the frustrated needs of the oedipal phase, the joyful assertiveness and affection of the child's entry into this phase, together with the expectation of confirmation and approval, must be mobilized in the transference. Again, for Kohut, it is not the Oedipus complex with its lust and hostility that needs to be enacted in the analysis but the selfobject needs associated with the child's entry into the oedipal phase.

Kohut believed that the analysis must retrace the steps of the neurosis to arrive at the thwarted developmental needs. Initially, there is a period of severe resistance to the Oedipus complex and castration anxiety. Once these resistances are worked through, the Oedipus complex with its hate, death wishes, and lustful longings appears. In Kohut's view, traditional analysis stops at this point and misses the crucial issues of the oedipally damaged neurotic patient, since the analyst has a preconceived notion that the Oedipus comlex is psychological bedrock. To Kohut, the appearance of the Oedipus complex masks resistances under which lies disintegration anxiety, the fear of the crumbling of the self, which now becomes apparent. Under the next mild level of anxiety lies a healthy, joyfully undertaken attempt to enter into the oedipal phase. That is, the analysis traces the developmental steps of the neurosis in reverse direction, beginning with the isolated drive fragments of the pathogenic Oedipus complex, then uncovering the failure of the oedipal phase selfobjects, and finally reaching the child's joyful anticipation of an assertive relationship with the parent of the opposite sex and an affectionate one with the same-sex parent.

With the mobilization of the child's joyful anticipatory entry into the oedipal phase, the crucial transference constellation has entered the analysis. The analyst's task is to understand that the patient's wish for affection and self-assertion are healthy, phase-appropriate childhood longings so that they do not become reburied under intense resistances. In Kohut's view, the traditional model mistakenly views such healthy wishes as defenses against lust and hostility, thereby mistaking the patient's struggling effort to complete the development of the self as a resistance to be overcome. By understanding and welcoming the patient's effort to unblock the development of the self, the analyst can help in the achievement of this goal. If these efforts are mistaken for resistances, they are in danger of becoming repressed once again and the development of the self remains incomplete.

Kohut provided no case descriptions of a self-psychologically informed analysis of a neurosis, but one can discern his concept of the treatment in his discussion of female agoraphobia mentioned earlier. Recall that Kohut stated that the failure of the paternal selfobject to welcome the little girl's affectionate and assertive strivings in the oedipal phase resulted in their conversion to lust and hostility. In addition, the failure of the maternal selfobject to provide soothing functions led to a gap in the child's ability to soothe herself and, consequently, to a tendency toward disintegration anxiety and an easily threatened self. The result was that the patient could not leave home without another woman to provide the soothing she was unable to provide for herself. It is clear from this formulation that Kohut's treatment approach would be to allow the development of the expected idealizing transference. As the transference becomes mobilized, the analyst would function to fill the gap in the self. The addiction to the woman should lessen as dependence on the analyst takes its place. The analytic process would then involve the patient's reactions to disappointments in the analyst and their interpretation. The transmuting internalization process, the means of resolution of all such transferences, would be expected to result in the internalization of self-soothing functions and the subsequent building up of self structure.

One can see that Kohut's views culminated in the belief that selfobject needs typify both the neuroses and the normal oedipal phase. This view raises the question of whether selfobject needs are ever totally overcome. Kohut (1984) maintained that selfobject needs continue throughout life. This aspect of his thought is critical because it reflects a shift in the goals of analysis away from the "independence morality" he believed the traditional theory had imposed on it. Kohut believed that the drive–ego model assumes that dependence is a negative trait and that the goal of analysis is to free patients from attachments and enable them to learn to achieve self-esteem without selfobject needs. Kohut believed that such a view of the human process is an illusion because even the psychologically healthiest individuals require positive responses from others to feel a strong sense of self. He came to believe that selfobjects are the oxygen of human life. Thus, the goal of analysis is not to free patients from all need for selfobject contact but to replace their "archaic" selfobject needs with "mature" selfobject needs and enable patients to evoke the needed responses from the mature selfobjects.

Kohut's extension of his treatment model to the neuroses raises the question of whether the self psychological model of treatment ought to replace the drive–ego model in the analysis of these milder disorders. While Kohut (1984) was reluctant to conclude that traditional analysis of neurotic patients should be replaced by self psychology, he increasingly believed in the applicability of the self-psychological model of cure even for these patients. The curative process for the neurotic patient involves selfobject transference and transmuting internalization, just as it does for the narcissistic patient. The difference lies in the developmental phase of the selfobject failure, which has no significant impact on the treatment process. Curtis (1985), in his criticism of self psychology, pointed out that although Kohut contended that the replacement of the classical model by self psychology was a question for the future, his reformulation of the treatment process accomplished this goal in the present.

The fact is that Kohut appeared to believe that the Oedipus complex could never be the cause of psychopathology of any type, since the intense affects of lust and hostility become issues only if the self is weakened, and that even the pathogenic sexual and aggressive conflicts in cases of neurosis are products of the breakdown of the self. Kohut did not believe that expression of a drive in and of itself resolves conflict. According to Kohut, chronic rage and sexual promiscuity are symptoms of a weak, enfeebled self that yearns for selfobject responses and will continue such behaviors until it gets them. Once the self becomes strengthened by the responsiveness of a selfobject, the "drive" needs are relieved.

It is clear from this conception of the psychoanalytic treatment of the neuroses that Kohut did not believe that making the unconscious conscious was the essence of psychoanalytic cure even for the structural neuroses. Indeed, he criticized this traditional concept of the analytic process as the imposition of the analyst's "truth morality" on the patient. Kohut advocated a shift in analytic priorities from the moralizing value system of the traditional analyst to the smooth functioning of the self. Making conscious the unconscious may or may not be necessary for the achievement of this goal in a given case. When the unconscious is made conscious, according to Kohut, it helps the neurotic patient, like the narcissistic patient, not because of the increased awareness to which it gives rise but because a selfobject has provided an experience of optimal frustration that culminates in the development of new self structures.

This view raises the question of why traditional analyses have had some success given the tendency of the traditional model to see healthy longings as resistances. Kohut's answer is that any model within the psychoanalytic tradition is successful to the extent that it provides understanding and explanation. According to Kohut, the classical analyst often conveys correct understanding and proceeds to offer incorrect explanations. Kohut (1984) gave as an example an interpretation by a Kleinian analyst, but the principle applies to traditional analysis as well. In the example, the patient's withdrawal after a cancelled session was interpreted as transference anger due to his view of the analyst as a bad breast. Kohut believed the interpretation to be incorrect but was surprised to learn that the patient felt much better in response to it. He explained this apparent anomaly by the fact that the analyst correctly understood the patient's withdrawal as a response to the canceled session; that is, empathic understanding provided relief despite the erroneous explanation invoking the bad breast. Thus, many contradictory theoretical schools can promote beneficial understanding. However, complete analytic cure requires both empathic understanding and accurate explanation.

Although Kohut was reluctant to state definitively that classical analysis should be abandoned in favor of a self-psychological approach in the treatment of neurosis, it is clear that he gave the drive–ego model no primary role in treatment. By approaching the analysis of neurotic conditions as the restoration of the self's normal developmental process, Kohut had, in essence, replaced the classical model with self psychology as both an explanatory system and a treatment method. By the time of his death in 1981, Kohut's views had evolved into a new psychoanalytic model encompassing development, psychopathology, and the treatment process.

SUMMARY: THE SELF PSYCHOLOGY MODEL

Ultimately, Kohut's thought led him to the creation of self psychology as a new model within the analytic framework. Freud (1915a) had developed psychoanalysis on the basis of the fundamental concept of the drive, a border concept between the biological and the psychological. For Kohut, not only can drives not be the basis for a psychology of complex mental states, but they cannot even be a part of such a psychology because they cannot be known by empathy and introspection. Psychological life begins, according to Kohut, with the empathy of the selfobject responding to the infant. The infant is born with innate potentials, and when these givens come into contact with the empathy of the first selfobject, a rudimentary nuclear self is born. Psychological development is from the beginning concerned primarily with the self, and the crucial factor in each phase is its relationship with its selfobjects. Optimally frustrating selfobjects give the self strength, harmony, and cohesion. Any faulty selfobject experience weakens the self and leaves it prone to pathology. With these concepts, Kohut reoriented psychoanalysis by directing its focus on the self, or, more precisely, the self–selfobject relationship.

Since the fundamental issue in psychological development is the growth of the self, pathology of whatever type is due to a developmental arrest that leaves the self weak, vulnerable, and prone to fragmentation. Defenses are often erected to protect a vulnerable self, but the essence of pathology does not reside in the use of defenses. In fact, defenses should be appreciated by the analyst as self-preservative maneuvers. With these concepts Kohut, echoing Winnicott's concept of pathology as blocked maturational process, replaced the drive–defense model with the pathology of developmental arrest. Since, in his view, the self depends on its relationship with selfobjects and since its defects are caused by disturbances in that relationship, all pathology ultimately derives from faulty selfobject empathy in crucial phases of development.

This reconceptualization of pathology fundamentally changes the nature of psychoanalytic treatment. Since pathology is arrested self development, the crux of analysis is not interpretation of defense but mobilization of the arrested self via empathic engagement and the resumption of self development by transmuting internalization. The analyst acts as a selfobject who functions as a part of the arrested self until he or she is internalized to complete its development. Interpretation is still the crucial tool of the analyst not so much because it makes the unconscious conscious but because it provides the optimal frustration necessary for the resumption of self development by transmuting internalization. Most crucially, to help the self complete the unfinished tasks of development the analyst functions in a manner analogous to how the parental selfobjects should have functioned. To the degree that the analyst allows himself or herself to be used to finish the developmental task, the analysis will be successful.

The fundamental attitude of the self-psychological analyst is markedly different from that of the classical analyst. The latter sets himself or herself in alliance with a part of the patient, the presumably healthy or observing part of the ego, in order to break through the patient's resistances by interpretation and thus reach the unconscious wishes that lie buried beneath the defenses. This concept has been a crucial component of the psychoanalytic model of treatment since Freud (1895) first began to trace associations back to the "pathogenic nucleus" of the neurosis. In Kohut's model there are no resistances, and so there is no alliance with one part of the patient's personality against another part. The self-psychological analyst does not oppose the patient, not even a part of the patient. Rather, the analyst's task is to be empathic with whatever material the patient brings to the treatment. If the patient is defensive, the analyst's role is not to interpret the defenses in order to get rid of them but to function as an empathic selfobject so that the defenses eventually become unnecessary.

Kohut's analytic posture is the decisive feature that sets his views into unalterable opposition to the classical model. The use of interpretation as a means for the achievement of transmuting internalization and the appreciation of defenses as phase appropriate combine to change the essence of analysis from the investigation of the unconscious to the completion of the self. Kohut, like Winnicott, believed that analysts must allow themselves to be used according to the patient's developmental needs of the moment. The essence of psychoanalysis, in this view, is not investigation but the development of the self, and the role of the analyst is not to convey knowledge but to be used as a selfobject. To the extent that the analytic relationship becomes problematic, the analyst has failed in this function, and it is incumbent upon the analyst to search for the empathic lapse rather than to interpret the deficit that caused the patient to need the analyst to be an unfailing selfobject. This concept of the psychoanalytic process has become the focal point for much of the expansion of self psychology by Kohut's followers, but before we discuss the growth of self psychology after Kohut, a critical assessment of some of his major views will be offered.

CRITIQUE

Kohut made an enduring contribution to psychoanalytic theory by introducing the concepts of the self and self-esteem in ways that have significant therapeutic value. He contributed to the movement to make psychoanalytic theory closer to patient experience with his distinction between "experience near" and "experience distant" theorizing and his application of it to his theory of self pathology. Kohut also introduced into psychoanalytic theory a far more detailed account of the development of the self and its vicissitudes than did any other theorist, including those who, like Guntrip, employed the concept of the self. Kohut also brought into psychoanalytic theory recognition of the need for relationships with others in the struggle to achieve self-esteem and of the importance of these relationships throughout life. A seminal clinical contribution is his recognition that much transference enactment, which in the classical model is considered resistance, is in fact the patient's expression of legitimate needs. Thus, Kohut furthered the movement toward appreciating the adaptive value of patients' defenses and their survival value in the treatment process.

Kohut's ability to extend this thinking to an alternative theory of development, pathology, and treatment has led to the most significant and comprehensive new model of psychoanalysis since Klein's formulation. In two ways Kohut's alternative model is more radical than Klein's: (1) self psychology attempts to establish psychoanalysis as a pure psychology, that is, without the assumption of biological drives, and (2) it proposes an alternative to the defense/resistance model. In this sense, Kohut's model is a revolutionary movement within the psychoanalytic tradition. Kohut's approach is a coherent, elegant alternative that fits the child development data much better than the classical model (see, e.g., Lichtenberg, 1983). Nonetheless, Kohut's model does have deficiencies that must be addressed if it is to endure as an alternative model or become the preeminent model within psychoanalysis. It has been widely criticized by more traditional analysts as being "unanalytic" (Kernberg, 1982; London, 1985; Curtis, 1985, 1986; Rubovitz-Seitz, 1988). Kohut's emphasis on the self rather than drives, on empathy rather than making the unconscious conscious, and on arrested development rather than defense interpretation have all been attacked as fostering defense and resistance rather than working them through. As indicated, Kernberg has been sharply critical of Kohut's work. The emphasis in our critique of Kohut's model will be on three major difficulties: confusion regarding the concept of the selfobject, the homogeneity of psychopathology, and the lack of clarity in the treatment approach.

Initially *selfobject* had a very specific meaning: an object used as a part of the self. In this sense, the selfobject is similar to Winnicott's notion of a transitional object (see chapter 4). In fact, when he was still focused exclusively on pathological narcissism, Kohut (1971, p. 33) referred to the selfobject as a transitional object. This definition of the term conflicts with Kohut's frequent tendency to equate selfobjects with people. Kohut's work is replete with references to pathogenic failures of early selfobjects. Sensitive to the criticism that he was leading psychology away from the psyche into interpersonal relationships, Kohut (1984) made a point of insisting that the selfobject was an intrapsychic concept, not an interpersonal one. One can, therefore, discern three definitions of the term: a transitional object, a person in certain roles, and an intrapsychic concept.

Wolf (1988) attempted to defend Kohut against the charge of "interpersonalism" by contending that Kohut always insisted that *selfobject* was an intrapsychic term. Kohut used the term to refer to parents and analysts in their behavior toward the child or patient. For example, Kohut (1984) attributed agoraphobia to "faultily responsive" paternal and maternal selfobjects and then went on to say, "The mother, in other words, was apparently not able to provide a calming selfobject milieu for the little girl, which via optimal failure, would have been transmuted into self-soothing structures capable of preventing the spread of anxiety" (p. 30). In this formulation of agoraphobia, Kohut used the term selfobject to refer to both parental behavior and a "milieu" provided by parental behavior. This dual usage is confusing, and neither is an intrapsychic usage of the term.

Kohut's treatment approach also contradicts his contention that *selfobject* is an intrapsychic term. Recall that in Kohut's view the selfobject transference is inevitably disrupted by the empathic failures of the analyst, which are disappointing to the patient. When these disturbances occur, Kohut believed, analysts should look for the ways in which they were unempathic to the patient. However, if the selfobject is intrapsychic, the analyst should seek the reasons for the disruption in the analysand's subjective experience. The clear implication of the recommendation that analysts look for their empathic failure is that the analyst as a selfobject is a real person who performs activities that have an impact on the patient.

According to Kohut, the result of a successful analysis of a narcissistic personality disorder is the ability "to evoke the empathic resonance of mature selfobjects and to be sustained by them" (Kohut, 1984, p. 66). If a mature selfobject can be evoked to empathic resonance and perform or fail to perform functions, it cannot be intrapsychic. To Kohut's credit, he was aware of the criticism that his usage of *selfobject* was confusing. His defense was that the reader had to understand that when he used self–selfobject relationship he meant the representations of "human surrounds" whether he explicitly said so or not. This defense is not satisfactory because in his statements regarding the origin of pathology, the selfobject component of treatment, and criteria for successful analysis, he used the term selfobject to refer to behavior rather than "representatives of the human surrounds."

Additionally, it is not at all clear that people without selfobjects necessarily lead impoverished lives. Indeed, people differ a great deal in their ability to withstand disapproval, unpopularity, and criticism. Some people are much more needful of others' approval and are willing to compromise themselves to get it. To say that people need selfobjects like they need oxygen is to oversimplify and mask crucial psychological differences among people. In this sense, one may say that the ability to live without selfobjects is a hallmark of self-esteem and self-cohesion. There is considerable evidence that people need both ties to others and self-enhancement, what Bakan (1966) calls the "duality of human existence." Bakan marshals evidence to demonstrate the need for both "agency" and "communion," and social psychological evidence tends to support this view (Carson, 1969). While Kohut understandably objected to the overemphasis on agency in the psychoanalytic value system, he overreacted to it and neglected the value of self-enhancement that is independent of echo, approval and admiration and even in opposition to them.

The failure to recognize individual differences among people in the extent to which they need others is a problem not only for the selfobject concept; it is a major weakness of Kohut's self psychology in general. By fitting all psychopathology into the category of self defects, Kohut homogenized emotional disorder both with analytically untreatable and with analytically treatable disorders. In the former category, which is less germane to his major ideas, he blended borderline disorders with psychotic conditions in arguing that the former are "really schizophrenic" but able to cover their psychosis with defense. This view is a serious, almost glib, distortion of borderline psychopathology, which, as those who work extensively with borderline patients know, is not a psychosis but a stable, severe personality disorder that is characterized by brief psychotic episodes under certain conditions. We saw ample evidence of this concept of the borderline personality in Kernberg's work (discussed in chapter 5), and this conception of the disorder is substantiated by most workers in the field of borderline pathology (for example, Masterson, 1976; Giovacchini, 1979; Adler, 1985). Why Kohut, who by his own admission had minimal clinical experience with this group, would maintain that borderline patients are "really schizophrenic" is difficult to discern. More important, Kohut is guilty of homogenizing all analyzable pathology into one type of problem: defects in the self. The treatment for all disorders is the same; namely, mobilization of the archaic self and interpretation of narcissistic injury, which promote transmuting internalization. This problem is similar to the difficulty we encountered in the work of Fairbairn and Guntrip, who homogenized all pathology in terms of the schizoid position. While Kohut has undoubtedly made a lasting contribution to the field with his emphasis on and understanding of self pathology, his single-minded approach risks losing the uniqueness of each case by assuming the existence of a self defect that must be filled in by the analyst. Alcoholic, depressive, obsessive–compulsive, hypochondriacal, and phobic patients, to name but a few, are all in danger of being understood as suffering from the same deficit. This approach risks missing those crucial aspects of each case that do not fit the model, the very consequence Kohut criticized in what he saw as the intent of classical analysis to make the patient fit the theory. Kohut's views themselves are in danger of repeating the same mistake.

This single-minded focus of treatment leads to the third major difficulty with Kohut's views. Kohut was quite sweeping in his enunciation of his principles of treatment. He believed the analyst should allow the archaic self to become mobilized and should interpret only failures and injuries. All disruptions are interpreted as the patient's experience of the analyst's failures. This technical approach is far too sweeping and potentially detrimental for patients who become "disrupted" and rageful for reasons other than the analyst's empathic failures. For example, Kohut's treatment model would be difficult to apply to patients who need to do battle and seek only the opportunity to do so; it is equally difficult to apply to patients who project their negative thoughts and feelings onto others, including the analyst. Undoubtedly, one could fashion a self-psychological explanation for such cases based on the empathic failures of the past and the patient's need to safeguard self-cohesion. However, to interpret these situations as the patient's "phase-appropriate" response to the analyst's failure does scant justice to the patient's pathology and risks submerging it by putting the focus on the analyst's supposed mistake. Many patients foster disruption and need to view others negatively in order to avoid more deeply felt anxieties. It is difficult to see how the patient's motive for the disruption and rage would be uncovered by an approach that focuses on the analyst's empathic failure to meet the patient's phase-appropriate needs. This is not to say that Kohut's approach is not valid in many clinical situations; it is only to say that his model is in danger of becoming a theoretical straitjacket that blurs critical clinical differences. In this sense, self psychology may be erecting another version of what Goldberg (1990) calls the psychoanalytic "prisonhouse."

Having said this, it should be noted that Kohut was responding to the traditional analytic posture of fostering regression and then criticizing the patient, even if subtly, by attacking resistances and adopting a moralizing, educational posture. Kohut was unalterably opposed to viewing patients' narcissistic needs as pathological entitlement and felt that analysts should adopt an empathic posture of accepting and understanding regression as an appropriate response to a given phase of pathology. While this approach has a great deal of validity, it cannot be used to justify a single-minded focus on the analyst's errors; part of a transference regression may well be the patient's need to cause disruption of the analysis and be rageful toward the analyst. It may be that Kohut's sweeping generalizations are an overreaction to the classical model that blurs the distinction between failures in analytic empathy and the patient's pathological needs for disruption.

One can question whether Kohut's views risk losing the value of transference analysis. In his view, the patient reacted in a realistic way to the parents in the past and reacts in a similar fashion to the analyst now; the current reaction is to be accepted as phase appropriate. When the analyst misunderstands, the patient's rage is accepted as understandable and, if interpreted at all, is seen only as an appropriate response to the analyst's "failure." This view seems to miss the most powerful therapeutic aspect of transference: the patient's equation of today's perceptions with past trauma. If the analyst is able to point out to the patient that whenever the analyst acts in any way similar to a figure from the patient's past, the patient reacts as if to the archaic figure, the analyst can help the patient understand the reaction while accepting its appropriateness in the past. The patient's transference reactions frequently are responses to the analyst's behavior, but the therapeutic action lies in the patient's recognition that his or her reaction is rooted in the past. This distinction is the most significant and therapeutically powerful component of transference and is crucial to helping patients understand the difficulties they have with many people in their current life. If analysts cannot differentiate past from present because they feels that their behavior is equivalent to that of the childhood figure, they are colluding with the patient's pathological perceptions and are not using the leverage of the transference to help the patient differentiate present echoes from past trauma and thereby master his or her current emotional life.

It has fallen to Kohut's followers to attempt to complete his mission by correcting problems in the model and continuing to develop it as the primary alternative to classical psychoanalysis. To complete our discussion of Kohut's work, we now turn to these followers to trace recent developments in the theory of self psychology and thereby grasp the state of the model at the present time.

THE SELF PSYCHOLOGISTS

Kohut's followers may be grouped into three broad categories: those who adopt his self psychology model and make only minor emendations to it; those who extend his model; and those who use Kohut's work as a beginning point for a new concept of psychoanalysis even more radical than self psychology.

Most of Kohut's followers fit into the first group. Wolf collaborated with Kohut on the delineation of disorders of the self in order to refine distinctions between different types of self pathology (Kohut and Wolf, 1978). They outlined four types of self pathology: (1) the understimulated self, which is bored and apathetic owing to the lack of selfobject responses in development and which seeks excitement by pathological means, such as sexual promiscuity, addictions, or perversions; (2) the fragmenting self, which has lost its continuity in time and space owing to the failure of selfobject responses and which resorts to hypochondriasis when selfobjects fail; (3) the overstimulated self, which avoids attention and receives no joy from success owing to its archaic fantasies of greatness, caused by extreme lack of empathy or phase-inappropriate selfobject responses and which cripples productivity; (4) the overburdened self, which suffers from diffuse anxiety and constantly maintains a hostile view of the world and reacts to selfobject failures with paranoia, pathology attributable to the inability of the childhood selfobjects to allow merger and provide self-soothing functions.

Kohut and Wolf also delineated three personality types that are not necessarily pathological: the mirror-hungry personality, the ideal-hungry personality, and the alter-ego personality. These personality styles are pathological only if they are extreme, reflecting a deep defect in the self. There are two such pathological personality styles: (1) the merger-hungry personality, which has such an intense need for merger that it lacks boundaries and is so intolerant of others' independence that it attempts to dominate others, and (2) the contact-shunning personality, which has the same intense needs but reacts to them by avoiding others. With these typologies, Kohut and Wolf hoped to differentiate the various types of pathology that Kohut (1971) grouped under the rubric "narcissistic personality and behavioral disorders" in his earlier work .

Wolf (1988), who prefers the expression "disorder of the self" to "narcissistic disorder," sharpened Kohut's transference typology by eliminating "mirror transference in the broad sense." Instead, he divided selfobject transferences into the following types: merger, mirror (formerly "mirror in the narrow sense"), alter-ego, ideal, and adversarial. He defines the latter as the expression of the patient's need for supportive, oppositional selfobjects that is, like other selfobject needs, lifelong. Wolf also attempted to define the selfobject needs of the life cycle, pointing out that there are, in addition to the archaic and oedipal selfobject needs discussed by Kohut, selfobject needs in the more advanced stages of the life cycle: in latency, selfobjects are needed as models for imitation whereas in prepuberty the need for selfobjects moves away from parents and toward teachers, friends, and symbols. Adolescents and young adults find selfobjects in peers, idols, and the subculture; and in marital relationships the spouse becomes the primary selfobject.

Apparently aware that Kohut's view of selfobjects as psychological oxygen can be criticized for failing to take into account people who appear to function well without approval or admiration—or even without others—Wolf points out that Kohut (1984) had extended the selfobject concept to activities, such as listening to music and reading. Wolf believes that selfobject needs are concrete only in infancy. As the self develops, selfobject needs become increasingly abstract: symbols or ideas can serve the purpose. Activities and ideas are symbolic replacements for the selfobjects of infancy. This view may explain why some people appear to function without selfobjects, since different experiences might work for them, but it creates new problems. First, Kohut defined selfobject in general as the "human surrounds" and more specifically as the echo, admiration, and approval of the human environment. If music and reading are categorized as selfobjects, one would have to say that they somehow serve to admire and approve. Since they clearly cannot do this, the selfobject concept has to be expanded to mean anything that makes people feel good. Thus, ultimately it can mean and explain nothing. In this broadened sense the selfobject concept can have no explanatory power; it can only label after the fact any positive experience as "selfobject." This does not help to understand individuals, nor does it advance the field. In this broadened sense the concept of selfobject is no different from the concept of reinforcement in behavioral theory; it simply labels what people do by means of a pseudoexplanatory theoretical construct.

Self psychologists have tended to underscore the value of empathic resonance in the therapeutic process. Basch (1985) considers "affective attunement" the paradigmatic self–selfobject relationship, applicable to the mother–infant dyad as well as the therapist–patient relationship. According to Ornstein and Ornstein (1985), the understanding phase of treatment constitutes acceptance of the patient's childhood wishes as legitimate, an experience that leads to belated maturation and growth. P. Tolpin (1988) considers the therapeutic action of psychoanalysis to be in the "optimal affective engagement" of the patient, a phenomenon tantamount to the therapeutic provision of selfobject functions. M. Tolpin (1983) elaborates Kohut's concept of the "corrective emotional experience": her view is that the mutative aspect of the analytic process lies in the working through of a new "transference edition" of the old self–selfobject unit. The interaction between patient and analyst, once the selfobject transference is established, is equivalent to a "corrective developmental dialogue" in which the patient's developmental needs are responded to in a new way; it is the patient's internalization of this "cohesion-fostering" selfobject tie that is the essence of the curative process. For Tolpin, who emphasizes this new experience as the essence of the change process, this is the self-psychological "corrective emotional experience."

One can see that those of Kohut's followers who apply his concepts closely tend to de-emphasize the "optimal frustration" aspect of insight in favor of a new "exchange" or experience between analyst and patient. This tendency is even more prominent in the second group of self psychologists, who tend to accept most of Kohut's principles but further shift the treatment focus from insight to the patient–analyst relationship. This view is best represented by Bacal and Newman (1990), who are in the minority among self psychologists both in their acknowledgment of the debt of self psychology to previous object relations theories and in their view of self psychology as one type of object relations theory. These theorists agree with Wolf and other self psychologists that the crucial contribution of self psychology is the selfobject concept. Unlike other self psychologists, however, they believe that self psychology is a "multi-body" theory because the self–selfobject relationship is an interpersonal relationship. Since the self is formed from the psychological meaning that grows out of self–selfobject interactions, the mutative aspects of the analytic process are considered to lie in the provision of selfobject functions. Bacal and Newman list five such functions: affective attunement, validation of subjective experience, tension regulation and soothing, organization and restoration of the self, and recognition of uniqueness. The task of the analyst is to provide these functions, and to the extent that he or she does, the analysis will be successful.

Bacal (1985) replaces Kohut's concept of optimal frustration with the concept of optimal responsiveness. According to Bacal, there is no inherent value in frustration and Kohut's use of the concept is a vestige of the drive model that is best removed from his theory. According to Bacal, if the child is responded to optimally, its self will grow; if not, growth will be delayed. Bacal and Newman point out that since Kohut rejected the view that the "untamed" infant must experience frustration in order to turn drives into structure, optimal frustration can have no role in his therapeutic model.

The upshot of the shift from optimal frustration to optimal responsiveness is to exchange the role of insight in the treatment process for the provision of selfobject functions. Bacal and Newman believe the patient needs to be responded to, not investigated. The value of explanation, in their view, is to verbalize affects—much as the mother names the child's experience to help the child organize it. However, if the analyst's only way of communicating understanding is to put feelings into words, the patient's experience may be invalidated, as patients cannot always use words. The analyst's way of talking, listening, and responding may provide the needed selfobject experience more effectively. It is this view of the analyst's task—that is, to provide selfobject functions rather than insight—that makes Bacal and Newman's formulations an extension of the self-psychological model rather than a refinement of it. For Kohut, the analytic process consists of the provision of insight, although its value lies not in the accretion of knowledge, but in the creation of new self-structure. For Bacal and Newman, the analytic process involves the provision of selfobject functions, which may or may not include insight.

There are two offshoots of self psychology that represent an even more radical departure from the drive-ego model. The first is the intersubjective model advanced by Stolorow and his followers (Stolorow and Lachmann, 1980; Stolorow, Brandchaft, and Atwood,

1988), who point out that Kohut's definition of psychoanalytic data as that which is gathered by empathy and introspection makes psychoanalysis a "pure psychology" (Stolorow, 1985). Stolorow and his colleagues agree with Kohut that drive is not a psychoanalytic concept because it is not accessible to the psychoanalytic method. They argue that once psychoanalytic theory is freed from the drive concept, one is left with "intersubjective contexts." According to Kohut, the traditional analyst cannot be empathic with the narcissistic patient because the material does not fit the analyst's preconceptions. Stolorow and his colleagues call this an example of the analyst's subjectivity failing to connect with the patient's subjectivity. Kohut believed he made progress with Miss F when he gave up his attempt to fit her material into the model of the Oedipus complex and heard her expectations as longings to meet a developmental need; Stolorow points out that such a clinical experience indicates that the analytic process is a meeting of two "subjectivities." He believes his intersubjective theory frees psychoanalysis from the last vestiges of the drive–ego model. The analyst's task is to understand the patient by attempting to grasp the material from the patient's point of view, the patient's subjective reality. Analysts have their own viewpoint from which they will interpret the patient's reality, but Stolorow's point is that the analyst's reality is no more objective than the patient's view and that it therefore has no claim to priority. He is supported in this view by Schwaber (1979), who sees "analytic listening" as the grasp of the patient's "subjective truth."

From the vantage point of their more radical phenomenological view, Stolorow and his colleagues agree with Kohut's emphasis on the centrality of self experience and its relationship with selfobjects, but they find fault with Kohut's concept of the self and its development (Stolorow et al., 1988). First, they point out that Kohut uses *self* to mean both the sense of personal agency and a structure that organizes experience. The first meaning confuses *self* with *person*. Second, they view the bipolar self as a simplification and reification. In Stolorow's view, ambitions and ideals are two affective meanings in a multidimensional self with a variety of affective meanings; moreover, the "tension arc" that allegedly spans them is not accessible to empathy and introspection. Third, Stolorow and his colleagues object to the notion that the self can break down, and have "disintegration products." They believe that such concepts are reifications, remnants of the old mechanistic metapsychology, and serve only to obscure the meaning and purpose of affects.

One can see from this critique that, in the Stolorow group's view, the self is organized around affects and the understanding of affects is crucial to the analytic process. To achieve its organization of affective meanings, the self requires the responsiveness of caregivers. Stolorow and his colleagues (1988) point out that the concept of optimal frustration is based on the drive–frustration model of development and that "transmuting internalization" is a mechanistic concept inaccessible to empathy and introspection. They agree with Bacal that the self requires responsiveness, not frustration. Stolorow and his coworkers replace the concepts of optimal frustration and transmuting internalization with the hypothesis that the self develops through integration of its affective meanings. Selfobjects, in their view, are functions that help the self to integrate affects into the organization of self-experience.

Stolorow and his colleagues (1988) describe four key selfobject functions performed by the parents: affect differentiation, the synthesis of affectively discrepant experience, toleratation of affects and their use as signals, and the "desomatization" and logical articulation of affects. If any of these selfobject functions are not performed in early development, the child's central affective states are not effectively responded to; as a result, they must be disavowed rather than integrated, and development is derailed. Such a self is vulnerable owing to its lack of integration of affects.

Although Stolorow tends to eschew diagnostic labels, clinical depression can be invoked to illustrate his viewpoint: if the child's depressive affects are not responded to in childhood, these affects are not integrated into the self structure; when grief reactions or depressive affects of any type are subsequently experienced, the self is threatened with dissolution. According to the Stolorow group, this threat is the basis of all psychogenic affective disorders. The crucial variable in the onset of affective disorder is the lack of calm caregiver responsiveness evoked by the depression.

If the parent is unresponsive but the child adapts to the parent to maintain the selfobject tie, guilt conflicts result (Stolorow, 1985). According to Stolorow, conflicts involving guilt are a product of what the child must do to maintain the tie to parents who are unable to adapt to the child. In this view, the superego is the child's perception of what is required to maintain the selfobject tie. If the child's autonomy is a threat to the parent, the child will feel that its own affects are threatening and will believe itself to be cruel and dangerous. This is Stolorow's concept of what Kernberg calls "superego forerunners" (see chapter 5). Structural conflict is always a product of selfobject failure.

In the view of Stolorow and his colleagues, more severe pathology has the same root, but the injury is so severe that affective strivings are abandoned in favor of self protection to prevent repeated trauma. Either the self is protected by rebellion or isolation or it submits and becomes chronically dependent; or it is tormented by ambivalence between these two states. Brandchaft and Stolorow (1984) view terms such as *borderline* as pejorative labels that reflect the clinician's failure to understand the patient's developmental needs. In keeping with their intersubjective approach, they contend that borderline pathology does not reside in the patient but is always codetermined by the intersubjective context. In such severely disturbed patients, it is difficult to comprehend the archaic intersubjective contexts in which the pathology arises, resulting in recourse to terms like *borderline*. The therapeutic process with such patients consists of the same process as Kohut described in the treatment of narcissistic disorders, but the "archaic intersubjective meaning context" is more difficult to find.

In accordance with this theoretical posture, the goal of psychoanalysis for Stolorow is the unfolding, illumination, and transformation of the patient's subjective world. Consequently, the task of the analyst is to facilitate the unfolding of developmental strivings. The stance of the analyst is determined by whatever helps achieve this goal; if abstinence does not facilitate this goal, it should not be part of the analytic stance. Stolorow believes that the optimal approach to facilitate the transformation of the patient's subjective world is sustained empathic inquiry. Such an attitude permits the structure of the past to gain expression in the analytic relationship. From this viewpoint, the transference is the organizing activity by which the patient subsumes the analyst into his or her view of the world. Stolorow objects to the concept of a temporal regression. Instead, he points to a universal striving to organize experience and understands psychopathology as the operation of the patient's past "structures of subjectivity" in the present.

Stolorow and his colleagues adopt Kohut's view that failures in selfobject experience are pathogenic, but they believe that conflict has a larger role in emotional disorder than Kohut ascribed to it. While Stolorow agrees with Kohut that selfobject failure results in developmental arrest, he points out that when the self is able to resume development by the establishment of a selfobject tie, such as occurs in analysis, the self will then be in conflict. Treatment may involve prolonged periods of empathy and understanding to establish the selfobject tie, but once it is so established, conflict can be addressed; when this bond is disrupted, deficits become prominent and conflict recedes.

Deficit and conflict are figure and ground, according to Stolorow, and each becomes the focus at different times in the treatment.

The therapeutic action of analysis in this view is the mutative effect of the selfobject tie. Initially, the patient is defensive out of fear of a faulty response from the selfobject. Once this resistance is analyzed, the emergence of the need for the original selfobject allows for the articulation of the patient's affective organization in the analytic setting. As the analyst becomes a part of this organization, the transference bond is established, and to the extent that it is protected from disruption, growth can occur. When disruptions take place, they are interpreted, thereby permitting the reestablishment of the tie and the resumption of arrested development. According to Stolorow, it is this transference tie that gives interpretations their mutative power; interpretations are part of this bond. The selfobject tie and transference cannot be separated. That is, in this view, all mutative moments in analysis entail some degree of "transference cure." This process is as applicable to the treatment of the so-called borderline as it is for the patient with structural conflict. Insight, affective bond, and psychological integration are critical components of every psychoanalysis. The resolution of this process occurs when the transference experience becomes integrated into the patient's psychological organization. When this happens, the patient's affective life is immeasurably enriched.

The other radical offshoot of self psychology is the approach of Goldberg (1990), who uses Kohut's concept of selfobject as the link between psychoanalysis and the modern philosophical and scientific view of man. In Goldberg's view, traditional psychoanalysis is still wedded to the outmoded subject–object distinction. That a person is not limited by his or her skin is, according to Goldberg, a conclusion of many disciplines. For example, memory is not a static "storehouse" but an active effort, a working upon the world; external objects activate neurons and the connections between neurons so that the object actually becomes part of the entire pattern of activating the brain. There is no storehouse of internal representations upon which people draw; what we call representations are ways of participating in the world. Heidegger's philosophy of man as being-in-the-world highlights the inherent, inextricable link between man and world.

In Goldberg's view, Stolorow's conception of separate "subjectivities" coming together is an advance but does not go far enough because it fails to appreciate that one's "subjectivity" is never separate, that there is no need to postulate a "coming together." Goldberg adopts Heidegger's view that we are inherently bound in a man–world relationship, and our particular relationship to the world and others is who we are. According to Goldberg, Kohut's concept of selfobject is the psychoanalytic dimension of this modern view of man. The implication of Kohut's view of the self–selfobject relationship is that the self is composed of the experience of others, selfobjects. Goldberg's view is that among psychoanalytic theories only Kohut's view of the self-selfobject relationship appreciates the inherent relationship between man and world. Freed from the outmoded self–object distinction, analysis can, Goldberg contends, become free to study the development of the self as it changes its composition by means of its self–selfobject relationships. In this view, transference is a form of Heidegger's being-in-the-world. The psychoanalytic process then becomes an effort to transcend the boundaries of the self, to find new ways of being. According to Goldberg, the essence of psychoanalysis is a mutual effort between patient and analyst to remake the patient's self via a verbal exchange. In Goldberg's conceptualization of the process, self-psychological concepts become a bridge between psychoanalysis and the phenomenological-existential view of man.

By way of summary, one can see that although the various offshoots of self psychology differ and even conflict in some areas, they have all tended to move self psychology further away from its roots in the drive-ego model. In this sense, self psychology is evolving toward a fundamental shift in the psychoanalytic conception of the nature of the human enterprise and its requirements for change. Even the more conservative tendencies of the self psychology movement have eschewed the drive model remnants in Kohut's theory in favor of emphasis on "affective engagement." Self psychologists whose theories are more sharply divergent from the classical model have shifted toward a relationship paradigm of psychoanalysis in opposition to an interpretive model of treatment. Further, the most radical branches of self psychology have used Kohut's conceptual reformulation of psychoanalytic thought as a springboard to a pure psychology of people-in-interaction with the world. This paradigmatic shift is the link between object relations theories such as self psychology and interpersonal theories of psychoanalysis, and it is to this latter school of thought that we now turn.

The Interpersonalists

THE INTERPERSONAL APPROACH TO PSYCHOANALYSIS WAS DEVELOPED between the 1930s and 1950s by Harry Stack Sullivan but was largely ignored by mainstream psychoanalysis until the growing influence of object relations theories led to recent interest in integrating it with more traditional models. A significant component of this shift is Greenberg and Mitchell's (1983) interpretation of object relations theories in terms of a "relational model" conceptually linked to Sullivan's interpersonal theory. Let us delineate the major concepts of interpersonal theory, ascertain its similarities to and differences from object relations theories, and assess its contribution to psychoanalytic thought. Since the interpersonal theory of emotional disorder began with Sullivan and all current versions of this model are influenced, if not rooted in, his theory, our discussion begins with his contribution.

THE WORK OF HARRY STACK SULLIVAN

Sullivan found Freud's metapsychology of impulses and psychic mechanisms to be too far removed from patients' experiences. The difficulties people have in living have to do with their interpersonal relations, he believed, not intrapsychic mechanisms. Sullivan's (1953) view is that human beings are inherently imbedded in such relationships to the point that one cannot understand them outside their relationships with others. The way one relates to others defines who one is. In Sullivan's view, this fact can be seen from the beginning of life. The baby cannot be conceived of without the mothering figure. And, however independent children may become, they define themselves by the way they relate to others. Freud's intrapsychic concepts—impulses, defenses, ego, superego, id, even the unconscious—only obfuscate understanding by artificially cutting off individuals from their relationship to the human environment.

In accordance with his concept of the nature of personality, Sullivan (1953) conceived of development as a series of stages of interpersonal relationships. The infant is born with "needs for satisfaction," which include both biological and emotional needs. A need produces tension, but the infant is completely incapable of satisfying the need by itself. The infant's tension elicits tension from the mothering figure, which leads her to satisfy the need. The mother's ministrations are experienced by the infant as tender behavior, and "these needs, the relaxation of which require the cooperation of another, thereupon take on the character of a general *need for tenderness*" (Sullivan, 1953, p. 40). That is, the generic needs of the child for the mother are subsumed under the need for tenderness, which becomes a primary emotional need. Even though many of the infant's needs involve biological tension, they are considered interpersonal because they can only be satisfied by tender behavior from another. Sullivan called this first relationship "maternal empathy" and believed that it characterized the first stage of development.

Life remains interpersonal as the infant develops because needs continue to require others for their satisfaction. In the first year the infant's emotional need is for bodily contact. Between ages one and four, the need is for others to be an "audience" for the child's behavior. For children ages four through eight the primary need is for learning both to compete and compromise with others. The primary need of the preadolescent, ages eight to puberty, is for a "chum" of the same sex with whom to be intimate, and in adolescence the need is for intimacy with the opposite sex. Each of these stages is defined by the type of relationship sought.

One can see from this view of personality development that Sullivan attributed much more importance to emotional needs than to biological needs. He acknowledged the pressure of biological tensions, especially in early development, but he pointed out that since these tensions immediately give rise to the need for another person, the need for tenderness predominates. It is the history of relations with the mother and then other persons that forms the personality. However, needs for satisfaction are not the only type of need. If the infant's needs elicit anxiety in the caretaker, the infant "catches" this anxiety and becomes fearful. Anxiety, for Sullivan, is different from tension because it has no identifiable object; it is difficult to describe in words but approximates an uncanny sense of dread. Sullivan's primary theorem regarding anxiety is that it is contagious, that is, it is exchanged through the empathic linkage between caretaker and child. When the child's needs produce tenderness in the mothering figure, the needs are met and the tendency is toward integration of the personality; when the needs produce anxiety in the caretaker, the child becomes anxious and the experience is "disintegrating."

According to Sullivan, the child's first distinction is between anxious and nonanxious states, and these global, diffuse conditions are experienced as "good mother" and "bad mother." These "prehensions" are not perceptions of the real mother; rather, all experiences of tenderness and need satisfaction, from however many people, are "good mother" while all experiences of anxiety and disintegration are "bad mother." Further, self- and object-images are not differentiated at this point. Only later, as the child matures, do these images and the particular characteristics of self and other become differentiated. As this differentiation occurs, the child develops a view of itself based upon its perceptions of the way it is being viewed and responded to by its caretakers. Sullivan terms these perceptions "reflected appraisals." The self is defined as what one "takes oneself to be," and this sense emerges from the interpersonal patterns of development. All experience consistent with others' appraisals becomes part of the self whereas experience diverging from these appraisals is excluded from this organization.

According to Sullivan, anxiety is the most unbearable feeling to which the human being is subject. Once anxiety is felt, the personality develops a strong need to avoid it. The need to avoid anxiety becomes the "need for security," the second basic human motivation. Because of its fear of anxiety, the child learns to anticipate which of its behaviors will produce anxiety in the caretaker and to pattern its interactions accordingly. Sullivan called the maneuvers used by the child, and later by the adult, to avoid anxiety "security operations." The initial security operations are means of restricting awareness. Behavior that gains caretaker approval, increases tenderness, and reduces anxiety in caretaker and child becomes organized into the "good me." Behavior that has the opposite effect, that results in the mothering figure's disapproval, reduces tenderness, and increases anxiety in both the child and caretaker, becomes organized into the "bad me." Sullivan added a third category of experience that produces such intense anxiety in caretaker and child that it cannot be allowed into awareness in any form; he called this experience the "not me or dissociative system." Experience of this type operates on the edge of awareness but is occasionally experienced by all people, the most common instance being nightmares. When "not me" experience breaks into awareness, it tends to be felt as dread or uncanny emotion. The personality attempts to keep all "bad me" and "not me" experiences out of awareness. Eventually, the mother is no longer necessary, as the self-system is sufficiently developed to reduce anxiety by restricting awareness only to what fits. As the child matures, it learns other forms of security operations, that is, other ways of reducing anxiety, most of

which involve a sense of superiority. The primary maneuvers discussed by Sullivan are the illusions of power, stature, and a sense
of specialness. The self-system for each individual is the set of security operations that effectively reduced anxiety in childhood, and
preserves the shape of the self.

Anger, in Sullivan's view, is a response to threat. The child's first
response to punishment is rage, but as it develops and learns foresight
it finds that anger is more useful. If anger is suppressed, the child may
continue to be rageful and have temper tantrums into the school
years. If the child is punished with no discernible cause, it will learn
that anger exacerbates the situation and will become chronically resentful. Resentment, in Sullivan's view, is anger that is not expressed
openly for fear of reprisal. Most children learn anger and many are
resentful to some degree, but the most debilitating form of anger
is what Sullivan called the "malevolent transformation." This pathological shift in the psychological organization comes about if the
child's need for tenderness is not only denied but met with a hurtful
response. If children are made to feel anxious or humiliated for the
expression of their need for tenderness, they will turn this need into a
malevolent attitude and not only refuse to show such a need but
refuse to allow anyone to act tenderly toward them. In these cases
hostile behavior becomes a significant component of the personality
and greatly interferes with interpersonal relationships. As can be seen,
Sullivan did not view anger or aggressiveness as inborn; he saw them
as reactions to situations of interpersonal anxiety. Anger is always a
response to threat, and since all people experience threats, they all
experience anger. It is not an emotion to be tamed, and it becomes
part of a pattern of emotional disorder only when it replaces the need
for tenderness.

Unlike most psychoanalytic theorists, both traditional and object-
relations-oriented, he did not accept Freud's theory of infantile sexuality. Adolescence begins what he called the "lust dynamism." Lust is
the need for satisfaction characteristic of this phase of development;
like all needs for satisfaction, it requires another for fulfillment. How
well it becomes integrated with the need for intimacy is a function of
the interpersonal experiences of this phase. The degree to which these
experiences are marked by anxiety is the degree to which the lust
dynamism becomes a disintegrating rather than an integrating tendency in personality development. Like anger, sex is not a drive to be
tamed but an interpersonal need that becomes growth enhancing to
the degree that it elicits tenderness as opposed to anxiety.

Human life, in Sullivan's view, revolves around the dialectic between the dual needs for satisfaction and security. When a need is associated with minimal or no anxiety, it will be satisfied; when anxiety interferes, the need for security interferes with satisfaction. The degree to which the need for security dominates the need for satisfaction is the degree of psychopathology in the personality. Since the anxiety that motivates security operations always has an interpersonal source, all psychopathology is ultimately traceable to anxiety-ridden interpersonal relationships. A pathological personality is a self that operates only, or primarily, out of the need for security. In such a personality the needs for power, status, and prestige predominate. Sullivan did not use traditional diagnostic categories, in keeping with his belief that psychopathology is a human process, not a "disease" that can be diagnosed. In his schema diagnosis is supplanted by an assessment of the interpersonal sources of the patient's security operations. All the traditional nosological categories, such as obsessive–compulsive and hysterical disorders, are viewed as markers for different security operations that were developed originally in childhood in response to anxiety and are maintained out of fear of its reappearance.

Negative or unhappy interpersonal experiences of childhood lead to security operations, but if these operations cannot protect against the experience of the "bad me," low self-esteem results. For Sullivan, this low self-esteem is the source of many traditional psychiatric syndromes. Since the "bad me" produces anxiety, new strategies of anxiety reduction must be developed. Low self-esteem, in Sullivan's view, inhibits what he called "conjunctive motivation," that is, integrating situations capable of bringing need satisfaction, such as falling in love. Consequently, other solutions are sought, resulting, for example, in "exploitive attitudes," which include behavior that would normally be classified as passive-dependent and masochistic. Sullivan equated the general characterological recourse to masochism to an indirectly exploitive use of others, as opposed to the more open efforts of exploitation used by the passive-dependent character. In lieu of exploiting others, individuals may tell themselves how abused they are or may envy others, and Sullivan called these strategies "substitutive processes." He also considered hypochondriasis on this continuum, as he believed it to be the personification of oneself as "customarily handicapped." People with low self-esteem may also involve themselves in situations in which they are taken advantage of in such a way that they are led to expose a weakness. For example, they may engage in relationships in which others entrap them into acknowledging something they would normally keep private; the result is chronic humiliation. When the exposed weakness is part of the person's "dissociative system," the experience is "attended by some measure of the uncanny emotions—awe, dread, loathing, and horror" (Sullivan, 1953, p. 359). In Sullivan's view, this experience of the uncanny is the closest one can get to the "not me," the dissociative part of the personality, without becoming schizophrenic. If the individual is unable to employ security operations against the previously dissociated component of the personality, it becomes the personified "not me." Sullivan calls this the "paranoid transformation," which in turn can degenerate into a schizophrenic process.

Sullivan explained all of what would normally be considered psychopathology in terms of various reactions to interpersonal anxiety that he believed corresponded to real experiences in childhood. This explanation encompassed even the most severe form of pathology, schizophrenia (Sullivan, 1962). Indeed, Sullivan applied much of his early theoretical and clinical effort toward advancing the view that schizophrenia is an understandable reaction to interpersonal anxiety, like any other form of pathology. He believed that schizophrenics had suffered such devastating anxiety in early life that their security operations could not be employed effectively against the dissociative component of the personality, and he labeled the resulting terror "schizophrenia."

Thus, Sullivan attempted to account for all difficulties in living without recourse to traditional psychoanalytic concepts, such as the unconscious, the ego, the id, defenses, and even internal objects. He substituted a dual system of human needs for Freud's dual drives and attempted to explain psychopathology on the basis of the relative balance between the need for security and the need for satisfaction.

Consistent with his interpersonal theory of development and pathology, Sullivan (1956) conceptualized the goals of treatment as the learning of more effective, flexible ways of interacting with other people. His focus was on what patients do in their interpersonal world in the present and on what can be done about it, rather than on uncovering the past. Thus, Sullivan's (1940) goal with all patients was to make them aware of their patterns of interpersonal relationships. Perhaps his most commonly quoted statement is that "one achieves mental health to the extent that one becomes aware of one's interpersonal relations" (Sullivan, 1940, p. 102).

Sullivan's use of the transference is puzzling. He recognized that the patient-therapist relationship is from a theoretical viewpoint, an interpersonal relationship, as he defined the role of the therapist as "participant observer." He believed that the therapist is inevitably a participant in the interaction and that no useful data could come from trying to adopt a "detached position." Sullivan (1954) adopted the theoretical position that the therapist must begin with the patient's external relationships and later move the treatment into the patient–therapist relationship. Despite this view, however, there is considerable evidence that he focused very little on transference and countertransference. While he recognized them in the form of resistances and asserted their importance, he in fact interpreted the transference very little (Havens, 1976).

Sullivan's technique seems to have been based on two strategies. The first is to help patients with their relationships outside of the patient–therapist interaction by attempting to help them gain awareness of their interpersonal patterns. The second strategy, which addresses the patient–therapist interaction, is the attempt to counteract, rather than interpret, the patient's perceptions. In his discussion of psychiatric interviewing, Sullivan (1954) described a variety of techniques, verbal and nonverbal, for demonstrating to the patient that what the patient feels as shameful and anxiety provoking is not so construed by the therapist. In addition, Sullivan made many statements derogating interpretation as a whole, not just transference interpretations. Havens (1976) termed Sullivan's technique "counter-projective," by which he meant that Sullivan actively combatted the patient's projections. It appears that Sullivan's attitude toward treatment was that patients need a new interpersonal relationship in which the other party is not as fearful of the patients' emotions as the patients are themselves. Nonetheless, Sullivan believed that the goal of treatment was the patient's awareness of the patterns of interpersonal relationships; one may infer that he believed his techniques of counterprojection would help the patient become more aware of these patterns, but this was not made explicit.

The fact that Sullivan made little use of unconscious mental processes and put little emphasis on interpretation in general or on transference interpretation in particular largely accounts for the fact that his thought received little attention outside Sullivanian circles for several decades, even among those favorably disposed to his interpersonal theory. For example, Guntrip (1961a), who lauded Sullivan's use of interpersonal concepts in lieu of drives, did not consider Sullivan a psychoanalyst because his theory was not a depth psychology. However, in recent years Sullivanian analysts, who adopt major tenets of Sullivan's interpersonal approach to development and pathology, have incorporated his theories into a system of psychoanalytic exploration and interpretation. These Sullivan-inspired models of the psychoanalytic process cannot be summarily dismissed as "nonanalytic." It is to these more contemporary outgrowths of Sullivanian analysis that we now turn.

THE WORK OF JAY GREENBERG AND STEPHEN MITCHELL

Greenberg and Mitchell (1983) view Sullivan's work as one of many versions of the "relational/structural" model, the others being the various object relations theories. All theories based on a view of man as inherently imbedded in human relationships fit this model in which is opposition to the "drive/structural" model of classical psychoanalysis. That is, Greenberg and Mitchell recognize two basic theoretical models of psychoanalysis: one that sees man as an interpersonal being motivated to relate to others as part of his very nature and one that considers the fundamental human motivator to be inborn drives and their vicissitudes.

Greenberg and Mitchell recognized that some object relations theories, such as Kernberg's, attempt to accommodate both models by viewing object relations as the primary preoedipal issue and drive/conflict as the appropriate model for the neuroses. They take the position that all such "strategies of accommodation" are doomed to fail: if the child is viewed as inherently imbedded in a relational matrix, the drives must be seen as fundamentally object relations and the drive/structural component never quite works, even for the neuroses in these hybrid theories. We saw that this was the case in the critique of Kernberg in chapter 5, where it was pointed out that Kernberg's theoretical model obviated the drive concept, although he himself had not drawn this conclusion. Greenberg and Mitchell opt for what they term a "strategy of radical alternative," replacing the drive model with the "relational/structural" model, with Sullivan's theory as one of many contributions to this model.

Mitchell (1988) has adopted the view that psychological reality is a relational matrix encompassing both the intrapsychic and interpersonal realms; he opposes this model to the "monadic view of the mind," which assumes that the self can operate independently of others. He considers the principal contributors to the relational model to be the interpersonal psychoanalysts, beginning with Sullivan and Fairbairn, and considers object relations theorists who emphasize self development, such as Kohut, to be "monadic" theorists because their basic units, such as the nuclear self, are intrapsychic. Mitchell is also critical of theorists like Kohut, Winnicott, and Guntrip, who viewed pathology as developmental arrest, for failing to appreciate both the inherent nature of human conflict and the relational nature of development. Mitchell's alternative is a "relational conflict" model, which recognizes the intrinsic nature of human conflict but sees its basic units as relational configurations, not drives and defenses against them. For Mitchell, mind does not need to *become* socialized: it exists only as a social product. Therefore, the units of psychoanalytic study are relational bonds and the matrices they form. One can see in this view the influence of Sullivan's interpersonal theory of mental life. However, unlike Sullivan, Mitchell is concerned with the meaning of experience to the individual and sees psychoanalysis as the process of elucidating meaning, especially as it manifests itself in the patient–therapist interaction. Thus, Mitchell draws out the clinical implications of Sullivan's interpersonal theory by proposing that meaning is embedded in a relational matrix and that the relationship between patient and analyst is the best place to discover the meaning of the patient's experience.

In accordance with his substitution of the relational model for the drive model, Mitchell does not view sexuality as a drive. He appreciates its biological "drivenness" and acknowledges its prominence in human life but points out that sexuality always gains expression in a relational matrix. Thus, sexuality does not derive its power from organ pleasure but from its meaning in a relational matrix. Although sexuality is an especially powerful motive, it is a vehicle for the expression of relational patterns and social roles. It does not create social meaning but derives its power from the social meaning with which it is relationally invested. Mitchell believes that sexuality is particularly apt to become the focus of psychopathology because its biological power and requirement of another makes it the most powerful medium for connection with other people and renders the individual potentially vulnerable to the needed other. Further, the privacy of the body makes sexuality a natural vehicle for the symbolization of object seeking.

If development has resulted in object seeking becoming a dangerous endeavor, sexuality becomes not an enriching experience, but "a search for symbolic reassurances and illusory guarantees" (Mitchell, 1988, p. 111). For example, the search for the elusive object may be concretized by the genitals, resulting in compulsive promiscuity. If demands from the primary object to be good and clean were excessive, sex may be associated with dirtiness; in an extreme outcome, only prostitutes or other "dirty" or "degraded" objects are exciting because they represent defiance of the primary object. Or, if submissiveness is felt to be a requirement to maintain connection to the partner, sexuality with the primary object may become deadened and sexual dominance in fantasy or reality with other objects may become the only means for independence. Mitchell gives other such examples to make his point that sexual difficulties of any form are sexualized expressions of relational conflicts.

Mitchell is critical of object relations theorists, such as Kohut and Winnicott, who conceive of the patient as a passive receptor rather than a creator of experience and who reify the patient's experience of himself or herself as a baby with their belief that patients who have a concept of themselves as a baby are arrested at an infantile life that lurks under the surface of adulthood. Mitchell views such a self as a strategy that permits interaction with others. Further, he regards relatedness as inherently conflictual and believes that the self-as-baby is a product of conflict rather than an unconflicted arrested self that needs only to be found. In addition, Mitchell believes that the needs expressed by the adult patient are not infantile needs but adult dependency needs fraught with anxiety. All human needs exist throughout the life cycle, and the developmental arrest hypothesis, in his view, conflates ongoing life cycle needs with their earliest expression.

In contradistinction to the developmental arrest view, Mitchell believes that patients willfully cling to their pathological patterns as the only types of relationships they know. According to Mitchell, all children have a range of possibilities and this range is limited by the parents not because of parental failure but because the child's anxiety and parental limitations require that the child use the parents as "anchor points." The child learns what it must do to engage the parents with a minimum of anxiety, and these modes of engagement become the child's interactional template for all subsequent relationships. Out of these patterns the individual weaves the tapestry of the self. The patterns learned in childhood are adhered to because they were formed to avoid anxiety; if they are threatened, the individual fears loss of contact, which is tantamount to loss of self and isolation. According to Mitchell (1988), "each person is a specifically self-designed creation, styled to fit within a particular interpersonal context" (p. 277). If certain of these relational configurations are in conflict with the predominant self-shaping relational patterns, they will not be woven into the "dominant themes of the tapestry" and will find hidden forms of expression, resulting in neurosis. Mitchell (1988) objects to the classical concept of psychopathology that patients fail to meet a standard of appropriate behavior and substitutes his view that "difficulties in living would be regarded with respect to the degree of 'adhesion' to one's early relational matrix and, conversely, the relative degree of freedom for new experience which that fixity allows" (pp. 277–278). It is the degree of rigidity of the relational configurations, that is, the extent of attachment to the archaic childhood objects, that determines the extent of maladjustment of the personality. Flexibility of the self-organization, the freedom to experience different relationships in different ways, is Mitchell's concept of mental health.

As a direct consequence of this position, the aim of analysis, according to Mitchell (1991), is to help the patient develop a more variegated sense of self. To achieve this goal, analysts have a twofold task. First, they must immerse themselves in the experiential world of the analysand, because it can be understood only from the inside. Here, too, Mitchell is critical of object relations theories, as he believes they attempt, much like the classical model, to understand the patient from an "external" perspective. In Mitchell's view, the analyst must inevitably become a part of the patient's relational world, and it is this immersion that provides the understanding of who the patient is. However, if analysts were to do only this much, they would be no different from others in the patient's life. What allows for therapeutic action, rather than simple repetition, is analytic inquiry. The analyst's second task is to wonder with the analysand why his or her way of relating is the *only* way he or she can form a relationship with the analyst. According to Mitchell, the analysand was forced to choose in childhood between his or her limited way of relating and total isolation. By finding neither inappropriateness nor incorrectness in the patient's construction of the analytic relationship but, rather, restrictiveness, the analyst creates the possibility of the patient's relinquishing old object ties and becoming open to new interpersonal experience. The aim is not to make the unconscious conscious, nor even to provide a new experience, but to alter the structure of the analysand's relational world.

In Mitchell's view, psychoanalysis as a treatment is a special type of dyadic relationship that has as its aim the broadening of the relational possibilities of one of the two participants. In the course of this process the other participant, the analyst, will also be changed. But the analyst's goal is to become both participant and observer of the analysand's relational world so that he or she can offer a different perspective on this world. The psychoanalytic encounter, then, creates the possibility of broadening the structure of the analysand's relational world beyond the narrow confines of childhood constraints.

A good example of Mitchell's concept of treatment is his approach to narcissism. He takes a position midway between Kohut and Kernberg. Mitchell (1988) views Kohut as understanding the childhood need for narcissistic illusion but as missing the defensive function of grandiose and idealizing illusions in both childhood and in the adult patient, and he views Kernberg as grasping the defensive nature of narcissistic illusion but missing its function in normal development. The child and the patient need both the illusion of narcissism and its eventual relinquishment. In normal childhood the parent understands the child's need for narcissistic illusion and engages in the child's play; at the same time, the parent knows the illusions are play and must eventually be given up. In Mitchell's view, the proper analytic stance requires an analogous mixture of engagement in the patient's narcissistic fantasies, which Kohut understood, and analytic scrutiny of their illusory status, which Kernberg understands. Mitchell advocates engaging the patient and exploring why such illusions represent the only way the patient can engage others. The combination of the analyst's participation in the "play" of the analysand's narcissistic illusions and his or her interpretations creates the possibility of experiencing a relationship with other dimensions.

Mitchell accepts Sullivan's interpersonal theory of human experience and his view of development as learning strategies of relating to others. However, he adapts this model to a treatment strategy that focuses on the patient–therapist relationship and aims to enrich the patient's ways of interacting through this relationship.

Greenberg has recently become quite critical of some aspects of the relational model he championed in the book he and Mitchell (1983) wrote on object relations. Greenberg (1991) accepts the importance of relationships but finds Mitchell and other relational theorists guilty of committing three fundamental errors: (1) neglect of the fact that relations are motivated by pre-experiential needs, (2) denial of the inherent nature of conflict in human existence, and (3) failure to recognize the need for separation as well as relatedness.

Greenberg (1991) criticizes Mitchell, Fairbairn, and Kohut for failing to appreciate that relatedness is not autonomous, but motivated by other needs. He uses Fairbairn's and Kohut's theories as examples of relational models that purport to view relations with others as autonomously motivated but implicitly assume underlying drives that fuel interpersonal contact. Fairbairn (1944) saw the infant as object seeking but, according to his theory, object contact is necessary for ego growth. Similarly, Kohut (1984) views the self–selfobject relationship as a means for the structuralization of the self. Greenberg argues that both models assume an underlying motive for object contact and therefore are implicitly drive models because relationships are motivated and motivation is ultimately reducible to drives. Greenberg's conclusion is that no psychoanalytic theory can be sufficiently explanatory without the concept of drives. Greenberg does agree with Mitchell and other relational theorists that the biological concept of drives is irrelevant to psychoanalysis, but he feels that these theorists make the mistake of throwing the baby out with the bath water by eliminating the drive concept entirely.

The second error Greenberg believes to be characteristic of relational theories is their tendency to see human motivation as unidirectional. Examples are Kohut's view of development as moving toward the structuralization of the self unless there is interference from an unempathic environment and Winnicott's belief in the natural unfolding of the maturational process unless arrested by impingements. Such theories, in Greenberg's view, deny the conflict inherent in the human condition. In his view, conflict is not only produced by an environmental counterforce but human motivation itself is inherently conflictual; thus, tension is experienced in the most benign environment. Greenberg believes that relational models tend to share the narrowness of the impulse/prohibition model of conflict by assuming that all conflict involves defense. He argues that people frequently experience conflicting motives without defense, that is, that the presence of human conflict extends well beyond the employment of defenses. Unidirectional relational theories are thus limited by their inability to account for the ubiquity of human conflict.

The third limitation of relational theories, in Greenberg's view, is their inability to appreciate the need to be separate and independent of others. Greenberg argues that such a need is as critical to development as the need for relations, all autonomy is not reducible to defense against object contact. Greenberg conceives of development as an oscillation between relating and autonomy. In this regard, his views bear a striking similarity to Mahler's (1975) separation–individuation model discussed in chapter 1.

Greenberg's alternative to previous relational theories is a nonsomatic drive/conflict model of motivation. He conceives of development as motivated by the dual needs for safety and effectance. Safety encompasses the needs for physical and emotional well-being and motivates relations with others. Effectance is the need to do and to learn how to do; it provides a sense of vitality and aliveness to the human experience but drives the individual away from others. Both are endogenous, pre-experiential, nonbiological drives with innate directedness. Both drives, in Greenberg's view, have immutable underlying tendencies, but they are decisively influenced by interpersonal events and therefore are expressed in a variety of behaviors. According to Greenberg, there is inherent tension between the two drives. Safety drives people to others, and effectance requires doing without others. The inborn nature of the two drives, therefore, explains the ubiquity of conflict in the human experience. While conflict may be caused by a negative response to the child's needs, such responses are not required for the experience of conflict; the needs themselves have opposing motivations. Greenberg illustrates this point with an example of a child's hunger. The child may need the hunger satisfied but may also feel the need to act autonomously. The result cannot be fully satisfying: if the mother meets the need for hunger she stifles the need for autonomy, and if she lets the child cry she preserves his need for distance but leaves him hungry.

Greenberg believes his dual-drive theory preserves the importance of relationships while resolving the three difficulties he finds in previous relational theories. Nonetheless, a major developmental implication of Greenberg's drive theory is a de-emphasis on the actual child–mother exchange. According to Greenberg, many factors influence the outcome of early experience, one of which is the relative strength of the drives. Consequently, the meaning of any particular developmental experience may result from perceptions of the parents based on the child's needs and may have little to do with the actual interaction between parent and child. Thus, Greenberg tends to weigh internal motivation more heavily than do other relational theorists.

In Greenberg's view, the center of initiative of the personality is best conceptualized as the ego, as Freud used the term, before the structural model, when he referred to the "dominant mass of ideas." Greenberg views the mind as an active container of ideas that cannot be a direct object of experience but can be represented. Self-representations and feeling states reciprocally influence each other and are the primary regulators of behavior: "the way we are feeling at any moment significantly affects how we imagine ourselves to be" (Greenberg, 1991, p. 171). In turn, the shape of the self-image profoundly influences affective responses. Since self-representations are multiply determined constructions, many ways of thinking of oneself are possible at any given time. However, a particular self-representation tends to be stable and dominant and decisively influences intentions, which in turn lead to wishes. Each wish consists of a self, an object, and a relationship between the two. Whenever the dominant self-representation is threatened, painful affects are experienced, stimulating repression to safeguard the integrity of the self. When development surpasses previous inabilities, the latter are "re-represented" as negative. For example, when a child learns to read, its previous inability to read is "re-represented" as shameful and repressed. All defense, for Greenberg, is directed against such "re-representations." According to Greenberg, the task of analysis is to understand the meanings of representations by bringing the unconscious "re-representations" into awareness. The patient will not be easily amenable to such broadened awareness because the repression of threatening self-representations produces a feeling of safety. Resistance, according to Greenberg, is motivated by the safety drive. In this regard, Greenberg's ideas are in agreement with the views of Weiss and Sampson (discussed in chapter 1) that resistance is an index of the lack of safety the patient feels with the analyst and that the analyst must first help the patient feel safe before interpretations will be accepted by the patient. Psychoanalysis, in this view, depends on the patient's feeling of safety with the analyst, which in turn allows rejected mental contents into awareness and thus broadens the patient's self-representations. Since self-representations lead to wishes, which involve both self- and object-representations, increasing the flexibility of the self-representational field expands the patient's motivations and allows for greater possibilities for effectance and ways of interacting with others. Like Mitchell, Greenberg sees pathology as rigidity and effective analysis as a broadening of the interactional field, allowing the patient to respond to different interpersonal situations in different ways.

Despite this similarity with Mitchell's thought, Greenberg differs from Mitchell and other interpersonal theorists in the greater emphasis he places on the patient's representational world. Because Greenberg believes that relational needs are half of the human motivational system and are motivated internally, he is, despite his theoretical divorce from the biological basis of psychoanalysis, closer to the classical model than any other interpersonal theorist.

EDGAR LEVENSON

Another major extension of the Sullivanian model is proposed by Levenson (1985) who, unlike Mitchell and Greenberg, accepts the major tenets of Sullivan's interpersonal theory. In contrast to Mitchell, Levenson sees a decisive difference between the interpersonal and object relations viewpoints; in fact, Levenson (1989) has attacked Mitchell's efforts to link the two models as an unwarranted ecumenicalism that threatens to subvert the interpersonal viewpoint (Levenson, 1989). In Levenson's (1981) view, the crucial distinction is not between the interpersonal and intrapsychic points of view but between "reality behind appearance" and "reality in appearance."

According to Levenson, the classical analytic model makes the error of proposing that the patient's fantasies, dreams, and other presumed manifestations of "the unconscious" are clues to the patient's psychic reality and that the task of the analyst is to decipher the meaning of symbols and appearances to uncover the "true" psychic reality. As opposed to this view, Sullivan's interpersonal theory sees the patient's difficulties as residing in interpersonal reality, the nature of which must be delineated by the analyst from the relationship between patient and analyst. Thus, the patient's problems in living are not an intrapsychic reality to be uncovered by decoding symbols and disguises but distortions produced by interpersonal anxiety experienced in the real world. Fantasies, in this view, are a reaction to real interpersonal anxiety rather than motivators of interpersonal perceptions. From the data of the analytic situation, the analyst attempts to discern the pattern of the interpersonal relationships causing the patient's problem. The aim of the analyst's delineation of interpersonal patterns is not to demonstrate the patient's projections from the past into the analytic setting but to show that the very interpersonal patterns currently occurring outside the analytic setting are also taking place within it.

In this context that Levenson takes issue with object relations theories. Because object relations theorists tend to seek to uncover the patient's psychic reality, whether this be thought of as a "true self," a "nuclear self," or a "regressed ego," these theories, according to Levenson, commit the same errors as does the drive model. That is, they seek a "truer" reality under appearance, rather than attempting to delineate the patient's interpersonal reality. For Levenson (1985), the distinction between which comes first, fantasy or reality, marks the critical division among the different psychoanalytic schools of thought.

One can see from this model that Levenson is attempting to adapt the Sullivanian interpersonal viewpoint to the clinical method of using the patient–therapist relationship as the primary analytic instrument. The Sullivanian model changes the principal analytic question from "What does it mean?" to "What's going on around here?" (Levenson, 1989). According to Levenson, the question is the same for object relations theory, as it is for the drive model: both seek meaning. The interpersonal analyst does not search for meaning but for understanding the interaction between patient and therapist.

From Levenson's viewpoint, object relations theorists, no less than classical analysts, ignore the reality of the patient's life. Like Sullivan, Levenson seeks to know in detail the realities of the life before him. In

discussing a case of Silverman's, Levenson (1987) criticized the therapist for neither discussing nor inquiring into the details of the
patient's life outside of therapy. Unlike Sullivan, Levenson believes in
paying close attention to the patient–therapist relationship as an
example of the patient's interpersonal pattern and as the best lever for
effective change.

These considerations have a number of clinical implications. While
the patient–therapist relationship is the critical factor in treatment, the
process does not depend on the analyst's correct interpretation of it.
Indeed, in Levenson's view, the analyst's perception of reality has no
privileged status over the patient's. The two form an interpersonal
reality in which neither party has a special claim as arbiter. Further,
the analyst is important not as a fantasied or transference object but as
a real person with real qualities. According to Levenson (1982), the
analyst will inevitably become caught in the patient's interactional
pattern, but this participation must be authentic, "not merely sincere."
Every interpretation is a form of participation in the interaction,
enlarging not only the communicational matrix between the two participants but, simultaneously, the relationship per se. Levenson (1982)
breaks down the distinction between speech and action: all speech is
action, and all action is structured like a language. Thus, for Levenson,
psychoanalysis becomes a semiotic science. Everything that takes
place between the participants is a communication and is coded like a
language. According to this model, speech is only one form in which
such coded communication takes place. It is Levenson's contention
that everything that is talked about between the two participants is
simultaneously enacted between them. Consider, for example, a sce-
nario in which the analyst points out that the patient is sensitive, and
the patient, upon hearing this, begins to cry. If the patient is masochistic, the analyst may feel benign and detached, that is, sadistic, or the
analyst may get angry at the patient and actually feel sadistic. In either
case, the sadomasochistic relationship is enacted (Levenson, 1982). In
opposition to the usual analytic posture, Levenson does not believe
that continual interpretation of this enactment will achieve an analytic
result. The therapeutic action, in his view, lies in "a changing, or at
least expanded, participation with the patient around the material. In
some way the therapist must operate with the patient so as to be
'heard'" (Levenson, 1982, p. 99).

Levenson (1991) acknowledges that this conceptualization of the
change process is obscure, but he believes that a certain degree of inef-
fability is inherent in therapeutic shifts. In Levenson's view, the
change process is stimulated not by information exchange but by

interpersonal "resonance," which is difficult to define. Although the precise nature of the process is unknown, the analyst delineates the authentic patterns of the patient–analyst interaction in such a way that he "resonates" with the patient's private experience and a patterning emerges. Levenson's (1991) concept of resonance gives his view a similarity to the self-psychological concept of therapeutic action as affect attunement (Kohut, 1984; Basch, 1984). Unlike self psychologists, however, Levenson believes that when moments of resonance occur, the patient experiences a sudden reconfiguration into which all the material seems to fit. Change, in this view, is discontinuous. Analytic technique cannot cause this repatterning to occur nor predict when it will happen; it can only attempt to stimulate the preconditions for its occurrence.

Levenson views the analytic task as an enriching human relationship in which there is no place for the analyst to employ "techniques," such as interpretation, or "corrective emotional experience" from outside the relationship. According to Levenson (1982):

> Corrective emotional experiences largely disappear in the tar pit of the patient's self-equilibrating system. I doubt that the patient grows because he is supplied with a nurturing environment. I suspect the patient must be engaged and experienced and responded to. If behavior is a language, then it must be heard. The therapist who is detached from an angry patient may hear him on the speech level but does not hear him on the action level [p. 100].

The patient is helped neither by a new truth, nor even by a new relationship; rather, the patient's experiential world is enriched by the analyst's authentic engagement in this world. In response, the patient gives up his or her wish to change in favor of a wish to be his or her authentic self. Psychoanalysis, from this viewpoint, is not a talking cure but an "experience cure." The interpersonal analyst in this view does not nurture the patient or "accept the patient's psychic reality" but engages the patient's world in a real way. One can see that Levenson's variant of the interpersonal model stretches the concept of psychoanalysis beyond both object relations theories and Mitchell's concept of the interpersonal model. Authentic engagement replaces interpretation and the meeting of childhood needs as the principal therapeutic instrument.

THE WORK OF MERTON GILL AND IRWIN Z. HOFFMAN

Another major extension of the interpersonal model has been proposed by Gill and Hoffman. Unlike Mitchell and Levenson, they do not begin from a Sullivanian theoretical base, although Gill (1981) has acknowledged the link between his "social model" and Sullivan's interpersonal theory. Gill theorizes primarily about the analytic process, with little reference to personality development or psychopathology. He contends that much analytic practice is of poor quality because analysts do not pay sufficient attention to the moment-to-moment here-and-now transference process owing to their failure to see the patient's veiled allusions to the transference. In Gill's view, Freud may have made this error himself since he did not believe all of a neurosis would necessarily translate into the transference neurosis. The history of psychoanalysis is replete with failures to see that seemingly nontransferential material is really a distorted allusion to the transference. This problem is serious, in Gill's view, because the extent to which the neurosis enters the transference is the extent to which it can be resolved.

It follows that the analyst's first task is to expand the transference within the analytic situation. This is accomplished by attempting to link external material to the relationship with the analyst. Patients talk about material external to the transference, which Gill considers frequently to be a form of resistance, and analysts often resist connecting this material to the transference because analysands may attribute attitudes to their analysts that make them uncomfortable. Nonetheless, analysis of resistance to the awareness of transference is a crucial phase of the treatment process. Gill points out that the analyst must be alert not only to the patient's attitudes but also to the attitudes the patient implicitly (that is, nonverbally) attributes to the analyst. Gill disputes the traditional technical stance of allowing the transference to unfold spontaneously. His contention is that the patient's resistance will prevent such an unfolding without interpretation of the resistance to awareness of the transference. The patient will of course react to the analyst's persisting efforts to frame transference interpretations, but the patient will likewise react to the analyst's silence. Any reaction of the patient to the analyst is "grist for the analytic mill" and should be interpreted.

The analyst must be careful not to increase resistance by telling the patient he is "really" referring to the analyst; rather, interpretations should emphasize the parallel between the external material and the analytic situation. When such a parallel exists, the analytic reference is the most relevant and has priority over all other material, including genetic interpretations, from an interpretive point of view. This principle applies at any point in treatment. The analyst need not wait for the development of the "therapeutic alliance," because transference interpretations will help foster that relationship and without such interpretations the patient's resistance may prevent its formation.

Once the patient is aware of the transference, Gill believes the crucial issue is to demonstrate to patients that their way of construing the analytic situation is not the only way. He disagrees with the traditional view that the patient is "distorting" the relationship, a view that reflects what he considers to be the positivistic classical view of the analytic situation, namely, that it has an objectively perceivable reality that the analyst knows and that the patient must come to see. In this regard, Gill's epistemological position is in agreement with that of both Mitchell and Levenson. In Gill's view, patients do not distort but they do not see what they are bringing to the relationship; Gill terms this "resistance to the resolution of the transference." This resistance is overcome when patients see that their version of the relationship is their own construction, which is not, however plausible, the only possible way of viewing the analyst's behavior and the analytic relationship in general.

Up to this point, Gill's views appear to apply only to the conduct of analysis. What shifts Gill's (1981) position from a purely technical to a theoretical model is his view that the transference is always connected to the real behavior of the analyst. In every analysis the analyst evinces both technical and personal behavior, and the patient responds to both. Gill believes there are major clinical implications in the view that the analyst's behavior, both technical and personal, is real and is responded to by the patient as both transference and reality. Because the transference is always connected to the real analytic situation, reference to it should be included in all transference interpretations. By pointing out what in the analyst's behavior has contributed to the patient's perceptions, the interpretation becomes more plausible and acceptable to the patient. Furthermore, if the analyst cannot find the connection between the transference perception and his or her actual behavior, the task is to uncover it.

One can see in Gill's view a shift from the typical analytic conceptualization of transference as the patient's projection of wishes and fantasies onto the analyst to an interpersonal model according to which the patient is always reacting to a real person and the transference is seen as an interactional phenomenon. Object relations theories and the drive-ego model tend to hold similar structural views of transference: it is what the patient projects from his past onto or into the analyst and the analytic situation. Gill, like the Sullivanians, opposes this concept of transference in favor of the interpersonal view that the real relationship between patient and analyst is inevitably implicated in the transference and its interpretation. The clinical implication is that the actual features of the analytic situation must be clearly delineated and even scrutinized. Gill (1981) sums up his view of the therapeutic action of psychoanalysis this way:

> The analyst suggests that the patient's conclusions are not unequivo-
> cally determined by the real situation. Indeed, seeing the issue in this
> way rather than as a "distortion" helps prevent the error of assuming
> some absolute external reality of which the "true" knowledge must be
> gained. The analyst need claim only that the situation is subject to vari-
> ous interpretations and that since the patient's conclusions are not
> unequivocally determined by the features of the situation which can be
> specified, he would be wise to investigate how his interpretation may in
> part be influenced by what he has brought to the situation [p. 118].

There is an even deeper level at which Gill's theory is interpersonal. For Gill (1983), the fact that the analytic relationship is interpersonal means that the analyst will inevitably "fall in" with the patient's transference wishes to some degree. Therefore, the meaning of the analyst's participation must be explored in every analysis. This investigation does not necessarily imply "countertransference confession," although such confession is not precluded in every situation. An exploration of the relationship between patient and therapist in which the participation of both is reflected on becomes a crucial component of the analysis. Like Mitchell and Levenson, Gill views the analyst as an inevitable participant in the patient's pathology, however, in opposition to those theorists, Gill believes that interpretation is the primary tool for the resolution of the transference neurosis. Gill agrees with the Sullivanians that the analyst is a participant but believes in the therapeutic efficacy of both the new experience and its interpretation. Gill's view is that analysis works best when what is being experienced between patient and analyst is simultaneously interpreted.

Hoffman (1991), who has collaborated with Gill on a study of transference, has emphasized the epistemological aspects of their shared viewpoint, which he believes leads to a "social-constructivist" model of the analytic process. He believes that the division in psychoanalysis is not so much between the drive and relational models as between the "positivist" and "constructivist" positions. He describes the positivist model in the same way Gill does: the myth of an objective reality knowable in some privileged fashion by the analyst. Like Mitchell and Levenson, Hoffman opposes such a view and believes, instead that the patient and analyst are coparticipants in an interactional drama in which together they are continually constructing an interpersonal reality. Every act by either party, such as an interpretation, shapes the interaction in a new, not totally foreseeable way. Each participant has a perspective on the "social construction," but neither has a privileged view of it. Hoffman agrees with the interpersonal emphasis of much of object relations and interpersonal theory, but he contends that these views do not follow through and embrace the proper epistemological perspective. He attacks such theories as latently positivistic because they imply that one can explore the patient's perceptions to "get at something already there" (Hoffman, 1991).

The alternative offered by Hoffman's social-constructivist model is for the analyst to recognize that any exploration may lead to something never before formulated that may affect both participants in unforeseeable ways. The explication of the patient-analyst relationship and the influence of each participant on the other create new meanings. In Hoffman's view, the adoption of this model implies a shift in the analyst's attitude toward a recognition that intervention cannot capture a "reality" and therefore shapes the process in unknowable ways. In Hoffman's (1991) view, this attitude leaves analysts freer to engage patients in a more open, authentic manner because they are not burdened with the myth of believing in a "right" interpretation that they must find but have, instead, the perspective that they cannot foresee the results but are ready to explore them. In Hoffman's view, this sort of analytic encounter differs from a simple, existential confrontation because such analysts continually reflect on themselves and their involvement. The aim of this process is "to affect some of the most deeply rooted ways in which patients experience themselves and others" (Hoffman, 1991, p. 96). Further, the patient is made aware that these patterns are relative rather than absolute and inevitable, and this constructivist attitude will be carried over to the rest of the patient's life.

SUMMARY OF THE INTERPERSONALISTS

One can see from this review that the interpersonalists differ in many ways but are united in the view that man is defined by his relationships with other people. With the possible exception of Greenberg, interpersonal theorists believe that the inherent nature of personal relationships is neither incidental nor even simply necessary for the achievement of human aims but the very substance of life. Gill and Levenson both invoke this principle as the key difference between the interpersonal and object relations models. All versions of the latter model see interpersonal relationships as necessary for the formation of psychological structure whereas the interpersonalists see man's very nature as inherently relational. Gill (1983) points out that for object relations theories pathological issues occur in the context of interpersonal relations whereas for interpersonal theories issues are a matter of interpersonal relations. If one views the drive–ego model as relatively *neglectful* of interpersonal relations and the object relations model as *emphasizing* them, the interpersonal model is the next step: a theory *based on* interpersonal relations.

In reviewing the interpersonal theories one is struck by the relatively minimal attention given to concepts of development and pathology. Sullivan is the only interpersonal theorist who had a detailed theory of development. Since Sullivan, interpersonal theory has tended to focus on man-in-relationships of various sorts, with relatively little attention to the phases and issues in development leading to their occurrence. One can see in the work of Levenson, Gill, and Hoffman a relative neglect of the developmental viewpoint in favor of the view that relational problems exist in the present and must be addressed as they manifest themselves in treatment. Mitchell gives more consideration to the influence of development on current problems but still focuses his treatment approach on the enrichment of current relationships in the patient's life. Greenberg is the exception, as he believes that the interpretation of "re-representation" of the past is crucial in helping to free the patient from rigid self-representations. Since Sullivan did not draw on his developmental theory in his treatment approach, Greenberg is the only major interpersonal theorist whose clinical strategy includes a significant role for interpretation of childhood experience.

Conceptualizations of psychopathology also tend to be absent from the post-Sullivanian interpersonalist theories. Sullivan himself addressed specific diagnostic categories from his interpersonalist perspective, but all major interpersonal theories since have concentrated on concrete interpersonal difficulties in living, not clinical syndromes. This focus is a direct product of the interpersonal principle that people are defined by their interpersonal relationships. Since this principle is no less applicable to people who seek help than to others, interpersonalist therapists tend to regard clusters of symptoms or character structure as being of little clinical relevance in comparison to the interpersonal strategies patients use to negotiate their lives. Common to all versions of the interpersonal paradigm is the idea that as these strategies are altered, existing difficulties will be simultaneously ameliorated. The "diagnosis," rather than invoking a traditional nosology, is framed in terms of interpersonal patterns, and such patterns are believed to be best seen in the patient's relationship with the analyst.

This emphasis on the interpersonal nature of human problems has led theorists in the post-Sullivan movement to place the patient–analyst relationship at the center of the analytic process, just as those who follow object relations theories or classical psychoanalytic technical theory do. However, there is a major difference in the way this relationship is construed. The interpersonalists locate the analyst's participation in the patient's issues at the center of the analytic process. Levenson (1981) even states that analysis begins when the participants experience what is talked about. Gill (1981) has quite correctly pointed out that this view of the analyst as participant separates the interpersonal theory of technique from both the classical and object relations models.

The interpersonal view leads logically to the question of the relative importance of experience versus interpretation in therapy. Theorists differ on this issue. Sullivan, of course, gave little role to interpretation (Havens, 1976). Levenson (1989, 1991) has concluded that authentic encounter is more conducive to change than is the accretion of knowledge or even the provision of a new relationship. Hoffman (1991) sees a role for interpretation but emphasizes authentic encounter. Mitchell (1988) believes in the importance of interpretation but not because it offers mutative insight; for Mitchell, the new relationship with the analyst is the most significant therapeutic factor and interpretations help consolidate this relationship by showing the patient "where the analyst stands." Again, Greenberg (1991) is traditional in his belief that interpretation is the center of the therapeutic action. Gill (1981) also gives interpretation the most significant role in the analytic process; in fact, Gill insists, much like a classical analyst, that everything that goes on ought to be interpreted as fully as possible. That is, although Gill, like all interpersonal theorists, sees a major role for the analytic relationship in effecting change, his focus is clearly on interpretation: the therapeutic relationship is optimally formed by consistent transference interpretation, and the new relationship is most effective when it is interpreted.

The exclusive focus on the interaction between patient and analyst has led interpersonal theorists to mount epistemological challenges to psychoanalytic theory. Since analyst and patient bring their respective backgrounds to a conjointly shaped relationship, the privileged epistemological position of the analyst is abandoned in favor of the view that neither participant has privileged access to the truth about what happens between them. In this sense, the interpersonal view is linked to certain extensions of self psychology, such as the intersubjective approach of Stolorow and his colleagues (1988) and Schwaber's (1983) view of analytic listening. According to all these theorists, the analyst is not the arbiter of reality but a coparticipant with a separate, frequently differing, viewpoint. Consequently, in Levenson's version of interpersonal theory the analyst offers not *the* truth, but only his or her experience of the situation. Gill and Hoffman, by contrast, hold to the primacy of interpretation but emphasize that the aim of the interpretive process is to open the patient to alternative perceptions. The epistemological issues raised by the interpersonalists are not abstract; they deeply influence the posture of the practicing analyst. Levenson and Hoffman both emphasize these implications of interpersonal thought.

Both interpersonal and object relations viewpoints shift psychoanalysis from a theory of intrapsychic wishes and defenses to a theory of development and pathology connected inevitably to interpersonal relationships. However, one can see from this review that despite the similarities in theoretical perspective between the interpersonal and the object relations/paradigms, there are clear distinctions between them that render the two models fundamentally different. First, in object relations theories interpersonal relationships are a means to an end, whether this end is conceived of as the formation of the self or as ego growth; in all object relations theories, personal relationships lead to psychological structure, and this structure defines the health or pathology of the personality. Each variant of interpersonal theory, on the other hand, views the interpersonal relationships themselves as actually constitutive of personality with little concept of psychological structure. This difference leads to distinct views of the analytic situation. In interpersonal theory the analyst is a co-participant in a relationship whereas in object relations theories, the relationship is primarily a construction of the patient, and the analyst's role is to understand it and sometimes meet the needs expressed through it. Gill believes that this difference—the analyst as a co-participant and the analyst as an interpreter of the patient's relational experience—is the key cleavage in modern psychoanalytic theory.

Second, all object relations theories include a theory of development and a concept of the relationship between developmental difficulties and subsequent types of pathology. One does not find such correlations in interpersonal theory; they are obviated by the emphasis on current interpersonal patterns. For object relations theories, developmental concepts are crucial because the analysis aims to achieve its goals by making contact with a part of the personality that was either arrested or inhibited by conflict at some point in development. Current problems are seen as having direct connection with developmental issues. In each variant of the interpersonal paradigm, with the exception of Greenberg's formulation, developmental issues are either largely ignored (for example, Levenson, 1985, and Gill, 1981) or related to current problems in a complex manner that does not have significant treatment implications (Mitchell, 1991). Greenberg's (1991) emphasis on re-representation in the interpretive process gives the past the most prominent role among interpersonal theories.

Third, the epistemological issue divides the object relations and interpersonal paradigms. Levenson (1989) and Hoffman (1991) believe that the division in psychoanalysis is between the "positivist" viewpoint of the analyst knowing "objective reality" and the view of reality as relative to the observer. Whatever epistemological position the various object relations theorists may adopt on the nature of an objective reality, they all see the role of the analyst as one of understanding the patient—whether that understanding is used for interpretation, the meeting of needs, or the formation of a new relationship. By contrast, the interpersonalists tend to view the analyst's role in terms of presenting a point of view and offering a potentially enriching relationship. Gill and Hoffman emphasize the analyst's role as interpreter more than other interpersonalists, but they, especially Hoffman, stress the relativity of the analyst's perspective. Thus, the goal of interpersonal psychoanalysis is to overcome problems by expanding, transforming, and enriching the nature of the analysand's world of human relationships; the aim of object relations analysis is to change the structure of the personality.

CRITIQUE OF THE INTERPERSONAL SCHOOL

The interpersonal viewpoint in psychoanalysis adds a significant dimension to the efforts of object relations theories to shift psychoanalytic theory and practice from an impersonal drive model toward a theory of the person relating to objects. As is clear from this review, the interpersonal theories, while sharing the interpersonal conception of personality and analytic process, form a widely divergent, often conflicting, group. They all point out that however much object relations theorists may purport to shift the concept of the analytic process from the drive model to a notion of the person in relation to others, they all retain a tendency to view the analyst solely as an interpreter of the patient's experience. Even Winnicott, who tended to view the analyst's role as active adaptation to the patient's needs, employed interpretation in the traditional manner of interpreting the patient's experience. By contrast, the interpersonal position is that the analyst is inherently a participant in the very process he or she seeks to understand.

Nonetheless, some of the later contributors to object relations theorizing have tended to emphasize the interactional role of the analyst. The tendency toward an interactional model in Kleinian thought, as seen most prominently in Racker's work, Stolorow's extension of self psychology to an "intersubjective" approach, and Green's application of Winnicott's thought are all examples of a movement in object relations theories toward a more interpersonally oriented view of the analytic process. Although these developments are a major connecting point between object relations and interpersonal theories, there is still a decisive difference between the two models. For the interpersonal school, the assessment and treatment of personality are a matter of interpersonal relationships. The object relations paradigm tends to view relationships as the primary influence on the development of psychological structure rather than as a substitute for it. Consequently, object relations theories tend to emphasize the role of early relationships in the formation of stable internalized perceptions of self and others whereas the interpersonal theorists either disregard development (Levenson, Gill and Hoffman) or view it as a series of relationships (Sullivan, Mitchell, Greenberg). In the conceptualization of the treatment process, the interpersonalists place far greater emphasis on the analyst's role in shaping the interaction than do even those theorists who propose an interactional extension of object relations theories.

Mitchell adds a great many specific conceptualizations to the general contributions of the interpersonal paradigm. He points out the significance of the relational matrix in development and contemporary problems in living. More than most other interpersonal theorists, he emphasizes the ubiquity and importance of conflict, thus blending interpersonal theory with the conflict model. Furthermore, Mitchell underscores the active role of the child in forming attachment to its parents, thus combining the environmental dimension of interpersonal problems with the child's contribution. Finally, Mitchell has made an invaluable contribution with his explicit recognition of the critical human need to adhere to the established sense of self and of the intense anxiety attendant upon threats to the self structure. While most object relations theorists recognize the importance of self structure, Mitchell has specifically emphasized the patient's investment in his or her sense of self as an element blocking analytic change.

Despite these contributions, there are some fundamental draw-backs to the several versions of interpersonal theory. First, the episte-mological position that reality is relative and that the analyst's view is no closer to *the* truth than any other tends to be contradicted in the work of each theorist who advocates it. Levenson (1989) contends that the analyst has no special claim to know the patient's reality but sees the task of analysis to be the exposing of the patient's distortions of interpersonal reality. Hoffman (1990) has pointed out that Levenson advocates a perspectivist position and then proceeds to treat his own interpretations as observations. For example, Levenson discusses a dream of one of Kohut's patients in which the patient plunges a knife into a straw doll and draws blood. Kohut interpreted that the patient was disappointed that the analyst was not the strong father he had hoped for. Levenson (1989), wishing to go beyond Kohut's interpreta-tion, asks if the dream could not mean "exactly what it says, namely, that the therapist is real, that he can be hurt, that he is vulnerable" (p. 549). Hoffman points out that although Levenson's interpretation is "cogent," it is only an interpretation (whereas Levenson himself regards it as "exactly what [the dream] says"). Hoffman finds this objectifying tendency to be a general problem with Levenson's approach. Further, Hoffman points out that Levenson tends to regard the patient's view as reality, and that in the dream example, the patient, according to Levenson, sees the "reality" that the analyst is ill and vulnerable and the analyst has no claim to a truer reality. This position reverses the classical view that the analyst is "right" and the patient "wrong" to a comparably positivistic stance in which the patient is "right" and the analyst "wrong."

Levenson (1990) replied to Hoffman that he is not a perspectivist and that he in fact erred in implying that he was. Levenson disagrees with Hoffman's view that reality is ineffable and that one can only have a plausible perspective on it. For Levenson, there is a reality, but it is obscured by distortions in the patient's life due to interpersonal anxiety and the analyst has no special claim to know it. He sees his own formulations as no "truer" but as efforts to grasp the "real experi-ence of the patient." As Levenson (1990) states, "The point is not that I believe that my perceptions are direct observations of interpersonal events, but that my observations focus attention *on* interpersonal events, not the patient's distortions" (p. 302). Levenson (1990) goes on to attack Gill and Hoffman's position that patients must see that there are plausible views of the analytic situation other than their own. He believes that this position, like Stolorow's, fails to take the final step of accepting the patient's perceptions not as a "point of view" but as a "valid basis for inquiry into real events in the patient's life and in the analysis" (p. 301). In Levenson's view, Gill and Hoffman "straddle the fence of reality" by accepting the patient's view as "plausible" but insisting that the patient see other views. According to Levenson, this position actually requires patients to see that their insistence on their point of view is wrong; analysts may not tell patients that they are wrong, but they communicate this very judgment by suggesting that there are other ways of looking at the situation. For Levenson (1990, 1991) this type of treatment is a form of persuasion.

One can see that in his attempt to defend himself against Hoffman's charges Levenson makes his position less clear. While insisting that the analyst has no privileged claim to know reality he says that the patient's problem is the *distortion* of reality and that the analyst's comments focus on interpersonal *events*, "not the patient's distortions." If the analyst has no claim to reality, how can he discern distortions and how can he have access to "real" interpersonal events? If he does not have "direct observations of interpersonal events" to offer, how can he make observations "*on* interpersonal events"? Levenson's position results in the conundrum that the analyst's task is to focus on interpersonal reality even though the analyst cannot claim to know it.

Despite this confusion in Levenson's epistemological position, he makes a valid criticism of Gill and Hoffman. Levenson (1989) points out that Gill and Hoffman claim to disavow any notion of a superior analytic view of reality but proceed to describe the transference as "not a distortion, but a misreading" (p. 302). Levenson contends that the type of analysis advocated by Gill and Hoffman is based on the following assumptions: there are right and wrong views for the patient to adopt; if the patient views the analyst in one particular way, he or she is "resisting," and this perception must be worked on until the patient sees that there are other views; the analyst's view that there are other "plausible" interpretations is clearly the view that the patient is enjoined to adopt. Hoffman (1991) even says that the patient has to become a "constructivist." For Levenson, such a prejudgment of analytic outcome raises the question of subtle persuasion.

Further, the very usage of the concept of resistance suggests an inconsistency in Gill's and Hoffman's epistemological position. There is no element more embedded in the psychoanalytic concept of the analyst as the arbiter of the patient's reality than the notion of resistance. Indeed, some theorists who are closer to the classical model than Gill have abandoned usage of resistance because of its judgmental connotation (for example, Giovacchini, 1979). However one may attempt to soften it, resistance means that the analyst knows that the patient is excluding something from his or her awareness, even if the analyst does not know what it is. If the patient disputes the analyst's interpretation, he is "resisting." Hence, the analyst is the arbiter of reality. One cannot meaningfully speak of the patient as "resisting" except in this sense of the analyst's judgment that the patient is excluding from awareness realities about himself.

To be sure, Gill and Hoffman attempt to address this problem by insisting that the patient's perception is plausible and that what the patient resists is not some "truer" way of experiencing but the mere consideration of other plausible ways. However, this rejoinder does not entirely solve the problem. First, it applies only to what Gill terms "resistance to the resolution of the transference," not to "resistance to the awareness of the transference." That is, the patient's failure to see an allusion to the transference in what he or she is saying or experiencing is itself deemed a form of resistance. The patient must be brought to accept the reality that the material is at minimum *also* a reference to the transference. And the analyst is arbiter of this reality.

Moreover, even in the context of "resistance to the resolution of the transference" the patient's refusal to adopt the analyst's view that there are other interpretations of the analyst's behavior is another example of how the patient fails to see "reality." Gill and Hoffman refer to the patient as resisting not any particular interpretation but the complementary "truths" of other ways of looking at the same situation. According to Gill and Hoffman, if patients persist in their positivistic commitment to their own "truth," they are resisting and the analyst's view, rooted in his or her superior constructivistic epistemology, may be taken to be correct.

There is still another inconsistency in the perspectivism advocated by Gill and Hoffman. While they insist that analysts can never know the validity of their interpretations, they also point out that some interpretations are better than others (Gill, 1991; Hoffman, 1991). The problem is that they make this claim while eliminating any epistemological basis for judging any interpretation as better than any other. If they believe that one interpretation is better than another, they must provide criteria by which "better" and "worse" can be assessed, criteria that then become the basis for the view of reality posited by the analyst and offered to the patient.

The same problem applies to Hoffman's (1991) effort to differentiate his view of analysis from existential encounter by citing the analyst's continual reflection on his or her participation in the process. Any criterion for such a reflection assumes a view of reality by which this process may be judged. Here one arrives at the fundamental problem with the constructivist view of the analytic process: either the constructivist must hold that there are no criteria for judging any particular interpretation as better than any other, in which case there can truly be no analysis, only one individual offering his or her experience to another in an existential encounter. Or, the constructivist must admit, as Gill and Hoffman have, that some interpretations are better than others, in which case they implicitly invoke, without admitting it, some criteria for making such a judgment, a position that is difficult to differentiate from the ordinary analytic view.

The reason Gill and Hoffman are given to these inconsistencies is that they are trapped in the conundrum of attempting to implement their constructivist philosophy without eliminating the very basis for analysis. Since they do not wish to reduce analysis to existential encounter, they are ultimately forced to utilize implicitly the very notions of reality and validity of interpretation that conflict with their constructivism. We found the same problem with Levenson's contention that while the analyst has no access to "reality," the analytic task is to focus on the patient's distortions of it. The interpersonal theorists have argued persuasively that analysis is inherently an interpersonal enterprise, but they have not been able as yet to successfully sustain the view that the interaction of two people with equally valid viewpoints is legitimate analytic treatment. Since each version of interpersonal theory ultimately wishes to defend the analytic model, each theory resorts to the very concepts of reality and validity of interpretation it purports to dispute. Interpersonal theory has yet to resolve this epistemological dilemma.

The epistemological position of interpersonal theory leads to the relative depreciation of the concept of psychopathology. Patients do not "have" an objectively ascertainable form of pathology that they bring to the analysis. This position fails to account for just why the patient has emotional problems. The concept of a pathological personality seeking relief conflicts with the interpersonalist notion that patients' problems inhere in their relationships. Since interpersonal theories tend to minimize the concept of psychopathology, they must develop an alternative view of why emotional distress occurs.

Mitchell's contributions are limited by this problem. Mitchell (1988) contends that there is no normative human personality against which people can be judged. Consequently, pathology is not a deviation but an extreme degree of "adhesion" to early relational patterns. As we have seen, Mitchell views maladjustment as rigidity of experience. However, this criterion does not hold up to scrutiny. Pathological patterns cause inherent difficulties in relating to others, leading to depression, anxiety, and distress, irrespective of their degree of flexibility. For example, borderline patients are far more pathological than neurotic or "normal" individuals not because their patterns are more rigid but because of the types of demands they make on others and the difficulties they have in functioning with others (Summers, 1988). Such patients become lonely and distraught not because they have only one way of relating but because that way does not allow them to form satisfactory bonds with others. If their one way of relating were more amenable to the formation of gratifying relationships, they would be far happier, even if limited. Neurotics may be equally rigid, but since their relational patterns do not cause as much difficulty in forming bonds, they are less disturbed. In short, Mitchell appears to confuse lack of resilience in personality patterns with maladjustment.

Mitchell's reluctance to acknowledge that some needs are pathological per se is illustrated by his view of patients with dependency needs. Such patients are not pathologically dependent, in Mitchell's view; these needs are "perfectly appropriate," as all people are dependent. The problem, as Mitchell sees it, is that the patient has excessive anxiety over normal dependency needs. Such a position is contradicted by the nature of the expectations and demands of many patients. For example, consider borderline patients, who make all manner of demands on the analyst—such as to hold and caress them, understand and gratify wants never expressed, and give them money and material goods—for immediate gratification of needs. The fact that such patients fall into despair if their needs are not met immediately underscores that these needs are not "perfectly appropriate" (Summers, 1988).

There are also difficulties with Mitchell's concept of neurosis as "loose threads" that do not fit into the tapestry of the personality. First, in neurotic character pathology, a healthy aspect of the personality is a "loose thread." Moreover, many neurotic patterns are woven well into the personality structure; as Mitchell himself points out, patients have great difficulty yielding these patterns precisely because they fit so well into the sense of self. This fact points out the contradiction in Mitchell's two criteria: if maladjustment is tantamount to rigidity of self experience, it is difficult to see how neurosis can be a "loose thread" that does not fit into the sense of self. Indeed, if neurosis really does not fit in, it should be easily amenable to change because it would not be part of the self that is the cause of pathological rigidity. In sum, Mitchell has made an impressive effort to explain "difficulties in living" without resorting to a judgment of psychopathology, but his two criteria are in conflict and neither can explain emotional problems satisfactorily.

The same problem of equating rigidity with pathology is inherent in Gill and Hoffman's variant of interpersonal theory. They offer no explicit developmental theory to account for the formation of emotional problems, but since their treatment focus is on inducing the patient to recognize other ways of perceiving the analyst, their concept of treatment is equivalent to a loosening of rigid interpersonal ways of perceiving. Their views thus fall prey to the same conflation of singularity of experience with pathological patterns. In fact, some patients acknowledge that there are other ways of viewing the analyst's behavior but still cling to their original view, which may be, for example, that the analyst does not like them. In these circumstances, it is the tendency to view people as hostile or assaultive that approaches the crux of the problem, not the rigidity with which this attitude is held. Even more tellingly, there are many characterologically disturbed patients who are inconsistent and even chaotic in their perceptions of the therapist. For such patients, a major component of the pathology is severe and unpredictable transference oscillations: the therapist is now an angel, later a devil; now a savior, later a persecutor (for example, Kernberg 1976, 1984; Summers, 1988). The pathology of such patients is best captured by the lack of correspondence of the perception to reality, not its inflexibility. Because Gill and Hoffman are reluctant to use the concept of reality in their explanations of pathology, they are confined to the criterion of rigidity.

Thus the problem of explaining emotional problems is unresolved in the interpersonal paradigm. Having abandoned the notion of psychopathology in favor of the concept of a person relating to other persons in a particular way, the interpersonalists are left to explain without making any judgments about pathology why some people do less well than others. The result is the attempt to employ concepts such as "rigidity" or "inability to fit into the personality structure" as explanations, but these issues can neither explain the differences among types of pathology nor differentiate adequately between pathological and healthy adaptation.

All of this explains why Mitchell (1988) and Levenson (1991) tend to view psychoanalysis not as a treatment but as an "enriching experience." This conclusion follows logically from their view that people's problems inhere in relationships and that these relationships may not be judged as reflecting personality disturbance per se. The point of analysis in such a view is the provision not so much of a new experience as of an "enriching" relationship that widens the patient's experience. This goal is not only unduly modest for many patients who seek and need more than enrichment, but also inappropriate for certain patients. Many depressed and anxious patients can have enriching relationships and still remain depressed and anxious. An enriching relationship would not reorganize the structure of a narcissistically disturbed patient unless such a relationship helped to facilitate understanding of his needs for idealization and grandiosity.

In sum, enriching relationships do not necessarily resolve the fundamental object relations conflicts that produce symptoms. For Levenson (1981), for example, the aim of pointing out the patient's interactions with the analyst is to connect these interactions with the patient's interpersonal patterns outside the analysis. It is difficult to see how the awareness of this connection would resolve the interactional pattern. Both Levenson and Mitchell have a limited concept of how pathology is actually resolved, and their view of analysis therefore seems quite restricted. Gill and Hoffman have a more elaborated concept of therapeutic change, but it is difficult to see how adoption by patients of a constructivist perspective necessarily resolves their problems; the acknowledgment of alternative possibilities cannot be expected to lead to the growth of the self, any more often than do other forms of "enriching experience."

The limited view of analysis advocated by the interpersonal school is in sharp contrast with the more ambitious aims of the object relations theorists. Because the latter do embrace the concept that pathology can be grasped by the analyst, they tend to believe that pathological patterns can be illuminated, worked through, and resolved. We have seen that the various object relations theories share the traditional analytic assumption of psychopathology residing in the patient but depart from classical analysis in the belief that pathology consists of object relations units. Apart from these presuppositions, object relations theories differ and even conflict among themselves. This diversity returns us to the question of whether one can discern a common object relations model of the analytic process that can serve as an alternative to the drive/conflict model. Having elucidated the main principles of the various interpersonal theories and differentiated them from object relations theories, we are now in a position to address this issue.

CHAPTER 8

An Object Relations Paradigm
For Psychoanalysis

THE MAJOR DIFFERENCES AMONG OBJECT RELATIONS THEORIES WOULD SEEM to militate against the concept of a unified object relations model. Nonetheless, these very real differences should not obfuscate the commonality of principles that differentiate an object relations approach from both the drive model and the interpersonal model. By a critical elucidation of principles one can delineate an object relations paradigm within which the various theories can fit as variations. Such a model cannot be constructed by an uncritical eclecticism nor by a preference for one particular theory to the exclusion of the others. The approach taken here is to build on the critical assessments of each theory to define an object relations concept of psychoanalytic theory and practice that fits no particular theory but illuminates object relations as a model differentiated from the drive-ego and interpersonal models.

The common principle of all object relations theories is the view that the fundamental human motivation is for object contact rather than drive discharge. As we have seen, both Klein and Kernberg adhere to the drive theory but view the importance of drives to be not so much in their ability to discharge tension as in their role in the formation of the object relations that become the building blocks of the psyche. It may be said that all object relations theories view the formation of object relations as the primary human motivation. Further, the concept of drives in both the Klein and Kernberg views does not hold up to scrutiny. Klein's view of drives is the same as Freud's: they are innate, biologically driven impulses for tension reduction. This concept does not fit the modern concept of drive as a hierarchical organization that is responsive to stimuli and able to adapt to changing circumstances (Tinbergen, 1951; Lorenz, 1963). Kernberg's (1976) notion of drives, unlike Klein's, is informed by modern conceptualizations. However, since in Kernberg's view a drive can only be expressed through an object relationship, the drive concept is obviated, especially since aggression, which is central to Kernberg's theory, does not fit the drive concept. When one eliminates the unnecessary concept of drives, the motivational concept in the theories of Klein and Kernberg corresponds to the concept in the theories of Fairbairn, Guntrip, Winnicott, and Kohut, namely, that the organism is inherently directed toward object contact.

PSYCHOLOGICAL STRUCTURE

Any object relations theory leads to a concept of the self, the development of which is linked to the vicissitudes of the object relations units. As André Green (1977) has pointed out, the complement of the object is not the ego but the self (see chapter 4). As we saw in chapter 2, Fairbairn (1944) used the word *ego*, but employed it to refer to the self, not the ego of the tripartite model. Since development is not a matter of the taming of drives, in object relations theories the importance of ego structure wanes in favor of the development of the self structure, which is a product of the internalization of attachments in the form of object relationships. In this way the object relations paradigm replaces the development of id and ego with self and object relations as the cornerstones of development. The way the self structure is experienced at any given moment is the sense of self; that is, the phenomenological experience of the self, the sense of self, is a reflection of the underlying self structure.

While it is implicit in most object relations theories that psychological structure is built with object relations units, Kernberg (1984) makes this point explicit and uses the concept of object relations structure to understand pathology. Furthermore, he is alone in pointing out that the psychological structure of the neurotic is composed of object relations units. However, for Kernberg the structure of object relationships is the structure of the ego. Given the data of child development, to be described shortly, suggesting that attachments rather than drives are primary and given the fact that the drive concept is unnecessary even in his theory, it makes more sense to conceive of the structure built from object relations units as self structure rather than ego structure.

The data from infant research do not support the concept of a separate id (White, 1963; Stern, 1985). There is a compelling quality to some of the infant's behavior, but this "drivenness" applies as much to searching for stimuli as to biological gratification (Lichtenberg, 1983). From the beginning of life the neonate will interrupt feeding to look at stimuli, but there is no need to postulate "independent ego energies," as the developmental data do not support giving primacy to drive gratifications. As we have seen, the evidence indicates that the infant is best conceived as programmed to seek contact and relationships of various types, only one of which involves the satisfaction of biological urges.

This view of psychological structure as self formed from object relationships leads to a different view of anxiety than that proffered by the drive-ego model. According to the latter, anxiety is a warning signal to the ego of threat from id or superego (Freud, 1926). While Freud did acknowledge that traumatic anxiety, the feeling of infantile helplessness, is characteristic of early infancy, nontraumatic anxiety encompasses most forms of anxiety. From the object relations viewpoint, anxiety is a threat to the sense of self, to one's sense of who one is. Consequently, object relations theories tend to describe anxiety as a threat to existence rather than as the eruption of particular contents into consciousness. This reconceptualization links Klein's "annihilation anxiety," Winnicott's "unthinkable anxiety," and Kohut's "disintegration anxiety," all of which refer to a threat to one's psychological existence. These terms were not used solely to describe severe pathology but were deemed relevant to development and pathology of almost any type. Mitchell (1988) and Greenberg (1991), from the viewpoint of interpersonal theory, also emphasize the threat to self (or self-representation in the case of Greenberg) in the experience of anxiety. Since, from the object relations viewpoint the self structure is composed of object relations units, any threat to the structure of those units is a threat to the self and will be experienced as anxiety. Therefore, the self may be threatened even in well-integrated personalities. This notion of anxiety also fits Sullivan's concept of anxiety as a threat to the self-system.

According to the drive-ego model, anxiety is caused by a threat of eruption of a particular content, such as a childhood wish eliciting guilt or shame, and defended against by a particular defense, such as repression. The problem with this view is that if the repressed content is made conscious, guilt or shame is felt; it is difficult to see why a guilt-invoking wish should evoke a sense of threat. Guilt is not a pleasant emotion, but it causes feelings of "badness" rather than threat. As we saw in chapter 2, this reasoning led Fairbairn and Guntrip to conclude that shame, rather than guilt, is at the source of most pathology. However, while shame is often a more painful, threatening feeling than guilt, it does not necessarily evoke anxiety. In fact, neither shame nor guilt can account for the threatening experience of anxiety. In the object relations paradigm, anxiety is a threat to one's sense of who one is, and this explains the sense of dread, or angst, even in the well-integrated neurotic individual.

The type of anxiety emphasized in object relations theories is closer to Freud's concept of "traumatic anxiety." However, Freud (1926) consigned this type of anxiety to the helplessness of the young infant whose ego is so weak that he or she becomes overwhelmed. This psychoeconomic concept defines anxiety in terms of quantity of stimuli in relation to the strength of the ego. The annihilation anxiety of object relations theories is most usefully considered a threat to the sense of self, the anchor point of one's existence.

DEVELOPMENT

The object relations view that attachment is autonomously motivated fits the research data on development much more closely than does the drive model. Three separate lines of research evidence support the view that the infant is inherently motivated to make contact with its caretaker rather than discharge tension. First, it seems that infants are programmed for human contact and are preadapted to form a relationship with the caretaker. Findings from experimental research show that the neonate turns to the source of human sounds, differentiates human from nonhuman sounds, reacts with distress if the sound source is disengaged from the view of the speaker's mouth, recognizes the human face, and behaves differently to human and nonhuman objects (Lichtenberg, 1983; Stern, 1985). In the first few weeks of life the infant's feeding behavior becomes regulated to the particular behavior of its caretaker. According to Stern (1985), the infant has an active "social" life from birth. Beebe, Jaffe, and Lachmann (1992) have demonstrated that the mother–child dyad develops its own mutually regulated rules of communication, which are not predictable from either partner separately. They conclude that the interactional sequence between both parties to the mother–child relationship is internalized by the child rather than by the mother as an object. Beebe and Lachmann (1992) provide convincing evidence that in the first months of life mother and child learn to match their affective direction and interpersonal timing in a variety of ways and that the child comes to expect this matching and reacts negatively if it is absent. Their data provide convincing evidence for the view that a presymbolic representational world consists of these mother–child interactions.

Evidence against the view of infant behavior as tension reducing comes from the fact that infants pursue objects visually from the beginning weeks of life and will even interrupt feeding to look at visually presented objects (White, 1963). The findings that infants actually seek stimuli and make active choices for preferred stimuli with no consequent tension reduction is strong evidence against the concept of the infant as a discharge-seeking organism (White, 1963; Stern, 1985). Infants will react aversively to noxious stimuli only. The view that emerges from the experimental data is of an infant programmed almost from birth to form a synchronous interaction with its caretaker and to regulate stimulation both by increasing and decreasing it (Lichtenberg, 1983).

The second primary source of evidence for the object relations view of motivation comes from naturalistic observation and experimental work with animals. John Bowlby (1969) marshaled an impressive array of ethological evidence demonstrating the existence of a powerful need for attachment among nonhuman primates. Newborn guinea pigs, lambs, and dogs will attach to physical objects or animals of other species if those are the only possibilities for contact without receiving other sources of gratification. Indeed, puppies isolated for three weeks and punished upon their only contact with a human will become more attached to that figure than will puppies receiving rewards for human contact. Equally compelling are Harlow's experiments with rhesus monkeys, which showed that baby monkeys attach to cloth model mothers and not wire models even when latter provide bottle feeding (Harlow and Zimmermann, 1959). Further, rhesus monkeys raised by a nonfeeding cloth mother surrogate will attach to the model mother and cling to it when alarmed or in a strange setting (Harlow, 1961). However, baby monkeys raised by a wire model that provides bottle feeding do not use the surrogate for comfort despite strange or dangerous conditions. Like lambs and puppies, monkeys cling intensely to the cloth mother in the face of danger and punishment, even if the danger is from the surrogate mother itself. Bowlby's evidence shows that nonhuman primates have an autonomous need for attachment irrespective of gratification of biological needs and that this attachment endures.

Bowlby's (1969) work also summarizes the third line of evidence: naturalistic data on children showing that they attach to figures who do not meet their physiological needs. Children in concentration camps reared without the opportunity to attach to a benign adult formed strong bonds with each other. A study of Scottish children showed that about one-fifth attached to adult figures who did not participate in their physiological care. Furthermore, Bowlby pointed out that there is as yet no evidence that human babies attach to adult figures because of their association with the meeting of biological needs. Bowlby (1969) summarized the evidence this way: "Such evidence as there is strongly supports the view that attachment behavior in humans can develop, as it can in other species, without the traditional rewards of food and warmth" (p. 218). This work extends the concept of the autonomous need for attachment to humans.

Ethological and child research evidence provides solid support for the object relations view that there is an autonomous human need to attach to significant figures very early and that this attachment tends to endure. These findings fit with Fairbairn's view of the infant as inherently object seeking rather than pleasure seeking. According to the experimental data, infants are preadapted to seek object contact and to form an interactional synchrony with the caregiver. The object relations view adds to the experimental data the concept that the human, being a symbolic animal, will at some point in development give meaning to these attachments and use them to develop a sense of self. According to this object relations model, the structure of the self is formed from the internalization of early attachment relationships and is based on the symbolic meaning the child gives to its early object ties. In this way these early object relationships not only endure but define the sense of self and influence later relationships with others.

Each object relations theory has a different way of understanding the process by which early object contact forms the sense of self. For Fairbairn and Guntrip, the ability to love without destruction and the degree of schizoid withdrawal resulting from fear of the destructiveness of object contact are crucial. For Klein and Kernberg the vicissitudes of aggression and its integration with good objects are the critical components in the formation of the self. For Winnicott, the availability of the "environmental mother" to provide background support for the natural unfolding of the self is central to the internalization of the good mother, which allows the maturational process to unfold. In Kohut's view, the gradual relinquishment of archaic grandiosity and idealization, fostered by the mixture of parental gratification and frustration, results in the structuralization of the self. Each object relations theory has a different concept of how the self develops and of the role the environment plays in its formation. While one cannot justifiably speak of a single object relations theory, each theoretical viewpoint is based on the general principle that autonomously motivated attachments to early figures become internalized and form the building blocks of the self.

In the object relations view of development, children navigate the interpersonal world by forming object attachments designed to minimize anxiety and pain. However, they will always prefer some attachment, no matter how painful it may be, to loss of contact. Mitchell (1988) has pointed out that children form the type of relationship they need to maintain contact with early objects and that these relationships play a crucial role in the formation of the self structure. As indicated, experimental evidence indicates that young subhuman primates will attach to animals who only cause pain if no other alternative is available (Bowlby, 1969); in fact, they will attach more strongly than will young animals who are not abused. According to the object relations paradigm, children prefer painful attachments to isolation in order to avoid the anxiety of annihilation. This principle is the object relations explanation for the observation that children and adults form intense, resilient bonds with harmful figures. Fairbairn pointed out that Freud's drive theory resorted to the "death instinct" to explain this phenomenon, an explanation that is exceedingly speculative and has few backers even within the classical tradition. In the object relations view, children form bonds to their caretaker early, the bond with an abusive adult tending to be even stronger than that with a benign adult. Further, early relationships are internalized to form a self structure that is then defended against all threats. Attachments to early negative figures and their persistence in childhood are explained by the need for bonding, as is the persistence of the effects of such attachments into adult life.

As Mitchell (1988) has pointed out, these internalized object relationships are not simply passive imprints of the relationships; they are the ways in which children construe the relationships and what they extract from them according to their defensive and adaptational needs. However, Mitchell (1988) is incorrect in attributing a passive view of the infant to object relations developmental arrest theories. Winnicott (1963a, b) emphasized the activity of even the very young infant in "creating" the object; while initially this "object creation" is purely fantastical, in later infancy and childhood the creation of the object out of "transitional space" plays a primary role in development. Similarly, Fairbairn emphasized the child's active object seeking in personality formation and pathology. While Kohut's views lend themselves to the interpretation of the child as a passive recipient of parental empathy or injury, he did see the child as defensively responding to parental failures.

All these theories take into account the child's response to disruptive environmental events and suggest that the way the child construes and responds to the environment plays a critical role in the formation of psychological structure. For example, if the parent is abusive, the child may be too traumatized to internalize the parent as attacking and sadistic, and may defend against this internalization by a defensive construction of the parent as benign; that is, the child internalizes an attacking, sadistic parent layered over by a defensive "benign" parent. Each such constructed internalization is a building block in the edifice of psychological structure. This process tends to become complex: object relations units that defend against others may conflict or harmonize with each other, and still other object relations units may be used to defend against such conflicts. The buildup of these object relations units in their variegated patterns forms the unique structure of each individual self.

Kohut (1971, 1977) emphasized more than any other theorist the construction of the self structure from the child's internalization of aspects of the parenting figures in both normal and pathological development. The emphasis in Kohut's theory was on the infantile self as bipolar, consisting of the poles of grandiosity and idealization, each of which must be supported by parental gratifications. With each experience in which the infant relinquishes some degree of its archaic narcissism, there is accretion of psychological structure. In Kohut's view, the key to emotional development is the formation of self structure. The data from infant research support Kohut's view that the gaze of the parent is an important aspect of development (Lichtenberg, 1983; Stern, 1985). At birth the infant sees best at eight inches, the right distance for breast- or bottle-feeding. Further, if the infants do not successfully elicit the parental gaze, they actively search for it, and if they cannot find it they will eventually withdraw. One may therefore conceive of the child as programmed for "mirroring" interaction with the caretaker. These findings support the importance of mirroring in development, though they do not support Kohut's emphasis on the mother as the sole initiator of the mirroring relationship. Kohut's view ignores the fact that the infant is primed for mirroring, and proceeds actively to seek it, rather than just being in need of it. Fairbairn's conceptualization of the infant as object seeking and Mitchell's (1988) view of the infant as actively seeking and forming relationships are better supported by the data from infant research.

The object relations view is that development hinges on the ability of the parent–child interaction to foster the growth-enhancing object relationships out of which a functional self is constituted. Winnicott and Kohut both recognized the importance of parental empathy and support in the development of the self, but Kohut underemphasized the child's role in the construction of the mother–child relationship. Infant research has underlined this emphasis by demonstrating that the child actively seeks out a synchronous parent–child interaction and by documenting the aversive response of the child to not receiving it (Lichtenberg, 1983).

PSYCHOPATHOLOGY

If the parent–child attachment does not foster growth-enhancing object relationships, the formation of the self will be arrested and its functioning crippled. For example, if the dominant attachment is to a denigrating parental figure, the child may well defend against the internalization of an object that devalues the self by adopting a superior, aloof posture to the now denigrated object. In this case, a significant portion of the self structure consists of "object devalues self" and "self devalues object." These object relations structures will interfere with efforts to achieve satisfying interpersonal relationships. In this situation the self consists of dysfunctional object relationships that impede effective functioning.

Each object relations theory has a different view of how crippling object relationships come about. For Fairbairn (1940) and Guntrip (1969), the mother's inability to accept the child's love leads to the internalization of "desirable deserters," against which the child must defend itself. For Klein and Kernberg, if the internalization of bad objects exceeds that of good objects, pathological processes such as splitting and projective identification ensue. In Winnicott's view, if the environment is unable to provide for the child's needs within the different phases of dependence, the internalization of the good mother is thwarted and the development of the self is arrested. According to Kohut, if the mother is unempathic with the child's needs for grandiosity and idealization, transmuting internalization is blocked, archaic grandiosity and/or idealization remain, and the self is not able to develop. In every variant of the object relations paradigm, psychopathology is a product of distorted object relationships that interfere with the structure and functioning of the self.

In this object relations paradigm, Freud's criteria of mental health— to love and work well—are assumed. The difference between this paradigm and Freud's conception lies in the reasons for the inability to operate well in these two arenas. In each variant of the object relations view, the integration and smooth functioning of the self allows for achievement and interpersonal satisfaction. Some versions of interpersonal theory also fit this view of adjustment. Mitchell's (1988) concept of psychological health as a well-integrated self formed from relational patterns is compatible with the object relations view. However, as pointed out in chapter 7, Mitchell's concept of pathology as rigidity of relational patterns and his concept of neurosis as a "loose thread" in the tapestry of the self are questionable and do not accord with the object relations root of neurotic symptoms. For example, Mitchell (1988) refers to Stern's view that because issues recycle throughout life, one cannot assume that a particular issue originates in a specific developmental phase. Mitchell concludes that issues frequently judged to be pathological, such as the dependence–autonomy conflict, are normal and that the patient's needs are "perfectly appropriate." This view misses the fact that it is not the existence of the conflict between dependency and autonomy that makes a personality pathological but the meaning of each need embedded in an unproductive object relations structure that makes dependence and individuation so difficult to achieve. When the object relations structure does not allow the meeting of one or both of these needs, the functioning of the self is impaired.

Fairbairn viewed all neurosis as a manifestation of the conflict between dependence and autonomy. However, he recognized that what makes an individual symptomatic is not the existence of the conflict, which is ubiquitous, but the inability of the individual to form a satisfactory object relationship with a separate object. Object contact threatens the self, and the individual withdraws. The conflict between the need for object contact and autonomy is not the source of the pathology; the neurosis arises from the fear of object contact, a fear that causes difficulties both for the attainment of autonomy and for the establishment of relationships. The following principle is recognized in all object relations theories: while any individual may be caught in conflicts between competing needs or desires, what makes such conflicts pathological for some is an underlying object relations structure that interferes with the achievement of satisfaction in one or both of the conflicting needs. In a similar fashion, Greenberg (1991) sees the fundamental human conflict as a battle between the need for safety, which motivates relationships, and effectance, the need for individuation. Greenberg's view of the human dilemma as a balancing act between these conflicting drives bears a striking similarity to Fairbairn's concept of conflict between the needs for dependence and autonomy. The difference is that for Greenberg the conflict itself is the cause of the pathology, with maladaptive relational patterns resulting from the conflicting needs.

While it is true that every object relationship limits the self in some way, the pathological individual has had to accept a malfunctioning self in order to achieve object attachment. Fairbairn and Guntrip see the result of the compromise in all pathology as an inability to relate to objects in an authentic manner. According to Klein and Kernberg, because the integration of aggression into the self is compromised, pathological mechanisms are used to preserve the self. For Winnicott, this compromise is viewed in terms of arrested maturation of the self. For Kohut, the price paid is a realistic sense of self-esteem that allows the achievement of healthy goals and ambitions.

An illustration of pathological self formation from the viewpoint of self psychology is Kohut's case of Miss F. As discussed in chapter 6, in analytic sessions this patient tolerated neither extended periods of silence nor any of Kohut's comments that went beyond a mere summary of her material. When Kohut attempted the latter, Miss F became enraged and felt the analysis was being ruined. Kohut reached the conclusion that these reactions were not resistance, but the emergence of the patient's grandiose self and the parallel need for mirroring. Through the development of a relationship in which she was only echoed, Miss F experienced the sense of strength and wholeness of self that was missing from her childhood. Because the only object contact of which she was capable consisted of the satisfaction of her need for mirroring, in order to achieve a sense of self she needed to experience the bolstering of her grandiose self by a selfobject. That is, her self was only minimally functional since it was able to operate only within the narrow parameters of a reliable selfobject who performed the mirroring function. Miss F's narcissistic pathology consisted of this severe impairment of self functioning and the consequent limitation of her goals and ambitions.

Guntrip's analysis of the schizoid character illustrates the extreme of compromise to maintain a minimal sense of self. As we saw in chapter 2, Guntrip's formulation was that schizoids are so hungry for love that they fear destroying the object with their desires for merger. Since all affect threatens to stimulate the hunger for merger, the patient removes affect from all interactions and assumes a defensive aloof posture in order to protect the object and the self. By this character defense of withdrawal the patient is able to maintain contact but at the cost of emotional poverty, emptiness, loneliness and apathy.

A case example of this schizoid compromise is Guntrip's patient, discussed in chapter 2, a young woman who worked through her traumatic rejection by her grandfather in her therapy. When her fear of trusting others was linked by Guntrip to her relationship with him, she began to withdraw from him. Guntrip then interpreted that she had been more trusting of him lately, and she responded by becoming cold and uncommunicative and said that she feared she could never respond to another human being. This cold, hardened attitude was the only way she could relate to others without feeling the terror of affective object contact.

Both Kohut's and Guntrip's cases demonstrate that even the internalization of painful object relations units helps to achieve a sense of self and allay anxiety. In some situations, the child is forced to internalize painful and even destructive object relationships in order to avoid anxiety and achieve a sense of self connected to others. The child will do so because the internalization is better than the alternative—annihilation anxiety. Analogously, all internalizations, no matter how seemingly healthy, have a cost because they restrict interactional patterns in the very process of anxiety avoidance. Thus, every accretion of self structure through object relationships has both an adaptive value and a limiting effect on the functioning of the self. Pathology and health are a question of the balance between the restrictive, dysfunctional aspects of object relations units and their benefits. The extent to which internalized object relationships inhibit the development and functioning of the self is the extent of pathology in the personality.

This view of pathology questions the conventional view, held even by some object relations theorists, that object relations theories apply to early, or preoedipal, issues and the drive-ego model applies to neurotic conditions, presumed to originate in the oedipal phase. Mitchell (1988) is critical of "developmental tilt" theorists who maintain the classical view that conflict between drives and defenses is the primary issue at the oedipal stage and who insert object relations "underneath" as the key to earlier development. This effort to accommodate object relations and drive theories characterizes Winnicott's (1963a) and Kernberg's (1984) view of the neuroses, as well as Kohut's (1971) early work. On the other hand, Fairbairn (1941), Guntrip (1969), Klein (1937), and Kohut (1977, 1984) in his later work all viewed the relationship between object and self as critical to all pathology, including neurosis. As Mitchell (1988) has pointed out, if development is a matter of the relationship between self and object, drives have no greater import in later stages than in earlier ones.

In the object relations paradigm proposed here, psychopathology is tantamount to an edifice built with dysfunctional object relations building blocks. This concept of psychopathology can accommodate the classical view of neurosis as conflict between wish and defense only if wish and defense are both conceived of as object relations units. This solution has been adopted by Kernberg (1984), who considers neurosis to be a result of psychic conflict and the elements of the conflict to be object relationships. We saw in chapter 5 that Kernberg's view of the inherent nature of object relationships from the earliest phase of psychological life óbviates the drive concept and defines neurosis in terms of conflicting object relations units. As we saw in chapter 5, Kernberg's clinical illustrations of analysis for neurotic conditions were difficult to distinguish from his treatment approach to character pathology because in both cases split object relations units were analyzed and then synthesized. In no case was Kernberg able to establish that defense against a wish resulted in a neurotic symptom.

If the self structure consists of object relations units, neurosis must be a matter of dysfunctional object relationships (Summers, 1993b). Even if the neurotic symptoms are manifestations of conflicts between object relationships, the units themselves must be defective in some manner to account for a symptomatic outcome. One is then left with the question of differentiating neurosis from other forms of psychopathology. On the basis of object relations theory, the criterion for this differentiation is the extent of dysfunction resulting from the object relations structure of the personality. In the borderline personality, severe impairment in the abilities to love and work results from the need to fuse with the other to complete the sense of self (Summers, 1988). The object relationships of fusion and hostile defiance to protect fragile self boundaries are sufficient to achieve a minimal sense of existence but leave little opportunity for effective functioning (Kernberg, 1975; Summers, 1988). The higher level characterologically disturbed patients gain more functional capacity from their object relations but are crippled in relationships, work, or both. Patients are labeled neurotic because their object relationships allow functioning in major areas of their lives but impede success and gratification. Severity of pathology is thus a matter of degree: the extent to which the object relations structure of the personality interferes with the functioning of the self is the degree of psychopathology to which an individual is subject.

In the object relations paradigm, then, neurotic pathology reflects a defect in the structure of the self. This view stands in opposition to Mitchell's metaphor of neurosis as a "loose thread" in the "tapestry" of the self, a notion that reflects the classical view of neurosis as symptomatic outcome in an integrated personality. But the loose threads metaphor does not adequately address the pain, suffering, and functional impairment of the neurotic individual. The self dysfunction typically labeled neurosis is more like a tear that weakens the fabric without ruining it completely. Thus, the aims of analytic treatment for the neurotic involve restructuring the self rather than reintegrating loosened components (Summers, 1993b). This view bears a kinship to

Kohut's (1984) later concept that neurosis consists of a cohesive sense of self that has been unable to achieve its life program. This notion fits closely the concept of neurosis as an adaptive object relations structure that impedes effective functioning. However, the underlying object relations structure that impedes the achievement of the "nuclear program" of the self is far more complex and variegated than is suggested by the concept of transmuting internalization of grandiosity and idealization. As noted, Stolorow, Brandchaft, and Atwood (1987) adopt a multimodal concept of self that moves self psychology closer to viewing psychopathology as a product of a complex object relations structure.

The mixture of adaptive functioning with pathological constraints explains the ubiquity of conflict in neurosis without putting it at the source. The functioning of the self is continually obstructed by pathological object relationships that pressure the self in a different direction. Neurotic conflicts result from these pulls in opposite directions; however, the pathology is not caused by the conflict itself but by the maladaptive object relations units. Clearly, object relations theories tend to de-emphasize the function of guilt in pathogenesis in comparison to the classical model, but they do consider the role of excessive guilt in neurotic conditions. The crucial question for the object relations paradigm is whether guilt interferes with the functioning of the self. To the extent that it does, it can be a pathogenic factor in neurosis—as well as in more severe pathology.

The reason guilt is so relatively underemphasized in object relations theories is that guilt is not frequently a significant element of crippling object relations structures. Recall that Fairbairn (1944) and Guntrip (1969) viewed guilt as a defense that provides the illusion of being in control when one in fact feels weak and ashamed. Kohut (1984) made a point of his belief that conceptualization of human dysfunction has shifted from Guilty Man, who denounces his own immorality, to Tragic Man, who is defective, weak, and incapable. Green (1977) expressed a similar belief in his statement that psychoanalysis has changed its paradigmatic figure from Oedipus to Hamlet. These views represent the shift to an object relations view in which pathology is rooted in dysfunctional self structure that produces feelings of shame and incapability, rather than in unacceptable wishes that give rise to guilt.

To be sure, the theories of Klein (1937), Winnicott (1960a), and Kernberg (1976) accord a more central role to guilt in pathology, especially neurosis. For these theorists, guilt originates in the anxiety of realizing one can injure the mother one loves and depends on. In this view, excessive guilt consists of disabling object relations. Thus, in the Kleinian concept of the depressive position and in Winnicott's emendation of it as the stage of concern, guilt is an outgrowth of anxiety rather than of superego strictures.

While Kernberg (1976, 1984) does seem to accept the classical view of neurotic guilt as oedipally formed and organized, he acknowledges that even in the neuroses the structure of the ego consists of units of object relations that must be modified and reorganized. Ultimately, even in object relations theories that include a potentially pathogenic role for guilt, the concept does not fit the drive-ego model of a structured superego in conflict with unacceptable wishes. When it is a factor in pathology, guilt is viewed as another form of defective object relationship inhibiting self functioning.

This conception of neurosis is illustrated by the case of a 40-year-old real estate developer who, despite a seemingly successful long-standing marriage and some professional success, entered analysis because he felt that something was wrong with his life and that he was a professional "underachiever." It turned out that he had been close to bankruptcy due to a business venture that was extremely undercapitalized and that he had several other tumultuous and unproductive business associations. Early in the analysis the patient complained, almost without noticing it, of most people in his life. The employees upon whom he most depended tended to be either highly volatile, unpredictable, and crisis prone or unresponsive and incompetent. Consequently, his business life was in constant turmoil, and he felt continually frustrated. His current business was making enough money to provide a comfortable living, but he was in continual debt and his success was far more limited than would have been expected given his situation. As a result, his life was beset with continual tension and anger.

Without entering into the details of a complex analysis, it may be pointed out that the patient's business difficulties were traced to a self-defeating pattern that manifested itself in a variety of ways, such as by not acquiring sufficient capital, failing to receive sufficient funds for costs, underselling his services, and hiring and keeping inadequate and difficult employees. This pattern was related to the internalization of his father as a mean, abusive alcoholic whom he feared but longed to please. Every move toward success meant a threat to his internalized father, who would be envious and depreciative of the son who longed to please him.

The object relations structure of the patient's bond with his father consisted of a longing to idealize the father as strong, a fear of his father as abusive, and the intense desire to please his father and gain his approval, which the patient defended against with anger. He was in fact deeply identified with his father, and his business career began with his entrance into his father's business. His father was a highly successful businessman, and the patient's identification with him led to a certain degree of business achievement. However, he was subjected to constant verbal abuse for trivial errors, and every successful step led to fear that his father would be threatened and would withdraw approval and depreciate him. The patient's attempts to be like his father and his fear that he would become an "abusive drunk" led to a lifetime of oscillation between success and defeat. To be unsuccessful would have displeased the father and subjected the son to vituperation, so the patient internalized the object relations unit of the "good boy" trying to gain approval from the successful father. However, every step of success threatened the internalized, envious father, thereby stimulating identification with the "abusive drunk" he did not wish to be. Consequently, the patient would achieve a certain degree of success and then sabotage his ventures. This pattern was on external reflection of his internalized ambivalent relationship with the father who both wished him success and was threatened by it.

This abbreviated formulation of one aspect of this analysis appears to fit the classical view of neurosis as unconscious conflict. The patient was most certainly in conflict between two object relations patterns involving himself and his father. However, the pathological pattern was not a product of the conflict between the internalized "good" father who wished him success and his fear of the threatened father who wished to see him struggling and ultimately defeated. It is this latter object relations unit, being pathological per se, that creates functional difficulty. The source of this patient's neurosis was not to be found in the conflict between the pathological and healthy components of the self but in the very existence of the pathological components. This case illustrates the concept of neurosis advanced here. The patient had a father–son object relations unit that allowed and even encouraged functioning—until the internalized father was threatened, at which point the son's professional success was inhibited. This layered father–son object relations structure fostered some success but did not allow for expansive professional or financial achievement; every time the patient made money, he found a way to lose it. The aspect of the father–son dyad that led him to please and identify with a successful father was highly adaptive and encouraged success, but the object relations unit that made him fear the abusive, denigrating father resulted in his self-defeating life pattern. The patient's external life of oscillating successes and defeats thus mirrored his internal world of productive and defeating object relationships. This structure corresponds to an adaptively neurotic pattern of functioning that falls short of realizing the potential of the self. Within this structure, neurotic conflict results from the coexistence of adaptive and maladaptive aspects of the personality; the conflict is not the cause of the unhealthy components of the self but their result.

This object relations paradigm of psychopathology has profound implications for psychoanalytic treatment, and it is to the clinical consequences that we now turn.

TREATMENT

It follows from the object relations paradigm of psychopathology that the aim of treatment is to change the structure of the patient's object relationships in such a manner that the self can function more effectively. The target of object relations analysis is neither the wish nor the interpersonal relationship but the object relationship. We have seen that most object relations theorists tend to depart from the classical model by questioning the exclusive role of interpretation. There is wide variation in the extent to which other interventions are advocated and interpretation is construed as offering a therapeutic experience as opposed to new knowledge. Only Klein and Kernberg have held to the classical concept that insight alone has therapeutic efficacy. But even Klein viewed the mutative factor as the internalization of the good object, and her followers (see Rosenfeld, 1978; Segal, 1981) have emphasized the patient–therapist relationship as a crucial therapeutic ingredient. In fact, a dominant theme in object relations theories is the role of the analytic relationship in effecting therapeutic outcome. Consequently, in the object relations paradigm there are two categories of intervention relevant to the aims of psychoanalysis: interpretation and the provision of a new relationship.

The Interpretive Model

The most direct and significant implication of the object relations paradigm for psychoanalytic interpretation is that interpretations are cast in terms of a self in relation to an object.

Analysts frame their interpretations not in terms of what the patient wishes for or desires but in terms of the self-affect-object unit, as Kernberg (1976) points out. Moreover, the elucidation of one such unit is only the beginning. Because each object relations unit is a component of the self structure, the eventual target of the analytic process is not a group of disparate units but the structure that they form and the sense of self to which they give rise. The patient is never angry without the anger directed at someone, and the self-angry-at-the-other is embedded within a structure of other such units. For example, the anger may be a defense against other, more threatening, object relationships, such as longing for or fear of the other; or the anger may be a means of seeking vengeance for the frustration of yet another object relationship, such as a grandiose self-superior-to-others. We may say that in this paradigm the analyst's task is to elucidate the object relations units, including the defenses against these units of experience, as they are enacted and reenacted with the analyst.

Since interpretations based on this paradigm are directed to a person in relation to another, the analyst points out to the patient what he or she is doing rather than that he or she has a wish. This implication is consistent with Schafer's (1976) notion of analytic interpretation as "action language." Eschewing the concept of psychic mechanisms, object relations analysts do not view the patient as enacting or subject to psychical forces but as a person navigating relationships with other people. Fairbairn (1943) referred to this type of intervention as the "personalization" of interpretations and pointed out that interpreting according to the drive model fosters defenses by distancing the patient from the material. This principle may well be adhered to by analysts who do not identify themselves with object relations theories, but insofar as this is the case such analysts are departing from the classical psychoanalytic paradigm with its emphasis on drives.

The most immediate and accurate path to the patient's object relations structure is the patient–analyst relationship. From the object relations perspective, transference is the perception of and interaction with the analyst according to the object relationships formed from the patient's early attachments. With the exception of Sullivan's approach, interpretations are geared as much as possible to the transference within all models of psychoanalytic treatment, but the object relations paradigm has a stronger theoretical reason to emphasize the centrality of transference interpretation. As Fairbairn (1944) pointed out, if the therapeutic action of psychoanalysis consists of interpretation of drives and defenses, as is claimed by the drive-ego model, it should not be crucial whether wishes are made conscious within or outside the relationship with the analyst. The acceptance of the technical principle that the patient's deficits and conflicts are best addressed and resolved within the analytic relationship is a tacit admission that they are imbedded in object relationships. From the object relations perspective, the patient's psychological structure, being a product of early attachments, is expected to manifest itself most clearly in its current relationships, most notably in the interaction with the analyst. Since pathology is viewed as a product of relationships as they are internalized and structured within the patient's personality, the clinical focus on the transference is theoretically grounded in the object relations perspective on development and pathology.

Although Sullivan (1953) and Levenson (1991) view pathology as a matter solely of external, interpersonal relationships and eschew the concepts of internalization and psychological structure, other aspects of interpersonal theory are compatible with the object relations viewpoint. Mitchell's (1988) relational/conflict model views the mind as a social product derived from transactional patterns and embodied in an internalized structure that patients bring into the analytic setting. Greenberg (1991), viewing psychological structure as a product of the dual drives of effectance and safety, believes that the patient's experience of safety with the analyst allows access to expanded self-representations. Gill's (1981) and Hoffman's (1991) concept of the transference also appears to be rooted in a view of man as bringing patterns of relating into the analytic relationship.

The object relations concept of transference is best appreciated by contrasting it to the transference as presented by the drive-ego model. Freud's (1912, 1915d) view was that the frustrated portion of drives seeks new objects which in later life become the targets upon which templates of the earlier frustrated objects are placed. In the Dora case, Freud (1905b) recognized that the patient notices some detail in the analyst's behavior that is similar to that of the past frustrating figure and that becomes the stimulus for the transference perception. Nonetheless, Freud did not develop this idea into a broadened concept of the transference but viewed the analyst's behavior as only the stimulus for the projection of a preexisting template of an early object of frustration onto the figure of the analyst. Because, in Freud's view, drive frustration is based largely in the Oedipus complex, the transference tends to take on the character of the frustrations of the unresolved portions of the oedipal struggle. Thus, he conceptualized Dora's transference as solely her frustrated erotic feelings for her father projected onto Freud. Later, as Freud (1920) modified his drive theory to include aggression, the concept of transference was expanded to involve both libidinal and aggressive frustrations, but the idea that transference is rooted in the frustration of endogenous drives was not altered.

As we saw in chapter 1, when Anna Freud (1936) and the ego

psychologists added the view that the patient's defenses against the drives also become manifest in the transference, defense interpretation became a major part of transference analysis. Despite this emendation, the motor of the transference continues to be frustration as only those aspects of the relationship with the analyst infiltrated by drive frustration and defense against it compose the transference and are, therefore, interpretable.

This view of the transference is narrow and reductionistic compared to its object relations counterpart. Frustration is not a necessary component of object relationships, as object contact is motivated by the early need to attach. The transference relationship is not reducible to frustrated drives, their psychological expression in wishes, or any other more primary motivation. Freed from a conflict-based theory of mental structure, the object relations paradigm opens exploration of all early attachments, whether conflictual or not, as contributions to self formation. Although differing on details, all object relations theories view the child as navigating early relationships with the minimum degree of anxiety possible to form a sense of self. These early bonds, with their associated affects, form the basis of the transference. In the object relations paradigm, the arena of transference interpretation is broadened significantly, since every aspect of the way the patient relates to the analyst is potentially interpretable as a manifestation of character structure.

To choose but two examples of this broadened concept of the transference, let us consider briefly Winnicott's (1963c) case of Miss X and Kohut's (1971) treatment of Mr. A. As reported in chapter 4, Miss X's therapeutic progress began in one crucial session during which she lay covered with a rug and said very little. The decisive event was Winnicott's understanding of what she needed without her having to tell him. Miss X needed Winnicott to "take over" her omnipotence, which allowed her the "disintegration" she needed to make contact with her "true self." Miss X transferred an early object relationship that had arrested the development of her self and could not be reduced to a libidinal or aggressive drive.

As we saw in chapter 6, the transference of Mr. A consisted of two primary demands: that the analyst share his values and confirm "through a warm glow" that the patient had lived up to the analyst's standards. When either of these needs was not met, Mr. A felt empty and trite no matter how moral his behavior was. Kohut concluded that the patient suffered from a "diffuse narcissistic vulnerability" due to a gap in the idealization of the superego, which Kohut believed was due to his thwarted efforts to idealize his father. The object relations pattern with the father was repeated in the patient's attempts to fill the gap in his psyche by receiving the "warm glow" from the analyst. As in Winnicott's case of Miss X, the needs expressed as the crucial components of the transference cannot be reduced to endogenous drives in any meaningful sense. Both cases illustrate the broadened, relational view of the transference that typifies the object relations paradigm.

The much narrower drive-ego model of transference separates it from character structure. From the object relations perspective, character structure and transference are indistinguishable. Character is equivalent to the structure of the self, an organization of object relationships that defines both the perceptions of and interactional patterns with others (Summers, 1993a). Transference is the character pattern, or self structure, as it gains expression in the analytic setting.

Each object relations theory emphasizes different types of object relations in the formation of the self and has a distinct view of how this process occurs. Consequently, they all emphasize different factors as crucial to the transference. For Fairbairn (1958), the transference is the patient's effort to bring the analyst into the closed system of inner reality formed to protect the patient against object contact. Guntrip (1969) equated transference with the regressed needs of the patient's ego. In Klein's (1952c) and Kernberg's (1976) views, the vicissitudes of the aggressive drive are the crucial feature. Winnicott (1963c) saw transference as the manifestation of early dependence needs. Kohut (1984) and the self psychologists view transference as the manifestation of early needs for grandiosity and idealization in the analytic setting. Each theorist emphasizes a different type of object relationship as critical to the transference, but all conceive of transference as early forms of object attachment manifested in the relationship with the analyst. Because character structure is a product of object relationships and the attachments to which they give rise, transference is not conceived from the object relationship perspective as projection upon a blank screen. As Gill (1981) has pointed out, the patient's attachments press for interaction with the analyst, since the form of attachment evokes an affective reaction from the analyst, and this response is a fundamental part of the object relationship. We have seen this shift in the conceptualization of the transference in several object relations theories. The major conceptual breakthrough in this shift to an interactional concept of analysis was the Kleinian concept of projective identification. As we saw in chapter 3, Rosenfeld (1978), Segal (1981), and Bion (1962) all transformed Klein's intrapsychic concept into an interactional process in which the patient evokes experiences in the analyst in order to communicate nonverbalized parts of the self and get rid of its unwanted aspects along with anxiety-pro-voking affects. Racker (1968) added the distinction between com-plementary and concordant countertransference to capture the difference between (1) the analyst as object and patient as self and (2) the analyst as self and patient as object. Kernberg (1988) consid-ers the use of projective identification to be one of the primary clini-cal implications of the object relations approach. Winnicott (1947, 1960c) also made use of projective identification; he felt that many patients communicate best by what they make the analyst feel and that sometimes it is useful to tell patients what feelings they have evoked. While Kohut did not make use of the analyst's responses to the patient in his clinical theory, some of his followers, most notably Stolorow, Brandchaft, and Lachmann (1988), have expanded self psychology into an intersubjective model in which the analyst's feelings play a prominent role in the treatment.

Kernberg (1988) has drawn out the clinical implications of the view that children internalize object relations units in which self and object can become reversed. Since the unit is internalized, rather than simply the object, the patient learns to operate accord-ing to the structure of the object relationship rather than on the basis of only one side of it. Consequently, patients may experience themselves as either the self or object part of an object relations unit. For example, the patient who frequently feels victimized may wantonly disregard the analyst and attempt to defeat the treat-ment, thus reversing roles by becoming the abuser and victimizing the analyst. Such a patient may have a conscious self-concept of a victim but in fact has a "victim–abuser" object relations unit as a primary component of the self structure and may enact either role. This view of the countertransference is another way in which the object relations paradigm broadens the concept of transference; it alerts analysts to their affective responses to the patient and the need to use them to understand the patient's psychological struc-ture. How the analyst feels in response to the patient is always a significant component of the transference, and sometimes the best clue to its nature.

The interpersonal concept of transference is a primary point of con-nection between the object relations paradigm and interpersonalist the-ory. Indeed, in this sense, the object relations approach is closer to the interpersonalist position than the classical model. Mitchell (1988), Greenberg (1991), Gill (1981), and Hoffman (1991) all view the analyst's reactions to the patient as a critical component of the transference.

Although patients defend against the awareness of their object relationships, it is not this type of defense that is the biggest obstacle to therapeutic success. As every therapist knows, pointing out the patient's object relations structure, even if accurately timed in the transference, does not mean that the structure will change. It is common for patients to see and even understand their experience of the analyst without being able to change it. Patients tend to be reluctant to yield any aspect of their pathology, and this resistance to change is especially true for the structure of the self. For patients to give up their object relations structure, they must yield their sense of self, of who they are. It is the patient's inability to modify his or her characteristic pattern of relating to the analyst despite insight into the pattern that constitutes resistance from the object relations perspective (Summers, 1993a). This position contrasts with the classical point of view, according to which resistance is defense against awareness of either wishes toward the analyst or the affect associated with them.

It should be emphasized that within the classical framework it has always been difficult to account for the phenomenon of the patient's refusal to change after awareness of affect. Freud (1937) attempted to account for it primarily with his concepts of the constitutional strength of the instincts and the deformation of the ego. He felt that the more pathology is due to the constitutional strengths of the instincts and the more the ego needs to be altered, the more difficult to change process will be. Freud (1937) considered the following to be the most recalcitrant obstacles to analytic success: (1) adhesiveness of the libido, the inability of the patient to withdraw investment in the object; (2) masochism, or the desire to be ill, which Freud attributed to the death instinct; (3) the fixity of the defenses, which leads to the pursuit of situations to justify the defenses, a phenomenon Freud called "resistance to resistance"; (4) the rigidity inherent in all mental processes, which Freud felt had unknown causes; and (5) the male's repudiation of femininity and the female's penis envy. Freud was quite pessimistic about the possibility of changing any of these phenomena inasmuch as the "quantitative factor" of the instincts was considered unalterable and the ego not amenable to change. Indeed, Freud considered most of these factors constitutional, and he offered little hope for altering those that are not, such as resistance to resistance. With these intractable resistances, Freud seemed to feel he had come upon psychological rock bottom.

The object relations belief in the amenability of resistance to psychoanalytic intervention highlights an advantage of the object relations paradigm as a pure psychology. From this perspective, the patient's attachment to the analyst is the way the self structure is maintained; the defenses are resilient because they are protecting the self. The patient is resistant to change even with awareness because awareness does not change the need to maintain the sense of self. To give up the attachment to the object is to face the feeling of not knowing who one is, that is, of annihilation anxiety. Two critical interpretive implications follow. First, the fact that the resistance is an object relationship makes it interpretable as a need to attach in a particular manner. The object relations paradigm approaches resistance by investigating the patient's need to form *this type* of relationship with the analyst, rather than viewing it as a constitutional given. Mitchell (1988) has pointed out the therapeutic power of patient and analyst exploring the question, Why is this the *only* way of relating to the analyst? Whereas the drive model hits analytic rock bottom, that is, reaches issues deemed unanswerable through analysis, object relations theories pursue analysis of the need for a given type of object relationship and the anxiety of giving it up. In the example presented earlier of the internalization of the victim–abuser object relationship unit, the analytic inquiry pursued why the patient could only experience the analyst as abuser or victim. There is no biological bedrock beyond which the analysis cannot be pursued.

This inquiry is of course likely to run into further defenses, and this renewed resistance leads to the second critical interpretive implication of the object relations view of resistance. The recalcitrance of the object relations structure, as noted, is due to the anxiety of yielding the sense of self and bearing the consequent annihilation anxiety. The working-through process from this perspective implies a continual confrontation with the threat to the sense of self during the process of structural change. All movement toward structural change evokes anxiety of loss of self and leads to the desire to conserve the old structure. Working through, from the object relations perspective, is the continual interpretation of this conservative tendency of the psyche. When the patient regresses from apparent therapeutic progress, the analyst identifies the primary cause of the regression as the anxiety of losing the sense of self. This working-through process of confrontation with the borders of the self continues until a new self is solidified. Thus, the confrontation and management of the anxiety evoked by the threat to the patient's object relations structure become crucial components of all psychoanalytic treatment based on the object relations perspective, irrespective of the severity of pathology.

These principles are illustrated in the analysis of the real estate developer discussed earlier. The analysis became especially painful to the patient when, after about one year of therapy, he became aware of how much he had compromised himself in his desperate efforts to maintain a relationship with his father. He had tolerated sustained, humiliating verbal abuse in order to maintain a sense of connection with his father and in the vain hope of winning his approval. Working for his father, the patient had felt subjected to the whims of an almost totalitarian presence from which he could not break loose. As he began to become aware of the intensity of his former need for his father, the patient acknowledged that he had begun "obsessing" about the relationship with the analyst, which he found abusive and humiliating. He feared that he was becoming excessively dependent on the analyst and that he had made himself vulnerable only to meet with no support. The patient felt intense anger at the analyst and concluded that it would be best to leave the relationship to arrest that process. The patient agreed with the interpretation that the analysis was being experienced as a repetition of his relationship with the father but said that it was for that very reason that the process was debilitating and that he must leave it. He then acknowledged that he had drunk excessively when he worked for his father to make the situation "tolerable" and maintained that the difference between analysis and the relationship with his father was that he no longer drank heavily; consequently, the analytic relationship was intolerable. He believed that in the analysis he was "throwing [himself] at a wall," just as he had with his father, to no avail. Remaining in analysis despite the lack of support from the analyst was experienced as futilely groveling to please his unresponsive father, and he did not wish to be humiliated a second time. While fully acknowledging that he was escaping the analytic relationship, the patient was convinced that flight from the relationship was his only self-respecting option.

The analytic process reached a critical juncture at this point. The patient ultimately decided to stay once he realized that fleeing was not an escape from his father but continued imprisonment in his emotional grip, which reaffirmed his pattern of relating only as a humiliated victim. Further, the patient realized that he had constructed the analytic situation as a stricture of unrelenting hard work according to which relaxation was "against the rules." Analysis had become another excessive life burden. His desire to flee from this internal prison led to an understanding of his life pattern of constant traveling. He now realized that many of his frequent trips were not business necessities but "escapes." His experience of himself as a victim at the hands of his business associates and now his analyst was clearly rooted in the paternal transference. It became evident at this point that continual escape was a part of the pattern. The patient acknowledged his terror of dependence on the analyst, which he associated with his futile attempts to win his father's love. His inability to leave his father had led to feelings of humiliation and guilt; he had compromised himself to the point of self-loathing out of fear of losing the connection. His escapes through traveling and alcohol were his efforts to maintain the self he had created of a victimized coward without becoming fully aware of its existence.

In the next session the patient reported that after the previous hour he had had the fantasy of being accosted by muggers, seizing their gun, shooting their legs out from under them as they ran away, and permanently damaging them. He connected this rage to his desire for vengeance against his father for having put him in the humiliating position of compromising so much in his effort to achieve a relationship. While he acknowledged that the fantasy signified continued anger at the analyst, he believed that this rage was about having to enter into a new relationship to resolve his issues. The blind rage and its injurious intent were not a product of an endogenous drive but a product of his complex past relationship with his father and his current relationship with the analyst and could not be understood outside the context of his willingness to pay a crippling emotional price for contact with his father.

The therapeutic action of the analysis consisted of the patient's confrontation with his unwillingness to yield his sense of himself as an overburdened, victimized, undeserving failure. In acknowledging his dependence on the analyst, he became terrified as he began to lose the sense of who he was. He realized that his view of himself was self-denigrating, tension producing, and self-defeating but felt that he would rather have that than face the terror of not knowing who he was. He feared success for its implication of a positive view of himself, and in this fear he included a sense of betrayal of both his parents. If he was not burdened by guilt, he experienced a terrifying loss of direction. The therapeutic action became the patient's continual confrontation with his fear of relating to others without being a victim or failure; he clung to his guilt, victimization, failure, humiliation, and self-loathing. Over and over he faced the fear of life without these ways of relating.

In confronting the barriers of his self the patient was already forming a new object relationship with the analyst and thereby a new sense of self. For the first time, he experienced a close relationship not based on self-loathing and humiliation and from which he did not need to escape. Many of his self-defeating, self-denigrating life patterns began to fall away as his sense of self started to crystallize in a new direction. At this point the patient began to discard many of his former business associates and demeaning business arrangements in favor of more lucrative, self-respecting ventures. He also began to experience both the analysis and external world with increasing joy and relaxation. In Winnicott's (1971) terms, he was more able to "play." This process of therapeutic change, this restructuring of the self organization so that the various symptoms and pathological features give way, is a manifestation of fundamental change in the patient's object relations structure.

The patient's progress is best summarized by a dream in which he got off a train and believed he had the wrong baggage because his suitcase was so light and he usually "travel[ed] heavy." He went back on the train to find his bags but could not; he decided he would have to "make do" and felt the worst part would be having to buy new underwear. The dream represents the beginning of a sense of a new, "lighter" self that had no need to carry the older, "heavy" baggage, but the desire to find the old, familiar baggage, reflects the self in formation. The new self included the ability to relax and enjoy life, as represented by the lighter baggage. Further, the "worst part" of the new life—"buying new underwear"—represents the rebuilding of the self from the inside out.

It must be underscored that from the objective relations perspective the patient's characteristic self structure promotes such functioning as the patient is capable of. In cases of severe character pathology, such as borderline conditions, such functioning may be tantamount to the sense of feeling alive and real (Summers, 1988) whereas in neurosis the self structure is able to cope at a higher level. In the case discussed here, the patient's compromise between his need to please the admired father and his fear of threatening him with success led to a mixture of success and self-defeat; the latter reduced the patient's anxiety over threatening the internalized father to the point that it allowed him to perform in many areas. That is, as long as the patient did not enjoy too much success, he could feel satisfied with some degree of achievement and live without crippling anxiety. The object relations paradigm suggests that the adaptive value of this self structure should be interpreted to the patient and that the transference should be seen in this light as well. Treatment is not simply a matter of confronting anxiety but also of interpreting to patients the reasons why they need the types of attachments they have formed. In all these ways, the object relations paradigm adopts a more optimistic approach to resistance and character change than does Freud's theory.

A major advantage of the object relations reformulation of the psycho-analytic process is the broadened interpretive field to which it gives rise. For this reason, all object relations theories have expanded the range of pathology considered analytically accessible to include character, and even borderline, pathology. While some theories emphasize a particular type of pathology, such as schizoid or borderline conditions—the Kleinians have even extended analytic treatment to psychotic states—all object relations theories share a paradigm that considers the structure of the personality, even in severe character disorders, potentially accessible to psychoanalytic treatment. As we have seen, the transference of the neurotic patient is as much a product of the self structure as is that of the more severely disturbed patient. Patients of both types are confronted with anxiety in the face of structural personality change and resist change despite awareness of transference motivations. The object relations paradigm opens a way to interpret and resolve this fundamental dilemma. Freud (1937) believed that treatment of the neurotic patient often ran into exasperating, perplexing, and even insurmountable obstacles when the male's repudiation of femininity and the female's penis envy were reached. From the object relations perspective, in both situations the patient is holding on to a precious sense of self and attempting to avoid anxiety; the analysis has not reached psychoanalytic bedrock but, rather, the anxiety of changing the sense of self, and this anxiety is interpretable to the patient. Thus the treatment of neurosis is conducted on the same basis as the treatment of other forms of pathology.

Despite this broadened arena of interpretation, the object relations paradigm rarely attributes therapeutic efficacy solely to making the unconscious conscious. Because object relations units are formed from early attachments, they typically require a new relationship for their modification. The analytic relationship is especially well suited to this task, since bringing to light the unconscious object relations structures, even with the attendant anxiety, creates the possibility of forming a new type of object relationship with the analyst. The object relations paradigm thus emphasizes the formation of a new relationship between patient and analyst as a critical component of the therapeutic action of the analytic process. We now turn to this aspect of the process.

The Analytic Relationship

Since patients' pathological object relations units arose in response to early inadequate attachments, new types of attachments present patients with opportunities to internalize more benign relationships and reorganize their psychological structure. Object relations theorists differ in their conceptualization of this process, but most see the analytic relationship, even if it is conceived on a purely interpretive basis, as a new type of object contact that can be productively internalized to form a more functional self.

The most obvious way the analytic relationship enters the treatment is in the interpretive process. Most object relations and interpersonal theorists point out that the relationship established by the analyst's interpretive posture is in itself new for the patient. Because the patient suffers from unhealthy early relationships that endure in the form of object relations units, this new relationship based on understanding, should have therapeutic benefit apart from the content of interpretations. Kohut (1984) and other self psychologists (for example, Basch, 1985; have given the greatest weight to analytic empathy in the formation of a therapeutically beneficial relationship; for them, analytic understanding, including its successes and failures, creates and sustains the relationship that is conducive to the creation of new psychological structure.

Winnicott (1960a), like Kohut, saw a parallel to the mother–child relationship in the analyst–patient interaction of understanding and failing to understand. Within the interpretive model, their views are remarkably similar. However, Winnicott (1954b, 1960a) believed that adaptation to developmental need must often go beyond interpretation to the provision of a relationship geared to developmental deficit whereas Kohut limited the gratification of unmet needs to analytic empathy. Nonetheless, both theorists emphasized the necessity of a phase of illusion that is sustained by the analyst's attunement and is only gradually relinquished, with the aid of the analyst's errors, in favor of reality.

Fairbairn (1958) ultimately came to the view that the greatest value of interpretation resides in its ability to break through the "closed system" of the patient to develop a new relationship. Guntrip (1969) saw the benefit of interpretation in its ability to reach the regressed, hidden part of the self. Even Klein (1952c), who adhered to the classical framework of offering only interpretations, saw as their ultimate value the internalization of the good object. Moreover, contemporary Kleinians, such as Rosenfeld and Segal, infer from this view of the analytic process that the analytic relationship must play a role in treatment in order to account for the internalization of the good object. Only Kernberg among object relations theorists gives no role to the relationship beyond the content of interpretations. With this exception, then, object relations theorists tend to ascribe the therapeutic efficacy of interpretations not solely to insight but also to their ability to serve as the instrument of a new relationship for the patient.

We have seen an example of the way interpretation begins the formation of a new relationship in our discussion of the analysis of the real estate developer referred to earlier. As the analysis focused on the patient's fear of yielding the sense of himself as victimized, humiliated, failing, and guilty, he became enmeshed in a dependent relationship with the analyst. A major component of the therapeutic action of the analysis consisted of the patient's struggle to remain in this relationship rather than flee it. The interpretations formed the bond that allowed the patient to remain connected to the analyst and fostered his dependence on the analysis. The decision of the patient, who was tempted to flee and almost did, to remain occurred in response to the interpretation of his pattern of escape from dependence and meaningful object contact. With that decision began his engagement in a new relationship, one in which he was dependent but freer to be himself without self-loathing and the need for escape. Thus, interpretations were the medium through which this new relationship was realized, but the experience of this relationship was in itself analytic progress.

Thus, it may be argued that interpretation is only one strategy for effecting the new relationship that is crucial to the reorganization of the personality. The view of interpretation as the instrument of a therapeutic relationship has led some object relations theorists to question the primacy, even the value, of interpretation. As we saw in chapter 4, this is exactly the conclusion Winnicott (1954b, 1960a) drew. He deemphasized interpretation in favor of the analyst's ability to make contact with the arrested portion of the patient's self in order to unblock the developmental process. According to Winnicott, this unblocking can take place via interpretation but if other experiences are more important for overcoming the developmental deficits, then provision of those experiences should be given priority. Winnicott's explicit belief that analysis is about the analyst's adaptation to, rather than interpretation of, the patient's needs is the most radical revision of the analytic process posited by object relations theories.

Guntrip (1969), who was strongly influenced by Winnicott, believed that the therapeutic action of analysis resided in the meeting of the patient's regressed needs, that while interpretation might be required to arrive at the point of developmental fixation, the meeting of the regressed needs might require noninterpretive intervention. Fairbairn (1958) was more cautious in questioning the central role of interpretation, but at the end of his life he seemed to be adopting the position that the personal relationship between analyst and patient is more important than the content of interpretation in breaking through the patient's "closed system" of object relationships. Kohut (1984), as we have seen, adhered to an interpretive approach but saw the value of interpretation in the type of relationship it created. Furthermore, Kohut believed the type of interpretation should be limited for a prolonged period so that the therapeutic relationship can be built. While the analytic behavior may be construed as interpretive in this phase, analysts' comments are limited to understanding, with explanation kept to a minimum. Understanding has therapeutic benefit owing to its ability to foster a new bond. Thus, while Kohut tended to emphasize interpretation, he gave great weight to a significant period of relationship building during which time there is little depth interpretation. Some of Kohut's followers, such as Bacal and Newman (1990), have questioned more radically the value of interpretation as opposed to the creation of the optimal relationship, suggesting a version of self psychology that is closer to Winnicott's concept of the analytic process.

While Klein (1952c) did not question the exclusive role of interpretation, she did see the aim of the analytic process to be the internalization of the good object. One may question, however, how Klein's strict adherence to making conscious bad internalized objects can lead to the internalization of the good object. This gap led some of her followers to become more flexible in seeing the relationship as a critical part of the treatment (Bion 1962; Rosenfeld, 1978; Segal, 1981). They tend to locate this flexibility primarily in the projective identification process, which leads to a focus on how analysts absorb the experiences patients project "into" them. They note that this interpersonal relationship between patient and analyst is important for the internalization of the good object, the goal of Kleinian treatment. One can see in this modification of Klein's theories a shift away from her exclusive reliance on interpretation. Again, Kernberg is most traditional in his view that the sole therapeutic benefit of analytic treatment resides in the content of interpretation, even though he emphasizes the analyst's feelings in the understanding of the patient.

It is clear, then, that the object relations theorists differ on the type of relationship they deem most helpful to the patient and on how this bond is formed. Nonetheless, the majority of object relations theorists draw from the equation of pathology with a dysfunctional object relations structure the implication that the relationship between patient and analyst is critical to the therapeutic action of the analytic process.

Emphasis on the analytic relationship as the primary instrument of therapeutic action is another point of intersection between object relations and interpersonal theorists. Interpersonal theory sees interpretation as inherently relationship building because interpretation is an interpersonal event. Even Greenberg (1991) who tends to view interpretation of representations as the primary therapeutic intervention, emphasizes strongly that interpretation is an interaction. As we have seen in chapter 7, Mitchell (1988) focuses on the analyst's expansion of the patient's relational configurations via the relationship he or she offers. Levenson (1991) takes an even more radical approach: he questions the value of depth interpretation in favor of expanded awareness of the applicability of relational patterns and believes change results more from authentic encounter than from interpretation. Gill (1979, 1981) gives more importance to interpretation than most interpersonalists, but he believes a large share of the power of interpretation resides in the fact that it forms a new relationship and thus extricates the analytic relationship from the patient's relational patterns. Hoffman (1991) tends to emphasize authentic analytic encounter as a significant component of the process. Thus, we can see that the interpersonal theorists tend to place an even greater emphasis on the patient–analyst relationship and less on interpretation than do object relations theorists. The two viewpoints are alike in their rejection of the classical model of technique, but the primary difference appears to be in the *kind* of relationship deemed most conducive to therapeutic change. The interpersonal viewpoint tends to stress authentic modes of engagement whereas the tendency of object relations theories is to see therapeutic change as the unblocking of developmental arrests via the formation of a relationship that in some way offers the patient the type of contact missing in the earlier pathogenic relationships.

According to the object relations paradigm, a component of this relationship is the affective response of the analyst to the patient. As mentioned earlier, the analyst's response to the patient subserves the interpretive process. Kernberg (1988) has emphasized this aspect of the use of countertransference. In addition, some of the Kleinians (Racker, 1968; Rosenfeld, 1978; Segal, 1981), along with Winnicott (1947, 1960c) and his followers (Green, 1977; Little, 1981), have pointed out that the analyst's absorption of the feelings engendered in him or her by the patient in itself constitutes a new relationship. Ogden (1982) has emphasized the importance of the therapist's ability to process and interpret the affects projected into him or her by the patient in order to reduce the anxiety associated with troublesome affects and allow their integration by the patient. The Kleinians' revision of projective identification to an interpersonal process implies that from the object relations perspective the analyst's affective response is not a problematic countertransference to be avoided, but a crucial communication from the patient that needs to be understood.

We have noted that one of the major implications of the view of mental structure as composed of object relations units is that the patient can be enacting either pole of such a unit while evoking the other pole in the analyst. Such a reversal means that the analyst is "absorbing" his or her response and using it as a communication rather than acting on it. This therapeutic response runs contrary to the patient's expectations based on past experience and helps promote a new, more benign and productive, relationship. For example, if the patient's behavior evokes a feeling of anger in the analyst, this affective response leads not to hostile behavior on the analyst's part but to the utilization of the angry response for understanding the interaction. Interpersonal theorists, such as Mitchell (1988), Gill (1979, 1983), and Hoffman (1991), have also stressed this point, thus providing another connection between the interpersonal and object relations paradigms. Gill (1979) has pointed out that the fact that the analyst responds to the patient's troublesome affects with an interpretation is contrary to the patient's expectations and therefore inherently beneficial. Further, Gill's (1981) social paradigm extends the interpersonal nature of the therapeutic process beyond projective identification, since it assumes that the patient's material is at least partly determined by the analyst's behavior. While the interpersonalists have made a significant contribution to the object relations model by emphasizing the interactional aspects of the analytic relationship, they tend to depart more sharply from the traditional model by conceptualizing the transference as mutual influence and interaction (for example, Mitchell, 1988; Levenson, 1991; Hoffman, 1991). In the most extreme versions of this model the analytic process seems to take on the character of an existential encounter. Levenson (1991) and, to a lesser degree, Hoffman (1991) view the analyst's authenticity as a crucial component of the therapeutic action of analysis. Although this component of interpersonal theory is not shared by object relations theorists, the interpersonalists in general underscore the object relations view that the patient communicates by interaction and that this aspect of the relationship may often be the heart of the analytic process. While Mitchell (1988) also sees a role for analytic engagement, his view of the interaction as a product of the patient's relational patterns is closer to the object relations paradigm. From the latter perspective, analysts offer a new relationship based on their assessment of the developmental fixation point of the object relations structure of the patient's self. Even

Winnicott's radical approach of giving priority to adaptation over interpretation is based on a careful understanding of the particular developmental arrest of each individual patient. Despite these differences in emphasis, the object relations and interpersonal paradigms are alike in departing from the classical approach by deeming the formation of a relationship between patient and analyst integral to the therapeutic action of psychoanalysis.

The object relations paradigm has a further kinship with the interpersonal model in that both are pure psychologies, in opposition to the biological basis of the drive-ego model, that see the relationship between patient and analyst as key to the treatment. Since object relations structures are seen as products of interpersonal relations and since these structures cannot be affected without a new relational contact, each object relations theory has a concept of some aspect of the self that needs to be contacted for growth to occur. Whether the unconnected part of the self is conceptualized as narcissistic illusion, the true self, a schizoid core, or split-off or repressed aggressive object relations, a major component of the self structure is distorted and out of contact with the world. Engaging this part of the self brings it into an interpersonal relationship that can now affect its structure. Thus, the primary analytic task is to find a way to recognize and communicate with the hitherto detached part of the self. As this engagement takes place, the crippling object relations structure is now involved in a new, growth-enhancing interaction. The internalization of this new attachment results in a new, more functional object relations structure.

Object relations theorists have tended to see the patient as unable to achieve personal contact in some fundamental manner. Fairbairn (1940) emphasized schizoid withdrawal in his application of the object relations viewpoint to the reconceptualization of psychopathology. Winnicott (1960a, 1963b) developed the notions of self arrestation in the "pre-reality" phases of dependence and a split between the "true" and "false" self. Even Klein (for example, 1960), while adhering to a drive model, saw forceful interpretation of the unconscious as the vehicle for making contact with pathological aspects of the patient's self. Klein's followers broadened this focus to making contact with the withdrawn parts of the self. For Kohut, the patient's archaic grandiosity and/or idealizing needs interfere with relationships, and the analyst's task is to help the patient resume development in these areas in the interest of forming and maintaining more mature interpersonal contacts and adopting more realistic ambitions and goals.

As noted, the object relations paradigm of psychoanalytic treatment is based on pure psychology. The starting point of this paradigm is the initial attachment between child and mother; its clinical theory derives from the fact that psychological life originates in this manner. The human psyche is conceived to be a product of early attachments, and psychopathology is understood to consist of defects resulting from the absence or malignant transformation of such attachments, with resulting problems in the internalization of healthy, self-sustaining attachments. Each object relations theory offers its own version of development and pathogenesis and a treatment approach claiming a degree of therapeutic success, but each view, in turn, has theoretical and clinical weaknesses. The object relations approach is still very much in the process of developing.

The object relations paradigm changes the interpretive model and goes beyond it. Whether interpretation or the nature of the therapeutic relationship is emphasized in any given object relations theory, all such theories view the clinician's task as one of connecting with the patient in a new way, contacting an unengaged part of the self, confronting the resulting annihilation anxiety, and thereby forming a new type of attachment that eventuates in more functional object relations structures. In this way, the implications of a pure psychology are carried through to the clinical process. Neither biological drives nor abstract psychological energies nor mechanisms have a place in this model. The patient is a person-in-interaction, and the analyst's task is to forge a connection in order to change fundamentally the nature of who the patient is and who that person may yet become.

References

Abraham, K. (1924), A short study of the development of the libido. In: *Selected Papers on Psycho-Analysis*. London: Hogarth Press, 1954, pp 418–502.

Adler, G. (1985), *Borderline Psychopathology and Its Treatment*. New York: Aronson.

Alexander, F. (1950), Analysis of the therapeutic factors in psychoanalytic treatment. In: *The Scope of Psychoanalysis: Selected Papers of Franz Alexander*. New York: Basic Books, 1961, pp. 261–275.

Arlow, J. (1963), Conflict, regression, and symptom formation. *Internat. J. Psycho-Anal.*, 44:12–22.

—— (1969), Unconscious fantasy and disturbances of conscious experience. *Psychoanal. Quart.*, 38:1–27

—— (1987), The dynamics of interpretation. *Psychoanal. Quart.*, 56:68–87.

—— & Brenner, C. (1964), *Psychoanalytic Constructs and the Structural Theory*. New York: International Universities Press.

—— & —— (1990), The psychoanalytic process. *Psychoanal. Quart.* 59:678–693.

Bacal, H. (1985), Optimal responsiveness and the therapeutic process. In: *Progress in Self Psychology, Vol. 1*, ed. A. Goldberg. New York: Guilford Press, pp. 202–226.

—— & Newman, K. (1990), *Theories of Object Relations: Bridges to Self Psychology*. New York: Columbia University Press.

Bakan, D. (1966), *The Duality of Human Existence*. Chicago: Rand McNally.

Balint, M. (1968), *The Basic Fault*. London: Tavistock.

Basch, M. (1984), Selfobject theory of motivation and the history of psychoanalysis. In: *Kohut's Legacy: Contributions to Self Psychology*, ed. P. Stepansky & A. Goldberg. Hillsdale, NJ: The Analytic Press, pp. 3–20.

—— (1985), Interpretation: Toward a developmental model. In: *Progress in Self Psychology, Vol. 1*, ed. A. Goldberg. New York: Guilford Press, pp. 33–42.

Beebe, B. & Lachmann, F. (1992), A dyadic systems view of communication. In: *Relational Perspectives in Psychoanalysis*, ed. N. Skolnick & S. Warshaw. Hillsdale, NJ: The Analytic Press, pp. 61–82.

—— Jaffe, J. & Lachmann, F. (1992), The contribution of mother-infant influence to the origins of self- and object-representations. In: *Relational Perspectives in Psychoanalysis*, ed. N. Skolnick & S. Warshaw. Hillsdale, NJ: The Analytic Press, pp. 83–118.

Bettelheim, B. (1972), Regression as progress. In: *Tactics and Techniques in Psychoanalytic Therapy*, ed. P. Giovacchini. New York: Science House, pp. 189–199.

Bibring, E. (1947), The so-called English school of psychoanalysis. *Psychoanal. Quart.*, 16:69–93.

—— (1954), Psychoanalysis and the dynamic psychotherapies. *J. Amer. Psychoanal. Assn.*, 2:745–770.

Bion, W. (1957), Differentiation of psychotic and non-psychotic personalities. In: *Melanie Klein Today: Vol. 1. Mainly Theory*, ed. E. Spillius. London: Routledge, 1988, pp. 61–80.
—— (1959a), Attacks on linking. In: *Melanie Klein Today: Vol. 1. Mainly Theory*, ed. E. Spillius. London: Routledge, 1988, pp. 87–101.
—— (1959b), *Experiences in Groups*. New York: Basic Books.
—— (1961), A theory of thinking. In: *Melanie Klein Today: Vol. 1. Mainly Theory*, ed. E. Spillius. London: Routledge, 1988, pp. 178–186.
—— (1962), *Learning from Experience*. New York: Basic Books.
Bowlby, J. (1969), *Attachment and Loss: Vol. 1. Attachment*. New York: Basic Books.
Brandchaft, B. & Stolorow, R. (1984), A current perspective on difficult patients. In: *Kohut's Legacy: Contributions to Self Psychology*, ed. P. Stepansky & A. Goldberg. Hillsdale, NJ: The Analytic Press, pp. 93–116.
Brenner, C. (1976), *Psychoanalytic Technique and Psychic Conflict*. New York: International Universities Press.
—— (1979), Working alliance, therapeutic alliance, and transference. *J. Amer. Psychoanal. Assn.*, 27(suppl.):137–158.
—— (1981), Defense and defense mechanisms. *Psychoanal. Quart.*, 50:557–569.
Carson, R. (1969), *Interaction Concepts of Personality*. Chicago: Aldine.
Celani, D. (1993), *The Treatment of the Borderline Patient: Applying Fairbairn's Object Relations Theory in the Clinical Setting*. Madison, CT: International Universities Press.
Curtis, H. (1985), Clinical perspectives on self psychology. *Psychoanal. Quart.*, 54:339–378.
—— (1986), Clinical consequences of the theory of self psychology. In: *Progress in Self Psychology, Vol. 2*, ed. A. Goldberg. New York: Guilford Press, pp. 3–17.
Fairbairn, R. (1940), Schizoid factors in the personality. In: *Psychoanalytic Studies of the Personality*. London: Tavistock, 1952, pp. 3–28.
—— (1941), A revised psychopathology of the psychoses and psychoneuroses. In: *Psychoanalytic Studies of the Personality*. London: Tavistock, 1952, pp. 28–58.
—— (1943), The repression and the return of bad objects (with special reference to the "war neuroses"). In: *Psychoanalytic Studies of the Personality*. London: Tavistock, 1952, pp. 59–81.
—— (1944), Endopsychic structure considered in terms of object-relationships. In: *Psychoanalytic Studies of the Personality*. London: Tavistock, 1952, pp. 82–136.
—— (1946), Object-relationships and dynamic structure. In: *Psychoanalytic Studies of the Personality*. London: Tavistock, 1952, pp. 137–151.
—— (1949), Steps in the development of an object-relations theory of the personality. In: *Psychoanalytic Studies of the Personality*. London: Tavistock, 1952, pp. 152–161.
—— (1951), A synopsis of the development of the author's views regarding the structure of the personality. In: *Psychoanalytic Studies of the Personality*. London: Tavistock, 1952, pp. 162–182.
—— (1954), Observations on the nature of hysterical states. *Brit. J. Med. Psychol.*, 27:116–125.
—— (1958), On the nature and aims of psycho-analytical treatment. *Internat. J. Psycho-Anal.*, 39:374–385.
Freud, A. (1927), Four lectures on child analysis. In: *The Writings of Anna Freud, Vol. 1*. New York: International Universities Press, 1974, pp. 3–69.
—— (1936), *The Ego and the Mechanisms of Defense*. New York: International Universities Press.
Freud, S. (1895), Studies on hysteria. *Standard Edition*, 2. London: Hogarth Press, 1955.
—— (1905a), Three essays on the theory of sexuality. *Standard Edition*, 7:135–243. London: Hogarth Press, 1953.

—— (1905b), Fragment of an analysis of a case of hysteria. *Standard Edition,* 7:7–122. London: Hogarth Press, 1953.

—— (1912), The dynamics of transference. *Standard Edition,* 12:97–108. London: Hogarth Press, 1958.

—— (1914), On narcissism. *Standard Edition,* 14:73–102.London: Hogarth Press, 1957.

—— (1915a), Instincts and their vicissitudes. *Standard Edition,* 14:117–140. London: Hogarth Press, 1957.

—— (1915b), Repression. *Standard Edition,* 14:143–158. London: Hogarth Press, 1957.

—— (1915c), The unconscious. *Standard Edition,* 14:166–204. London: Hogarth Press, 1957.

—— (1915d), Observations on transference love. *Standard Edition,* 12:157–168. London: Hogarth Press, 1958.

—— (1917), Mourning and melancholia. *Standard Edition,* 14:243–258. London: Hogarth Press, 1957.

—— (1920), Beyond the pleasure principle. *Standard Edition,* 18:7–64. London: Hogarth Press, 1955.

—— (1923), The ego and the id. *Standard Edition,* 19:12–59. London: Hogarth Press, 1966.

—— (1926), Inhibitions, symptoms and anxiety. *Standard Edition,* 20:87–172. London: Hogarth Press, 1959

—— (1937), Analysis terminable and interminable. *Standard Edition,* 23:216–253. London: Hogarth Press, 1964.

—— (1940), An outline of psycho-analysis. *Standard Edition,* 23:144–207. London: Hogarth Press, 1964.

Geleerd, E. (1963), Evaluation of Melanie Klein's "Narrative of a Child Analysis." *Internat. J. Psycho-Anal.,* 44:493–513.

Gill, M. (1954), Psychoanalysis and exploratory psychotherapy. *J. Amer. Psychoanal. Assn.,* 2:771–797.

—— (1979), The analysis of the transference. *J. Amer. Psychoanal. Assn.,* 27 (suppl.):263–288.

—— (1981), *Analysis of the Transference, Vol. 1.* New York: International Universities Press.

—— (1983), The interpersonal paradigm and the degree of the therapist's involvement. *Contemp. Psychoanal.,* 19:200–237.

—— (1991), Discussion of *Psychoanalytic Theory and Its Relation to Clinical Work* (by E. Schwaber). Meeting of Chicago Psychoanalytic Assn., October, Chicago, IL.

—— & Hoffman, I. (1982), The analysis of transference, Vol. II. Studies of nine audiorecorded psychoanalytic sessions. *Psychological Issues,* Monogr. 54. New York: International Universities Press.

Giovacchini, P. (1979), *Treatment of Primitive Mental States.* New York: Aronson.

Gitelson, M. (1962), The curative factors in psychoanalysis. *Internat. J. Psycho-Anal.,* 43:194–205.

Glover, E. (1937), Theory of the therapeutic results of psychoanalysis: A symposium. *Internat. J. Psycho-Anal.,* 18:125–132.

—— (1945), *Examination of the Kleinian System of Child Psychology.* New York: International Universities Press.

Goldberg, A., ed. (1978), *Self Psychology: A Casebook.* New York: International Universities Press.

—— (1990), *The Prisonhouse of Psychoanalysis.* Hillsdale, NJ: The Analytic Press.

Gray, P. (1973), Technique and the ego's capacity for viewing intrapsychic activity. *J. Amer. Psychoanal. Assn.,* 21:474–494.

—— (1982), Developmental lag in the evolution of technique for the psychoanalysis of neurotic conflict. *J. Amer. Psychoanal. Assn.*, 30:621–656.

—— (1987), On the technique of analysis of the superego: An introduction. *Psychoanal. Quart.*, 56:130–154.

—— (1990), The nature of therapeutic action in psychoanalysis. *J. Amer. Psychoanal. Assn.*, 38:1083–1097.

Green, A. (1975), The analyst, symbolization and absence in the analytic setting. *Internat. J. Psycho-Anal.*, 56:1–19.

—— (1977), The borderline concept. A conceptual framework for the understanding of borderline patients: Suggested hypotheses. In: *Borderline Personality Disorders*, ed. P. Hartcollis. New York: International Universities Press, pp. 15–46.

—— (1978), Potential space in psychoanalysis. In: *Between Reality and Fantasy*, ed. S. Grolnick & L. Barkin. New York: Aronson, pp. 167–190.

Greenberg, J. (1991), *Oedipus and Beyond*. Cambridge, MA: Harvard University Press.

—— & Mitchell, S. (1983), *Object Relations in Psychoanalytic Theory*. Cambridge, MA: Harvard University Press.

Grolnick, S. (1990), *The Work and Play of Winnicott*. Northvale, NJ: Aronson.

—— & Barkin, L. (1970), *Between Reality and Fantasy*. New York: Aronson.

Grotstein, J. (1986), *Splitting and Projective Identification*. Northvale, NJ: Aronson.

Guntrip, H. (1961a), *Personality Structure and Human Interaction*. New York: International Universities Press.

—— (1961b), The schizoid problem, regression and the struggle to preserve an ego. In: *Schizoid Phenomena, Object Relations, and the Self*. New York: International Universities Press, 1969, pp. 49–86.

—— (1962), The clinical-diagnostic framework: The manic–depressive problem in the light of the schizoid process. In: *Schizoid Phenomena, Object Relations, and the Self*. New York: International Universities Press, 1969, pp. 130–164.

—— (1969), *Schizoid Phenomena, Object Relations, and the Self*. New York: International Universities Press.

—— (1971), *Psychoanalytic Theory, Therapy, and the Self*. New York: Basic Books.

—— (1975), My experience of analysis with Fairbairn and Winnicott. In: *Essential Papers on Object Relations*, ed. P. Buckley. New York: New York University Press, pp. 447–468.

Harlow, H. (1961), The development of affectional patterns in infant monkeys. In: *Determinants of Infant Behavior, Vol. 1*, ed. B. Foss. New York: Wiley, pp. 75–88.

—— & Zimmerman, R. (1959), Affectional responses in the monkey. *Science*, 130:421–432.

Hartmann, H. (1939), *Ego Psychology and the Problem of Adaptation*. New York: International Universities Press.

—— (1953), Contribution to the metapsychology of schizophrenia. *The Psychoanalytic Study of the Child*, 8:177–198. New York: International Universities Press.

—— Kris, E. & Lowenstein, R. (1949), Notes on the theory of aggression. *The Psychoanalytic Study of the Child*, 3/4:9–36. New York: International Universities Press.

Havens, I. (1976), *Participant Observation*. New York: Aronson.

Hendrick, I. (1942), Instinct and the ego during infancy. *Psychoanal. Quart.*, 11:33–58.

—— (1943), Work and the pleasure principle. *Psychoanal. Quart.*, 12:311–329.

Hoffman, I. (1990), In the eye of the beholder: A reply to Levenson. *Contemp. Psychoanal.*, 26:291–304.

—— (1991), Discussion: Toward a social constructivist view of the psychoanalytic situation. *Psychoanal. Dial.*, 1:74–103.

Hughes, J. (1989), *Reshaping the Psychoanalytic Domain*. Berkeley: University of California Press.

Jacobson, E. (1954), Transference problems in the psychoanalytic treatment of severely depressed patients. *J. Amer. Psychoanal. Assn.*, 2:595–606.

——— (1964), *The Self and the Object World*. New York: International Universities Press.

Kernberg, O. (1972), A critique of the Kleinian school. In: *Tactics and Techniques in Psychoanalytic Therapy, Vol. 1*, ed. P. Giovachini. New York: Science House, pp. 62–93.

——— (1975), *Borderline Conditions and Pathological Narcissism*. New York: Aronson.

——— (1976), *Object Relations Theory and Clinical Psychoanalysis*. New York: Aronson.

——— (1980), *Internal World and External Reality*. New York: Aronson.

——— (1982), Self, ego, affects, and drives. *J. Amer. Psychoanal. Assn.*, 30:893–918.

——— (1984), *Severe Personality Disorders*. New Haven, CT: Yale University Press.

——— (1988), Object relations theory in clinical practice. *Psychoanal. Quart.*, 57:481–504.

———, Bernstein, E., Coyne, L., Appelbaum, A., Horwitz, L. & Voth, H. (1972), Psychoanalysis and psychotherapy: Final report of the Menninger Foundation Psychotherapy Research Project. *Bull. Menn. Clin.*, 36:1–275.

———, Selzer, M., Koenigsberg, H., Carr, C. & Appelbaum, A. (1988), *Psychodynamic Psychotherapy of Borderline Patients*. New York: Basic Books.

Khan, M. (1960), Clinical aspects of the schizoid personality: Affects and technique. In: *The Privacy of the Self*. New York: International Universities Press, 1974, pp. 136–167.

——— (1962), Dream psychology and the evolution of the psychoanalytic situation. In: *The Privacy of the Self*. New York: International Universities Press, 1974, pp. 27–41.

——— (1963), The concept of the cumulative trauma. In: *The Privacy of the Self*. New York: International Universities Press, 1974, pp. 42–58.

——— (1964), Ego-distortion, cumulative trauma and the role of reconstruction in the analytic situation. In: *The Privacy of the Self*. New York: International Universities Press, 1974, pp. 59–68.

——— (1971), Infantile neurosis as a false self organization. In: *The Privacy of the Self*. New York: International Universities Press, 1974, pp. 219–233.

——— (1974), *The Privacy of the Self*. New York: International Universities Press.

Klein, M. (1926), The psychological principles of early analysis. In: *Love, Guilt and Reparation, 1921–1945*. New York: Free Press, 1975, pp. 128–138.

——— (1928), Early stages of the Oedipus conflict. In: *Love, Guilt and Reparation, 1921–1945*. New York: Free Press, 1975, pp. 186–198.

——— (1933), The early development of conscience in the child. In: *Love, Guilt and Reparation, 1921–1945*. New York: Free Press, 1975, pp. 248–257.

——— (1935), A contribution to the psychogenesis of manic-depressive states. In: *Love, Guilt and Reparation, 1921–1945*. New York: Free Press, 1975, pp. 262–289.

——— (1937), Love, guilt and reparation. In: *Love, Guilt and Reparation, 1921–1945*. New York: Free Press, 1975, pp. 306–343.

——— (1940), Mourning and its relation to manic-depressive states. In: *Love, Guilt and Reparation, 1921–1945*. New York: Free Press, 1975, pp. 344–369.

——— (1945), The Oedipus complex in the light of early anxieties. In: *Love, Guilt and Reparation, 1921–1945*. New York: Free Press, 1975, pp. 370–419.

———, (1946), Notes on some schizoid mechanisms. In: *Envy and Gratitude, 1946–1963*. New York: Dell, 1975, pp. 1–24.

——— (1948a), On the theory of anxiety and guilt. In: *Envy and Gratitude, 1946–1963*. New York: Dell, 1975, pp. 25–42.

——— (1948b), *The Psychoanalysis of Children*. London: Hogarth Press.

——— (1950), On the criteria for the termination of psychoanalysis. In: *Envy and Gratitude, 1946–1963*. New York: Dell, 1975, pp. 43–47.

———— (1952a), On observing the behavior of young infants. In: *Envy and Gratitude, 1946–1963*. New York: Dell, 1975, pp. 94–121.

———— (1952b), Some theoretical conclusions regarding the emotional life of the infant. In: *Envy and Gratitude, 1946–1963*. New York: Dell, 1975, pp. 61–93.

———— (1952c), The origins of transference. In: *Envy and Gratitude, 1946–1963*. New York: Dell, 1975, pp. 48–56.

———— (1952d), The mutual influences in the development of the ego and id. In: *Envy and Gratitude, 1946–1963*. New York: Dell, 1975, pp. 57–60.

———— (1957), Envy and gratitude. In: *Envy and Gratitude, 1946–1963*. New York: Dell, 1975, pp. 176–235.

———— (1958), On the development of mental functioning. In: *Envy and Gratitude, 1946–1963*. New York: Dell, 1975, pp. 236–246.

———— (1959), Our adult world and its roots in infancy. In: *Envy and Gratitude, 1946–1963*. New York: Dell, 1975, pp. 247–263.

———— (1960), *Narrative of a Child Analysis*. New York: Free Press, 1975.

Kohut, H. (1959), Introspection, empathy, and psychoanalysis: An examination of the relationship between mode of observation and theory. *J. Amer. Psychoanal. Assn.*, 7:459–483.

———— (1966), Forms and transformations of narcissism. *J. Amer. Psychoanal. Assn.*, 14:243–272.

———— (1968), The psychoanalytic treatment of narcissistic personality disorders. *The Psychoanalytic Study of the Child*, 23:86–113. New York: International Universities Press.

———— (1971), *The Analysis of the Self*. New York: International Universities Press.

———— (1972), Thoughts on narcissism and narcissistic rage. *The Psychoanalytic Study of the Child*, 27:360–400. New York: Quadrangle Books.

———— (1977), *The Restoration of the Self*. New York: International Universities Press.

———— (1979), The two analyses of Mr. Z. *Internat. J. Psycho–Anal.* 60:3–27.

———— (1982), Introspection, empathy, and the semi-circle of mental health. *Internat. J. Psycho-Anal.* 63:395–407.

———— (1984), *How Does Analysis Cure?* ed. A. Goldberg & P. Stepansky. Chicago: University of Chicago Press.

———— & Wolf, E. (1978), The disorders of the self and their treatment: An outline. *Internat. J. Psycho-Anal.*, 59:413–425.

Levenson, E. (1981), Facts or fantasies: On the nature of psychoanalytic data. *Contemp. Psychoanal.*, 17:486–500.

———— (1982), Language and healing. In: *Curative Factors in Dynamic Psychotherapy.*, ed. S. Slipp. New York: McGraw Hill, pp. 91–103.

———— (1985), The interpersonal (Sullivanian) model. In: *Models of the Mind: Relation to Clinical Work.*, ed. A. Rothstein, New York: International Universities Press, pp. 49–67.

———— (1987), An interpersonal perspective. *Psychoanal. Inq.*, 7:207–214.

———— (1989), Whatever happened to the cat? *Contemp. Psychoanal.* 25:537–553.

———— (1990), Reply to Hoffman. *Contemp. Psychoanal.*, 26:299–304.

———— (1991), *The Purloined Self*. New York: William Alanson White Institute.

Lichtenberg, J. (1983), *Psychoanalysis and Infant Research*. Hillsdale, NJ: The Analytic Press.

Little, M. (1981), *Transference Neurosis and Transference Psychosis*. New York: Aronson.

———— (1985), Winnicott working in areas where psychotic anxieties predominate. *Free Associations*. 3:9–42.

London, N. (1985), Appraisal of self psychology. *Internat. J. Psycho-Anal.*, 66:95–107.

Lorenz, K. (1963), *On Aggression*. New York: Bantam Books.

Mahler, M. (1952), On child psychosis and schizophrenia: Autistic and symbiotic infantile psychoses. *The Psychoanalytic Study of the Child.* 7:286–305. New York: International Universities Press.

―――― (1968), *On Human Symbiosis and the Vicissitudes of Individuation.* New York: International Universities Press.

―――― (1971), A study of the separation-individuation process. *The Psychoanalytic Study of the Child,* 26:403–424. New York: Quandrangle Books.

―――― (1972), Rapprochement subphase of the separation-individuation process. *Psychoanal. Quart.,* 41:487–506.

―――― (1975), On the current status of the infantile neurosis. *J. Amer. Psychoanal. Assn.,* 23:327–333.

――――, Pine, F. & Bergman, A. (1975), *The Psychological Birth of the Human Infant.* New York: Basic Books.

Masterson, J. (1976), *Psychotherapy of the Borderline Patient.* New York: Brunner/Mazel.

Mitchell, S. (1988), *Relational Concepts in Psychoanalysis.* Cambridge, MA: Harvard University Press.

―――― (1991), Contemporary perspectives on the self: Toward an integration. *Psychoanal. Dial.,* 1:121–147.

―――― (1993), Interaction in psychoanalysis. Presented at annual spring meeting of the Division of Psychoanalysis, American Psychological Association, New York City.

Ogden, T. (1982), *Projective Identification and Psychotherapeutic Technique.* New York: Aronson.

Ornstein, P. (1978), The evolution of Heinz Kohut's psychoanalytic psychology of the self. In: *The Search for the Self,* ed. P. Ornstein. New York: International Universities Press, pp. 1–106.

―――― & Ornstein, A. (1985), Clinical understanding and explaining: The empathic vantage point. In: *Progress in Self Psychology. Vol. 1,* ed. A. Goldberg. New York: Guilford Press, pp. 43–61.

Racker, H. (1968), *Transference and Countertransference.* New York: International Universities Press.

Rapaport, D. (1951), The theory of ego autonomy. In: *The Collected Papers of David Rapaport,* ed. M. Gill. New York: Basic Books, 1967, pp. 357–367.

―――― (1954), Clinical implications of ego psychology. In: *The Collected Papers of David Rapaport,* ed. M. Gill. New York: Basic Books, 1967, pp. 586–593.

―――― (1957), The theory of ego autonomy: A generalization. In: *The Collected Papers of David Rapaport,* ed. M. Gill. New York: Basic Books, 1967, pp. 722–744.

Rayner, E. (1991), *The Independent Mind in British Psychoanalysis.* Northvale, NJ: Aronson.

Rosenfeld, H. (1965), *Psychotic States: A Psychoanalytic Approach.* London: Hogarth Press.

―――― (1971), A clinical approach to the psychoanalytic theory of the life and death instincts: An investigation into the aggressive aspects of narcissism. *Internat. J. Psycho-Anal.,* 52:169–175.

―――― (1978), Notes on the psychopathology and psychoanalytic treatment of some borderline patients. *Internat. J. Psycho-Anal.,* 59:215–221.

―――― (1983), Primitive object relations and mechanisms. *Internat. J. Psycho-Anal.,* 64:261–267.

―――― (1987), *Impasse and Interpretation.* London: Tavistock.

Rubovitz-Seitz, P. (1988), Kohut's method of interpretation: A critique. *J. Amer. Psychoanal. Assn.,* 36:933–960.

Schafer, R. (1976), *A New Language for Psychoanalysis.* New Haven, CT: Yale University Press.

Schwaber, E. (1979), On the "self" within the matrix of analytic theory. *Internat. J. Psycho-Anal.,* 60:467–479.

—— (1983), Psychoanalytic listening and psychic reality. *Internat. Rev. Psycho-Anal.*, 10:379–392.

Scott, J. (1958), *Aggression*. Chicago: University of Chicago Press.

Segal, H. (1980), *Klein*. London: Karnac Books.

—— (1981), *The Work of Hannah Segal*. New York: Aronson.

—— (1983), Some clinical implications of Melanie Klein's work. *Internat. J. Psycho-Anal.*, 64:269–276.

Spitz, R. (1965), *The First Year of Life*. New York: International Universities Press.

Stern, D. (1980), The early development of schemas of self, of other, and of various experiences of "self with other." Presented at Symposium on Reflections on Self Psychology, Boston.

—— (1985), *The Interpersonal World of the Infant*. New York: Basic Books.

Stolorow, R. (1985), Toward a pure psychology of inner conflict. In: *Progress in Self Psychology, Vol.1*, ed. A. Goldberg. New York: Guilford Press, pp. 194–201.

—— Brandchaft, B. & Atwood, R. (1988), *Psychoanalytic Treatment: An Intersubjective Approach*. Hillsdale, NJ: The Analytic Press.

—— & Lachmann, F. (1980), *Psychoanalysis of Developmental Arrests*. New York: International Universities Press.

Stone, L. (1954), The widening scope of indications for psychoanalysis. *J. Amer. Psychoanal. Assn.*, 2:567–594

Sullivan, H. (1940), *Conceptions of Modern Psychiatry*. New York: Norton.

—— (1953), *The Interpersonal Theory of Psychiatry*. New York: Norton.

—— (1954), *The Psychiatric Interview*. New York: Norton.

—— (1956), *Clinical Studies in Psychiatry*. New York: Norton.

—— (1962), *Schizophrenia as a Human Process*. New York: Norton.

Summers, F. (1988), Psychoanalytic therapy of the borderline patient: Treating the fusion–separation contradiction. *Psychoanal. Psychol.*, 5:339–355.

—— (1993a), Implications of object relations theories for the psychoanalytic process. *The Annual of Psychoanalysis*, 21:225–242. Hillsdale, NJ: The Analytic Press.

—— (1993b), Object relations theories and neurotic pathology: Toward a new paradigm. Presented at annual spring meeting of the Division of Psychoanalysis, American Psychological Association, New York City.

Sutherland, J. (1980), The British object relations theorists: Balint, Winnicott, Fairbairn, Guntrip. *J. Amer. Psychoanal. Assn.*, 28:829–860.

Tinbergen, N. (1951), *The Study of Instincts*. New York: Oxford University Press.

Tolpin, M. (1983), Corrective emotional experience: A self-psychological reevaluation. In: *The Future of Psychoanalysis*, ed. A. Goldberg. New York: International Universities Press, pp. 255–271.

Tolpin, P. (1988), Optimal affective engagement: The analyst's role in therapy. In: *Learning from Kohut: Progress in Self Psychology, Vol. 4*, ed. A. Goldberg. Hillsdale, NJ: The Analytic Press. pp. 160–168.

Waelder, R. (1937), The problem of the genesis of psychical conflict in earliest infancy. *Internat. J. Psycho-Anal.*, 18:406–473.

Weiss, J. (1971), The emergence of new themes: A contribution to the psychoanalytic theory of therapy. *Internat. J. Psycho-Anal.*, 52:459–467.

—— (1988), Testing hypotheses about unconscious mental functioning. *Internat. J. Psycho-Anal.*, 69:87–94.

White, R. (1963), Ego and reality in psychoanalytic theory. *Psychological Issues*, Monogr. 11, Vol. 3, No. 3. New York: International Universities Press.

Winnicott, D. (1945), Primitive emotional development. In: *Through Paediatrics to Psychoanalysis*. New York: Basic Books, 1975, pp. 145–156.

effectance
x9

——— (1947), Hate in the countertransference. In: *Through Paediatrics to Psychoanalysis*. New York: Basic Books, 1975, pp. 194–203.

——— (1949), Mind and its relation to the psyche-soma. In: *Through Paediatrics to Psychoanalysis*, New York: Basic Books, 1975, pp. 174–193.

——— (1950), Aggression in relation to emotional development. In: *Through Paediatrics to Psychoanalysis*, New York: Basic Books, 1975, pp. 204–218.

——— (1951), Transitional objects and transitional phenomena. In: *Through Paediatrics to Psychoanalysis*, New York: Basic Books, 1975, pp. 229–242.

——— (1952), Psychoses and child care. In: *Through Paediatrics to Psychoanalysis*, New York: Basic Books, 1975, pp. 219–228.

——— (1954a), The depressive position in normal emotional development. In: *Through Paediatrics to Psychoanalysis*. New York: Basic Books, 1975, pp. 262–277.

——— (1954b), Withdrawal and regression. In: *Through Paediatrics to Psychoanalysis*, New York: Basic Books, 1975, pp. 255–261.

——— (1954c), Metapsychological and clinical aspects of regression within the psycho-analytical set-up. In: *Through Paediatrics to Psychoanalysis*. New York: Basic Books, 1975, pp. 278–294.

——— (1956a), Primary maternal preoccupation. In: *Through Paediatrics to Psychoanalysis*. New York: Basic Books, 1975, pp. 300–305.

——— (1956b), The anti-social tendency. In: *Through Paediatrics to Psychoanalysis*, New York: Basic Books, 1975, pp. 306–315.

——— (1958), The capacity to be alone. In: *The Maturational Processes and the Facilitating Environment*. New York: International Universities Press, 1965, pp. 29–36.

——— (1959), Classification: Is there a psycho-analytic contribution to psychiatric classification? In: *The Maturational Processes and the Facilitating Environment*. New York: International Universities Press, 1965, pp. 124–139.

——— (1960a), The theory of the parent–infant relationship. In: *The Maturational Processes and the Facilitating Environment*. New York: International Universities Press, 1965, pp. 37–55.

——— (1960b), Ego distortion in terms of true and false self. In: *The Maturational Processes and the Facilitating Environment*. New York: International Universities Press, 1965, pp. 140–152.

——— (1960c), Counter-transference. In: *The Maturational Processes and the Facilitating Environment*. New York: International Universities Press, 1965, pp. 158–165.

——— (1962a), A personal view of the Kleinian contribution. In: *The Maturational Processes and the Facilitating Environment*. New York: International Universities Press, 1965, pp. 171–178.

——— (1962b), Ego integration in child development. In: *The Maturational Processes and the Facilitating Environment*. New York: International Universities Press, 1965, pp. 56–63.

——— (1963a), From dependence toward independence in the development of the individual. In: *The Maturational Processes and the Facilitating Environment*. New York: International Universities Press, 1965, pp. 83–92.

——— (1963b), The development of the capacity for concern. In: *The Maturational Processes and the Facilitating Environment*. New York: International Universities Press, 1965, pp. 73–82.

——— (1963c), Dependence in infant care, in child care, and in the psycho-analytic setting. In: *The Maturational Processes and the Facilitating Environment*. New York: International Universities Press, 1965, pp. 249–260.

——— (1963d), Psychotherapy of character disorders. In: *The Maturational Processes and the Facilitating Environment*. New York: International Universities Press, 1965, pp. 203–216.

————— (1963e), Psychiatric disorder in terms of infantile maturational processes. In: *The Maturational Processes and the Facilitating Environment*. New York: International Universities Press, 1965, pp. 230–241.

————— (1965), *The Maturational Processes and the Facilitating Environment*. New York: International Universities Press.

————— (1971), *Playing and Reality*. London: Routledge.

Wolf, E. (1988), *Treating the Self: Elements of Clinical Self Psychology*. New York: Guilford Press.

Zetzel, E. (1951), The depressive position. In: *Affective Disorders*, ed. P. Greenacre. New York: International Universities Press, pp. 84–116.

————— (1956), An approach to the relation between concept and content in psychoanalytic theory. *The Psychoanalytic Study of the Child*, 11:99–121. New York: International Universities Press.

————— (1964), The analytic situation. In: *Psychoanalysis in the Americas*. ed. R. Litman. New York: International Universities Press, 1966, pp. 86–106.

Index

A

Abraham, K., 25, 28
Abreaction, 216
Adaptive point of view, 356, 371
Addictions. *See* Substance abuse.
Adler, A., 49
Adler, G., 300
Affective attunement in analysis, 304-5, 327-28
Affects: Kernberg on, 192-93; Stolorow on, 307
Agency: Bakan's concept of, 299; Klein's concept of, 89; Winnicott's concept of, 153
Aggression: Fairbairn on, 31, 33, 40; Guntrip on, 49; Hartmann on, 6; Kernberg on, 193-94, 200-2, 206, 239-43; Klein on, 73-75, 90, 120, 350, 365; Kohut on, 262; neutralization of, 6; Winnicott on, 142-43, 145-46, 152-53, 160, 176-81; Sullivan on, 314
Agoraphobia: Fairbairn on, 39; Kohut on, 268-69, 298
Alcoholism. *See* Substance abuse.
Alexander, F., 183
Ambivalence toward objects: Fairbairn on, 30-31, 37-38; Klein on, 88-91; Winnicott on, 147, 152-54, 176-81
Anality: Fairbairn on, 29-30; Klein on, 100
Analyst's participation in the therapeutic process: Gill on, 331, 334-35, 365-66, 377; Hoffman on, 332, 340-41; Levenson on, 327, 334, 344, 376, 377; Stolorow on, 308-9, 335; Sullivan on, 316
Analytic empathy: Kernberg on, 218; Kohut on, 270, 275-77, 281, 295-97, 301, 328, 373; Winnicott on, 163, 169-70, 180
Analytic "failures," Kohut on, 270, 275, 284, 296, 298, 300-1
Analytic regression. *See* Therapeutic regression.
Analyzability: Fairbairn on, 43, 46; Kernberg's view of, 215; Klein's approach to, 106; and object relations paradigm, 372
Anger. *See* Aggression.
Annihilation anxiety, 74, 347
Antisocial personality: Kernberg on, 198, 201; Klein on, 92; Kohut on, 264, 265; Winnicott on, 167-68, 172
Anxiety of engulfment, 39

L